The Anthropology of Sport and Human Movement

The Anthropology of Sport and Human Movement

A Biocultural Perspective

Edited by Robert R. Sands and Linda R. Sands

LEXINGTON BOOKS
A division of
Rowman & Littlefield Publishers, Inc.
Lanham • Boulder • New York • Toronto • Plymouth, UK

Published by Lexington Books
A division of Rowman & Littlefield Publishers, Inc.
A wholly owned subsidiary of
The Rowman & Littlefield Publishing Group, Inc.
4501 Forbes Boulevard, Suite 200, Lanham, Maryland 20706
http://www.lexingtonbooks.com

Estover Road, Plymouth PL6 7PY, United Kingdom

British Library Cataloguing in Publication Information Available

The hardback edition of this book was previously cataloged by the Library of
Congress as follows:

Library of Congress Cataloging-in-Publication Data

The anthropology of sport and human movement : a biocultural perspective /
edited by Robert R. Sands, Linda R. Sands.
    p. cm.
Includes bibliographical references and index.
1. Sports—Anthropological aspects. 2. Human mechanics. I. Sands, Robert R.
II. Sands, Linda R. GV706.2.A56 2010
612.7'6—dc22   2010000725

ISBN: 978-0-7391-2939-5 (cloth : alk. paper)
ISBN: 978-0-7391-2940-1 (pbk. : alk. paper)
ISBN: 978-0-7391-4941-6 (electronic)

Printed in the United States of America

Contents

Preface

For many years, one of the editors struggled against the lack of attention his discipline paid to sport and culture. From a promising beginning in the early 1970s, anthropologists joined other social scientists and founded the Anthropological Association for the Study of Sport and Play (TAASP). Yearly conferences were held and volumes were generated from these conferences. However, interest in this kind of scholarship never caught on beyond a few anthropologists, including Norbeck, Blanchard, and Cheska. The subject of sport, and sport and culture as it relates to the human condition, were eventually adopted by the sister fields of the social sciences.

When dealing with sport and culture, sociologists, historians, and psychologists tracked to the traditional foci of their individual fields and the signature trademarks of anthropology: holism, ethnography, and the comparative method, as well as the interest in all facets of the human condition were never fully realized. Granted, ethnography has become of late a method utilized by any number of fields and professions, and it has been used by those in fields that do research in sport and culture, especially in cultural studies, feminist and queer studies, and now recently, sports studies. Sands, Klein, Brownell, Bolin, Granskog, Moore, and a few other anthropologists, continue to do singular work, never really seeing anthropology embrace the phenomenon of sport despite its universal appeal. The growth of a truly global appeal of sport and the recent resurgence in indigenous sport forms and subjects such as Kenyan running would have benefited from an anthropological perspective.

This volume was birthed from a series of discussions Robert and Linda Sands and Philip Moore had in 2007 that bemoaned the state, or lack thereof, of the field of sport and anthropology. The impact of postmodernism has lessened in and out of anthropology, and these discussions involved optimism that some of the key tenants of an involved anthropology, both in social conscience and the span of the human condition, could engage new perspectives. Elsewhere in anthropology, as there is a new round of discussion that looks at the fracturing of the traditional four field approach, Alan Goodman and others have suggested a biocultural approach that reflects the perspective of humans as the sum of biology and culture.

To the editors of this volume, our condition as humans is the result of culture as it impacts our biology, and in ways how our biology might indeed impact our culture. This perspective excited the anthropologist Robert Sands and microbiologist Linda Sands and sport enthusiasts from running to surfing. Sport cannot fully be appreciated as part of the human condition without looking at it from the perspective of human movement and the unique evolution of culture and biology that has existed for millions of years and still continues today. Movements early in human evolution were shaped by competing selective agents such as the environment, to include climate, geology, and the fate of other species. However, later cultural evolution engineered its own set of selections and movement became an interface between both the physical and social-cultural environment. This is evident in the examples of the Kenyan running culture. In Kenya, due to the success of Kalejin runners in national and international competitions[1] (both in status and economic gain), there is now a strong movement where running in organized and unorganized running camps has produced a wave of running to win. Whereas earlier in the prehistory of this Kenyan group, selection pressures for running were for transport, communication and cattle raiding that would produce status and gain, running now performs a similar role in contemporary Kenyan culture. Running as movement retains its singular importance in the culture and as such, the biological aspects that make a good runner are powerfully selected and retained in cultural institutions and lifeways.

This volume represents an initial foray in exploring the biocultural foundation of human movement patterns as it relates to the human propensity of sport in all of its manifestations, from health and human well-being, to human performance, to even extending performance through genetic engineering. However, the implications of such a biocultural foundation can extend far beyond the study of movement and athletic performance. As Clifford Geertz wrote in his other seminal work republished in *Interpretations of Culture*, one cannot divorce, in any study of the human condition, our biology from our culture.

Certainly, how culture now impels humans to move or, for that matter, to not move through their cultural and physical environments has profound ramifications on human biology. Consider living at altitudes, the impacts of globalization, and world markets on indigenous subsistence strategies, and the onslaught of video games and its influence on reducing physical activity in many of the planet's cultures. Humanity's revolutionary success over the last four million or so years reflects the critical importance of the evolution of our movement patterns. How humans survive the next decade, the next century, the next millennium in part is certainly dependent on the role movement patterns play in that future.

NOTES

1. Kenyan running success and ability has been ascribed to both genetic and environmental factors, see part 3 of this volume.

Acknowledgments

Indeed, when an author or authors write that their words are a product of a "labor of love" perhaps only volume editors can truly appreciate the significance of that phrase. We hope the volume this effort birthed will be a significant work in establishing a more anthropological perspective on the study of sport and human movement.

We would like to thank the contributing authors for their scholarship and willingness to be a part of this volume. Special note goes to Philip Moore for providing initial thoughts on the direction of this volume.

One final but certainly not in passing acknowledgement is saved for Alyce Cheska. This book marks the close of the second decade of research and publishing in anthropology and sport for Robert Sands; I continue to find passion for my work through the enthusiasm Alyce displayed in her own career and the lasting influence she had on me starting out more than twenty years ago, as first my advisor and mentor and later as good friend and confidant. She continues to be a living inspiration.

Part 1

FOUNDATIONS

Foundation is perceived as a framework, a primary support, or even in construction terms, the slab in which the rest of the structure rests. The next three chapters are just that, foundations for a biocultural exploration of sport and human movement.

Robert R. Sands provides an initial scaffolding for this perspective in the introductory chapter, "Anthropology Revisits Sport through Human Movement." Anthropology, as a discipline, has never warmed up to the notion that sport is an important cultural domain worth studying, while sister disciplines in the social sciences have embraced sport as important in looking at human behavior. Sands, among several anthropologists, such as Blanchard, Cheska, Klein, Brownwell and others, had in the past, published on sport and culture, but their work never resonated within the academy. Anthropology currently is engaged in a renaissance of the integration of biology and culture that previously was denied by a postmodern emphasis. Sands suggests that anthropology in its traditional holistic enterprise, including biology, culture, comparative nature, and grounded ethnographic fieldwork, offers a perfect tableau for viewing sport within the human condition.

Sport is certainly a cultural and universal expression of humankind, its importance to human interaction, indeed its reflection of human culture, is readily apparent to the most uninterested in cultural research. However, one cannot ignore the evolutionary and contemporary significance of human biology, to include human movement, that is part of this expression. Our genetic makeup has developed the anatomy and physiology that has

1

produced uniquely human movements that have an antiquity of millions of years in our evolution. These "biological" features have and continue to influence this universal cultural expression. Sands' chapter is a call for anthropology to "revisit" the importance of sport in human behavior, and to use the tools of the discipline to promote a more informed perspective of sport and human movement.

Play seems to be a basal animal behavior upon which humankind has expanded into a variety of cultural manifestations to include sport. From a different perspective, a biocultural framework to consider human behavior, including sport, was found in one of the earliest publications of Clifford Geertz, unlikely given Geertz's trajectory as a symbolic anthropologist.

As evidenced in chapter 1, the path to a biocultural perspective in anthropology includes the engaged socially conscious view by Goodman as well as the contemporary evolutionary psychology view of a Paleolithic wiring of genes and modules that inform human behavior and indeed form culture. This is not surprising as anthropology has for the last three decades been sequestered in a post-modern relativism that at its height in the 1980s and 1990s denied the applicability of science, or even questioned the existence of science in investigating the concept of culture. Yet what is surprising is that the voice of interpretive anthropology and "thick" description, Clifford Geertz, was one of the earliest advocates in the discipline that suggested the impacts of biology and culture were not distinct and separate in human evolution, nor considered separate when looking at contemporary humankind.

Writing in 1966, Geertz posited a uniquely different perspective on the separated towers of anthropological interests, biology and culture when it came to the origins of "man." In "The Impact of Culture on the Concept of Man" Geertz sought to marry the two disciplines. Historically, Geertz was attempting to frame a new concept of humanity, not so much to situate origins in a new light, but to reconcile the disparate views that entrenched anthropology theory, that of the "Enlightenment approach of human nature" (Harman 2007: 59), where humans lay distinct and below their customs and the cultural relativism of Ruth Benedict that was espoused by her mentor, Franz Boas. This relativistic view where biology was considered inconsequential to culture was in response to the biological deterministic view inherent in the cultural evolutionism of nineteenth-century thinkers E. B Tylor and L. H. Morgan in particular. Geertz also eschewed the mechanistic and layered or what Geertz labeled as a "stratigraphic" strategy engaged by the functionalists Wissler, Malinowski, and Kluck-holn that viewed the construct of man as first a superficial layer of culture that hid the "structural and functional regularities of social organization" (Harman: 59), that in turn superimposed a deeper layer of psychological processes, and finally, if excavated to the core, revealed the biological es-sence of Man, informed by anatomy, physiology, and so forth.

What Geertz intuited, according to Harmon, was a view that brought together both culture and biology in an evolutionary process where de-velopment did not operate separately and distinctly on each, but where evolution created a unique animal integrating both. The cultural relativism of Boas and Benedict threatened to bury the existence of universal "man" and the classical theorists attempted to build a model that brought biol-ogy and culture together in the stratigraphic relationship of unconnected layers. Geertz, in his treatise, turned away from both, suggesting that universals used by the classicists and the extreme variation called out by the relativists were paths gone awry. In fact, it is the "systematic relation-ships" connecting cultural variation that are built upon the evolutionary development of humans that are important to understand.

Here, Geertz journeys into an area at the time that was void of any physical "evidence" to justify the assertion that culture springs from a biocultural framework. Invoking the metaphor of culture as a computer program, software if you like, Geertz saw human behavior controlled through sets of "plans, recipes and rules and instructions" (Geertz 1973: 44) and culture as a governance mechanism. As such, culture represents an extreme "general response capacity" (Harman 2007: 62) in humans that is less directed by their biology and for Geertz, humans are precisely humans because of the development of this outside the skin, "extrage-netic" control mechanism that is culture. In essence, biology and culture rode in on the same evolutionary horse that culture allowed humans to evolve beyond basic genetically determined behavior, but it was biology that set up humans to develop evolutionary software that would allow for general response capabilities, in which culture is the extreme rule-governed program. In this chapter, Geertz hinted at his future interests in interpretive anthropology by allowing that culture is based on symbols and the information they carry, both simple and compelling, and domains of culture, language, beliefs, knowledge, and more visible manifestations such as art and music, and for this volume especially, ritual and human movement are all generated in response to and expressed through the control mechanism that is culture. Geertz would write, "without men, no culture, certainly, but equally and more significantly, without culture, no men" (1973: 49).

In "From Landscapes to Playscapes: The Evolution of Play in Humans and Other Animals," Kerrie P. Lewis explores the relationship between animal and human play and offers perspectives on the role play had in human evolution and the role play continues to have on human lifestyles. Lewis first defines play (always an elusive task), characterizes the different types, explores the various theories for the origins of play, and suggests as a potential theory, that of social and cognitive enhancement, which would involve brain-behavior co-evolution. Lewis looks at play in humans, specifically children, and the influence of culture on shaping child's play, to include gender, ritual, and spirituality. Although manifestations of human play involve cultural elaboration, there seem to be universals that remain a legacy between animals and humans. Lewis further explores the relationship between the biological and neurobiological aspects of play and their roles in human evolution. She writes, "The rules of culture may be reiterated or bent during play, and thus, may shape future culture."

BIBLIOGRAPHY

Geertz, Clifford. "The Impact of the Concept of Culture on the Concept of Man" in *New Views of the Nature of Man*, ed. J. Platt. (Chicago: University of Chicago Press, 1966): 93–118.

Geertz, C. *Interpretation of Cultures*. New York: HarperCollins Publishers, 1973.

Harman, O. S. "Powerful Intuitions: Re-reading Nature versus Nurture with Charles Darwin and Clifford Geertz." *Science in Context* 20:1 (2007): 49–70.

Lewis, Kerrie P. "From Landscapes to Playscapes: The Evolution of Play in Humans and Other Animals" in *The Anthropology of Sport and Human Movement: A Biocultural Perspective*, edited by Robert R. Sands (Lanham, Md.: Lexington Press, 2010): 51–76.

Anthropology Revisits Sport through Human Movement

Robert R. Sands

This introductory chapter will provide a framework for establishing a biocultural perspective as it applies to human movement and sport, echoing similar movements in other fields of anthropology. First, it will present a brief look at the recent relationship between anthropology and sport, and some of the reasons, both in the past and recently, why anthropology has not been a major contributor to the study of sport and culture. This chapter will then briefly look at the biocultural movement in contemporary anthropology and its impact on the discipline; provide a summary of the development of such a movement; and then explore how this movement applies to the study of human movement and sport from an anthropological perspective. The chapter will outline the contents of this volume and their relation to the biocultural perspective. In conclusion, it will be suggested that in the biocultural movement, anthropologists finally have a vehicle to advance good, novel, and meaningful research on the importance of human movement and sport to the study of the human condition.

In this volume, human movement is more than patterns of movement that are the sole function of anatomy and physiology. These patterns are also influenced by human behavior, and as such, offer a tantalizing perspective of the relationship of culture and biology throughout human evolution and ongoing today. It is clear that the crucible of our evolution produced a human biped capable of movements, and suites of movements, quite unique to mammals. These movements, found in human walking, running, feeding, and play, became instrumental in adapting to selective agents in the environment over the last four million years. Only recently in human evolution, many of these movement patterns have been co-opted by culture and are now featured in spiritual systems, games and sport. Running, which was made possible by a crucial anatomical development perhaps as early as two million years ago, has now become part of a human universal that is sport, and as such, a critical international, national and cultural phenomenon. Yet, the biology of movements such as running still carry with its expression a legacy of behavior spawned by adaptation—just as today the cultural manifestations of running found in sport, no longer crucial for survival, act as cultural selection agents for continued importance of that behavior.

Sport is ubiquitous, it transcends culture and is woven into all cultural fabric, but even more so, movements that are so integral to sport shape culture. The definitions of sport are many, much like the array of definitions of the concept "culture." Features agreed on by many are a form of competition, with winners and losers, usually limited to a physical expression, molded by rules and with achievement awarded with some reward of socially accepted value. Sports have been proposed by Guttmann (1979) to be a subset of larger categories of games and could possibly be considered a form of play. Siegal (2007) suggests that sport falls on a continuum that features play, games and athletics. The global prevalence of sport in particular, both the recent movement to return to indigenous sport as well as the huge growth of global "western" sport, does indicate a universality that transcends cultural specificity. In fact, as parents, educators, and others bemoan the growth in computer-based games, it is interesting to note that many of them are based in virtual "human movements" as well as actually incorporating human movement in the "game" itself (examples include tennis, golf, and even dance games). What seem to be common to these different "behaviors" are movement patterns that are prominently featured in our biology, both past and in the present.

Anthropologists tend to ignore or marginalize the human prevalence of play, games, and sport, and yet these universal tendencies helped shape our evolution and continue to command cultural visibility. Lately, traditional academic fields that have studied sport (sociology, psychology, philosophy, and history to name a few) have given rise to endeavors that either study specifically sport (i.e., sports studies), or include the study of sport in their "field of focus" (i.e., feminist and queer studies). The "gaze" of these fields is aligned more or less to the view of the traditional disciplines that spawned them, intent on present or recent past, focused on "western" sport forms and even more specifically at times on the influence of a globalized capitalism on athletes and sport.

A MURKY PAST

In 2002, Alan Klein called out the need to develop a critical "anthropology of sport," disparaging the anthropologists inability to use the "diagnostic" capability of the discipline to study sport in the context of culture and society. Comparing and contrasting the paucity of work, outside a few committed (perhaps in his mind, committable) anthropologists, with that of sociology and the emerging movement of sports studies, Klein wrote of the need to emphasize those central components of anthropology and its inquiry, cross-cultural "holism" and ethnographic method as separating anthropological study of sport from the a "western" or Euro-American look at sport defining other social sciences approaches. Ruminating on the seminal importance of Geertz's article on the Balinese cockfight (1973), Klein wondered, based on the importance of that work in general anthropological circles, how that also did not stand in as a clarion call to illuminate the importance of sport to help explain culture and society.

Elsewhere, Sands (1999a and 2002) and Moore (2006) have touched on or elaborated Klein's treatise. As Klein does, both offer a variety of reasons for anthropologists not to follow this direction: tenure, being seen as less than professional, even marginalized as anthropologists, and work on sport being considered an auxiliary field, a "sidebar" at best. The few anthropologists involved in sport have experienced in some ways the "marginalization" of their work that Klein described.

In addition, the legacy of the anthropological imperative that formed around the foundation of the "exotic" other and recent emphasis of the effect of globalization on developing countries and their indigenous populations has continued to eclipse even the slightest interest in sport and for that matter the study of human movement overall. Yet, those anthropologists that work in the field of sport and culture no doubt wonder why such a popular human endeavor that generates billions of dollars shared by billions of people, commands the largest global and cross-cultural stage every four years, and often times is a critical component of foreign diplomacy is ignored by anthropology as being a viable course of study. From a different perspective, considering the holism of anthropology, it is also difficult to square that sport in all its expression of the human biological condition is not considered a viable investigation as it is in exercise science and kinesiology.

Pioneer anthropologists of sport, Kendell Blanchard and Alyce Cheska, along with Edward Norbeck and others of the 1970s, founded the Anthropological Association for the Study of Sport and Play (TAASP, then later TASP). Blanchard and Cheska published the first-ever text on the subject, *The Anthropology of Sport* (1985), and Blanchard followed up with a revised edition in 1995. However, the text and TAASP's relevance faded as other disciplines such as sociology and history continued to engage the study of sport (and at times culture in sport) more rigorously. In essence, the study of sport was claimed by sociologists and an emerging field of sports studies that included a narrow focus illuminating and addressing social, economic, and gender inequality in western and global sport. Good ethnographies, however, were a bright spot; Klein authored several, from bodybuilding to baseball (1991, 1993, 1997), Sands wrote on collegiate sprinters and football players (1994 and 1999b), Brownell's (1995) work on sport in China was invigorating. Edited volumes such as Sands (1999a), Dyck (2000) and Bolin and Granskog (2003) signaled a growing interest and Sands (2002) authored an ethnographic methods text.

However, Klein, and as such, others, including myself, and with other social scientists involved in sport, may have been seduced by the interpretive and postmodern movement that swept through many of the social sciences, anthropology included, in the last twenty years. The direction of study in the arena of sport was to look at sport as an entity of singular focus or as embedded in culture and society. This direction also included the relevance or importance of sport as a cultural and social behavior, as a cultural and social identity marker, and through its structure and within human interactions of the participants, a reflection of the larger culture or society.

Many sport researchers were drawn to the flame of the postmodern sensitivity to positivism, no matter the generalized and humanistic nature of that positivism, and reflected in the singular focus of sports studies (seen in the feminist and Marxist approaches and the denial of positivism through its qualitative method, Silk et al. 2004) and sport anthropology became a contested or, even worse, ignored field of legitimate inquiry. This intersection of activism, the study of cultural space and sport, and the hegemonic-derived inequalities consistent with sport in a globalized context continue to be at the forefront in sport studies and, to a lesser extent, sociology of sport. Interestingly enough, the field of sports studies—a loosely defined collection of researchers that originate from many different traditional disciplines such as sociology, history, philosophy, a cultural geographer or two and anthropology—lacks the framework or body of knowledge for a true discipline (Sands 2008, Crawford 2005, Moore 2006), and even those who acknowledge working within such a discipline agree that the field has yet to take on a unifying focus (i.e., Silk et al. 2004).

Within the last three years, the number of anthropologists who include the study of sport and games as part of their research agendas has increased. Faculty Web pages feature topics that include all facets of sport and culture. A sample of publications explicate if not so much a renaissance of an earlier time, but a resurgence of interest in sport by anthropologists. In his review of Bale and Christensen's 2004 volume *Post Olympism? Questioning Sport in the Twenty-First Century*, Crawford states, "The anthropology of sport is growing, if one accepts the number of publications as an indicator. Another indicator could be the number of anthropologists involved in academic research concerning sport phenomenon" (2005: 382). Susan Brownell's recent book (2007), *Beijing's Games: What the Olympics Mean to China*, is a thoughtful and reflective treatise on the history of sport in China and the impact the Games will have not only on sport, but also other facets of Chinese culture. A recent edited volume, co-authored by two sociocultural anthropologists and a sociologist, *America's Game(s): A Critical Anthropology of Sport* (Eastman et al. 2007) provides a cross-cultural view of America's sports as they are "translated" to other nations and other cultures, including football in Europe, basketball in Senegal, and baseball in the Dominican Republic.

However, Klein was right in his assessment of the study of sport lacking even a muddy anthropological perspective, but anthropologists failed to see the forest because of the trees. Anthropologists are still working the margins of the study of sport and culture and will continue to do so in at least the near future, without a clear foundation or calling—the 2007 American Anthropological Association (AAA) meetings did not feature a session, let alone a paper, devoted to sport and society or culture.

This volume suggests a different perspective, one that matches well with the traditional tenets of anthropology, not just a holistic enterprise and cross-cultural or comparative method, but also featuring research and method that is grounded in both good ethnographic method and an engaged science that implicates the entire human condition, including cultural and biological dimensions. The foundation of sport and leisure, play, games, exercise and competition is embedded in human movement and the human condition. Sport is a pan-human behavior in recent and contemporary society, but more than a cultural behavior, sport is also a form of human movement that features a kinesthetic biology (biomechanical, neurobiological) and phylogenetic foundation that has a long and rich history in non-human primate and human evolution. This is reflected in the biology of humanity and the intimate relationship of biology with the evolution and proliferation of human cultures.

The intersection of biology and culture reveals a more complete and certainly complex picture of a species of "homobiles" (Renson 2001) that initially evolved for movement through landscapes of ecological opportunity that now supports movement gladiators in many world cultures that engage in a stunning array of movement patterns (sport and leisure) for any number of exclusive or inclusive reasons: money, fame, health, spirituality, or social and cultural solidarity, the list is long. Sport and play are certainly visible expressions of the relationship of biology and culture and as such hold clues for understanding the evolution of human movement and the evolution of our species. We live in a global world, we also live in a world where our behaviors are still in some part defined by local ecology (physical, social, and cultural) and we, as humans, are still modifying, creating, and responding to that ecology, which is expressed and manifested in our movement patterns.

In addition, the extent of plasticity found in the human brain can alter inborn and genetic behavior; in other words, genetic behavior can be influenced ("rewiring" or modifying neurobiological pathways) by cultural patterns of behaviors. There are certain behaviors that are genetic in origin (e.g., obsessive compulsive disorder); however, the suggestion can be made that movement patterns embedded in cultural behaviors can indeed modify biology (movements found in dance, different sports or even new sports, such as extreme sport), or as we are finding out, lack of movement patterns today that were once essential to our evolution can lead to health impacts on our biology, and along with cultural propensity for increases in certain dietary components, can lead to diseases such as obesity and diabetes.

For any student of anthropology or other discipline or field that explores the nature of human evolution and the development of culture, the legacy of an African beginning cannot be denied, just as the evolutionist cannot profitably deny the importance of the dynamic interplay between culture and biology for more than two million years of our evolution, or the complex relationship that existed between paleoecology and behavior even earlier, if we explore the development of bipedalism in hominin evolution prior to four million years ago. The study of anthropology spans the human condition and it is this scope that offers a critical and discerning perspective on the complex calculus involving human biological and cultural variation that produces human movement and performance.

Anthropology, as a discipline, is perfectly suited for such a thematic exploration. In their book, *Building a New Biocultural Synthesis*, Alan Goodman and Thomas Leatherman note that "anthropology with its dual emphasis on biology and culture, is—or should be—the discipline suited to the study of the complex interactions between these aspects of our lives" (1998: 5). Indeed, the divide between culture and biology has been bridged in such disciplines as biology, genetics, and anthropology (Goodman et al. 2003). Research has been done to show how such a biocultural perspective engages and modifies such human behaviors as language and knowledge systems (Maffi 2001) or how culture impacts menopause (Sievert 2006) or reproductive fertility (Wachter and Bulatao 2003). Goodman's Presidential Address to the annual AAA meetings was titled "Bringing Biology Back into Anthropology" (Goodman 2007) and, as such, cast an engagement of a biocultural perspective that can very well provide a framework to explore the dynamic relationship between the machinations of cultural behavior and such supporting institutions and the biology of humans that lies "underneath the skin." It is apparent that anthropology will not lose its social and cultural "conscience" that has developed since the advent of a postmodern agenda, and well it should not, but Goodman and others strike a harmonious chord with that conscience while acknowledging, certainly advocating, the necessity of considering the many facets of the human animal. Goodman's biocultural anthropology is one that has and promises to continue to be an anthropology that engages a radically different science, "how sociocultural and political-economic processes affect human biologies, and then how compromised biologies further threaten the social fabric" (Goodman and Leatherman 1998: 5).

Goodman's biocultural perspective is just one of several academic "cousins" that have developed in response to the "culture only" framework espoused by anthropology in the context of a social and political upheaval in the 1970s. The next section briefly charts two developments as it applies to such an emergence. The first is the very recent and contemporary debate within anthropology about the nature of the discipline as it struggles with the continued division between a cultural and a biological enterprise; this struggle certainly is engaged by the development of biologically based or influenced views of human behavior. It will be suggested that the biocultural perspective will certainly play a major role in determining what that future will look like for emerging research foci, such as anthropology of sport and, more generally, human movement. The second related discussion will explore the development of "biologic" views of human cultural behavior in not only anthropology, but as well in evolutionary biology, sociobiology, and other views of behavioral ecology, from gene-based views to Goodman's "under the skin" view. This discussion will then frame the later exploration of developing an initial "biocultural perspective" of human movement and sport.

THE STATE OF THE STATE OF ANTHROPOLOGY: A BIOCULTURAL FUTURE?

Anthropology in the United States is mired in a painful self-reflection on the viability of a four-field holistic approach to the study of humankind. Perhaps as a consequence of the rise and dominion of postmodernism in the construction and maintenance of an interpretive anthropology and the metaphoric four-letter word—to most anthropological positivists— postmodernism, anthropology finds itself in some departments a sharply divided intellectual enterprise teetering on the brink of extinction, scattering its four subfields to the winds of new and still viable interdisciplinary endeavors, such as cultural studies, evolutionary biology, and behavioral ecology, to name a few. Academic departments such as Duke and Stanford, with Harvard wavering, illustrate this deepening divide by splitting into departments reflecting a biological and social and/or cultural perspective, perhaps also reflecting epistemological differences as well.

However, there are other departments who have engineered integration across the divides of culture and biology and stress a holistic perspective on studying human nature. Integration means reaching across the traditional "fields" rather than strengthening each and frequent collaborative efforts in both research and the classroom. Emory University, University of Pennsylvania and University of Florida are committed to either a four-field approach or strong integration within the traditional parameters of anthropology. Arizona State has created the most radical of transformations, generating a School of Human Evolution and Social Change (Shenk 2006), which includes, in addition to anthropologists, computer sciences, economists, geographers and sociologists. Research focuses around themes that feature human origins, interaction between societies and the natural environment, and natural, cultural and social dimensions of human health (Shenk 2006).

Within an introspective contemporary anthropology, perhaps the last social science that still clings to the mantra, "the most scientific of the humanities, and the most humanistic of the sciences" (Wolf in Smith 2006), there exists a movement to heal the fracture between the cultural and the biological created by the pendulum swing of interpretive anthropology that swept through the discipline in the 1980s and 1990s. Echoing the foundation created by sociobiology, itself a discipline divider in the 1970s, and a more muted Fox-Tiger call for integration in cultural and biological approaches, and then later a rebirth in the guise of evolutionary psychology that brought a number of non-anthropologists together with anthropologists to explore the evolution of human behavior, there exists now an iteration of this ever-present theme, that of a "biocultural" anthropology. This contemporary perspective "combines theory from ecology and evolutionary biology with ethnographic methods and theory from the social sciences (Smith 2006: 8).

The fields of medical anthropology and, as of late, applied medical anthropology engage a rigorous biocultural approach—that has included theory built on an empiricism explicating social and cultural processes of health and illness, of care and prevention in a cross-cultural framework—while maintaining links to medicine, a comparative lens and a strong ethnographic method. There has always been a relationship between medicine and anthropology; however, there was an interlude where medicine was overly concerned with an empiricism that required clinical and laboratory research and the anthropology, through ethnography, of medicine systems among indigenous and other groups of people was less appealing. Although the link between medicine and anthropology was never fully severed, twentieth-century medical anthropology can trace its roots back to the engagement of anthropology in the postmodern era and the challenge of accepting non-western systems of medicine and including its practitioners and behaviors and rituals as systems of healing beyond just a cultural artifact. The area of folk medicine highlighted the culturally diverse means by which indigenous cultures participated in such systems and field research was engaged to discover the array and limits of medicine—considered as well was the role of ritual and the relationship between science and religion.

Applied medical anthropology has taken on a more advocate role, as other applied fields in anthropology, of introducing and then providing culturally resonating health care systems that look to incorporate facets of traditional prevention and healing and their specialists into community health programs. Other related interests such as ethnobotany and human nutrition routinely consider implications of biology on culture or culture on biology. Included in contemporary theoretical and applied medical anthropology are the social, cultural and biological factors that influence health and illness in the individual and community and even clearly guide the construction of cultural health care systems. Indeed, there is clear realization that a biocultural approach is crucial to understanding the human condition. Examples of this approach also include work done in evolutionary medicine (Trevathan 2007 and Trevethan et al. 2008) as well as work done in human sexuality concerning biological and cultural expressions (Bolin and Wheelen 2008).

Other approaches such as environmental anthropology and cultural ecology benefit from this collaboration. Thomas (2006) sees anthropology and the biocultural perspective as essential to face present and near future "global" changes, rapid as they are and may be in the future. Anthropology, as a discipline, is perfectly suited for such a thematic exploration. "Anthropology . . . is in an exceptional position to bring together the disparate aspects of an interconnected and increasingly tangled world—one where human biology, social relations, ideology and environment are bound together" (Thomas 2006: 11).

This debate is by no means tied to recent commentary. Brown and Yoffee (1992), Holden (1993), Peacock (1995), and Weiner (1995) highlighted a fractious anthropology landscape showing myriad signs of coming apart at the seams. Perhaps, an even more compelling reason for anthropology to heed the call of a "tangled world" from this and following generations are the pluralistic approaches to diversity apparent, and not so transparent, in cultural and biological dimensions of humanity and anthropology's acceptance of "non-western systems of knowledge as valid" (Thomas 2006).

Academic programs found at Arizona State (previously mentioned), Washington State University's Evolutionary Anthropology program, and the National Science Foundation (NSF)–funded Washington State University and University of Washington collaborative Integrative Graduate Education and Research Traineeship (IGERT) Program of Evolutionary Modeling (IPEM) represent the current academic trend of exploring biological concepts in concert with the cultural aspects of human behavior. These programs include evolutionary anthropology and ecology, behavioral ecology, cultural ecology, biocultural anthropology, and archaeology, and feature work on reproduction and kinship, ecological demography, hunter-gatherer societies, computational modeling, and cultural transmission. For example, the IPEM features work on reproductive "conflicts of interests" between males and females, even within socially monogamous pairs, while seeking explanations based on genetic transmission and Darwinian fitness. The IGERT program also features prominent cultural anthropologists, such as John Bodley, whose work in cultural ecology features indigenous peoples and environmental adaptation.

It is apparent that there is a growing interest within anthropology to return to a more anthropological science that stands in stark contrast to the postmodern assertion that reality exists only in perception and language, "while 'postmodern' anthropology may have had tremendous currency in the late 1980s and first half of the 1990s, there is substantial evidence that this is not the case today" (Mascia-Lees 2006: 13). Where before using science and culture in the same sentence, let alone the same paper, was heresy, the acknowledgement that culture can certainly influence and/or modify biology and that behavior that is observed within a culture may be based on biology does make a return to a more empirically based process more palatable.

It seems that an endeavor such as the current "Goodman" biocultural perspective would naturally depend not only on a holistic perspective of the interplay between culture and biology, but as well engage a healthy empiricism as this interplay is explored to define cultural and biologic variables "reliable and systematic knowledge" (Smith 2006: 10) that operate to produce behavioral reality. Only in knowing the gain and modulation of such variables can one begin to assess how the variables and/or conditions can be addressed, altered, or mitigated to improve quality of life. In this exercise, explicating the variables, as well as working to assist in addressing the condition, demands all kinds of anthropology and anthropologists (applied as well), from sociocultural and cultural, to biological anthropologists to even include archaeologists.

THE ROAD TO CULTURE AND BIOLOGY IN ANTHROPOLOGY

This section is not meant to be more than a brief review of the last fifty years of the development of movements that now look at the relationship of human evolution, genes, behavior, biology and culture in some form or fashion. Biocultural anthropology, as do the fields of human behavioral ecology and evolutionary psychology, owes its pedigree to several innovative and early evolutionary thinkers, among them Williams, Hamilton, Chomsky, Tiger, Fox, and so on. The greater academic and popular world at large were awakened to a re-engagement of the biological influence on human behavior with E. O. Wilson's interdisciplinary magnum opus, *Sociobiology: The New Synthesis* (1976) and the follow-up work, *On Human Nature* (1979), in exploring the relationship between genes and human behavior.

Sociobiology

In the nineteenth century, biologists led by Darwin literally hunted the origin of species while nascent anthropologists such as Morgan and Tylor sought the origins of social institutions such as marriage, kinship, family, and religion. Quests that tied behavior to human origins fell to the wayside, and rightly so, due to a lack of empirical data and the influence of Boas and historical particularism and Malinowski's functionalism subverting the cultural evolutionary paradigm and its unilineal and racist stance. At the turn of the twentieth century, Boas and Malinowksi brought a natural sciences ardor to the study of human culture and society, yet both and others realized the stringent requirements of empirical verifiability made natural studies of human behavior difficult. Instead, fieldwork—leading to the construction of theories of culture and society based on basic human needs, metacultural needs, personality types, gender roles, cultural ecology, energy consumption, symbols, creating and interpretation of cultural texts, and more—was emphasized and anthropologists became the global gypsies of the social sciences.

An increased interest in a Darwinian approach to the origins of human behavior was revived in the 1970s with the emergence of such theories as sociobiology, whose main proponent was Edward O. Wilson. His work built on earlier work of Robin Fox and Lionel Tiger and a *biogrammar*, or biosocial theory of the origins of human behavior. Like Wilson, both Fox and Tiger said that human behavior was indeed genetically encoded. They wrote of a Chomskian-like culture-acquisition device that allowed a bio-grammar for human behavior, "human wiring for culture . . . the genetic qualities that favored scientific activity or associative learning, general intelligence or the ability to inhibit present gratifications for future wants, or the propensity to obey rules, would be subject to selection as much as the muscular qualities that facilitated the striding walk" (1971: 19). If not sounding too familiar, Fox and Tiger posited the wiring to be a legacy of our Paleolithic ancestry, "civilized man is an evolutionary afterthought. . . . [A]griculture and industrial civilizations have put nothing into the basic wiring of the human animal" (1971: 22). Laying a foundation for Wilson, Fox and Tiger were evolutionary biologists such as George Williams and William Hamilton who initiated a return to a Darwinian selectionist theory. Williams especially clarified a modern relationship between selection and adaptive design, operating at the genetic level and initiated a scientific rigor into deciding the calculus of function leading to adaptation (Tooby and Cosmides 1992, 2005).

Let it be said that Wilson's sociobiology tread on waters of decades-old established doctrine of cultural relativism and the initial sowing of seeds of an anti-colonial postmodernism. With the recent exploration into the human genome still decades away, Wilson's approach, explored in the final chapter of his classic work, *Sociobiology: The New Synthesis*, and later follow-up work, *On Human Nature*, posited simple gene-driven models of human behavior that were found to be less prescriptive when cultural and environmental factors were discerned. Basically, human and non-human social and individual behaviors are the result of natural selection and can be inherited, just as physical traits evolve. Over time, evolutionary successful behaviors (complex social processes that can reflect complex combinations of genes in the behavior's expression), like traits, will survive, if providing for the evolutionary fitness of the individual or group, more specifically, aiding the preservation of one's genes from one generation to the next. In essence, the foundation of sociobiology rests on the assertion that certain behavioral traits were a function of natural selection and thus are inheritable and are an adaptive response to the species-evolved environment. Thus, the evolutionary mechanism for the reproducibility of these behaviors is genetic.

The publication of *Sociobiology* created an academic and then popular firestorm of controversy, and as such the criticisms were interdisciplinary in nature; Gould and Lewontin in evolutionary biology, Sahlins and many other anthropologists; neurobiologist Steven Rose and a host of scientists found fault with the mechanism (Bethell 2001), the reductionist nature and to many of the "culturalists" of the day, the implied correlation between human behavior and propensities and genes (read "race"). To the extreme, sociobiology was labeled Social Darwinism, aligned with the Eugenics movement, and became an unwitting central tenet in the IQ controversy of the 1970s. So vitriolic was the rhetoric, even within academe, within the same Harvard department—Gould and Lewontin and Wilson represented the academic and political divide—thirty-five prominent scientists led by Gould and Lewontin formed the Sociobiology Study Group of "Science for the People" (Bethell 2001) and unleashed a "leftist" critique of what Lewontin was to characterize as *Genomania*. This movement espoused political and social statements that certainly overshadowed necessary and well-founded critique. In retrospect, perhaps due to the nature of its subject and as well the social and political climate that Wilson was writing in, the interactive relationship of culture and biology was overlooked or lost in the debate.

Work by William Hamilton on kin selection (1964), Robert Trivers (1971, 1972) on reciprocal altruism, and Richard Dawkins' *Selfish Gene* (1990) promoted the Darwinian gene connection and laid the foundation for future advancement of evolutionary sciences. Dawkins followed genes with "memes," later evolutionary psychologist and cognitive scientist Steven Pinker (1999, 2002) introduced "modules," both units derived from the view of genes being the replicators of behavior, tried and true, through natural selection. The range of the gene-correlated behavior theory to explain human nature was attractive due to ease of applicability to any number of disciplines, any number of circumstances, and any number of animals. To critics it was the panacea to explain all. Gould and Lewontin's *Just so Stories* explanation (Bethell 2001)—the inability to measure the benefits but through observation of the behavior that rely on the adaptationist premise to explain the existence of the behavior—through a hazy tie from Paleolithic "stone age" mental structure to the contemporary mind and other critiques were and still are very debatable.

Yet, in the end, then and still now, torching sociobiology meant questioning Darwin and perhaps, as evidenced by Gould's eventual tepid acknowledgement of the position itself, the house that Darwin planned was better left a sound structure by maintaining one of the internal columns that held up the roof. Perhaps serenely ignorant of the need for an accepted tenet of science, the need for falsifiability, those gene-bent see a theory that has reached an almost scientific omnipotence, where belief can be considered secularized, scientific "faith" in the power of the gene to explain away the variability of human behavior. The Human Genome project certainly has provided the reason, for some the hope, for exploring at last, over sixty years after the coming out party for DNA, the relationship between all things phenotypic and all things genotypic, including more understanding of what motivates behavior.

A BRIEF HISTORY OF THE RISE OF CULTURE, GENES AND BIOLOGY IN EXPLANATORY MODELS

Human Behavioral Ecology

Sociobiology continues to exert the applicability and power of explanation of Darwinian or natural selection paradigm giving rise to a number of related "movements." Human behavioral ecology (HBE), using evolutionary ecology models and concepts to explain human behavioral diversity, began in the late 1970s on the heels of sociobiology (Cronk 1995). "Human behavioral ecology may be defined as the study of the evolutionary ecology of human behavior. Its central problem is to discover the ways in which the behavior of modern humans reflects our species' history of natural selection" (Cronk 1991: 25). Human behavioral ecologists develop hypotheses that speak to variation in individual behavior (strategies) that seem to maximize their inclusive fitness; "in many studies the central focus is on reproductive consequences of behavior" (Hames 2001: 6947). Originally keen to topics such as human-foraging strategies, mating systems, and spatial organization and competition, human behavioral ecology looks for environmental and social *factors* that affect behavioral variability within and between populations.

The central focus seems to be on the consequences of human economic, reproductive, and social behavior using a "neodarwinian theory" (Tucker and Taylor 2007: 181) allied with theory from ecology and economics while using ethnographic methodology to explicate explanation. Recent work in HBE has explored its use in applied anthropology. In August 2007, a full issue of the journal *Human Nature* was devoted to exploring human behavioral ecology as a tool(s) to aid anthropologists' "application of [HBE] to significant world issues through the design and critique of public policy and international development projects" (Tucker and Taylor 2007:181). Examples highlighted in this issue are an exploration of how a new national park in Madagascar will impact livelihood strategies of rural residents (Tucker 2007); tradeoffs of Fijian urban mothers meeting children's nutritional needs, long-term investments in skill-based learning (Neill 2007); and family-planning decisions among Indian groups such as the Khasi and Bengali with voluntary fertility reduction through contraception (Leonetti, Nath and Heman 2007).

Evolutionary Psychology

Evolutionary psychology is a sister field of human behavioral ecology (Barkow et al. 1995, Tooby and Cosmides 1992) where the primary focus is illuminating "high resolution models of the evolved [neural] mechanisms that collectively constitute universal human nature" (Tooby and Cosmides 2005: 5). Elsewhere referred to as "mental modules" (Pinker 1999, 2002), evolutionary psychologists see the human mind composed of a neural architecture that incorporates "circuit logic" (Tooby and Cosmides 2005: 6) or programs that process sensory information and causally elicit behavior. This circuit logic (modules) has been tested over time through Darwinian selection (to evolutionary psychologists, the only physical process that can "build" functional design into a species). However, given the short period of evolutionary time since the human species were ancestral Paleolithic hunters and gathers or in the environment of evolutionary adaptedness (EEA), the circuits' code for adaptively selected behavior is based on an environment that certainly was far different and less technologically complex than the culturally modified third millennium of today.[1] "Our minds are collections of mechanisms designed to solve adaptive problems posed by the ancestral world" (Tooby and Cosmides 2005: 11). The functional design of logic is adapted to the "recurrently structured ancestral world" more than the "fitness striving of individuals" that is customized to ongoing unique circumstances.

Psychological mechanisms (read behavior) are evolved adaptations, plain and simple. Tied to foundation precepts of evolutionary biology are the development of information theory and advances in neurosciences that presuppose human mental activity as in the structured informational relationships as part and parcel of physical structural components and systems in the brain. It is obvious to evolutionary psychologists that these behaviors and related physical components are girded by genes and, thus, are the currency of selective adaptation.

Dual Inheritance Theory

Robert Boyd and Peter Richerson (1985, 2001) posited what has been commonly referred to as the Dual Inheritance theory, a culture-gene co-evolutionary model that looks at humans as a dynamic interaction between culture and genes. Dual Inheritance theory follows initial work by geneticists Cavelli-Sforza and H. R. Feldman (1981) on quantifying cultural evolution. Basically genes affect cultural evolution by influencing psychological predispositions for learning, while culture will create ecological situations where genes may be selected for their success in that cultural environment. Cultural traits or memes are very similar to genes in the sense they are replicators "that use vehicles (bodies) to transmit themselves across generations" (Hames 2001) and, thus, are subject to selective agents or forces. Henirich and McElreath (2003) posited a social-learning model, while others recently have elaborated on topics that touch on culture, society, and history using a similar evolutionary culture-genes model.

Biocultural Human Biology

Biological anthropologist Alan Goodman along with Thomas Leatherman and George Ellison (Goodman and Leatherman 1998, Goodman et al. 2003, Ellison and Goodman 2006) and others have extended the reach of culture into biology, exploring fundamentally "the roots of human biological conditions, which are traced to the interaction of political-economic processes and local conditions" (Goodman and Leatherman 1998: 5). Certainly cognizant of the legacy of biological determinism implicit in early sociobiology and later evolutionary psychology, Goodman and others' approach is to bridge the divide between evolutionary anthropology and the sociocultural anthropologists by seeking a common ground between biology and culture.

Following the movement of addressing social and cultural inequality, Goodman sees a real benefit, almost a necessity, of intertwining human biology of fertility, mortality, "skinfolds, blood pressures, stress hormone levels and rates of amnesia [that] . . . adds an integral layer of information that is too often missed" (Goodman and Leatherman 1998: 6) to explicate and sharpen the anthropology of human "struggles" to cope and eventually affect global suffering.

Acknowledging the importance of a postmodern movement away from the perceived infallibility, westernized dominant authority and sterile problem-solver mantle applied to the human sciences, biocultural human biologists look to sensitize their work to the divide between biology and culture in anthropology departments specifically—spelled out earlier in this chapter—and to the models and theories in general and across disciplines that build on the more precise and advanced methodology now available to human biologists. This leads to the development of models that incorporate the dynamics between culture and biological systems. In other words, scientific methodology allows a greater window into the workings of human biological organisms, and Darwinian ecological theories explicate the increased interaction and influence of ecology, both natural and social, on human behavior. Yet, Goodman and others see the need to develop a lens that peers into the how and why humans engage in political-economic behavior and thus how humans perceive and define such behavior and differences that lie within. By adding in the biological systems, this biocultural view becomes a more complete explanation of the relationship between culture and biology. Using this approach, Ellison and Goodman's 2006 volume, *The Nature of Difference*, explores how humans differ, the causality of human difference, and what these differences mean. The nature of human difference is more than just biological or cultural, but the sum of both.

BIOCULTURAL PERSPECTIVE OF
SPORT AND HUMAN MOVEMENT

The noted physical anthropologist Robert Malina advocated a biocultural approach in response to work done in the 1980s and 1990s on race and sport. However, the clarion call for an integrated look at both human biology and culture(s) was espoused by none other than Clifford Geertz in a 1966 paper titled "The Impact of the Concept of Culture on the Concept of Man" (see chapter 2 in this volume). This paper was later reprinted in his foundational *The Interpretation of Cultures* (1973), even though Geertz himself would move away from an interest in the relationship between culture and biology as his work developed a more interpretive path. Geertz may not have envisioned his words being co-opted by endeavors such as an anthropology of sport or even human movement that exists well outside a cockfight ring. However, biocultural approaches such as that of Fox and Tiger (and later Wilson's sociobiology) were yet to be elaborated on when Geertz was writing the "impact" paper and the extent of the influence of our Paleolithic ancestors and their environment on today's human was at the time not well understood, nor very popular.

An engaged biocultural perspective, one that combines the intent of human behavioral ecology and the issues-centric nature of biocultural human biology, offers a platform for addressing real world issues and concerns of the species that lie at the heart of human "dissonance," such as health, nutrition and welfare; understanding many levels of human ancestry; providing an understanding of the nature of cultural and biological difference in human populations (as it extends to behavior); and biological impacts of economic and political inequality, to name a few. Developing a biocultural perspective in looking at human movement—one that is holistic in nature as anthropology has offered and promises to continue to offer—provides an integrated and diverse view of human movement in the contexts of both culture and biology. Critical to the success of this endeavor is an engaged and rigorous positivistic ethnography (Sands 2008) that explicates not only agency but also offers a truthful lens of biocultural reality.

Included in this perspective is the acknowledgement of human adaptability in biology and culture to past and contemporary physical and social-cultural ecologies. Examples of this perspective are the role of human

movement in our species' evolution and the implications of the evolution
of those patterns in contemporary issues of concern such as health; to
include diet, obesity, and the sedentary nature of recent human evolution;
describing and documenting the natural and cultural ecology of movement patterns, to include looking at the foundation of play in human and
non-human primates and play in contemporary human culture; the role
of movement patterns in extant cultures, such as the East African "running" cultures (Kenyan and Ethiopian) as performance in professional and
international running events become powerful "selection" agents on the
shape of culture and running biology; and the integration of movement
patterns into the development of human religion and faith systems in human evolution and, as well, in contemporary society. These are just some
of many general or specific issues that confront and energize a biocultural
perspective of human movement and are represented by the contributions
included in this volume. The following sections will outline just a few of
these issues where a biocultural perspective does and can offer insight and
analysis to ongoing research programs.

SPORT AND PERFORMANCE, GENES AND ENVIRONMENT

Within this energized perspective is that of human movement as it relates to performance in sport and games. Beyond the notion of "leisure,"
the influence of sport, its performance, behavior and meaning to world
cultures and societies and the role it has on globalization is unmistak-
able and pervasive. Performance, both in superior performance by the
athlete as well as performance as it relates to the construction and maintenance of cultural and social markers of identity and reification of that
identity, seems to be a thread that weaves through movement patterns in
many cultures. Recent work on human performance in, at first glance,
superficially disparate areas of human and non-human play, evolution
of human running, ultra-running, surfing, dance, and athletic training
has established the intimate relationship between biology and culture in
performance. However, what is emphasized here is that this relationship
is a two-way street, culture and behavior can perhaps override certain
biological traits, and even more so, can also act to "rewire" brain circuitry and its neurochemistry (Downey 2004). This is a particularly
timely focus as some scholars begin to consider both the potential and

bioethcs of twenty-first-century gene manipulation to enhance athletic performance (see Miah in this volume).

With an infancy tarnished by racist intentions, studies in sport from a biocultural approach have tended to focus more narrowly on specific issues, rather than developing an overall theoretical framework. Previous works included research on sprinting and endurance running, perhaps spurred on by the appearance of Jon Entine's 2000 popular publication, *Taboo*. Even before and since the publication of *Taboo*, a large body of work in both popular press and scholarly journals has been on the Kenyan dominance in world distance running (see Bale and Sang 1996; Entine 2000; Mayes 2005; Manners 1997; Burfoot 1999; see also Pitsiladis et al. 2006). However, work carried out within a biocultural perspective has not been well received in some quarters, and criticism (e.g., Hoberman 1997; St. Louis 2003, 2004) has focused on allegations of scientific racism and the lack of a sound theoretical foundation and/ or credible data in support of the arguments, even offering doubt on the legitimacy of conducting investigations in an effort to understand all aspects of the human condition, including sport and human movement. However, recent work on the evolution of human running is a prime example of this application of culture and biology (Bramble and Lieberman 2004, Lieberman et al. 2006, Sands and Sands 2009), opening up avenues of exploration for the selective forces that operated on the evolution of running and movement in human prehistory and the legacy of this system in contemporary human running.

The often times acrimonious and highly charged debate on genes, race, and performance continues and the nature and extent of this debate harbors the importance of why such a debate occurs at all, or the fact that it continues to be inserted in popular and academic circles in much that same way that the subject of origins of homosexuality has claimed a similar fate. Yet, probing the genome and shedding light on the contribution of genes to human disease and suffering is sufficient reason enough to continue to explore the relation of genes to human movement patterns, and in specific, human performance. Anthropology is perfectly suited to approach and explore this very complex issue, containing within its boundaries the very tools and perspectives needed to systematically explore the relationships of genes and performance and behavior, while maintaining and sensitizing the meanings, both empirical and cultural, that the investigation and continuing refinement of results will have on the human condition.

MOVEMENT AND HUMAN EVOLUTION

Amplifying the understanding of our species evolution through both extant human movements, as well as through the exploration of those movement patterns in paleoanthropology, paleoneurology, and paleoecology, provides a more discerning look at the adaptation of a running biology to the paleoecology of Pleistocene hominins (see Sands and Heinrich this volume). Work in this area, initiated by Carrier's 1984 treatise on running, followed by Heinrich (2001), and Bramble and Lieberman (2004), Lieberman and colleagues (2006), and Liebenberg (2006) posited running as a primary biocultural adaptation (scavenging and later hunting) to the paleoecology of the African Pleistocene.

As work continues to identify the pathways of neurochemical responses in contemporary movement in mammals, research is beginning to look at these responses in human movement in areas such as play, exercise, running, and extreme sport. What research in movement "studies" specific to human origins (in all its ramifications of paleoanthropology and paleoneurology, including primate studies on play and movement patterns) strongly suggests is that what many typically ascribe as solely a cultural foundation to the expression of play, sport, and games has very much a biological component. This area of research can prove to be very beneficial to understanding not only its importance in the evolution of our species, but as well the role of such movement patterns in contemporary human society as we move more into a technologically enhanced human future, where movement is subsumed by innovation. It is this intersection of human behavior with now cultural rather than biological selection that will have an impact on how movement will shape human biology.

PLAY DEVELOPMENT AND EXPRESSION

Much work has been done on the ontogeny of play as well as play development in human children (see Lewis this volume). Comparative work in play with other animals, specifically mammals and non-human primates, has provided both field and laboratory data that document playful behavior as a foundation for social behavior. However, recent investigations of playfulness in non-mammalian species have suggested that play behavior reaches further back into the phylogeny of animal species. Play behavior is seen as braking "serious" behavioral elements through context and the "braking" or neutralizing the seriousness of play behaviors seems to involve activated as well as advanced neurological control. As technology allows a more in-depth picture of brain function, the observed play patterns in concert with neurological function may produce a more refined and accurate model of play function. With a more complete picture of play function, continued investigations into play behavior in mammal and non-mammalian species will offer insights and suggest clear models of the evolution of play.

Perhaps with further insights into play beginnings, extrapolations on the importance and kind of play behavior in hominin evolution can be made. In addition, as the influence of the brain on play behavior is further documented, in non-human primates as well as humans, further understandings of the importance of contemporary play in humans from a cross-cultural perspective is critical. As diet and nutrition become problematic for the human species, especially during childhood, decreases in physical activity in all stages of ontogeny, especially during childhood, leads to more sedentism and obesity. Ramifications of less physical movement in childhood impact the development of the interconnections between neurobiology and movement, indicating that the concerns for the acceleration of culture and technology on human development are real.

RITUAL, SPIRITUALITY, AND RELIGION IN HUMAN MOVEMENT AND SPORT

The importance of faith, in the guise of both spirituality and formalized religion, to world cultures cannot be overstated. Physical movement is integral to human ritual, as in all mammals, and as such, physical movement is integral to human spirituality and religion. Work by Jones (2004), Sands (2008b, 2008c), and Sands and Sands (2009), among others, suggests that spirituality and, later, sport evolved from the dynamic interaction of ritual and movement patterns and perhaps could have coincided with the material manifestation of art and symbolism in the Upper Paleolithic, if not preceding the symbolic representation found on cave walls, portable art, and rock shelters.

Work in sport and religion has centered on topics such as Christian Evangelism and western sport, sport as a secular religion, and even sport as a central tenet for religiosity in culture (Ladd and Mathisen 1999, Putney 2003). However, there is a dearth of work done on human movement and sport from a biocultural perspective. With the advent of neurotheology popularized in works such as evolutionary psychology, the biology of religious thought and expression has become, through the use of brain scans and other technologies and even the unmasking of the human genome, a central focus and galvanizing concern to academics and the popular media.

The role and biology of human movement in religion and spirituality has thus far escaped any rigorous inquiry, although there are countless books and publications that draw comparisons between western and contemporary sport and formalized religion (Prebish 1992, Kotler 2007, Cooper 2004), even some classics on sport as secular religion (Novak 1976). Human movement has been detailed generally, and sport specifically, to spirituality and religion in human prehistory and history, in the cultures of indigenous groups such as American Indians, Australian aborigines, and the Mayan culture, not to mention the integral tie between Greek and Roman sport and spectacle and ritual and religion (Kyle 2006, Crowther 2007). Peter Nabakov's *Indian Running* (1981) delves into the role running played in the spirituality of Native Americans in the American Southwest and northwest Mexico, and Indian lacrosse (Vennum 1994) has been described and historically contextualized. Archaeological excavations have uncovered ball courts in Hohokam sites in Arizona, and Mayan excavations have uncovered similar features of ball courts. Ethnohistorical accounts describe ritual-laced performances of the ball players, with sacrifice of athletes more common than not. Certainly, within the last ten thousand years of human evolution, coinciding with the advent of a more settled existence of the human species, and all of its cultural and social ramifications as the result of a global and local climate-induced environmental change, movement patterns evolved into a formalized and religious-based system we label today as sport.

Speculative work on physical activities, such as running and surfing, based on research just beginning on neurochemical release systems, have tied movement with neurobiological release to promote an emotive state that is said to resemble those found in spiritual and religious states (see Jones 2004, Csikszentmihalyi 1991, 1998; Dietrich 2004; Sands 2008a; Sands and Sands 2009; Gunn 2006). Understanding the role that movement plays in religious and spiritual expression, from both a phylogenetic view as well as a contemporary cross-cultural perspective, provides a potential common understanding of the foundation of all human systems of belief and faith. As human movement and physical activity (sport, recreation and games) introduces new alternate movement expressions (alternate sport, extreme sports, ecotourism) that interface and even modify the environment in new ways, faith and belief systems will play a major role in incorporating that movement into culture and biology, as well as formalizing and legitimizing such expression.

HUMAN MOVEMENT AND SPORT
IN AN ENVIRONMENTAL CONTEXT

Human movement leaves large footprints on the surface of the planet. Movement joins other human behaviors in creating larger and larger destructive footprints, many of which have irreversible consequences on the planet's ecology, including impact to local and global biospheres and their wildlife inhabitants. Global warming or climate-induced environmental change has provoked international concern for the following: rising ocean levels from melting polar ice packs and the impact on ocean currents already impacting coastal Pacific islands in and around New Guinea, ratcheting up of weather patterns to include increased severity of hurricanes, cyclones, and tornadoes, and increased areas stricken and potential victims of increased drought; these impacts direct and indirect are staggering. Conservation, the cost of energy and the non-renewability of current energy sources, and population growth are intertwined to present an uncertain future of life as we know it in the near and not-too-distant future.

As an ever-increasing number of our species interact with the environment, our destructive footprint continues to grow and impact the global ecosystem. Searching for ways to slow down and reverse this impact is necessary. Going *green* is now popular and better business. The intersection of human movement, sport, games, and leisure activities and the environment proves to be one of those "ways" where footprint and environmental awareness can be contradictory activities. Ecotourism is on the rise, extreme or alternate sports that incorporate the natural environment into their expression are many; snowboarding, surfing, mountain biking, extreme trail running, rock climbing and mountain climbing now cater to a larger, more affluent participatory audience, and these are just a few that involve terra firma. Some alternative sports occur up to a mile or more above the earth's surface, ski surfing, paragliding, and ultra-lite flying to name a few, leaving little visible impacts on the earth's surface; however, greenhouse gas emissions are still generated. Other recreational pursuits leave a much larger footprint on the environment, to include off-road all-terrain vehicles such as motorcycles and quads.

Theories abound for the dramatic growth in these pursuits; those include socioeconomic, accounting for more affluence, leisure time, and technological advances. However, as risk seems to be one of the defining attributes of many of these activities, testing the limits of human potential, and perhaps including an addictive elements as well, initial work, certainly speculative in many cases, have advanced the Type T personality that includes neurobiological underpinnings and perhaps an adaptability of that constellation of behaviors either in our contemporary lifestyle, or recent and even not so recent past. It is however certain that these alternate and in some cases extreme sports happen in places, spaces and areas that feature pristine or protected landscapes.

CONCLUSION

The previous sections are just a sample of areas where an anthropological biocultural study of human movement and sport can provide meaningful and important insight on issues confronting the human species as well as further discovery into human origins. Anthropology is a field whose power of description can lead to generation of explanatory models. As indicated earlier, anthropology in some institutions has cleaved into biological and cultural entities, the emergence of—to some a rebound from the radicalized postmodernism—a more holistic approach in many fields (such as anthropology and biology and the development of new movements such as sociobiology, human behavioral ecology, evolutionary anthropology, and dual inheritance theory to name a few). Currently, the study of human behavior has included the realization that human culture and biology are more than mere disinterested bedfellows. The trail of most qualitative work being done in the social science study of sport is not anthropology, nor does it consider any of the other facets of movement and sport that could be undertaken by both biological and cultural anthropologists. The gaze of sport sociologists and those involved in sports studies is too focused and narrow, it marginalizes—through magnification of its current focus—what sport and human movement can tell us about human behavior, biology, and human evolution. We do not disallow the tools and methods of our trade, such as ethnography, nor the continued work in the cultural realm of sport and human movement. As Eric Alden Smith writes about a biocultural perspective, it "combines theory from ecology and evolutionary biology with ethnographic methods and theory from the social sciences" (2006: 9). In fact, operating under such a paradigm, there is ample opportunity for collaboration across the subdisciplines of anthropology, including what has been till recent and continues in some form or fashion today the schism between the cultural and the biological.

A recent example of such an engaging and more encompassing "gaze" of the dynamic relationship between biology, culture, and society in human movement and sport was the in-depth volume, *East African Running: Toward a Cross-Disciplinary Perspective* (Pitsiladis et al. 2006). Three of the authors included in that volume, Noakes, Pitsiladis, and Christensen, are featured in this volume as well. Bringing together a host of research on the diet, altitude, culture, biology, to include physiology and the byplay between the genetic and the environment, and history and prehistory of East Africans, *East African Running* produced a very informed and complete look at how running has been and continues today to be highly integrated into the biology and culture of the inhabitants of East Africa. This volume is an attempt at bringing this emergent "bioculturalism" anthropological perspective to the study of human movement in general and sport specifically. From a broader breadth and scope than *East African Running*, this volume explores what can be a critical and noteworthy engagement of anthropology in the study of human movement and sport and one which anthropologists can finally, without being apologists or ignorant of the value of peering into this complex human behavior, wrapped in our unique human biology and expressed in our past and contemporary culture, claim as a viable academic endeavor.

This volume dovetails on this thematic biocultural exploration and represents a collection of work that reveals and explores the sometimes dramatic relationship of our biology and culture that is inextricably woven into a tapestry of movement patterns and cultural expression. Some of the chapters deal specifically with movement and culture in sport, yet that is not the extent or scope of this volume. Other chapters explore the underpinning of human movement, reflected in play, sport, games, and human culture from an evolutionary perspective and contemporary expression of sport and human movement. As in any "movement," there are differing perspectives and therefore a variety of theories and this volume reflects each, perspective and theory. There are no "neat" and unencumbered conclusions—it does seem clear that there is a complex relationship between human biology and culture. Yet, anthropology offers through its holistic lens cross-cultural application, and ethnographic tradition a means to frame this relationship in ways that can reveal how human movement patterns can both influence culture as well as be influenced by culture. Indeed this volume offers an initial formulation of the promise of this exploration.

NOTES

I would like to thank Annie Bolin and David McConnell for reading drafts of this chapter and offering very pertinent reviews.

1. Earlier work by Irven Devore and Richard Lee introduced serious attempts at setting the Paleolithic stage and conditions and hence reconstructed lifeways of ancestral humanity. DeVore's systematic studies of primate social systems in natural conditions and with Richard Lee, the Kalahari San project that created the empirically based investigations of living hunters and gathers provided necessary focus on the dynamics of ecology and human behavior.

BIBLIOGRAPHY

Bale, John and Mette K. Christensen. *Post Olympism? Questioning Sport in the Twenty-First Century*. London: Berg, 2004.

Bale, John and Joe Sang. *Kenyan Running: Movement Culture, Geography and Global Change*. London: Frank Cass and Co. Ltd, 1996.

Barkow, Jerome, Leah Cosmides and John Tooby. *The Adapted Mind: Evolutionary Psychology and the Generation of Culture*. New York: Oxford University Press, 1995.

Bethell, Tom. "Against Sociobiology." *The Journal of Religion, Culture, and Public Life* 109 (2001): 18–24.

Blanchard, Kendall and Alyce Taylor Cheska. *The Anthropology of Sport: An Introduction*. South Hadley, Mass.: Bergin & Garvey, 1985.

Blanchard, Kendall. *The Anthropology of Sport: An Introduction (revised edition)*. Westport, Conn.: Bergin & Garvey, 1995.

Bolin, Anne and Jane Granskog. *Athletic Intruders: Ethnographic Research on Women, Culture, and Exercise.* Albany, N.Y.: SUNY Press, 2003.

Bolin, Anne and Patricia Wheelen. *Interdisciplinary Perspectives on Human Sexuality: Biological, Psychological, and Cultural Understandings.* London: Routledge Press, 2008.

Boyd, Robert and Peter J. Richerson. *Culture and the Evolutionary Process.* Chicago: University of Chicago Press, 1985.

———. "Built for Speed, Not for Comfort: Darwinian Theory and Human Culture." *History and Philosophy of the Life Sciences* 23 (2001): 423–63.

Bramble, Dennis M. and Daniel E. Lieberman. "Endurance Running and the Evolution of Homo." *Nature* 432, no. 7015 (2004): 345–52.

Brown, Peter J. and Norman Yoffee. "Is Fission the Future of Anthropology?" *Anthropology Newsletter* 33, no. 7 (1992): 1–21.

Brownell, Susan. *Training the Body for China: Sports in the Moral Order of the People's Republic.* Chicago: University of Chicago Press, 1995.

———. *Beijing's Games: What the Olympics Mean to China.* New York: Rowman & Littlefield Publishers, 2007.

Burfoot, Amby. "African Speed, African Endurance." *Anthropology, Sport, and Culture,* edited by Robert R. Sands. Westport, Conn.: Bergin & Garvey, 1999: 53–63.

Carrier, D. R. "The Energetic Paradox of Human Running and Hominid Evolution." *Current Anthropology* 25, no. 4 (1984): 483–95.

Cavalli-Sforza, Luigi. L. and M. W. Feldman. *Cultural Transmission and Evolution: A Quantitative Approach.* Princeton, N.J.: Princeton University Press, 1981.

Cooper, Andrew. *Playing in the Zone: Exploring the Spiritual Dimensions of Sports.* Boston: Shambhala, 2004.

Crawford, Peter. "Book Review: Post-Olympism? Questioning Sport in the Twenty-First Century." *Journal of the Royal Anthropological Institute* 11, no. 2 (2005): 382–83.

Cronk, Lee. "Human Behavioral Ecology." *Annual Review of Anthropology* 20, no. 1 (1991): 25–53.

———. "Is There a Role for Culture in Human Behavioral Ecology?" *Ethology and Sociobiology* 16, no. 3 (1995): 181–205.

Crowther, Nigel B. *Sport in Ancient Times.* Westport, Conn.: Praeger Publishers, 2007.

Csikszentmihalyi, Mihaly. *Flow: The Psychology of Optimal Experience.* New York: Harper Perennial, 1991.

———. *Finding Flow: The Psychology of Engagement with Everyday Life.* New York: Basic Books, 1998.

Dawkins, Richard. *The Selfish Gene (second edition).* New York: Oxford University Press, 1990.

Downey, Greg. *Learning Capoeira: Lessons in Cunning from an Afro-Brazilian Art.* New York: Oxford University Press, 2004.

Dyck, Noel, ed. *Games, Sports and Cultures.* Oxford: Berg, 2000.

Eastman, Benjamin, Sean Brown, and Michael R. Majumdar. *America's Game(s): A Critical Anthropology of Sport.* London: Routledge Press, 2007.

Ellison, George T. and Alan H. Goodman, eds. *The Nature of Difference: Science, Society and Human Biology.* New York: Taylor & Francis Books, 2006.

Entine, Jon. *Taboo: Why Black Athletes Dominate Sports and Why We Are Afraid to Talk About It*. New York: Public Affairs Books, 2000.

Fox, Robin and Lionel Tiger. *The Imperial Animal*. New York: Holt, Rinehart and Winston, 1971.

Geertz, Clifford. "The Impact of the Concept of Culture on the Concept of Man." Pp. 93–118 in *New Views of the Nature of Man*, ed. J. Platt. Chicago: University of Chicago Press, 1966.

———. *The Interpretation of Cultures*. New York: Basic Books, 1973.

Goodman, Alan H. "Bringing Biology Back into Anthropology." Presidential Address presented at the annual meeting of the American Anthropology Association, Washington, D.C., December 2007.

Goodman, Alan H. and Thomas L. Leatherman, eds. *Building a New Biocultural Synthesis: Political-Economic Perspectives on Human Biology*. Ann Arbor: University of Michigan Press, 1998.

Goodman, Alan H., Deborah Heath, and M. Susan Lindee, eds. *Genetic Nature/Culture: Anthropology and Science Beyond the Two-Culture Divide*. Berkeley: University of California Press, 2003.

Gunn, William F. Jr. *Rhythmic African Spirituality in Sports, Dance, Music and Art*. Kemetic Institute for Leadership and Human Development, 2006.

Guttmann, Allen. *From Ritual to Record*. New York: Columbia University Press, 1979.

Hames, Robert. "Human Behavioral Ecology." *International Encyclopedia of the Social & Behavioral Sciences*, edited by N. J. Smelser and P. B. Baltes. New York: Elsevier, 2001: 6946–51.

Hamilton, William D. "The Genetical Evolution of Social Behaviour I and II." *Journal of Theoretical Biology* 7 (1964): 1–16 and 17–52.

Heinrich, B. *Why We Run: A Natural History*. New York: HarperCollins Publishers, 2001.

Henrich, J. and R. McElreath. "The Evolution of Cultural Evolution." *Evolutionary Anthropology* 12 (2003): 123–35.

Hoberman, John. *Darwin's Athletes: How Sport Has Damaged Black America and Preserved the Myth of Race*. New York: Mariner Books, 1997.

Holden, Constance. "Failing to Cross the Biology-Culture Gap." *Science* 262 (1993): 1641–42.

Jones, Peter N. "Ultrarunners and Chance Encounters with 'Absolute Unitary Being.'" *Anthropology of Consciousness* 15, no. 2 (2004): 39–50.

Klein, Alan M. *Little Big Men: Bodybuilding Subculture and Gender Construction*. Albany: State University of New York Press, 1991.

———. *Sugarball: The American Game, the Dominican Dream*. New Haven, Conn.: Yale University Press, 1993.

———. *Baseball on the Border: A Tale of Two Laredos*. Princeton, N.J.: Princeton University Press, 1997.

———. "The Anthropology of Sport: Escaping the Past and Building a Future." *Theory, Sport and Society*, edited by Joseph Maquire and Kevin Young. Amsterdam: Elsevier Science Ltd, 2002: 129–49.

Kotler, Steven. *West of Jesus: Surfing, Science, and the Origins of Belief.* London: Bloomsbury, 2007.

Kyle, Donald G. *Sport and Spectacle in the Ancient World.* New York: Wiley Blackwell, 2006.

Ladd, Tony and James Mathison. *Muscular Christianity: Evangelical Protestants and the Development of American Sport.* Ada, Mich.: Baker Books, 1999.

Leonetti, Donna, Dilip C. Nath and Natabar S. Hemam. "In-law Conflict: Women's Reproductive Lives and the Roles of Their Mothers and Husbands among the Matrilineal Khasi." *Current Anthropology* 49, no. 2 (2007): 861–90.

Liebenberg, Louis. "Persistence Hunting by Modern Hunter-Gatherers." *Current Anthropology* 47, no. 5 (2006): 1017–26.

Lieberman. Daniel E., David A. Raichlen, Herman Ponzer, Dennis M. Bramble and E. Cutright-Smith. "The Human Gluteus Maximus and Its Role in Running." *The Journal of Experimental Biology* 209, no. 11 (2006): 2143–55.

Maffi, Luisa, ed. *On Biocultural Diversity: Linking Language, Knowledge and the Environment.* Washington, D.C.: Smithsonian Institution Press, 2001.

Manners, John. "Kenya's Running Tribe." *The Sports Historian* 17, no. 2 (1997): 14–27.

Mascia-Lees, Fran. "Can Biological and Cultural Anthropology Coexist?" *Anthropology News* 47, no. 1 (2006): 9–13.

Mayes, Ruben E. *The Cybernetics of Kenyan Running: Hurry, Hurry Has No Blessing.* Durham, N.C.: Carolina Academic Press, 2005.

McElreath, R. and J. Henrich. "Modeling Cultural Evolution." *Oxford Handbook of Evolutionary Psychology*, edited by R. Dunbar and L. Barrett. Oxford: Oxford University Press, 2008: 571–85.

Moore, Philip. "Scouting an Anthropology of Sport." *Anthropologica* 46 (2006): 37–46.

Nabokov, Peter. *Indian Running.* Berkeley: University of California Press, 1981.

Neill, Dawn B. "Indo-Fijian Children's BMI: In the Context of Urbanization, Embodied Capital, and Food Choice Trade-offs." *Human Nature* 18, no. 3 (2007): 209–24.

Novak, Michael. *The Joy of Sports: End Zones, Bases, Baskets, Balls, and the Consecration of the American Spirit.* New York: Basic Books, 1976.

Peacock, James. "Claiming Common Ground." *Anthropology Newsletter* 4, no. 1 (1995): 3.

Pinker, Stephen. *How the Mind Works.* New York: W. W. Norton & Company, 1999.

———. *The Blank Slate: The Modern Denial of Human Nature.* New York: Viking, 2002.

Pitsiladis, Yannis, John Bale, Craig Sharp and Timothy Noakes. *East African Running: Toward a Cross-Disciplinary Perspective.* London: Routlege, 2006.

Putney, Clifford. *Muscular Christianity: Manhood and Sports in Protestant America, 1880–1920.* Cambridge, Mass.: Harvard University Press, 2003.

Prebish, Charles S. *Religion and Sport: The Meeting of Sacred and Profane.* Westport, Conn.: Greenwood Press, 1992.

Renson, Roland. "Messages from the Future: Significance of Sport and Exercise in the Third Millennium." *European Journal of Sport Medicine*, no. 1 (2001): 1–17.

Sands, Robert R. *Instant Acceleration: Living in the Fast Lane: The Cultural Identity of Speed*. Lanham, Md.: University Press of America, 1994.

———. *Anthropology, Sport and Culture*. Westport, Conn.: Greenwood Press, 1999a.

———. *GutCheck! An Anthropologist's Wild Ride into the Heart of College Football*. Carpinteria, Calif.: Rincon Hill Press, 1999b.

———. *Sport Ethnography*. Champaign, Ill.: Human Kinetics Press, 2002.

———. *Sport and Culture at Play in the Fields of Anthropology*. Needham, Mass.: Ginn Press, 2002.

———. "Ethical Ethnography: The Epistemology of Good Intentions." *Tribal Play: Subcultural Journeys through Sport*, edited by Michael Atkinson and Kevin Young. London: JAI Press, 2008a: 353–77.

———. "Play Deep: Speculations on the Evolutionary Relationship between Nature, Spirituality and Deep Play." Paper presented at the International Society for the Study of Religion, Nature, and Culture in Morelia, Mexico, January 2008b.

———. "*Homo Cursor*: Running into the Pleistocene." Paper presented at the Central States Anthropological Association meetings, Indianapolis, March, 2008c.

Sands, Robert R. and Linda R. Sands. "Running Deep: Speculations on the Evolution of Running and Spirituality in the Genus Homo." *Journal for the Study of Religion, Nature and Culture* 3, no. 4 (2009): 552–77.

Shenk, Mary. "Models for the Future of Anthropology." *Anthropology News* 47, no. 1 (2006): 6–7.

Siegal, Donald. "Play, Games, Sport, and Athletics." www.science.smith.edu/exer_sci/ESS200/Play/PlayH01.htm (accessed May 4, 2007).

Sievert, Lynnette Leidy. *Menopause: A Biocultural Perspective*. Piscataway, N.J.: Rutgers University Press, 2006.

Silk, Michael L., David L. Andrews and Daniel S. Mason. "Encountering the Field: Sports Studies and Qualitative Research." *Qualitative Methods in Sports Studies*, edited by David L. Andrews, Daniel S. Mason and Michael L. Silk. Oxford: Berg, 2004: 65–103.

Smith, Eric Alden. "Anthropological Schisms." *Anthropology News* 47, no. 1 (2006): 8–11.

St. Louis, Brett. "Sport, Genetics and the 'Natural Athlete': The Resurgence of Racial Science." *Body & Society* 9, no. 2 (2003): 75–95.

———. "Sport and Common-sense Racial Science." *Leisure Studies* 23, no. 1 (2004): 31–46.

Thomas, R. Brooke. "Anthropology for the Next Generation." *Anthropology News* 47, no. 1 (2006): 9–13.

Tooby, John and Leda Cosmides. "The Psychological Foundations of Culture." *The Adapted Mind: Evolutionary Psychology and the Generation of Culture*, edited by Jerome H. Barkow, Leda Cosmides and John Tooby. New York: Oxford University Press, 1992: 19–136.

———. "Conceptual Foundations of Evolutionary Psychology." *The Handbook of Evolutionary Psychology*, edited by D. M. Buss. Hoboken, N.J.: Wiley, 2005: 5–67.

Trevathan, Wenda R. "Evolutionary Medicine." *Annual Review of Anthropology* 36 (2007): 139–54.

Trevathan, Wenda R., E. O. Smith, and J. J. McKenna, eds. *Evolutionary Medicine and Health: New Perspectives*. New York: Oxford University Press, 2008.

Trivers, Robert L. "The Evolution of Reciprocal Altruism." *Quarterly Review of Biology* 46 (1971): 35–57.

———. "Parental Investment in Sexual Selection." *Sexual Selection and the Descent of Man, 1871–1971*, edited by Bernard G. Campbell. Chicago: Aldine, 1972: 136–79.

Tucker, Bram. "Applying Behavioral Ecology and Behavioral Economics to Conservation and Development Planning: An Example from the Mikea Forest, Madagascar." *Human Nature* 18, no. 3 (2007): 190–208.

Tucker, Bram and Lisa Rende Taylor. "The Human Behavioral Ecology of Contemporary World Issues: Applications to Public Policy and International Development." *Human Nature* 18, no. 3 (2007): 181–89.

Various. "How Successful is Sociobiology?" 2001. www.firstthings.com/article.php3?id_article=2167 (accessed September 6, 2007).

Vennum, Thomas, Jr. *American Indian Lacrosse: Little Brother of War*. Washington, D.C.: Smithsonian, 1994.

Wachter, Kenneth W. and Rodolfo A. Bulatao. *Offspring: Human Fertility Behavior in Biodemographic Perspective*. National Academies Press 2003. www.nap.edu/catalog.php?record_id=10654 (accessed September 5, 2007).

Weiner, Annette B. "Culture and Our Discontents." *American Anthropologist* 97 (1995): 14–21.

Wilson, Edward O. *Sociobiology: The New Synthesis*. Cambridge, Mass.: Harvard University Press, 1976.

———. *On Human Nature (25th Anniversary Edition)*. Cambridge, Mass.: Harvard University Press, 2004.

2

Impact of the Concept of Culture on the Concept of Man

Clifford Geertz

I

Toward the end of his recent study of the ideas used by tribal peoples, *La Pensée Sauvage* (1962), the French anthropologist Claude Lévi-Strauss, remarks that scientific explanation does not consist, as we have been led to imagine, in the reduction of the complex to the simple. Rather, it consists, he says, in a substitution of a complexity more intelligible for one which is less. So far as the study of man is concerned, one may go even further, I think, and argue that explanation often consists of substituting complex pictures for simple ones while striving somehow to retain the persuasive clarity that went with the simple ones.

Elegance remains, I suppose, a general scientific ideal; but in the social sciences, it is very often in departures from that ideal that truly creative developments occur. Scientific advancement commonly consists in a progressive complication of what once seemed a beautifully simple set of notions but now seems an unbearably simplistic one. It is after this sort of disenchantment occurs that intelligibility, and thus explanatory power, comes to rest on the possibility of substituting the involved but comprehensible for the involved but incomprehensible to which Lévi-Strauss refers. Whitehead once offered to the natural sciences the maxim: "Seek simplicity and distrust it"; to the social sciences he might well have offered "Seek complexity and order it."

Certainly, the study of culture has developed as though this maxim were being followed. The rise of a scientific concept of culture amounted to, or at least was connected with, the overthrow of the view of human nature dominant in the Enlightenment—a view that, whatever else may be said for or against it, was both clear and simple—and its replacement by a view not only more complicated but also enormously less clear. The attempt to clarify it, to reconstruct an intelligible account of what man is, has underlain scientific thinking about culture ever since. Having sought complexity and, on a scale grander than they ever imagined, found it, anthropologists became entangled in a tortuous effort to order it. And the end is not yet in sight.

The Enlightenment view of man was, of course, that he was wholly of a piece with nature and shared in the general uniformity of composition which natural science, under Bacon's urging and Newton's guidance, had discovered there. There is, in brief, a human nature as regularly organized, as thoroughly invariant, and as marvelously simple as Newton's universe. Perhaps some of its laws are different, but there *are* laws; perhaps some of its immutability is obscured by the trappings of local fashion, but it *is* immutable.

A quotation that Lovejoy (whose magisterial analysis I am following here) gives from an Enlightenment historian, Mascou, presents the position with the useful bluntness one often finds in a minor writer:

> The stage setting [in different times and places] is, indeed, altered, the actors change their garb and their appearance; but their inward motions arise from the same desires and passions of men, and produce their effects in the vicissitudes of kingdoms and peoples (Lovejoy 1960: 173).

Now, this view is hardly one to be despised; nor, despite my easy references a moment ago to "overthrow," can it be said to have disappeared from contemporary anthropological thought. The notion that men are men under whatever guise and against whatever backdrop has not been replaced by "other mores, other beasts."

Yet, cast as it was, the Enlightenment concept of the nature of human nature had some much less acceptable implications, the main one being that, to quote Lovejoy himself this time, "anything of which the intelligibility, verifiability, or actual affirmation is limited to men of a special age, race, temperament, tradition or condition is [in and of itself] without truth or value, or at all events without importance to a reasonable man" (Ibid: 80). The great, vast variety of differences among men, in beliefs and values, in customs and institutions, both over time and from place to place, is essentially without significance in defining his nature. It consists of mere accretions, distortions even, overlaying and obscuring what is truly human—the constant, the general, the universal—in man.

Thus, in a passage now notorious, Dr. Johnson saw Shakespeare's genius to lie in the fact that "his characters are not modified by the customs of particular places, unpracticed by the rest of the world; by the peculiarities of studies or professions, which can operate upon but small numbers; or by the accidents of transient fashions or temporary opinions" (Johnson 1931). And Racine regarded the success of his plays on classical themes as proof that "the taste of Paris . . . conforms to that of Athens; my spectators have been moved by the same things which, in other times, brought tears to the eyes of the most cultivated classes of Greece" (Racine 1674).

The trouble with this kind of view, aside from the fact that it sounds comic coming from someone as profoundly English as Johnson or as French as Racine, is that the image of a constant human nature independent of time, place, and circumstance, of studies and professions, transient fashions and temporary opinions, may be an illusion, that what man is may be so entangled with where he is, who he is, and what he believes that it is inseparable from them. It is precisely the consideration of such a possibility that led to the rise of the concept of culture and the decline of the uniformitarian view of man. Whatever else modern anthropology asserts—and it seems to have asserted almost everything at one time or another—it is firm in the conviction that men unmodified by the customs of particular places do not in fact exist, have never existed, and most important, could not in the very nature of the case exist. There is, there can be, no backstage where we can go to catch a glimpse of Mascou's actors as "real persons" lounging about in street clothes, disengaged from their profession, displaying with artless candor their spontaneous desires and unprompted passions. They may change their roles, their styles of acting, even the dramas in which they play; but—as Shakespeare himself of course remarked—they are always performing.

This circumstance makes the drawing of a line between what is natural, universal, and constant in man and what is conventional, local, and variable extraordinarily difficult. In fact, it suggests that to draw such a line is to falsify the human situation, or at least to misrender it seriously.

Consider Balinese trance. The Balinese fall into extreme dissociated states in which they perform all sorts of spectacular activities—biting off the heads of living chickens, stabbing themselves with daggers, throwing themselves wildly about, speaking in tongues, performing miraculous feats of equilibration, mimicking sexual intercourse, eating feces, and so on—rather more easily and much more suddenly than most of us fall asleep. Trance states are a crucial part of every ceremony. In some, fifty or sixty people may fall, one after the other ("like a string of firecrackers going off," as one observer puts it), emerging anywhere from five minutes to several hours later, totally unaware of what they have been doing and convinced, despite the amnesia, that they have had the most extraordinary and deeply satisfying experience a man can have. What does one learn about human nature from this sort of thing and from the thousand similarly peculiar things anthropologists discover, investigate, and describe? That the Balinese are peculiar sorts of beings, South Sea Martians? That they are just the same as we at base, but with some peculiar, but really incidental, customs we do not happen to have gone in for? That they are innately gifted or even instinctively driven in certain directions rather than others? Or that human nature does not exist and men are pure and simply what their culture makes them?

It is among such interpretations as these, all unsatisfactory, that anthropology has attempted to find its way to a more viable concept of man, one in which culture, and the variability of culture, would be taken into account rather than written off as caprice and prejudice and yet, at the same time, one in which the governing principle of the field, "the basic unity of mankind," would not be turned into an empty phrase. To take the giant step away from the uniformitarian view of human nature is, so far as the study of man is concerned, to leave the Garden. To entertain the idea that the diversity of custom across time and over space is not a mere matter of garb and appearance, of stage settings and comedic masques, is to entertain also the idea that humanity is as various in its essence as it is in its expression. And with that reflection some well-fastened philosophical moorings are loosed and an uneasy drifting into perilous waters begins.

Perilous, because if one discards the notion that Man with a capital "M," is to be looked for "behind," "under," or "beyond" his customs and replaces it with the notion that he uncapitalized, is to be looked for "in" them, one is in some danger of losing sight of him altogether. Either he dissolves, without residue, into his time and place, a child and a perfect captive of his age, or he becomes a conscripted soldier in a vast Tolstoian army, engulfed in one or another of the terrible historical determinism with which we have been plagued from Hegel forward. We have had, and to some extent still have, both of these aberrations in the social sciences—one marching under the banner of cultural relativism, the other under that of cultural evolution. But we also have had, and more commonly, attempts to avoid them by seeking in culture patterns themselves the defining elements of a human existence which, although not constant in expression, are yet distinctive in character.

II

Attempts to locate man amid the body of his customs have taken several directions, adopted diverse tactics; but they have all, or virtually all, proceeded in terms of a single overall intellectual strategy: what I will call, so as to have a stick to beat it with, the "stratigraphic" conception of the relations between biological, psychological, social, and cultural factors in human life. In this conception, man is a composite of "levels," each superimposed upon those beneath it and underpinning those above it. As one analyzes man, one peels off layer after layer, each such layer being complete and irreducible in itself, revealing another, quite different sort of layer underneath. Strip off the motley forms of culture and one finds the structural and functional regularities of social organization. Peel off these in turn and one finds the underlying psychological factors—"basic needs" or what have you—that support and make them possible. Peel off psychological factors and one is left with the biological foundations—anatomical, physiological, neurological—of the whole edifice of human life.

The attraction of this sort of conceptualization, aside from the fact that it guaranteed the established academic disciplines their independence and sovereignty, was that it seemed to make it possible to have one's cake and eat it. One did not have to assert that man's culture was all there was to him in order to claim that it was, nonetheless, an essential and irreducible, even a paramount, ingredient in his nature. Cultural facts could be interpreted against the background of non-cultural facts without either dissolving them into that background or dissolving that background into them. Man was a hierarchically stratified animal, a sort of evolutionary deposit, in whose definition each level—organic, psychological, social, and cultural—had an assigned and incontestable place. To see what he really was, we had to superimpose findings from the various relevant sciences—anthropology, sociology, psychology, biology—upon one another like so many patterns in a *moiré*; and when that was done, the cardinal importance of the cultural level, the only one distinctive to man, would naturally appear, as would what it had to tell us, in its own right, about what he really was. For the eighteenth-century image of man as the naked reasoner that appeared when he took his cultural costumes off, the anthropology of the late nineteenth and early twentieth centuries substituted the image of man as the transfigured animal that appeared when he put them on.

At the level of concrete research and specific analysis, this grand strategy came down, first, to a hunt for universals in culture, for empirical uniformities that, in the face of the diversity of customs around the world and over time, could be found everywhere in about the same form, and, second, to an effort to relate such universals, once found, to the established constants of human biology, psychology, and social organization. If some customs could be ferreted out of the cluttered catalog of world culture as common to all local variants of it, and if these could then be connected in a determinate manner with certain invariant points of reference on the subcultural levels, then at least some progress might be made toward specifying which cultural traits are essential to human existence and which merely adventitious, peripheral, or ornamental. In such a way, anthropology could determine cultural dimensions of a concept of man commensurate with the dimensions provided, in a similar way, by biology, psychology, or sociology.

In essence, this is not altogether a new idea. The notion of a *consensus gentium* (a consensus of all mankind)—the notion that there are some things that all men will be found to agree upon as right, real, just, or attractive and that these things are, therefore, in fact right, real, just, or attractive—was present in the Enlightenment and probably has been present in some form or another in all ages and climes. It is one of those ideas that occur to almost anyone sooner or later. Its development in modern anthropology, however—beginning with Clark Wissler's elaboration in the 1920s of what he called "the universal cultural pattern," through Bronislaw Malinowski's presentation of a list of "universal institutional types" in the early 1940s, up to G. P. Murdock's elaboration of a set of "common denominators of culture" during and since World War II—added something new. It added the notion that, to quote Clyde Kluckhohn, perhaps the most persuasive of the *consensus gentium* theorists, "some aspects of culture take their specific forms solely as a result of historical accidents;

others are tailored by forces which can properly be designated as univer-sal" (Kroeber 1953: 516). With this, man's cultural life is split in two: part of it is, like Mascou's actors' garb, independent of men's Newtonian "inward motions"; part is an emanation of those motions themselves. The question that then arises is, Can this halfway house between the eigh-teenth and twentieth centuries really stand?

Whether it can or not depends on whether the dualism between empiri-cally universal aspects of culture rooted in subcultural realities and em-pirically variable aspects not so rooted can be established and sustained. And this, in turn, demands (1) that the universals proposed be substantial ones and not empty categories; (2) that they be specifically grounded in particular biological, psychological, or sociological processes, not just vaguely associated with "underlying realities"; and (3) that they can convincingly be defended as core elements in a definition of humanity in comparison with which the much more numerous cultural particularities are of clearly secondary importance. On all three of these counts it seems to me that the *consensus gentium* approach fails; rather than moving to-ward the essentials of the human situation it moves away from it.

The reason the first of these requirements—that the proposed universals be substantial ones and not empty or near empty categories—has not been met is that it cannot. There is a logical conflict between asserting that, say, "religion," "marriage," or "property" are empirical universals and giving them very much in the way of specific content, for to say that they are em-pirical universals is to say that they have the same content, and to say they have the same content is to fly in the face of the undeniable fact that they do not. If one defines religion generally and indeterminately—as man's most fundamental orientation to reality, for example—then one cannot at the same time assign to that orientation a highly circumstantial content, for clearly what composes the most fundamental orientation to reality among the transported Aztecs, lifting pulsing hearts torn live from the chests of human sacrifices toward the heavens, is not what comprises it among the stolid Zuñi, dancing their great mass supplications to the benevolent gods of rain. The obsessive ritualism and unbuttoned polytheism of the Hindus expresses a rather different view of what the really real is really like from the uncompromising monotheism and austere legalism of Sunni Islam. Even if one does try to get down to less abstract levels and assert, as Kluck-hohn did, that a concept of the afterlife is universal, or as Malinowski did, that a sense of Providence is universal, the same contradiction haunts one.

To make the generalization about an afterlife stand up alike for the Confucians and the Calvinists, the Zen Buddhists and the Tibetan Buddhists, one has to define it in most general terms, indeed—so general, in fact, that whatever force it seems to have virtually evaporates. So, too, with any notion of a "sense of Providence," which can include under its wing both Navaho notions about the relations of gods to men and Trobriand ones. And as with religion, so with "marriage," "trade," and all the rest of what A. L. Kroeber aptly called "fake universals," down to so seemingly tangible a matter as "shelter." That everywhere people mate and produce children, have some sense of mine and thine, and protect themselves in one fashion or another from rain and sun are neither false nor, from some points of view, unimportant; but they are hardly very much help in drawing a portrait of man that will be a true and honest likeness and not an untenanted "John Q. Public" sort of cartoon.

My point, which should be clear and I hope will become even clearer in a moment, is not that there are no generalizations that can be made about man as man, save that he is a most various animal, or that the study of culture has nothing to contribute toward the uncovering of such generalizations. My point is that such generalizations are not to be discovered through a Baconian search for cultural universals, a kind of public-opinion polling of the world's peoples in search of a *consensus gentium* that does not in fact exist, and, further, that the attempt to do so leads to precisely the sort of relativism the whole approach was expressly designed to avoid. "Zuñi culture prizes restraint," Kluckhohn writes. "Kwakiutl culture encourages exhibitionism on the part of the individual. These are contrasting values, but in adhering to them the Zuñi and Kwakiutl show their allegiance to a universal value; the prizing of the distinctive norms of one's culture" (Kluckholn 1962: 280). This is sheer evasion, but it is only more apparent, not more evasive, than discussions of cultural universals in general. What, after all, does it avail us to say, with Herskovits, that "morality is a universal, and so is enjoyment of beauty, and some standard for truth," if we are forced in the very next sentence, as he is, to add that "the many forms these concepts take are but products of the particular historical experience of the societies that manifest them" (Herskovits 1955: 364)? Once one abandons uniformitarianism, even if, like the *consensus gentium* theorists, only partially and uncertainly, relativism is a genuine danger; but it can be warded off only by facing directly and fully the diversities of human culture, the Zuñi's restraint and the Kwakiutl's exhibitionism, and embracing them within the body of one's concept of man, not by gliding past them with vague tautologies and forceless banalities.

Of course, the difficulty of stating cultural universals which are at the same time substantial also hinders fulfillment of the second requirement facing the *consensus gentium* approach, that of grounding such universals in particular biological, psychological, or sociological processes. But there is more to it than that: the "stratigraphic" conceptualization of the relationships between cultural and non-cultural factors hinders such a grounding even more effectively. Once culture, psyche, society, and organism have been converted into separate scientific "levels," complete and autonomous in themselves, it is very hard to bring them back together again.

The most common way of trying to do so is through the utilization of what are called "invariant points of reference." These points are to be found, to quote one of the most famous statements of this strategy—the "Toward a Common Language for the Areas of the Social Sciences" memorandum produced by Talcott Parsons, Kluckhohn, O. H. Taylor, and others in the early 1940s:

> in the nature of social systems, in the biological and psychological nature of the component individuals, in the external situations in which they live and act, in the necessity of coordination in social systems. In [culture] . . . these "foci" of structure are never ignored. They must in some way be "adapted to" or "taken account of."

Cultural universals are conceived to be crystallized responses to these unevadable realities, institutionalized ways of coming to terms with them.

Analysis consists, then, of matching assumed universals to postulated underlying necessities, attempting to show there is some goodness of fit between the two. On the social level, reference is made to such irrefragable facts as that all societies, in order to persist, must reproduce their membership or allocate goods and services, hence the universality of some form of family or some form of trade. On the psychological level, recourse is had to basic needs like personal growth—hence the ubiquity of educational institutions—or to panhuman problems, like the Oedipal predicament—hence the ubiquity of punishing gods and nurturant goddesses. Biologically, there is metabolism and health; culturally, dining customs and curing procedures. And so on. The tack is to look at underlying human requirements of some sort or other and then to try to show that those aspects of culture that are universal are, to use Kluck-hohn's figure again, "tailored" by these requirements.

The problem here is, again, not so much whether in a general way this sort of congruence exists, but whether it is more than a loose and indeterminate one. It is not difficult to relate some human institutions to what science (or common sense) tells us are requirements for human existence, but it is very much more difficult to state this relationship in an unequivocal form. Not only does almost any institution serve a multiplic-ity of social, psychological, and organic needs (so that to say marriage is a mere reflex of the social need to reproduce, or that dining customs are a reflex of metabolic necessities, is to court parody), but there is no way to state in any precise and testable way the interlevel relationships that are conceived to hold. Despite first appearances, there is no serious attempt here to apply the concepts and theories of biology, psychology, or even sociology to the analysis of culture (and, of course, not even a suggestion of the reverse exchange) but merely a placing of supposed facts from the cultural and subcultural levels side by side so as to induce a vague sense that some kind of relationship between them—an obscure sort of "tailoring"—obtains. There is no theoretical integration here at all but a mere correlation, and that intuitive, of separate findings. With the levels approach, we can never, even by invoking "in variant points of refer-ence," construct genuine functional interconnections between cultural and non-cultural factors, only more or less persuasive analogies, parallelisms, suggestions, and affinities.

However, even if I am wrong (as, admittedly, many anthropologists would hold) in claiming that the *consensus gentium* approach can produce neither substantial universals nor specific connections between cultural and non-cultural phenomena to explain them, the question still remains whether such universals should be taken as the central elements in the definition of man, whether a lowest common denominator view of hu-manity is what we want anyway. This is, of course, now a philosophical question, not as such a scientific one; but the notion that the essence of what it means to be human is most clearly revealed in those features of human culture that are universal rather than in those that are distinctive to this people or that is a prejudice we are not necessarily obliged to share. Is it in grasping such general facts—that man has everywhere some sort of "religion"—or in grasping the richness of this religious phenomenon or that—Balinese trance or Indian ritualism, Aztec human sacrifice or Zuñi rain dancing—that we grasp him? Is the fact that "marriage" is universal (if it is) as penetrating a comment on what we are as the facts concerning Himalayan polyandry, or those fantastic Australian marriage rules, or the elaborate bride-price systems of Bantu Africa? The comment that Cromwell was the most typical Englishman of his time precisely in that he was the oddest may be relevant in this connection, too: it may be in the cultural particularities of people—in their oddities—that some of the most instructive revelations of what it is to be generically human are to be found; and the main contribution of the science of anthropology to the construction—or reconstruction—of a concept of man may then lie in showing us how to find them.

III

The major reason why anthropologists have shied away from cultural particularities when it came to a question of defining man and have taken refuge instead in bloodless universals is that, faced as they are with the enormous variation in human behavior, they are haunted by a fear of historicism, of becoming lost in a whirl of cultural relativism so convulsive as to deprive them of any fixed bearings at all. Nor has there not been some occasion for such a fear: Ruth Benedict's *Patterns of Culture,* probably the most popular book in anthropology ever published in this country, with its strange conclusion that anything one group of people is inclined toward doing is worthy of respect by another, is perhaps only the most outstanding example of the awkward positions one can get into by giving oneself over rather too completely to what Marc Bloch called "the thrill of learning singular things." Yet the fear is a bogy. The notion that unless a cultural phenomenon is empirically universal it cannot reflect anything about the nature of man is about as logical as the notion that because sickle-cell anemia is, fortunately, not universal, it cannot tell us anything about human genetic processes. It is not whether phenomena are empirically common that is critical in science—else why should Becquerel have been so interested in the peculiar behavior of uranium?—but whether they can be made to reveal the enduring natural processes that underly them. Seeing heaven in a grain of sand is not a trick only poets can accomplish.

In short, we need to look for systematic relationships among diverse phenomena, not for substantive identities among similar ones. And to do that with any effectiveness, we need to replace the "stratigraphic" conception of the relations between the various aspects of human existence with a synthetic one; that is, one in which biological, psychological, sociological, and cultural factors can be treated as variables within unitary systems of analysis. The establishment of a common language in the social sciences is not a matter of mere coordination of terminologies or, worse yet, of coining artificial new ones; nor is it a matter of imposing a single set of categories upon the area as a whole. It is a matter of integrating different types of theories and concepts in such a way that one can formulate meaningful propositions embodying findings now sequestered in separate fields of study.

In attempting to launch such an integration from the anthropological side and to reach, thereby, an exacter image of man, I want to propose two ideas. The first of these is that culture is best seen not as complexes of concrete behavior patterns—customs, usages, traditions, habit clusters—as has, by and large, been the case up to now, but as a set of control mechanisms—plans, recipes, rules, instructions (what computer engineers call "programs")—for the governing of behavior. The second idea is that man is precisely the animal most desperately dependent upon such extragenetic, outside-the-skin control mechanisms, such cultural programs, for ordering his behavior.

Neither of these ideas is entirely new, but a number of recent developments, both within anthropology and in other sciences (cybernetics, information theory, neurology, molecular genetics) have made them susceptible of more precise statement as well as lending them a degree of empirical support they did not previously have. And out of such reformulations of the concept of culture and of the role of culture in human life comes, in turn, a definition of man stressing not so much the empirical commonalities in his behavior, from place to place and time to time, but rather the mechanisms by whose agency the breadth and indeterminateness of his inherent capacities are reduced to the narrowness and specificity of his actual accomplishments. One of the most significant facts about us may finally be that we all begin with the natural equipment to live a thousand kinds of life but end in the end having lived only one.

The "control mechanism" view of culture begins with the assumption that human thought is basically both social and public—that its natural habitat is the house yard, the marketplace, and the town square. Thinking consists not of "happenings in the head" (though happenings there and elsewhere are necessary for it to occur) but of a traffic in what have been called, by G. H. Mead and others, significant symbols—words for the most part but also gestures, drawings, musical sounds, mechanical devices like clocks, or natural objects like jewels—anything, in fact, that is disengaged from its mere actuality and used to impose meaning upon experience. From the point of view of any particular individual, such symbols are largely given. He finds them already current in the community when he is born, and they remain, with some additions, subtractions, and partial alterations he may or may not have had a hand in, in circulation there after he dies. While he lives he uses them, or some of them, sometimes deliberately and with care, most often spontaneously and with ease, but always with the same end in view: to put a construction upon the events through which he lives, to orient himself within "the ongoing course of experienced things," to adopt a vivid phrase of John Dewey's.

Man is so in need of such symbolic sources of illumination to find his bearings in the world because the non-symbolic sorts that are constitutionally ingrained in his body cast so diffused a light. The behavior patterns of lower animals are, at least to a much greater extent, given to them with their physical structure; genetic sources of information order their actions within much narrower ranges of variation, the narrower and more thorough-going the lower the animal. For man, what are innately given are extremely general response capacities, which, although they make possible far greater plasticity, complexity, and on the scattered occasions when everything works as it should, effectiveness of behavior, leave it much less precisely regulated. This, then, is the second face of our argument: Undirected by culture patterns—organized systems of significant symbols—man's behavior would be virtually ungovernable, a mere chaos of pointless acts and exploding emotions, his experience virtually shapeless. Culture, the accumulated totality of such patterns, is not just an ornament of human existence but—the principal basis of its specificity—an essential condition for it.

Within anthropology some of the most telling evidence in support of such a position comes from recent advances in our understanding of what used to be called the descent of man: the emergence of *Homo sapiens* out of his general primate background. Of these advances three are of critical importance: (1) the discarding of a sequential view of the relations between the physical evolution and the cultural development of man in favor of an overlap or interactive view; (2) the discovery that the bulk of the biological changes that produced modern man out of his most immediate progenitors took place in the central nervous system and most especially in the brain; (3) the realization that man is, in physical terms, an incomplete, an unfinished, animal; that what sets him off most graphically from non-men is less his sheer ability to learn (great as that is) than how much and what particular sorts of things he *has* to learn before he is able to function at all. Let me take each of these points in turn.

The traditional view of the relations between the biological and the cultural advance of man was that the former, the biological, was for all intents and purposes completed before the latter, the cultural, began. That is to say, it was again stratigraphic: Man's physical being evolved, through the usual mechanisms of genetic variation and natural selection, up to the point where his anatomical structure had arrived at more or less the status at which we find it today; then cultural development got underway. At some particular stage in his phylogenetic history, a marginal genetic change of some sort rendered him capable of producing and carrying culture, and thenceforth his form of adaptive response to environmental pressures was almost exclusively cultural rather than genetic. As he spread over the globe, he wore furs in cold climates and loin cloths (or nothing at all) in warm ones; he didn't alter his innate mode of response to environmental temperature. He made weapons to extend his inherited predatory powers and cooked foods to render a wider range of them digestible. Man became man, the story continues, when, having crossed some mental Rubicon, he became able to transmit "knowledge, belief, law, morals, custom" (to quote the items of Sir Edward Tylor's classical definition of culture) to his descendants and his neighbors through teaching and to acquire them from his ancestors and his neighbors through learning. After that magical moment, the advance of the hominids depended almost entirely on cultural accumulation, on the slow growth of conventional practices, rather than, as it had for ages past, on physical organic change.

The only trouble is that such a moment does not seem to have existed. By the most recent estimates the transition to the cultural mode of life took the genus *Homo* more than a million years to accomplish; and stretched out in such a manner, it involved not one or a handful of marginal genetic changes but a long, complex, and closely ordered sequence of them.

In the current view, the evolution of *Homo sapiens*—modern man—out of his immediate pre-*sapiens* background got definitely under way nearly two million years ago (editor's note: contemporary research indicates hominid evolution began at least four million years ago; however, *Homo sapiens* evolution began no more than two thousand years ago) with the appearance of the now famous Australopithecines—the so-called ape men of southern and eastern Africa—and culminated with the emergence of *sapiens* himself only some one to two hundred thousand years ago. Thus, as at least elemental forms of cultural, or if you wish protocultural, activity (simple tool making, hunting, and so on) seem to have been present among some of the Australopithecines, there was an overlap of, as I say, well over a million years between the beginning of culture and the appearance of man as we know him today. The precise dates—which are tentative and which further research may later alter in one direction or another—are not critical; what is critical is that there was an overlap and that it was a very extended one. The final phases (final to date, at any rate) of the phylogenetic history of man took place in the same grand geological era—the so-called Ice Age—as the initial phases of his cultural history. Men have birthdays, but man does not.

What this means is that culture, rather than being added on, so to speak, to a finished or virtually finished animal, was ingredient, and centrally ingredient, in the production of that animal itself. The slow, steady, almost glacial growth of culture through the Ice Age altered the balance of selection pressures for the evolving *Homo* in such a way as to play a major directive role in his evolution. The perfection of tools, the adoption of organized hunting and gathering practices, the beginnings of true family organization, the discovery of fire, and, most critical, though it is as yet extremely difficult to trace it out in any detail, the increasing reliance upon systems of significant symbols (language, art, myth, ritual) for orientation, communication, and self-control all created for man a new environment to which he was then obliged to adapt. As culture, step by infinitesimal step, accumulated and developed, a selective advantage was given to those individuals in the population most able to take advantage of it—the effective hunter, the persistent gatherer, the adept toolmaker, the resourceful leader—until what had been a small-brained, protohuman *Homo australopithecus* became the large-brained fully human *Homo sapiens*. Between the cultural pattern, the body, and the brain, a positive feedback system was created in which each shaped the progress of the other, a system in which the interaction among increasing tool use, the changing anatomy of the hand, and the expanding representation of the thumb on the cortex is only one of the more graphic examples. By submitting himself to governance by symbolically mediated programs for producing artifacts, organizing social life, or expressing emotions, man determined, if unwittingly, the culminating stages of his own biological destiny. Quite literally, though quite inadvertently, he created himself.

Though, as I mentioned, there were a number of important changes in the gross anatomy of genus *Homo* during this period of his crystallization—in skull shape, dentition, thumb size, and so on—by far the most important and dramatic were those that evidently took place in the central nervous system; for this was the period when the human brain, and most particularly the forebrain, ballooned into its present top-heavy proportions. The technical problems are complicated and controversial here; but the main point is that though the Australopithecines had a torso and arm configuration not drastically different from our own, and a pelvis and leg formation at least well launched toward our own, they had cranial capacities hardly larger than those of the living apes—that is to say, about a third to a half of our own. What sets true men off most distinctly from protomen is apparently not overall bodily form but complexity of nervous organization. The overlap period of cultural and biological change seems to have consisted in an intense concentration on neural development and perhaps associated refinements of various behaviors—of the hands, bipedal locomotion, and so on—for which the basic anatomical foundations—mobile shoulders and wrists, a broadened ilium, and so on—had already been securely laid. In itself, this is perhaps not altogether startling; but, combined with what I have already said, it suggests some conclusions about what sort of animal man is that are, I think, rather far not only from those of the eighteenth century but from those of the anthropology of only ten or fifteen years ago.

Most bluntly, it suggests that there is no such thing as a human nature independent of culture. Men without culture would not be the clever savages of Golding's *Lord of the Flies* thrown back upon the cruel wisdom of their animal instincts; nor would they be the nature's noblemen of Enlightenment primitivism or even, as classical anthropological theory would imply, intrinsically talented apes who had somehow failed to find themselves. They would be unworkable monstrosities with very few useful instincts, fewer recognizable sentiments, and no intellect: mental basket cases. As our central nervous system—and most particularly its crowning curse and glory, the neocortex—grew up in great part in interaction with culture, it is incapable of directing our behavior or organizing our experience without the guidance provided by systems of significant symbols. What happened to us in the Ice Age is that we were obliged to abandon the regularity and precision of detailed genetic control over our conduct for the flexibility and adaptability of a more generalized, though of course no less real, genetic control over it. To supply the additional information necessary to be able to act, we were forced, in turn, to rely more and more heavily on cultural sources—the accumulated fund of significant symbols. Such symbols are thus not mere expressions, instrumentalities, or correlates of our biological, psychological, and social existence; they are prerequisites of it. Without men, no culture, certainly; but equally, and more significantly, without culture, no men.

We are, in sum, incomplete or unfinished animals who complete or finish ourselves through culture—and not through culture in general but through highly particular forms of it: Dobuan and Javanese, Hopi and Italian, upper-class and lower-class, academic and commercial. Man's great capacity for learning, his plasticity, has often been remarked, but what is even more critical is his extreme dependence upon a certain sort of learning: the attainment of concepts, the apprehension and application of specific systems of symbolic meaning. Beavers build dams, birds build nests, bees locate food, baboons organize social groups, and mice mate on the basis of forms of learning that rest predominantly on the instructions encoded in their genes and evoked by appropriate patterns of external stimuli: physical keys inserted into organic locks. But men build dams or shelters, locate food, organize their social groups, or find sexual partners under the guidance of instructions encoded in flow charts and blueprints, hunting lore, moral systems, and aesthetic judgments: conceptual structures molding formless talents.

We live, as one writer has neatly put it, in an "information gap." Between what our body tells us and what we have to know in order to function, there is a vacuum we must fill ourselves, and we fill it with information (or misinformation) provided by our culture. The boundary between what is innately controlled and what is culturally controlled in human behavior is an ill-defined and wavering one. Some things are, for all intents and purposes, entirely controlled intrinsically: we need no more cultural guidance to learn how to breathe than a fish needs to learn how to swim. Others are almost certainly largely cultural; we do not attempt to explain on a genetic basis why some men put their trust in centralized planning and others in the free market, though it might be an amusing exercise. Almost all complex human behavior is, of course, the vector outcome of the two. Our capacity to speak is surely innate; our capacity to speak English is surely cultural. Smiling at pleasing stimuli and frowning at unpleasing ones are surely in some degree genetically determined (even apes screw up their faces at noxious odors); but sardonic smiling and burlesque frowning are equally surely predominantly cultural, as is perhaps demonstrated by the Balinese definition of a madman as someone who, like an American, smiles when there is nothing to laugh at. Between the basic ground plans for our life that our genes lay down—the capacity to speak or to smile—and the precise behavior we in fact execute—speaking English in a certain tone of voice, smiling enigmatically in a delicate social situation—lies a complex set of significant symbols under whose direction we transform the first into the second, the ground plans into the activity.

Our ideas, our values, our acts, even our emotions, are, like our nervous system itself, cultural products—products manufactured, indeed, out of tendencies, capacities, and dispositions with which we were born, but manufactured none the less. Chartres is made of stone and glass. But it is not just stone and glass; it is a cathedral, and not only a cathedral, but a particular cathedral built at a particular time by certain members of a particular society. To understand what it means, to perceive it for what it is, you need to know rather more than the generic properties of stone and glass and rather more than what is common to all cathedrals. You need to understand also—and, in my opinion, most critically—the specific concepts of the relations among God, man, and architecture that, having governed its creation, it consequently embodies. It is no different with men: they, too, every last one of them, are cultural artifacts.

IV

Whatever differences they may show, the approaches to the definition of human nature adopted by the Enlightenment and by classical anthropology have one thing in common: they are both basically typological. They endeavor to construct an image of man as a model, an archetype, a Platonic idea or an Aristotelian form, with respect to which actual men—you, me, Churchill, Hitler, and the Bornean headhunter—are but reflections, distortions, approximations. In the Enlightenment case, the elements of this essential type were to be uncovered by stripping the trappings of culture away from actual men and seeing what then was left—natural man. In classical anthropology, it was to be uncovered by factoring out the commonalities in culture and seeing what then appeared—consensual man. In either case, the result is the same as tends to emerge in all typological approaches to scientific problems generally: the differences among individuals and among groups of individuals are rendered secondary. Individuality comes to be seen as eccentricity, distinctiveness as accidental deviation from the only legitimate object of study for the true scientist: the underlying, unchanging, normative type. In such an approach, however elaborately formulated and resourcefully defended, living detail is drowned in dead stereotype: we are in quest of a metaphysical entity, Man with a capital "M," in the interests of which we sacrifice the empirical entity we in fact encounter, man with a small "m."

The sacrifice is, however, as unnecessary as it is unavailing. There is no opposition between general theoretical understanding and circumstantial understanding, between synoptic vision and a fine eye for detail. It is, in fact, by its power to draw general propositions out of particular phenomena that a scientific theory—indeed, science itself—is to be judged. If we want to discover what man amounts to, we can only find it in what men are: and what men are, above all other things, is various. It is in understanding that variousness—its range, its nature, its basis, and its implications—that we shall come to construct a concept of human nature that, more than a statistical shadow and less than a primitivist dream, has both substance and truth.

It is here, to come round finally to my title, that the concept of culture has its impact on the concept of man. When seen as a set of symbolic devices for controlling behavior, extra-somatic sources of information, culture provides the link between what men are intrinsically capable of becoming and what they actually, one by one, in fact become. Becoming human is becoming individual, and we become individual under the guidance of cultural patterns, historically created systems of meaning in terms of which we give form, order, point, and direction to our lives. And the cultural patterns involved are not general but specific—not just "marriage" but a particular set of notions about what men and women are like, how spouses should treat one another, or who should properly marry whom; not just "religion" but belief in the wheel of karma, the observance of a month of fasting, or the practice of cattle sacrifice. Man is to be defined neither by his innate capacities alone, as the Enlightenment sought to do, nor by his actual behaviors alone, as much of contemporary social science seeks to do, but rather by the link between them, by the way in which the first is transformed into the second, his generic potentialities focused into his specific performances. It is in man's *career,* in its characteristic course, that we can discern, however dimly, his nature, and though culture is but one element in determining that course, it is hardly the least important. As culture shaped us as a single species—and is no doubt still shaping us—so too it shapes us as separate individuals. This, neither an unchanging subcultural self nor an established cross-cultural consensus, is what we really have in common.

Oddly enough—though on second thought, perhaps not so oddly—many of our subjects seem to realize this more clearly than we anthropologists ourselves. In Java, for example, where I have done much of my work, the people quite flatly say, "To be human is to be Javanese." Small children, boors, simpletons, the insane, the flagrantly immoral, are said to be *ndurung djawa,* "not yet Javanese." A "normal" adult capable of acting in terms of the highly elaborate system of etiquette, possessed of the delicate aesthetic perceptions associated with music, dance, drama, and textile design, responsive to the subtle promptings of the divine residing in the stillnesses of each individual's inward-turning consciousness, is *sampun djawa,* "already Javanese," that is, already human. To be human is not just to breathe; it is to control one's breathing, by yoga-like techniques, so as to hear in inhalation and exhalation the literal voice of God pronouncing His own name—*hu Allah.*" It is not just to talk, it is to utter the appropriate words and phrases in the appropriate social situations in the appropriate tone of voice and with the appropriate evasive indirection. It is not just to eat; it is to prefer certain foods cooked in certain ways and to follow a rigid table etiquette in consuming them. It is not even just to feel but to feel certain quite distinctively Javanese (and essentially untranslatable) emotions—"patience," "detachment," "resignation," "respect."

To be human here is thus not to be Everyman; it is to be a particular kind of man, and of course men differ: "Other fields," the Javanese say, "other grasshoppers." Within the society, differences are recognized, too—the way a rice peasant becomes human and Javanese differs from the way a civil servant does. This is not a matter of tolerance and ethical relativism, for not all ways of being human are regarded as equally admirable by far; the way the local Chinese go about it is, for example, intensely dispraised. The point is that there are different ways; and to shift to the anthropologist's perspective now, it is in a systematic review and analysis of these—of the Plains Indian's bravura, the Hindu's obsessiveness, the Frenchman's rationalism, the Berber's anarchism, the American's optimism (to list a series of tags I should not like to have to defend as such)—that we shall find out what it is, or can be, to be a man.

We must, in short, descend into detail, past the misleading tags, past the metaphysical types, past the empty similarities to grasp firmly the essential character of not only the various cultures but the various sorts of individuals within each culture, if we wish to encounter humanity face to face. In this area, the road to the general, to the revelatory simplicities of science lies through a concern with the particular, the circumstantial, the concrete, but a concern organized and directed in terms of the sort of theoretical analyses that I have touched upon—analyses of physical evolution, of the functioning of the nervous system, of social organization, of psychological process, of cultural patterning, and so on—and, most especially, in terms of the interplay among them. That is to say, the road lies, like any genuine quest, through a terrifying complexity.

"Leave him alone for a moment or two," Robert Lowell writes, not as one might suspect of the anthropologist but of that other eccentric inquirer into the nature of man, Nathaniel Hawthorne.

> Leave him alone for a moment or two,
> and you'll see him with his head
> bent down, brooding, brooding,
> eyes fixed on some chip,
> some stone, some common plant,
> the commonest thing,
> as if it were the clue.
> The disturbed eyes rise,
> furtive, foiled, dissatisfied
> from meditation on the true
> and insignificant (Lowell 1964: 39).

Bent over his own chips, stones, and common plants, the anthropologist broods, too, upon the true and insignificant, glimpsing in it, or so he thinks, fleetingly and insecurely, the disturbing, changeful image of himself.

BIBLIOGRAPHY

Herskovits, M. J. *Cultural Anthropology*. New York: Alfred A. Knof, Inc., 1955: 364.

Johnson, S. *Preface to Shakespeare*. London: Oxford University Press, 1931: 11–12.

Kluckholm, C. *Culture and Behavior*. New York: Free Press of Glencoe, a division of The Macmillan Co., 1962: 280.

Kroeber, A. L., ed. *Anthropology Today*. Chicago: University of Chicago Press, 1953: 516.

Lévi-Strauss, Claude. *La Pensée Sauvage*. Paris: Plon, 1962.

Lovejoy, Arthur O. *Essays in the History of Ideas*. New York: G.P. Putnam's Sons, Capricorn Books, 1960. © 1948 by The Johns Hopkins Press.

Lowell, R. *For the Union Dead*. Reprinted by permission of Farrar, Straus, & Giroux, Inc., Faber & Faber, Ltd.

Parsons, Talcott, Talcott C. Kluckhohn, J. T. Dunlop, M. P. Gilmore, and O. H. Taylor. "Toward a Common Language for the Area of Social Science." Cambridge, Mass. Mimeographed. (Central section of this paper is published in *Essays in Sociological Theory*, by Talcott Parsons [Glencoe, Ill.: The Free Press, 1949]: 42–52.)

Racine, J. From the Preface to *Iphigénie*. 1674.

3

From Landscapes to Playscapes: The Evolution of Play in Humans and Other Animals

Kerrie P. Lewis

Play behavior has fascinated researchers and casual observers for centuries, but it remains a misunderstood behavior. Furthermore, there exists considerable disagreement concerning the functions of play. However, play seems to be an important part of an infant's physical, mental, and emotional development, and may be a contributory factor to some crucial learning skills. For humans, play can take many forms and mean many things: sports, gambling, video games, power, the antithesis of work or obligation, frivolity, relaxation, self-identity, creativity, and so on (Bateson 2005; Burghardt 2005; Power 2000). But play is not unique to humans. It has long been recognized that mammals play, and recent advances in play research demonstrate its occurrence in non-mammals also, such as turtles, octopuses, and perhaps even fish (Burghardt 2005). Humans are animals, and much can be learned from addressing play from an evolutionary standpoint. If we can understand play in other animals, perhaps we can understand its contribution to human behavior, development, and evolution.

DEFINING THE INDEFINABLE

Play is a behavior traditionally defined by the inability to satisfactorily define it. The difficulty appears to lay in the fact that it is easy to recognize play when we see it, but identifying what makes play *playful* can be an altogether trickier task. Play repertoires and their complexities vary widely across different species. Play is additionally confusing because it frequently resembles behavior patterns familiar to us from other more "serious" behaviors, such as sex, aggression, or predation. In play however, these serious patterns and sequences are scrambled in various ways, thus changing their context.

History has seen several working definitions of play, but I currently prefer Burghardt's set of careful criteria, that when met, enable confident identification of play in any species. Burghardt's (2001; 2005) criteria are summarized thus: "Play is repeated, incompletely functional behavior differing from more functional versions structurally, contextually, or ontogenetically, and occurring voluntarily when the animal is in a relaxed or low stress setting." More specifically, these criteria state: (1) Play is incompletely functional in the context in which it appears in that it does not contribute to current survival. It is not work, and there is no tangible goal (other than to keep playing). (2) Play is spontaneous and voluntary. You cannot force an animal or a child to play; play must derive from its own motivation. Play is also intentional behavior and appears to be pleasurable and rewarding. Indeed, Huizinga (1955: 3) noted that fun "characterizes the essence of play." Play differs from other more serious behaviors in that it is modified or exaggerated in form. However, the elements of play behavior may appear similar to other behaviors. For example, many species deliver neck bites in predatory or aggressive contexts. A neck bite during play looks similar, but the intention to do harm is inhibited, thus changing the context of the behavior. (4) Play has repeated elements but does not demonstrate abnormal stereotypic and repetitive behaviors that occur in distressed animals, such as pacing or self-scratching. In play, motor patterns such as rapid hopping or swinging are commonplace, and these rapid, repetitive movements convey excitability and perhaps even "fun" (5). Play requires stress-free conditions to occur naturally. Stressors can take many forms, such as lack of food, confinement, predation pressure, social instability, illness, and even inclement weather (Burghardt 1984). In times of stress, play behavior evaporates. This is an interesting phenomenon given that, in spite of such stressors, animals remain strongly motivated to engage in play. This demonstrates both the robustness and the fragility of play. Burghardt (2005) describes the necessity of this "relaxed field." In other words, play occurs when animals are warm, fat, and happy.

CATEGORIES OF PLAY

Play is traditionally described in terms of three basic categories: solitary locomotor-rotational play, object play, and social play. Solitary locomotor-rotational play comprises the usually vigorous motor acts that are performed alone, such as children running and skipping, deer bucking and leaping, or monkeys somersaulting (Müller-Schwarze 1984; Sommer and Mendoza-Granados 1995).

Object play, which involves the use of an inanimate object, can be solitary or social, such as a cat batting at a ball of twine, or two dogs tussling with a stick (Burghardt 2005). Recent research demonstrates that captive octopuses (*Octopus vulgaris*) play with Lego™ toy bricks (Kuba et al. 2006). Children's object play is often with toys such as dolls, blocks, toy trucks, and stuffed animals, but many children are equally happy digging in the dirt with a stick, or banging rocks together playfully (Pellegrini and Gustafson 2005). Indeed, Japanese macaques (*Macaca fuscata*) and kookaburras (*Dacelo novaeguineae*) like to bang stones together or smack them against trees (Nahallage and Huffman 2007; Watson 1992), and herring gulls (*Larus argentatus*) play drop-catch games with rocks (Gamble and Cristol 2002). Object play may be especially important for developing hand-eye coordination; this category of play is particularly prevalent in predator species like carnivores such as canids, felids, and ursids. For example, crab-eating foxes (*Cerdocyon thous*) play tug-of-war with sticks and hoard objects as toys in their dens (Biben 1982; 1983), cats chase autumn leaves (Thompson 1851: 63), and captive spectacled bears (*Tremarctos ornatus*) twirl broomsticks (Burghardt 2005: 207). Social play involves two or more individuals playing with one another, such as chasing and wrestling in humans, monkeys, rats, and other animals (Sommer and Mendoza-Granados 1995; Panksepp 1980). Play-fighting, or rough-and-tumble (R&T) play, is probably the most common social play behavior, and is described in many species. Furthermore, social play between two species may also occur. Inter-specific play is most common between humans and other animals, usually in a captive or domestic setting (Watson 1998; Rooney et al. 2000), but inter-specific play occasionally occurs among wild animals also. For example, inter-specific play has been reported between red-necked wallabies (*Macropus rufogriseus*) and Australian magpies (*Gymnorhina tibicen*) (Watson 1998), and between black and white colobus monkeys (*Colobus guereza*) and vervet monkeys (*Cercopithecus aethiops*) (Rose 1977). Baboons (*Papio* spp.) also play with vervet monkeys, in addition to chimpanzees (*Pan troglodytes*) and jackals (*Canis aureus*) (Altmann and Altmann 1970; Saayman 1970; van Lawick-Goodall 1967). In humans, play has several extended categories, and the classic types of play frequently overlap. For example, children's locomotor play can be solitary or social, such as chasing or swinging next to one another. Similarly, pretend or fantasy play, such as pretending to be a doctor, or pretending that a cardboard tube is a rocket, can be solitary or social also. Although many play behaviors, such as R&T, can at times be difficult to recognize, fantasy play is easily recognizable (Pellegrini 1988; Smith et al. 2004). Gomez and Martín-Andrade (2005) argue that apes trained in language experiments appear to exhibit human-like fantasy play, possibly because these "enculturated" apes had the opportunity to do so. One chimpanzee, Washoe, bathed and fed dolls while another, Austin, ate imaginary food with pretend cutlery. Koko the gorilla (*Gorilla gorilla*) held a rubber tube to her head as she made the sign for elephant, and placed a sock on a toy cat's head while signing "hat" (Gomez and Martín-Andrade 2005). Generally, discussions of fantasy play are limited to humans.

Another human play category is constructive play, which involves building something with objects, such as making a tower from blocks. Verbal or language play may involve making rhymes or vocalizations. Children also play rule-based games, which may be formally structured like soccer, or informally structured, where the children agree on a set of parameters for a game of tag, for example (Smith 2005). It should be noted that games following rules, including sports, often do not meet most definitions of play in the way many people casually believe (e.g., Burghardt 2005; Thorpe 1966). For this reason, many researchers consider rule-based games and sports separately from discussions of true play (e.g., Pellegrini et al. 2002). Whereas play is flexible with negotiated rules that are not usually set in advance, games are rule governed, those rules are set in advance, and breaking the rules is not tolerated and fraught with consequences (Pellegrini et al. 2002). Since keeping track of rules and potential outcomes is cognitively demanding, children's play is likely to develop and help promote social and cognitive competence (Pellegrini et al. 2002). Indeed, since play occurs consistently within and between species, it likely plays an important role in the development of motor, social, and cognitive skills (Lewis 2000). This is particularly likely given the specific time frame of play behavior across species.

DEVELOPMENTAL TIMING OF PLAY

It has long been recognized that play is important developmentally, and its timing is of crucial interest (Byers and Walker 1995; Fagen 1981; Groos 1898; Piaget 1962; Vygotsky 1967). Entering adulthood is a serious business. The developmental stages preceding adulthood are therefore key to ensuring that the individual reaches maturity as well prepared as possible. Developing the body and brain prior to adulthood is vital. Thus, infancy and juvenility represent critical periods of both growth and learning. Indeed, play is predominantly a behavior of the pre-adult period. It begins early in postnatal life, reaches a peak during the early juvenile period, and declines with the onset of adolescence and adulthood (Bekoff and Byers 1985; Fagen 1993; Byers and Walker 1995; Fairbanks 2000; Lewis 2005). In humans, R&T play in boys tends to become more competitive by early adolescence, and in many cases sports may replace other forms of play (Pellegrini 2006). Certainly, priorities and motivations change as a child ages. A younger child may enjoy sporting activities for physical activity, whereas older children and adolescents may engage in sports competitively for peer status or to emulate sporting heroes. College-aged sporting activities may be tied to scholarships or career opportunities, and thus an activity that was formerly playful may become more like work (Forencich 2003; Freysinger 2006). The same may be true of physical exercise generally, for example a shift from locomotor *play* to *work*ing out for health or physical appearance with increasing age (Forencich 2003).

In non-human primates and other mammals, a double spike in play frequency occurs. The first spike appears soon after play begins during infancy, and the second appears at, or just before, weaning (Lewis 2005). In humans, infants engage in self-exploration of the body and sensorimotor play types that become slowly replaced by increasingly elaborate play as children are weaned and start to develop gross motor skills (Garner and Bergen 2006). Most forms of play follow an inverted U-shaped trajectory in humans. Play increases steadily as self-exploration starts to decrease, and continues to increase throughout childhood; play then decreases with puberty and adolescence (Pellegrini and Gustafson 2005). The specific developmental timing of peaks and troughs in play frequency may have evolved to ensure that the body and brain are honed through the exhibition of appropriate behaviors at critical developmental periods (Byers and Walker 1995; Lewis and Barton 2004).

Although adults sometimes play, play behavior is generally considered the behavioral currency of the young. By engaging in play, a young animal may gain essential experience in formulating novel behavior patterns that may assist its adaptation to its environment (Burghardt 2005; Fagen 1981, Špinka et al. 2001; Sutton-Smith, 1997). Pellegrini and colleagues (2007) further suggest that in learning and practicing new behaviors within the safe confines of play, animals may influence their own adult phenotypes (in terms of increased co-operation, strength, and dominance status), which consequently may influence their genotypes. Pellegrini and colleagues (2007) thus turned Haeckel's old adage upside down and posited that, through play, ontogeny may actually influence phylogeny. The timing of play and the importance of juvenility are recurring themes in play research, and many functional explanations of play derive from this observation. That said, however, play in its entirety is probably not used purely as practice behavior for adult skills. In order to understand play further, we need to understand something about its function.

FUNCTIONS OF PLAY

Understanding the function of a behavior is considered of prime importance. But how do we understand the function of a behavior that for so long was described as "functionless" (Bekoff and Allen 1998)? While it is the case that some elements of play appear non-adaptive, it is important to remember that simply because a behavior does not have an immediately measurable or recognizable function, does not mean that there is no function. Indeed, Burghardt's first criterion is that play is incompletely functional in the context in which it appears. Also, since play incorporates elements from other behaviors, it is imperative to have a good working knowledge of a species' normal behavioral repertoire if we are to understand and fully recognize play. In other words, we need better ethology.

The adaptive significance of play behavior is less well understood than say, sex or fighting (Fagen 1981). If there is no function in playing, it might be assumed that any costs incurred through play would lead to selection against it (Martin and Caro 1985). However, the true functions of play are widely disputed. Play was long considered a practice behavior to learn the skills of adulthood. Children in traditional environments learn and develop work-related skills primarily through observation and play, rather than through formal teaching (Bock 2005; Lancy 1996; Pellegrini et al. 2007). For example, girls in an agropastoral community in the Okavango Delta in Botswana learn how to process grain by playful imitation of adults involved in the work of grain pounding. Through play, they become increasingly competent in the skill with age, and the activity gradually moves from play to work (Bock 2005; Pellegrini et al. 2007). Although play may contribute to learning (Singer et al. 2006), not all learning occurs through play (Martin and Caro 1985), and traditional views couching play as preparation for adulthood have to be tempered by the fact that adults of many species, including humans, play. Furthermore, young animals deprived of play still learn adult skills. However, juveniles that play may grow up to be more competent adults compared with their play-deprived counterparts (Hol et al. 1999). For example, children who engage in lots of R&T play tend to be more socially competent in non-play situations (Pellegrini 1993). Perhaps play might occur, not so much as practice, but to stimulate vigorous complex actions that give an individual experience in combining its brain, muscles, and sensory systems to respond to different or varying conditions (Burghardt 2001; Špinka et al. 2001). Thus, play may assist in, or contribute to, the development of permanent effects on the central nervous system.

In attempting to understand the functions and adaptive significance of play, discussions of costs and benefits have been prominent. Costs associated with playing include injury from falls or aggressive retaliation, reduction in time spent in survival behaviors such as foraging, and reduced vigilance, which may increase the risk of predation. Benefits are usually considered as long-term and delayed benefits, and include enhanced agility, familiarity with the environment, and social bonding. Immediate benefits might include enjoyment (Fagen 1992), immediate social bonds (Špinka et al. 2001), and immediate learning enhancement. It is possible that immediate benefits may also contribute to ultimate individual fitness, although perhaps delayed benefits may have more of an effect. Nonetheless, if playing reduces juvenile mortality through enhanced social integration, then both immediate and delayed benefits are important to play's behavioral evolution. However, most of these assertions are theoretical, rather than based on experimental observation (Burghardt 2005). Proximate causes for behaviors are also important. Play may occur because it is fun. Long-term benefits may accrue as a result of experiencing pleasure in the short term. So it is with other natural rewards; long before the availability of synthetic drugs, the brain evolved to experience rewards from natural behaviors such as food, sex, and exercise—and perhaps also play (Balcombe 2006). Thus, the experience and perception of pleasure from these activities represents a stable strategy to ensure that they occur (e.g., Rhodes et al. 2005). Understanding the adaptive significance of play is a tricky area, and one that requires both experimental and comparative synthesis. Although play probably did not evolve specifically to provide physical and cognitive benefits to an individual, the effects of such benefits are probably advantageous by-products of earlier evolutionary events (Burghardt 2005).

THEORETICAL APPROACHES TO THE STUDY OF PLAY

Surplus Resource Theory

Energy and physiology are important to consider in the evolution of play behavior (Burghardt 1982; 1984; 2001; 2005). Animals with very low metabolic rates (e.g., sloths [Choloepidae]) tend to play less. Similarly, small animals with high metabolic rates (e.g., shrews [Soricidae]) tend not to be playful because they have large surface-to-mass ratio, thus high metabolic costs. The surplus resource theory (Burghardt 1984) posits that due to such constraints, some animals simply may not have sufficient energy to devote to behaviors that are not directly related to survival. Some of the most playful species share certain traits such as slow development, parental care, large brains, and high resting metabolic rates (Lewis 2003; Burghardt 2005). It is possible that such traits may account for selection for behaviors and cognitive complexities that are apparent in endothermic (i.e., warm-blooded) animals (Burghardt 1984; 2005). Endothermy is costly in terms of energy and metabolism, but endotherms have aerobic metabolisms with quick access to energy reserves. In other words, warm-blooded animals are able to spring into motor activity spontaneously. Ectotherms such as reptiles, however, have anaerobic metabolisms that rely on behavioral adaptations to maintain thermoregulation, such as basking in the sun to raise the body temperature sufficiently for activity. As such, ectotherms quickly tire, whereas endotherms can prolong activity for far longer (Burghardt 1984; 2005). Burghardt (1984) states that since play only occurs when animals are in a "relaxed field," play probably originated under conditions in which animals were able to regulate their body heat efficiently, had sufficient metabolic resources, and could accumulate more energy than what was required for growth and maintenance alone. In addition, such animals probably had stable juvenile environments with high offspring survival rates and an innate mechanism for curiosity and exploration. Play is more prevalent after a feeding bout (Burghardt and Burghardt 1972) suggesting that the increase in energy following a meal can be diverted toward play. Human infants are more likely to initiate playful encounters with their mothers after feeding (Burghardt 2005: 155). This may be a key time for brain stimulation, given the extra energy and close mother-infant contact.

Metabolism certainly poses a constraint on the exhibition of play behavior. The time and energy devoted to play is typically reported at less than 10 percent of a species' daily active time budget (Bekoff and Byers 1992). The relationship between metabolic rate, thermoregulation, body size, and brain size are likely to be complex and are ill-understood in many animals (Nagy 1994). Although body size and brain size share a close allometric relationship, and body size and metabolic rate are related, McNab and Eisenberg (1989) and Barton (1999) warn that there is little evidence for a strong relationship between brain size and metabolic rate, as some variables affect an animal's overall metabolic rate without affecting the brain. Primates for example, may allocate 9–20 percent of their metabolism to the brain; in most other mammals the figure stands closer to 5 percent (Bennett and Harvey 1985). More important, variation in metabolism can usually be explained by differences in body size and phylogeny, although factors such as diet, seasonality and temperature may also contribute to this variance (Nagy 1994; 2005). Basal metabolic rate (BMR) not only varies with diet, but also varies considerably with climate; species in more tropical zones typically have lower BMR than species in colder climates (McNab 1989). This, of course, is connected to diet and food availability, but in any case, future studies of play should aim to include the latitude of the species' population as a variable. The locomotor behavior of a species also has a considerable impact on energetic constraints. For example, running or walking consumes more energy than swimming or flying (McNab 2002). In other words, a 10g bird expends 30 times less energy flying than a 10g mouse does walking. However, mice are probably more playful than hummingbirds (Burghardt 2005). This may have huge significance for the evolution of play in humans, given a transition from arboreality to bipedalism in hominin evolution.

Social and Cognitive Enhancement

A further view is that play behavior occurs in social animals to help facilitate social bonds (but see Sharpe 2005). Juvenile animals play most with their littermates (e.g., Nunes et al. 2004). This may be because littermates are the most readily available play partners of appropriate ages. In many cases, however, it may also be that social play helps to facilitate social bonds among conspecifics and may even promote cooperative behavior (Bekoff 2001; Sussman et al. 2005). Indeed, many species hunt cooperatively or defend territories and home ranges together. Although it is not necessarily the case that playmates later become adult allies, social play during development arguably provides important social experience that might facilitate learning how to form coalitions and alliances, especially in social species. Among children, the most socially dominant individuals appear to be highly social and cooperative with both their peers and their educators, and are generally not perceived as aggressive; however, they seem to be quite effective in using aggression to access resources (Pellegrini 2008). Additionally, play among littermates assists in familiarization, and may help eliminate inbreeding between siblings since playmates tend to avoid one another sexually in adulthood (Charlesworth and Charlesworth 1987). Diamond (2000) demonstrated that the cerebellum is involved not only with various aspects of motor control and coordination, but also with cognition, and Lewis and Barton (2004) found that evolutionary elaborations in cerebellum size correlate with increases in social play frequency in primates and carnivores (Lewis 2003). Social play, involving strong motor patterns, in addition to cognitive complexity, may reflect this mosaic pattern of brain-behavior co-evolution.

Motor Training Hypothesis

Another theory, the motor-training hypothesis, proposes that animals play for physical exercise or to develop and maintain physical skills (Brownlee 1954). The adaptive function of play in this context is to modify the developing neuromuscular system (Bekoff and Byers 1981; Byers and Walker 1995). Byers and Walker (1995) found that play during the critical period of development may actually be timed to occur to hone skeletal muscle fiber and cerebellar synaptogenesis; two true effects of play because the effects are permanent. Nevertheless, not all physical and neural responses are permanent; physical training improves physical skills at any age, but these increments may be lost as training ceases. Byers and Walker (1995) maintain that it is important to consider how much an animal plays in comparison with how much exercise it needs to increase strength and endurance. However, the amount of exercise needed to maintain physical skills is probably higher than the amount gained through play alone; thus play probably does not function for "getting into shape" (Byers 1998). Additionally, if play functions for physical exercise, we would expect adults to play more frequently.

Adult Play

Adult play has posed a problem for many researchers, since its occurrence does not fit neatly with traditional views of play as preparatory behavior. Adults play in many species, especially in adult-infant interactions, but usually at far lower frequencies than non-adults. Adult-infant play, such as tickling in monkeys, or peek-a-boo in humans, is probably most common between kin. However, unrelated adults may also play with the infant, perhaps granting some level of status to an adult while simultaneously demonstrating a "goodwill gesture" to the infant's mother. Adult play may have certain benefits in terms of assisting the development of offspring and may be considered a form of parental investment or assessment (Chiszar 1985). In adult male polar bears (*Thalarctos maritimus*), for example, play-fighting may serve as a means to assess the strength of potential competitors (Latour 1981). Adult humans may play in a competitive manner for peer-recognition and status. Adult-adult play between males and females may occur as courtship behavior and mate assessment. This may help to dilute tension between unfamiliar partners, especially in non-gregarious species (no animal is truly solitary) (Pellis and Iwaniuk 1999; 2000).

A PLAYFUL ENVIRONMENT

The environment is undoubtedly important to a juvenile's later development. Although the brain is somewhat robust in terms of sensitivity to nutritional deficiencies (Guesry 1998), marked malnutrition during critical periods in development may adversely affect brain and retinal development, especially in terms of skill acquisition (Gordon 1997). It is argued that provided the developing infant receives sufficient psychomotor stimulation, the brain should develop normally (Guesry 1998). If this is the case, then perhaps play acts as a buffer against certain aspects of malnutrition, particularly early in ontogeny (Lewis 2003). Play may provide a sufficient stimulus for psychomotor development, and arguably could protect the process of myelination from the deleterious effects of malnutrition. Myelin is a fatty insulating sheath that covers nerve fibers, and is especially associated with brain conductivity. Myelination, therefore, is considered to be one key indicator of intellectual performance (Miller 1994). In other words, the thicker the myelin, the better the brain. Myelin synthesis is sensitive to nutritional effects, and severe malnutrition may lead to fewer fibers becoming myelinated (Gordon 1997). "More intelligent" brains are argued to be more energy efficient (Parks et al. 1988). Haier and colleagues (1988) showed that individuals who were considered to be highly intelligent, and who performed well in a variety of neuropsychological tasks, also had thickly myelinated axons. Conversely, individuals who performed less well had thinly myelinated axons. Thickly myelinated axons additionally consume far less glucose in comparison with thinly myelinated axons (Haier et al. 1988). Diamond (1988) found that rats raised in an enriched environment, which improves maze-learning abilities, also had lower glucose utilization in certain neural regions. Thus, thicker myelin is associated with faster reaction times and skill acuity and, importantly, its developmental trajectory appears to correspond with the honing of certain skills and stages of developmental advancement (Miller 1994). Additionally, myelination is considered to be one marker for, and explanation of, improved intelligence through juvenility and into adulthood (Miller 1994). It may be the case that encouraging psychomotor development through play at crucial periods of neural development assists the honing of the central nervous system (see Fairbanks 2000). This may have an additional purpose of combating variance in the environment (Lewis 2003).

THE PLAY OF CHILDREN

Various authors have demonstrated that smart species are also those that are especially playful, and that includes humans (Lewis 2000; Lewis and Barton 2004; 2006; Iwaniuk et al. 2001). Although other big-brained animals, such as dolphins (Delphinidae), play games that appear to have rules (DeLong 1999), the nature of human play appears to extend beyond that which we see in other animals. As in other primates, human play begins in infancy, and it is argued that play, even at this early age, builds on developing cognitive abilities. This is demonstrated in contingency play, which relies on the infant's understanding that actions create contingent effects (Parker 1984). For example, the sound of a rattle is contingent upon it being dropped or shaken. Through social contingency games, like peek-a-boo, infants realize that their own laughs or smiles result in a tickle or a smile from their caregiver. This is argued to be vital to understanding the turn-taking required for human social interactions, such as conversations (Parker 1984). Turn-taking in this way is unique to humans. Although great apes engage in role-reversal during play-fighting, such as from dominant to submissive or from chaser to chased, turn-taking per se is not a natural behavior in other primates. Great apes even engage in simple mother-infant contingency play, such as tickling or dangling, but the interactions rarely encompass the intensity of face-to-face play that is universal in humans (Parker 1984). Both social and physical contingency play is likely to be important in developing social relationships, spatial awareness, and object perception. It is argued that contingency play may be an adaptation for tool use (Parker and Gibson 1979; Parker 1984). This view is especially compelling given that the great apes use various tools (Van Schaik et al. 1999) and engage in contingency play.

Another play category of note is that of aimed throwing. Hall (1904) noted the prevalence of throwing in human play and postulated its importance in terms of survival during human evolution. Early throwing attempts may be initially fairly inaccurate in terms of aim (Parker 1984), but arguably, babies are fairly efficient at gaining attention from their caregivers by throwing toys and food from their strollers and highchairs. Initial throwing attempts may begin as solitary object play, but throwing becomes increasingly social with age, developing from toss-catch play into more complex games and sports. By seven years old, children develop mature throwing patterns, including arm rotation and leverage (Parker 1984). By the same age, sex differences in throwing skill are also apparent, and appear to correlate with sex differences in shoulder-hip ratio. Certainly, boys are more likely than girls to play ball games (Pellegrini et al. 2002). Boys and men, with broader chests and longer forearms, even by age seven, consistently show greater accuracy in aimed throwing relative to girls and women (Parker 1984; Westergaard et al. 2000). This has important implications for human evolution. That greater skill in aimed throwing is a benefit to hunting pursuits is apparent. Speed and accuracy in throwing would have provided dividends for ancestral hominins, and such skills may have been subject to sexual selection pressures, ultimately giving modern male humans the advantage in aimed throwing (Watson 2001). Certainly, related social play behaviors such as R&T play or team games with rules may have provided important social bonding experiences which, among other things, may facilitate cooperative behaviors such as hunting large prey. Indeed, chimpanzees, our closest living relatives, appear to work together in a cooperative fashion to hunt red colobus (*Procolobus badius*) monkeys and other medium-sized prey (e.g., Boesch 2002). Additionally, Lewis and Barton's (2004) finding that the cerebellum shares a co-evolutionary relationship with social play, and Paulin's (1993) finding that that the cerebellum is involved with following the trajectory of objects, further supports the hypothesis that play has been selected to occur to support developing body-brain circuitry prior to adulthood.

Notable among humans is the performance of pretend or fantasy play. Piaget (1962) and others have noted that children typically play out familiar scenes from their perceptions of adult lives and in many cases specifically imitate adult activities such as housework, intimate activities, and social activities such as gossiping. Boys and girls also tend to imitate adults of their own sex (Gosso et al. 2005). For example, !Kung girls in the Kalahari Desert imitate mother-infant behavior such as cradling and cooing, and use melons as baby dolls (Gosso et al. 2005). Parakanã Indian men in Brazil hold evening meetings to socialize and to discuss community matters. In their play, Parakanã boys gather in the same meeting house and imitate such meetings, including singing, dancing, and using a stick as a pretend cigar (Gosso et al. 2005). Cross-culturally, young children play marriage games, which often include a complete ceremony. Among Parakanã children, variations on the game include discovering infidelity and beating an unfaithful spouse (Gosso et al. 2005). In many cases, fantasy play of children may be an accurate copy of adult society, suggesting that children understand both public and private adult worlds.

THE CRUELTY OF PLAY

"Children are cruel": a phrase we have all uttered at some point in our adulthood. The cruelty of children can frequently be seen in the context of play. The relationship between bullying and play is quite interesting. For example, R&T play among boys seems to be a good predictor of social cognitive status (Pellegrini 2006). For boys popular with their peers, R&T play predicts social status and cognitive problem solving; for boys rejected by their peers, R&T play is more closely associated with aggression and anti-social behavior. Most boys probably use R&T play as a way to learn social and cooperative skills, particularly through solving disputes within play. But it may be the case that bullies use R&T play to dominate others, for example through identifying other boys unable or unwilling to stand up to them. Bullying may also occur through exclusion of a peer from play (Pellegrini 2006).

Play can sometimes be pointlessly violent. As children, my brother and I played "slapsies." Opponents stand facing one another, with their own hands pressed together (as if to pray). Each player takes it in turns to try to clap their hands on their opponent's closed hands. If the attacker misses, the opponent gets a free slap. Although this game was painful, it was, bizarrely, cooperative. We agreed on the rules and we followed them, perhaps even self-handicapping the full force of our hand-slapping to keep it in the realms of playfulness and to be somewhat fair (and certainly to avoid parental punishment). Other games may be classified as painful, pointless, disgusting, or just plain silly, such as Chinese burns (twisting the skin on an opponent's forearm), attempting to touch one's nose with one's tongue, and blowing up balloons with one's nostrils. Such games may also be reminiscent of sibling rivalry or the phenomenon of fraternity hazing. These somewhat ritualized games of endurance tend to be more commonplace among males and may serve to both develop and test competitive personalities. It may be argued that these games assist in dealing with shame, pain, punishment, and confrontation, all of which are a part of the adult world. Similarly, through such games, social bonds and collaborative and co-operative friendships may also develop. The development of trust, respect, perhaps even fairness, may all justifiably accompany such apparently harsh games (Caillois 1961; 2001). Indeed, overcoming certain fears associated with these cruel play situations may be especially beneficial with increasing age. Peers testing one another prior to entering the adult world may serve as social and physical assessment for the perceived right to enter adulthood. In this vein, many aspects of human play seem inextricably linked to ritualistic behavior, rites of passage, and culture.

PLAY AND CULTURE

Sex and Violence

Herbert Spencer (1898) believed that animal play was a precursor to art and aesthetics in that neither play nor art were essential to survival. He noted that the existence of "inferior" animals was dominated by survival activities, whereas "superior" animals had increasing time to devote to non-essential ends, better nutrition, and extra time that could be devoted to leisure pursuits. Such pursuits, he claimed, were performed because they were pleasurable and provided exercise. Pleasure, reward, and fun are important elements to the experience of play, but also to other behaviors such as eating, exercise, and sex. The word "play" comes from the Old English *plegen* (to move briskly) and the Anglo-Saxon *plega* (to fight). Thus, semantically at least, human play hints at ritualized violence (Turner 1982). Play behavior occupies a continuum of behaviors including sex and aggression, and this is further demonstrated in that even words for play are the root of words for sex, love, violence, combat, and religious rites. For example, the Sanskrit word for copulation, *kridaratnum*, means "the jewel of games" (Ackerman 1999). Play incorporates activities that convey social meaning, cooperation, confrontation, and symbolism: in other words, culture.

The rules of culture may be reiterated or bent during play and thus may shape future culture. For adults, sexual behavior is arguably playful. In humans and other animals, playful encounters between consorting adults may be important for courtship and mating. Pellis and Iwaniuk (2002) showed that adult-adult play may be essential for overcoming unfamiliarity, particularly in the context of mate assessment; this further points to the evolutionary origins of adult play. Turner (1982: 34) suggests that sexual activity is divided between the "work" of procreation and the "fun" of fore*play*. Children's play, much like the play of young animals, is often sexual in nature. This is play, not abuse, and occurs across cultures (Gosso et al. 2005). Sexual play behavior in non-adults is typically referred to as "pseudo-sexual" play, because players lack sexual maturity and are unable to produce offspring. In this way, the divisions of sexual behavior and play behavior are blurred. Similarly, play-fighting and true aggression may also have unclear boundaries, especially with the onset of adolescence and adulthood when play may start to incorporate increasing competitiveness.

Indeed, juvenility represents a "limbo" period (Pagel and Harvey 1993) in development. The individual is nutritionally independent from its caregivers, but as yet not fully developed in terms of adult size and experience. Given this behavioral immaturity, young animals often engage in risky behaviors (Spear 2000). Juvenility and adolescence, then, are periods of considerable danger. In humans, adolescents as a group represent a high-risk, sensation-seeking proportion of the population (Trimpop et al. 1999). Risk-taking and anti-social behaviors (theft, vandalism, drug use, unprotected sex, etc.) are reported at high levels in the eleven-and-a-half to fifteen-year-old age range (Maggs et al. 1995). And with increased levels of risky behavior comes also increased mortality rates (Irwin 1993; Irwin and Millstein 1992); indeed, violent or accidental death in humans is highest during late juvenility and early adolescence (Irwin 1989). Such behaviors may be spurred by peer pressure or curiosity and, although the risks are sometimes immeasurably high, the rewards associated with such risks may be equally high in terms of self-esteem or access to the adult world and the perceived advantages therein (Silbereisen and Reitzle 1992). Fortunately for most, high levels of risk taking in humans tend to be restricted to this developmental period and are usually transitory. For young animals, including humans, curiosity is part of the business of being a juvenile; but avoiding predation and other hazards is part of the business of reaching adulthood—or more specifically, surviving long enough to reproduce. Play behavior need not specifically amount to the other risky behaviors engaged in by teenagers, but risky behaviors (and perhaps enjoyment of associated social prowess) may simply be "fun" (Maggs et al. 1995). And fun is often sufficient motivation to engage in any behavior or activity.

Ritual and Spirituality

Children's play often imitates adult society fairly accurately, even in the details of cultural ceremonies or rituals. The stylized violence of children's play may also hint at ritualized behaviors. Boyer and Lienard (2006) suggest that the development of ritualistic behaviors may have arisen as a coping strategy to deal with situations that may affect potential fitness. In other words, fear creates ritual. It is conceivable that aspects of human culture arose from animal play behaviors. Consider the vigorous energetic movements of an animal engaged in locomotor play. He runs and leaps and twists oblivious to everything around him. Could this be akin to human dancing? Dance is considered a primal activity, and one closely aligned with ritual and trancelike states (Forencich 2003). Humans may dance for cultural purposes, but it is also fun and exhilarating. However, humans are not the only species to dance. Some chimpanzees dance during thunderstorms and heavy rains, while others have been observed dancing at waterfalls, swaying and lifting each foot deliberately and rhythmically, and appearing as if in a trancelike state (Bekoff 2007: 62). Black rhinoceroses (*Diceros bicornis*) run and leap with abandon (Bekoff 2007: 61) and even beavers (*Castor canadensis*) appear to dance (Burghardt 2005). Play, movement, and pleasure are closely bounded. Spoken language and non-verbal thought are additionally linked to motor behavior and thus movement, intelligence, and culture seem intimately connected. With regard to human adults, Ackerman (1999) discusses the idea of "deep play": being so embedded in a pleasurable or creative activity that it creates deep exhilaration and relaxed concentration, perhaps even a spiritual "high" (but see also Geertz 1972). Sands and Sands (this volume) capture this idea with regard to endurance running. We may anthropomorphize similar activities in the soaring of eagles or the running of deer—something, perhaps, that stirs in us an appreciation for the nature that surrounds us. This is a compelling idea, although it is difficult to measure. There does however seem to be a neurological basis for deep pleasure, especially that which is connected to physical activity, and this may assist our understanding of the evolution of behavior. For example, concentrated and extended physical exercise appears to elevate levels of dopamine in the brain, a neurochemical most associated with pleasurable experience. Animals considered "smart" such as primates, cetaceans, and corvid birds appear to have dense dopaminergic innervation in key brain regions that may underlie or promote various cognitive abilities. Previc (1999) states that the big leap forward in human intelligence in our Paleolithic past coincided with the expansion of dopaminergic brain systems. Such expansion must have given rise to behavior that we specifically associate with human culture; that, for example, of ritual, symbolism, and language.

IMPLICATIONS FOR HUMAN EVOLUTION

The role of dopamine in human evolution is intriguing. Dopamine is the primary neurotransmitter for combating hyperthermia in hot conditions, and hypothermia in cold conditions. Certainly, human ancestors lived in thermally stressful environments, due in part to climatic changes associated with the formation of the East African rift system, and also with persistence hunting. Persistence hunting, or "chase" hunting, involves chasing prey to the point of exhaustion, and is still practiced by modern African Bushmen. Chasing a wildebeest (*Connochaetes* spp.) in the hot sun until it collapses from heat stress represents a true physical endurance ability, and does not rely on sophisticated hunting technologies (Previc 2006). Such hunting practices, however, are possible due to specific physiological adaptations to combating thermal stress. For example, bipedalism reduces radiant heat from the head, and may serve as a buffer against hyperthermia. Similarly, humans have increased surface-to-mass ratio, relative hairlessness, and an increased number of sweat glands, all of which help to dissipate heat from the body, providing a thermoregulatory system that functions quickly and efficiently during physical exhaustion. Previc (1999) argues that human reliance on persistence hunting underlies these adaptations. Of course, in addition to physiological adaptations, it is also necessary for the ambient temperature to be appropriate to cause sweating. Consequently, our ancestors also would have had to have been able to access water to replace bodily fluids lost through sweating. Both such conditions are the consequence of the ancestral environment. Previc (1999) posits that the dopaminergic expansion in the central nervous system would have made these physiological adaptations possible. Indeed, dopamine would have been affected by environmental changes that are likely to have taken place in early hominin evolution. Increasing aridity of the environment would have placed a premium on physical endurance and adaptation to hyperthermic stress, both of which depend on dopaminergic systems. Recent evidence on mice suggests that selection for such adaptations could have been selected for in very few generations (Rhodes et al. 2003; 2005).

Running was important in human evolution. Indeed, it was likely that movement through walking and running were key to our survival. Early human ancestors evolved as prey, rather than predator species (see Hart and Sussman 2005), and running may well have enabled survival. Later human ancestors probably scavenged food in addition to hunting through chasing down prey, and they also migrated great distances. While running itself is not always play behavior, it may share some of the underlying motivational elements of play. Like some humans, rodents have a yen for running, especially in wheels, and research suggests that voluntary wheel running may be autotelic and naturally rewarding, even addictive. It may in many cases be locomotor play. Rhodes et al. (2003) recently took this evidence a step further. They compared the brain regions of control mice against strains that were selectively bred for their motivation to voluntarily run in wheels. The voluntary aspect is important since the mice do not run to their full exercise capacity. The difference therefore seems to be in their brains, rather than in their heart, lungs, or muscles (Rhodes et al. 2005). The authors posit that brain regions may evolve in response to selection for increased motivation for wheel running. Specifically, they implicate the role of the caudate-putamen, medial frontal cortex, and lateral hypothalamus in the motivation to run. These brain regions are similarly implicated in play behavior in terms of voluntary locomotion, experiencing reward, and underlying pleasure (Gordon et al. 2002). High levels of dopamine suggest that running or other high levels of exercise may be a form of addiction. Moreover, mice bred for their high voluntary wheel running have a neurological profile similar to that of humans with Attention Deficit Hyperactivity Disorder (ADHD), as well as humans with high motivation for exercise. ADHD and high motivation for other rewards such as food, sex, and drugs are associated with changes in dopamine function. Indeed, when mice had access to a wheel, they ran more each day, increasing their revolutions on the wheel until about three weeks, when the running stabilized. Rather than increasing the time they spent on the wheel, the mice increased their revolutions by running faster or more often. When they were given dopamine blockers, the effect was a decrease in speed, but not duration (Rhodes et al. 2005). Perhaps dopamine had a similar effect on human ancestors, controlling short, sharp bursts of energy for travel, foraging, or hunting? Clearly, we have to be extremely cautious in attempting to reconstruct the past. This is especially the case for research involving brains and behavior, since neither fossilizes. Certainly, however, dopamine plays a role in voluntary movement and predatory aggression in wheel-running mice (Rhodes et al. 2005).

LOOKING AHEAD

In humans, play all too often is seen as a waste of time that could be better spent in productive activities like work and education. This might explain the ebbing away of recess times in schools in the last few decades. Curbing play in schoolchildren may be due in part to adult confusion, in particular between R&T play and aggression. While it may be the case that play behavior and aggression occupy places on the same continuum of behaviors, it is imperative to keep in mind that the contexts are quite distinct—and especially in the minds of children (Pellegrini 2006). Although games such as "slapsies" and others may strike parents and educators as pointlessly violent, the general motivation of children to engage in vigorous play episodes remains an important consideration, especially when recess times are filed down further and further. R&T play is not only an important physical activity and release of energy, but it may also be important in facilitating social relationships and cooperation. Recess may offer one of few opportunities for schoolchildren to engage freely in peer-interactions, and such social interactions are crucial for developing social competence (Pellegrini et al. 2002). In other words, through play, children learn to work together (Golinkoff et al. 2006). In America and other industrialized nations, the issue of surplus energy may be especially poignant with the rise in obesity rates among children. Indeed, obesity, both in adults and children, has reached epidemic proportions worldwide in the last two decades. It is estimated that 25 percent of U.S. children are overweight and 11 percent are obese (Dehghan et al. 2005). While both causes and solutions are debated, a daily hour of recess devoted to R&T play would certainly help redress the balance.

Modern humans typically have a diet that, in comparison to our hominin ancestors, is higher in fat and lower in protein, while strenuous exercise is atypical for the vast majority of people. Bortz (1985) went so far as to say that in terms of physiology, we are "playing a dangerous game with our heritage." Perhaps we should be more aware of the benefits of physical activity, especially that of play, as we watch our pets, and engage and encourage our children to play. It would seem that playfulness has been an important part of our human heritage. I leave the reader with this closing thought from Forencich (2003: 204), who says, "Absence of play is not a sign of maturity, it is a sign of pathology."

NOTE

Many thanks to Jeff Graham, Lorrie Hale, Michelle Hamilton, Hillary Huber, Laura Lewis, Tony Pellegrini, Rob Sands, Stephanie Schnorr, and Desserae Shepston for helpful comments on earlier drafts of this manuscript. Special thanks to Jeff and Huxley for reminding me daily of the importance of play.

BIBLIOGRAPHY

Ackerman, Diane. *Deep Play*. New York: Random House, 1999.

Altmann, Stuart A. and Jeanne Altmann. *Baboon Ecology: African Field Research*. Chicago: University of Chicago Press, 1970.

Balcombe, Jonathan. *Pleasurable Kingdom: Animals and the Nature of Feeling Good*. New York: Macmillan, 2006.

Barton, Robert A. "The Evolutionary Ecology of the Primate Brain" in *Comparative Primate Socioecology*, edited by Phyllis C. Lee. Cambridge: Cambridge University Press, 1999: 167–203.

Bateson, Patrick. "The Role of Play in the Evolution of Great Apes and Humans" in *The Nature of Play: Great Apes and Humans*, edited by Anthony D. Pellegrini and Peter K. Smith. New York: Guilford, 2005: 13–24.

Bekoff, Marc. "The Evolution of Animal Play, Emotions, and Social Morality: On Science, Theology, Spirituality, Personhood, and Love." *Zygon* 36 (2001): 615–55.

———. *The Emotional Lives of Animals*. Novato, Calif.: New World Library, 2007.

Bekoff, Marc and Colin Allen. "Intentional Communication and Social Play: How and Why Animals Negotiate and Agree to Play" in *Animal Play: Evolutionary, Comparative and Ecological Perspectives*, edited by Marc Bekoff and John A. Byers. Cambridge, Mass.: Cambridge University Press, 1998: 97–114.

Bekoff, Marc and John A. Byers. "A Critical Re-analysis of the Ontogeny and Phylogeny of Mammalian Social and Locomotor Play: An Ethological Hornet's Nest" in *Behavioural Development*, edited by K. Immelmann, G. Barlow, M. Main, and L. Petrinovich. Cambridge, Mass.: Cambridge University Press, 1981: 296–337.

———. "The Development of Behavior from Evolutionary and Ecological Perspectives in Mammals and Birds." *Evolutionary Biology* 19 (1985): 215–86.

———. "Time, Energy, and Play." *Animal Behaviour* 44 (1992): 981–82.

Bennett, Peter M. and Paul H. Harvey. "Brain Size Development and Metabolism in Birds and Mammals." *Journal of Zoology* 201 (1985): 491–509.

Biben, Maxeen. "Object Play and Social Treatment of Prey in Bush Dogs and Crab-eating Foxes." *Behaviour* 79 (1982): 201–11.

———. "Comparative Ontogeny of Social Behavior in Three South American Canids: The Maned Wolf, Crab-eating Fox, and Bush Dog: Implications for Sociality." *Animal Behaviour* 31 (1983): 814–26.

Bock, John. "Farming, Foraging, and Children's Play in the Okavango Delta, Botswna" in *The Nature of Play: Great Apes and Humans*, edited by Anthony D. Pellegrini and Peter K. Smith. New York: Guilford, 2005: 254–81.

Boesch, Christophe. "Cooperative Hunting Roles Among Taï Chimpanzees." *Human Nature* 13 (2002): 27–46.

Bortz, Walter M. II. "Physical Exercise as an Evolutionary Force." *Journal of Human Evolution* 14 (1985): 145–55.

Boyer, Pascal and Pierre Lienard. "Why Ritualized Behavior? Precaution Systems and Action-parsing in Developmental, Pathological and Cultural Rituals." *Behavioral and Brain Sciences* 29 (2006): 1–56.

Brownlee, A. "Play in Domestic Cattle in Britain: An Analysis of its Nature." *British Veterinary Journal* 110 (1954): 48–68.

Burghardt, Gordon M. "Comparison Matters: Curiosity, Bears, Surplus Energy and Why Reptiles Don't Play." *Behavioral and Brain Sciences* 5 (1982): 159–60.

———. "On the Origins of Play" in *Play in Animals and Humans*, edited by Peter K. Smith. New York: Blackwell, 1984: 5–41.

———. "Play: Attributes and Neural Substrates" in *Developmental Psychobiology*: Vol. 13, *Handbook of Behavioral Neurobiology*, edited by Elliott M. Blass. New York: Kluwer Academic/Plenum, 2001: 327–66.

———. *The Genesis of Animal Play: Testing the Limits*. Cambridge, Mass.: MIT Press, 2005.

Burghardt, Gordon M. and Lorraine S. Burghardt. "Notes on the Behavioral Development of Two Female Black Bear Cubs: The First Eight Months" in *Bears—Their Biology and Management*, edited by Stephen Herrero. Morges, Switzerland: International Union for the Conservation of Nature and Natural Resources (IUCN), 1972: 255–73.

Byers, John A. "Biological Effects of Locomotor Play: Getting into Shape, or Something More Specific?" in *Animal Play: Evolutionary, Comparative and Ecological*

Perspectives, edited by Marc Bekoff and John A. Byers. Cambridge: Cambridge University Press, 1998: 205–20.

Byers, John A. and Curt Walker. "Refining the Motor Training Hypothesis for the Evolution of Play." *American Naturalist* 146 (1995): 25–40.

Caillois, Roger. *Man, Play and Games*. (Meyer Barash, trans. 1961). Urbana and Chicago: University of Illinois Press, 2001.

Charlesworth, D. and B. Charlesworth. "Inbreeding Depression and Its Evolutionary Consequences." *Annual Review of Ecological Systems* 18 (1987): 237–68.

Chiszar, David. "Ontogeny of Communicative Behaviors" in *The Comparative Development of Adaptive Skills: Evolutionary Implications*, edited by Eugene S. Gollin. Hillsdale, N.J.: Lawrence Erlbaum, 1985: 207–38.

Dehghan, Mahshid, Noori Akhtar-Danesh, and Anwar T. Merchant. "Childhood Obesity: Prevalence and Prevention." *Nutrition Journal* (September 2005): 4–24.

DeLong, Theia C. "Observations of Free-play Behavior in Captive Juvenile Bottlenose Dolphins (*Tursiops truncatus*)." *Play and Culture Studies*, 2, *Play Contexts Revisited* (1999): 219–36.

Diamond, Adele. "Close Interrelation of Motor Development and Cognitive Development and of the Cerebellum and Prefrontal Cortex." *Child Development* 71 (2000): 44–56.

Diamond, Marian C. *Enriching Heredity: The Impact of the Environment on the Anatomy of the Brain*. New York: The Free Press, 1988.

Fagen, Robert M. *Animal Play Behavior*. Oxford: Oxford University Press, 1981.

———. "Play, Fun and the Communication of Well-being." *Play and Culture* 5 (1992): 40–58.

———. "Primate Juveniles and Primate Play" in *Juvenile Primates—Life History, Development, and Behavior,* edited by Michael E. Pereira and Lynn A. Fairbanks. Oxford: Oxford University Press, 1993: 182–96.

Fairbanks, Lynn A. "The Developmental Timing of Primate Play: A Neural Selection Model" in *Biology, Brains, and Behavior: The Evolution of Human Development,* edited by Sue Taylor Parker, Jonas Langer, and Michael L. McKinney. Santa Fe: SAR Press, 2000: 131–58.

Forencich, Frank. *Play as if Your Life Depends on It: Functional Exercise and Living for Homo Sapiens*. Seattle, Wash.: GoAnimal, 2003.

Freysinger, Valeria J. "Play in the Context of Life-span Human Development" in *Play from Birth to Twelve: Contexts, Perspectives, and Meanings* (2nd edition), edited by Doris Pronin Fromberg and Doris Bergen. New York: Routledge, 2006: 53–62.

Gamble, Jennifer R. and Daniel A. Cristol. "Drop-catch Behaviour is Play in Herring Gulls, *Larus Argentatus*." *Animal Behaviour* 62 (2002): 339–45.

Garner, Barbara P. and Doris Bergen. "Play Development from Birth to Age Four" in *Play from Birth to Twelve: Contexts, Perspectives, and Meanings* (2nd edition), edited by Doris Pronin Fromberg and Doris Bergen. New York: Routledge, 2006: 1–11.

Geertz, Clifford. "Deep Play: Notes on the Balinese Cockfight." *Daedalus* 101 (1972): 1–38.

Golinkoff, Roberta Michnick, Kathy Hirsh-Pasek, and Dorothy G. Singer. "Why Play = Learning: A Challenge for Parents and Educators." in *Play = Learning: How Play*

Motivates and Enhances Children's Cognitive and Social-Emotional Growth, edited by Dorothy G. Singer, Roberta Michnick Golinkoff, and Kathy Hirsh-Pasek. Oxford: Oxford University Press, 2006: 3–12.

Gomez, Juan-Carlos and Beatriz Martín-Andrade. "Fantasy Play in Apes" in *The Nature of Play: Great Apes and Humans*, edited by Anthony D. Pellegrini and Peter K. Smith. New York: Guilford, 2005: 139–72.

Gordon, N. "Nutrition and Cognitive Function." *Brain and Development* 19 (1997): 165–70.

Gordon, Nakia S., Sara Kollack-Walker, Huda Akil, and Jaak Panksepp. "Expression of C-fos Gene Activation During Rough and Tumble Play in Juvenile Rats." *Brain Research Bulletin* 57 (2002): 651–59.

Gosso, Yumi, Emma Otta, Maria de Lima Salum e Morais, Fernando José Leite Ribeiro, and Vera Silvia Raad Bussab. "Play in Hunter-Gatherer Society" in *The Nature of Play: Great Apes and Humans*, edited by Anthony D. Pellegrini and Peter K. Smith. New York: Guilford, 2005: 213–53.

Groos, Karl. *The Play of Animals*. New York: D. Appleton, 1898.

Guesry, P. "The Role of Nutrition in Brain Development." *Preventative Medicine* 27 (1998): 189–94.

Haier, Richard J., Benjamin V. Siegel, Keith H. Nuechterlein, Erin Hazlett, Joseph C. Wu, Joanne Paek, Heather L. Browing, and Monte S. Buchsbaum. "Cortical Glucose Metabolic Rate: Correlates of Abstract Reasoning and Attention Studied with Positron Emission Tomography." *Intelligence* 12 (1988): 199–217.

Hall, G. Stanley. *Adolescence: Its Psychology and Its Relations to Physiology, AnthroPology, Sociology, Sex, Crime, Religion, and Education*. New York: Appleton, 1904.

Hart, Donna and Robert W. Sussman. *Man the Hunted.* New York: Westview, 2005.

Hol, T., C. L. Van den Berg, J. M. Van Ree, and B. M. Spruijt. "Isolation During the Play Period in Infancy Decreases Adult Social Interactions in Rats." *Behavioural Brain Research* 100 (1999): 91–97.

Huizinga, Johann. *Homo Ludens: A Study of the Play Element in Culture.* (R. F. C. Hull, trans.) Boston: Beacon Press, 1955.

Irwin Jr., Charles E. "Risk Taking Behaviors in the Adolescent Patient: Are They Impulsive?" *Pediatric Annals* 18 (1989): 122–33.

———. "Adolescence and Risk Taking: How are They Related?" in *Adolescent Risk Taking,* edited by Nancy J. Bell and Robert W. Bell. Newbury Park, Calif.: Sage, 1993: 7–28.

Irwin Jr., Charles E. and Susan G. Millstein. "Correlates and Predictors of Risk-Taking Behavior During Adolescence" in *Self-Regulatory Behavior and Risk Taking: Causes and Consequences,* edited by Lewis P. Lipsitt and Leonard L. Mitnick. Norwood, N.J.: Ablex, 1992: 3–21.

Iwaniuk, Andrew N., John E. Nelson, and Sergio M. Pellis. "Do Big-Brained Animals Play More? Comparative Analyses of Play and Relative Brain Size in Mammals." *Journal of Comparative Psychology* 115 (2001): 29–41.

Kuba, Michael J., Ruth A. Byrne, Daniela V. Meisel, and Jennifer A. Mather. "When do Octopuses Play? Effects of Repeated Testing, Object Type, Age and Food Deprivation on Object Play in *Octopus vulgaris*." *Journal of Comparative Psychology* 120 (August 2006): 184–90.

Lancy, David F. *Playing on the Mother Ground: Cultural Routines for Children's Development*. New York: Guilford, 1996.

Latour, Paul B. "Interactions Between Free-ranging, Adult Male Polar Bears (*Ursus Maritimus* Phipps): A Case of Social Play." *Canadian Journal of Zoology* 59 (1981): 1775–83.

Lewis, Kerrie P. "A Comparative Study of Primate Play Behaviour: Implications for the Study of Cognition." *Folia Primatologica* 71 (2000): 417–21.

———. "Comparative Analyses of Play Behaviour in Primates and Carnivores." PhD diss., University of Durham, U.K., 2003.

———. "Social Play in the Great Apes" in *The Nature of Play: Great Apes and Humans*, edited by Anthony D. Pellegrini and Peter K. Smith. New York: Guilford, 2005: 27–53.

Lewis, Kerrie P. and Robert A. Barton. "Playing for Keeps: Evolutionary Relationships between the Cerebellum and Social Play Behaviour in Non-human Primates." *Human Nature* 15 (2004): 5–22.

———. "Amygdala Size and Hypothalamus Size Predict Social Play Frequency in Non-human Primates: A Comparative Analysis Using Independent Contrasts." *Journal of Comparative Psychology* 120 (2006): 31–37.

Maggs, Jennifer L., David M. Almeida, and Nancy L. Galambos. "Risky Business: The Paradoxical Meaning of Problem Behavior for Young Adolescents." *Journal of Early Adolescence* 15 (1995): 344–65.

Martin, Paul and Tim M. Caro. "On the Functions of Play and Its Role in Behavioural Development." *Advances in the Study of Behaviour*, 15 (1985): 59–103.

McNab, Brian K. "Basal Rate of Metabolism, Body Size, and Food Habits in the Order Carnivora" in *Carnivore Behavioural Ecology and Evolution*, edited by John L. Gittleman. London: Chapman and Hall, 1989: 335–54.

———. *The Physiological Ecology of Vertebrates: A View from Energetics*. Ithaca, N.Y.: Comstock, 2002.

McNab, Brian K. and John F. Eisenberg. "Brain Size and Its Relation to the Rate of Metabolism in Mammals." *American Naturalist* 133 (1989): 157–67.

Miller, Edward M. "Intelligence and Brain Myelination: A Hypothesis." *Personality and Individual Differences* 17 (1994): 803–833.

Müller-Schwarze, Dietland. "Analysis of Play Behavior: What Do We Measure and When?" in *Play in Animals and Humans*, edited by Peter K. Smith. Oxford: Basil Blackwell, 1984: 147–58.

Nagy, Kenneth A. "Field Bioenergetics of Mammals: What Determines Field Metabolic Rates?" *Australian Journal of Zoology* 42 (1994): 43–53.

———. "Field Metabolic Rate and Body Size." *Journal of Experimental Biology* 208 (2005): 1621–25.

Nahallage, Charmalie A. D. and Michael A. Huffman. "Age-Specific Functions of Stone Handling, a Solitary Object Play Behavior, in Japanese Macaques (*Macaca Fuscata*)." *American Journal of Primatology* 69 (2007): 1–15.

Nunes, Scott, Eva-Maria Muecke, Zaira Sanchez, Rebekah R. Hoffmeier, and Lesley T. Lancaster. "Play Behavior and Motor Development in Juvenile Belding's Ground Squirrels (*Spermophilus Beldingi*)." *Behavioral Ecology and Sociobiology* 56 (2004): 97–105.

Pagel, Mark D. and Paul H. Harvey. "Evolution of the Juvenile Period in Mammals" in *Juvenile Primates—Life History, Development, and Behavior,* edited by Michael E. Pereira and Lynn A. Fairbanks. Oxford: Oxford University Press, 1993: 528–37.

Panksepp, Jaak. "The Ontogeny of Play in Rats." *Developmental Psychobiology* 14 (1980): 327–32.

Parker, Sue T. "Playing for Keeps: An Evolutionary Perspective on Human Games" in *Play in Animals and Humans*, edited by Peter K. Smith. Oxford: Basil Blackwell, 1984: 271–93.

Parker, Sue T. and Kathleen R. Gibson. "A Developmental Model of the Evolution of Language and Intelligence in Early Hominids." *Behavioral and Brain Sciences* 2 (1979): 367–407.

Parks, Randolph W., David A. Loewenstein, Kathryn L. Dodrill, William W. Barker, Fumihito Yoshii, Jen Y. Chang, Ali Emran, Anthony Apicella, William Sheramata, and Ranjan Duara. "Cerebral Metabolic Effects of a Verbal Fluency Test: A PET Scan Study." *Journal of Clinical and Experimental Neuropsychology* 10 (1988): 565–75.

Paulin, M. G. "The Role of the Cerebellum in Motor Control and Perception." *Brain, Behavior and Evolution* 41 (1993): 39–50.

Pellegrini, Anthony D. "Boys' Rough-and-Tumble Play, Social Competence and Group Composition." *British Journal of Developmental Psychology* 11 (1993): 237–48.

———. "Elementary School Children's Rough-and-Tumble Play and Social Competence." *Developmental Psychology* 24 (1988): 802–6.

———. "Rough-and-Tumble Play from Childhood through Adolescence: Differing Perspectives." *Play from Birth to Twelve: Contexts, Perspectives, and Meanings* (2nd edition), edited by Doris Pronin Fromberg and Doris Bergen. New York: Routledge, 2006: 111–18.

———. "The Roles of Aggressive and Affiliative Behaviors in Resource Control: A Behavioral Ecological Perspective." *Developmental Review* (2008, in press).

Pellegrini, Anthony D., Danielle Dupuis, and Peter K. Smith. "Play in Evolution and Development." *Developmental Review* 27 (2007): 261–76.

Pellegrini, Anthony D. and Kathy Gustafson. "Boys' and Girls' Use of Objects for Exploration, Play, and Tools in Early Childhood" in *The Nature of Play: Great Apes and Humans*, edited by Anthony D. Pellegrini and Peter K. Smith. New York: Guilford, 2005: 113–35.

Pellegrini, Anthony D., Kentaro Kato, Peter Blatchford, and Ed Baines. "A Short-Term Longitudinal Study of Children's Playground Games Across the First Year of School: Implications for Social Competence and Adjustment to School." *American Educational Research Journal* 39 (2002): 991–1015.

Pellis, Sergio M. and Andrew N. Iwaniuk. "The Problem of Adult Play-Fighting: A Comparative Analysis of Play and Courtship in Primates." *Ethology* 105 (1999): 783–806.

———. "Adult-Adult Play in Primates: Comparative Analyses of Origin, Distribution, and Evolution." *Ethology* 106 (2000): 1083–104.

———. "Brain System Size and Adult-Adult Play in Primates: A Comparative Analysis of the Roles of the Non-visual Cortex and the Amygdala." *Behavioural Brain Research* 134 (2002): 31–39.

Piaget, Jean. *Play, Dreams and Imitation in Childhood.* New York: Norton, 1962.

Power, Thomas G. *Play and Exploration in Children and Animals.* Mahwah, N.J.: Lawrence Erlbaum, 2000.

Previc, Fred H. "Dopamine and the Origins of Human Intelligence." *Brain and Cognition* 14 (1999): 299–350.

———. "The Role of Extrapersonal Brain Systems in Religious Activity." *Consciousness and Cognition* 15 (2006): 500–539.

Rhodes, Justin S., Stephen C. Gammie, and Theodore Garland Jr. "Patterns of Brain Activity Associated with Variation in Voluntary Wheel Running Behavior." *Behavioral Neuroscience* 117 (2003): 1243–56.

———. "Neurobiology of Mice Selected for High Voluntary Wheel-Running Activity." *Integrated Computational Biology* 45 (2005): 438–55.

Rooney, Nicola J., John W. S. Bradshaw, and Ian H. Robinson. "A Comparison of Dog-Dog and Dog-Human Play Behaviour." *Applied Animal Behaviour Science* 66 (2000): 235–48.

Rose, M. D. "Interspecific Play between Free Ranging Guerezas (*Colobus Guereza*) and Vervet Monkeys (*Cercopithecus Aethiops*)." *Primates* 18 (1977): 957–64.

Saayman, G. S. "Baboon's Brother Jackal." *Animals* 12 (1970): 442–43.

Sharpe, Lynda L. "Play Does Not Increase Social Cohesion in a Cooperative Mammal." *Animal Behaviour* 70 (2005): 551–58.

Silbereisen, Rainer K. and Matthias Reitzle. "On the Constructive Role of Problem Behavior in Adolescence: Further Evidence on Alcohol Use" in *Self-Regulatory Behavior and Risk-Taking: Causes and Consequences*, edited by Lewis P. Lipsitt and Leonard L. Mitnick. Norwood, N.J.: Ablex, 1992: 199–217.

Singer, Dorothy G., Roberta Michnick Golinkoff, and Kathy Hirsh-Pasek, eds. *Play = Learning: How Play Motivates and Enhances Children's Cognitive and Social-Emotional Growth.* Oxford: Oxford University Press, 2006.

Smith, Peter K. "Social and Pretend Play in Children" in *The Nature of Play: Great Apes and Humans*, edited by Anthony D. Pellegrini and Peter K. Smith. New York: Guilford, 2005: 173–209.

Smith, Peter K., Rebecca Smees, and Anthony D. Pellegrini. "Play Fighting and Real Fighting: Using Video Playback Methodology with Young Children." *Aggressive Behavior* 30 (2004): 164–73.

Sommer, Volker and Domingo Mendoza-Granados. "Play as an Indicator of Habitat Quality: A Field Study of Langur Monkeys (*Presbytis Entellus*)." *Ethology* 99 (1995): 177–92.

Spear, Linda P. "The Adolescent Brain and Age-Related Behavioral Manifestations." *Neuroscience and Biobehavioral Reviews* 24 (2000): 417–63.

Spencer, Herbert. *The Principles of Psychology*, vol. 2, part 2. New York: D. Appleton, 1898.

Špinka, Marek, Ruth C. Newberry, and Marc Bekoff. "Mammalian Play: Training for the Unexpected." *Quarterly Review of Biology* 76 (2001): 141–68.

Sussman, Robert W., Paul A. Garber, and James M. Cheverud. "Importance of Cooperation and Affiliation in the Evolution of Primate Sociality." *American Journal of Physical Anthropology* 128 (2005): 84–97.

Sutton-Smith, Brian. *The Ambiguity of Play*. Cambridge, Mass.: Harvard University Press, 1997.

Thompson, Edward P. *The Passions of Animals*. London: Chapman Hall, 1851.

Thorpe, W. H. "Ritualization in Ontogeny: I. Animal Play." *Philosophical Transactions of the Royal Society of London*. Series B. *Biological Sciences* 251 (December 1966): 311–19.

Trimpop, R. M., J. H. Kerr, and B. Kirkcaldy. "Comparing Personality Constructs of Risk-taking Behavior." *Personality and Individual Differences* 26 (1999): 237–54.

Turner, Victor. *From Ritual to Theatre: The Human Seriousness of Play*. New York: PAJ, 1982.

van Lawick-Goodall, Jane. "Mother-Offspring Relationships in Free-Ranging Chimpanzees" in *Primate Ethnology*, edited by Desmond Morris. London: Weidenfeld & Nicolson, 1967: 287–346.

Van Schaik, Carel P., Robert O. Deaner, and Michelle Y. Merrill. "The Conditions for Tool Use in Primates: Implications for the Evolution of Material Culture." *Journal of Human Evolution* 36 (June 1999): 719–41.

Vygotsky, Lev S. "Play and Its Role in the Mental Development of the Child." *Soviet Psychology* 12 (1967): 62–76.

Watson, Duncan M. "Object Play in a Laughing Kookaburra (*Dacelo Novaeguineae*)." *Emu* 92 (1992): 106–8.

———. "Kangaroos at Play: Play Behaviour in the *Macropodoidea*" in *Animal Play: Evolutionary, Comparative and Ecological Perspectives*, edited by Marc Bekoff and John A. Byers. Cambridge: Cambridge University Press, 1998: 61–95.

Watson, Neil V. "Sex Differences in Throwing: Monkeys Having a Fling." *Trends in Cognitive Sciences* 5 (March 2001): 98–99.

Westergaard, G. C., C. Liv, M. K. Haynie, and S. J. Suomi. "A Comparative Study of Aimed Throwing by Monkeys and Humans." *Neuropsychologia* 38 (October 2000): 1511–17.

Part 2

EVOLUTION OF HUMAN RUNNING: THE PRECURSOR TO SPORT

Movements seen in most western or global sports are based on running, even when the sport is focused on the use of implements, to include diverse-sized balls, bats, racquets, and gloves, or simply movement across space, such as all types of track and field events, cross-country running, skiing and many others. Granted, there are many sports, especially extreme sport, where running is not featured as a foundational movement; yet, sports such as surfing and skateboarding, BMX, and others depend on movements that are a result of the unique human anatomy and physiology derived from the evolution of bipedalism, then the evolution of running.

Sport is featured in ancient civilizations such as the Mayans, Greeks and Romans. Evidence for the origins of sport is seen in the Middle East at the dawn of the Neolithic. Sport, in these examples, seems to have been connected directly or indirectly with religion and ritual. Running seems to have played a crucial role in these early instances and is still seen in indigenous sports, such as Indian running and lacrosse. Speculations for the development of sport in the evolution of human culture are many; however, it seems that a more sedentary lifestyle, based around the eventual development of agriculture, might have been the engine for the development of religion, and rituals associated with religion could have been the catalyst for the origins of sport.

Yet, the success of our species and all other hominids is predicated on not only the development of bipedalism, but the evolution of running. Our physical abilities, as seen in human anatomy, physiology, and neurology, that were crucial to subsistence, as well as other facets of early human culture, are now culturally, rather than environmentally selected for by a variety of means, including sports. The following chapters explore the evolution of human movement through a biocultural lens.

Bernd Heinrich's "Endurance Predator" (originally published in *Outside Magazine* on the eve of the 2000 Olympics) is a look at running in human evolution with respect to the role it played in hunting. Henirich's respected publication *Why We Run* (2001) focused on a natural history of running in human evolution and suggested through a highly informative narrative that subsistence, specifically hunting in Africa, was one of the prime selective agents for the development of running in humans. In this chapter, Bernd Heinrich briefly discusses the legacy of humans as running predators, but also explores this legacy in terms of performance in living populations of humans and technological advances that support this performance. Heinrich also writes on the necessity of the human spirit to aspire to improve, which he sees as a legacy to when humans inhabited the African landscape and pursued their prey through time and over distance—to chase their dreams of the fleet antelope. Today, those dreams are records and performances that are set by the gifted few, the human antelopes that are chased by the many.

The next two chapters by Timothy Noakes and Robert Sands explore aspects of the evolution of human running as well as the expression of these aspects in contemporary human populations. Both Noakes and Sands provide similar accounts of the evolution of running that include anatomical-biological and cultural responses to the plaeoenvironment. Whereas Noakes concentrates more on running's adaptive value to human evolution in terms of subsistence-hunting, Sands suggests running as a behavior that was interlaced throughout early human culture and as such became a critical behavior in ritual, communication, travel, play, and other facets.

In "Thermoregulation and Hydrating Strategies in Human Evolution," Timothy Noakes suggests that humans evolved as long-distance runners well adapted to the initial arid African environment through a well-functioning thermoregulatory system. He joins authors such as Carrier, Bramble and Lieberman, and Lieberberg in posting that this unique running ability among primates and most other mammals promoted "persistence" hunting of those same mammals that lacked or had under-developed thermoregulatory systems. This has novel implications to the applicability of the theory that humans should hydrate frequently and sufficiently during prolonged physical exercise such as running to replace water lost through perspiration. Noakes suggests that humans evolved as "delayed drinkers" with the ability to exercise without the need to replenish liquid and that this ability is retained by contemporary humans.

Robert R. Sands concludes this section with "*Homo cursor*: Running into the Pleistocene," a look at the evolution of human running and current theory that explores the origins of not only a running anatomy, but as well as environmental and cultural selection for running. Sands presents a summary of work, both recent and relevant, on the origins of running in human evolution. Whereas the origins of bipedalism have been explored for decades, and has rendered several theories, the evolution of human running has been a recent exploration. Carrier's (1984) *Current Anthropology* article pushed the subject of running into the foreground, and Heinrich's 2001 book (previously discussed) promoted hunting as a powerful driver for running; however, Bramble and Lieberman's (2004) selection laid out the anatomical requisites and fossil evidence for running in the genus *Homo*. This has been followed up by work exploring the energetics of running versus other modes of locomotion, structural adaptations as well as limitations posed by running, and more recently, the neurobiology of running. The theory of persistence hunting, basically running prey into exhaustion, has been promoted by several researchers as motivation for the evolution and further refinement of running, and has been supported (depending on one's perspective) by ethnography of San hunters in the Kalahari (Lieberberg 2006), although running would have also made scavenging more efficient for early *Homo*.

Sands' chapter inventories research and publications on the development of running, to include fossil anatomical and paleoenvironmental evidence. However, Sands suggests that running was integrated into *Homo erectus* (*H. erectus*) lifeways in many other facets, and perhaps running as a multipurpose human behavior was crucial for the success of hominin species beginning with *H. erectus*. Briefly using analogy with recent and contempory running cultures of the Tarahumara of the Sierra Madre and the Kalenjin of the Great Rift, Sands concludes that past and recent ethnography, along with future ethnography, can provide further insight into the question of the origin of running.

BIBLIOGRAPHY

Bramble, D. M. and D. E. Lieberman. "Endurance Running and the Evolution of Homo." *Nature* 432 (2004): 345–52.

Carrier, D. R. "The Energetic Paradox of Human Running and Hominid Evolution." *Current Anthropology* 25, 4 (1984): 483–95.

Heinrich, B. *Why We Run: A Natural History*. New York: HarperCollins Publishers, 2001.

———. "Endurance Predator." *Outside Magazine* (September 2000).

Liebenberg, L. "Persistence Hunting by Modern Hunter-Gatherers." *Current Anthropology* 47, 5 (2006): 1017–26.

4

Endurance Predator

Bernd Heinrich

I'm standing in ancient landscape in East Africa. All around me white and yellow flowering acacia trees are abuzz with bees, wasps, and colorful cetoniid beetles. Baboons and impalas roam in the miombe bush. Herds of wildebeests and zebras thunder by; in the distance, elephants and rhinoceroses lumber over the rolling hills like prehistoric giants. Little seems to have changed in the last few million years. Caught up in searching for insects, I happen to peek under an inauspicious rock overhang and am taken aback by what I see. Painted on the wall is a succession of sticklike human figures, clearly in full running stride. All are clutching delicate bows, quivers, and arrows, and all are running in one direction, left to right across the rock canvas. It's a two- or three-thousand-year-old pictograph, with nothing particularly extraordinary about it—until I notice something that sends my mind reeling: The figure leading the procession has his hands thrust upward in what seems to me to be the universal sign of athletic victory. As both a former ultramarathoner and a biologist, I know this gesture to be reflexive in runners and other competitors who have fought hard and then feel the exhilaration of triumph over adversity.

This happened several years ago, in Zimbabwe's Matobo National Park (formerly Matopos Park), but it remains for me an iconic reminder that the roots of our competitiveness go back very far and very deep. Between the marketing hype, the melodramatic background stories, and the sprawling spectacle of the millennial Olympic Games this September in Sydney will lurk the real reason we will tune in: an intense, innate, even visceral appreciation for the magnificence of the serious athlete's body. The modern

95

Olympics represent the ultimate test of our ancient faculties. We thrill to see athletic skill—abilities that most of us possess to a degree—raised to the utmost level. The Olympics are a product both of our dreams and of our indomitable drive for perfection, the best of what the mortal human body can achieve.

Looking at that African rock painting made me feel like I was witness to a kindred spirit, a man who had long ago vanished yet whom I understood as if we'd talked just a moment earlier. I was not only in the same environment and of the same mind as my unknown Bushman, I was also in the place that most likely produced our common ancestors. The artist had been here hundreds of generations before me, but that was only the blink of an eye compared to the aeons that have elapsed since a bipedal intermediate between our apelike and recognizably human ancestors left the safety of the forest for the savanna some four million years ago.

It wasn't an easy transition. Indeed, it had fateful physiological and psychological consequences that are still deeply embedded in our bodies and our psyches. Standing before that long-lost victor in the struggle to survive, I was reminded of what I was, still am, and perhaps what we will forever be as long as we are human.

We were all runners once. Although some of us forget that primal fact, comparative biology teaches us that life on the plains generates arms races between predators and prey—and our ancestors definitely weren't into unilateral disarmament. Meat was abundant, for those who could catch it or wrest it from the competition, such as leopards and lions, not to mention hyenas, jackals, and vultures. Because we primates weren't superb runners, we needed alternatives to sheer speed to eat in the wide-open spaces. So we traveled in groups, racing overland to fresh-killed carcasses and chasing off scavengers. These skirmishes, as well as infighting with our own species—that is, our first true competitors—became the bridge to hunting live prey. The faster you could run, the more valuable you became in the new social groups based on the hunt.

In 1961 I spent a year collecting birds in Africa for Yale's Peabody Museum, and I experienced, I think, what ancient hunters were up against. I'll never forget my feelings of dreary claustrophobia during the months we spent in dense, dripping forests, nor, alternatively, the feeling of glorious exhilaration out on the open steppes. To catch even small birds, I had to wander extensively, half of each day, just as our ancestors must have done. By about two to three million years ago, they had a leg and foot structure almost identical to our own, and it's reasonable to assume that they walked and ran like we do. While other predators rested, I was able to continue, albeit slowly, because we humans have one major physical advantage: We can sweat, copiously, which allows us to manage our internal temperature and extend our endurance. Most animals have no such mechanism. Through the ages and across the continents there are examples of men actually chasing down beasts that are much faster. In fact, there are modern reports of the Paiutes and Navajos of North America hunting pronghorn antelope on foot, patiently running down a stray till it drops in its tracks from exhaustion and then reverently suffocating the animal by hand.

A quick pounce and kill requires no dream. Dreams are the beacons that carry us far ahead into the hunt, into the future, and into the marathon. We have the unique ability to keep in mind what is not before the eye. Visualizing far ahead, we see our quarry, even as it recedes over the hills and into the mists. Those ancient hunters who had the longest vision—the most imagination—were the ones who persisted the longest on the trail and therefore were the ones who left more descendants. The same goes these days: Human beings with the longest vision tend to make the biggest mark. Vision allows us to reach into the future, whether it's to kill a mammoth or an antelope, to write a book, or to achieve the record time in a race.

Now we chase each other rather than woolly mammoths. But the basic body movements required for hunting and for warfare—running, throwing, jumping—have become ritualized in the track and field events, which are still the heart and soul, the very essence, of the Olympics. The Games are simply mock wars waged in the spirit of camaraderie, though they retain the intensity of their origins. The difference is that in a contest with prey there is always an endpoint: We get it, or it gets away. In our races against one another, in our constant striving to better our achievements and set new records, there is no apparent end. Where, then, are the limits?

World and Olympic records have been kept for more than a century, but over that span there never has been a year in which records have not been broken. Performances that were world-class only fifty years ago are almost routine now. Again and again, feats thought physiologically impossible have been surpassed. In 1954, Roger Bannister ran the mile in 3:59.40 to break the four-minute barrier and stun the world. But within six weeks even that improbable mark fell. Fast-forward to 1999 and Moroc-can Hicham El Gerrouj lowered the record to 3:43.13.

So it goes: In the Mexico City Olympics of 1968, Bob Beamon shat-tered Ralph Boston's world long-jump record of twenty-seven feet, four and one-quarter inches with a jump of twenty-nine feet, two and a half inches. For nearly twenty-three years Beamon's record was considered to be beyond unbreakable, until the 1991 World Championships in Tokyo, where Carl Lewis came within one inch of it and Mike Powell actually beat it by two inches at the same meet.

The first modern record for the 100-meter dash was 11.0 seconds, set by Great Britain's William MacLaren in 1867. It got chipped away over the next several decades until American Charles Paddock dropped it to 10.2 seconds in 1921. His time didn't see a major improvement until 1956, when countryman Willie Williams ran a 10.1. Then, in 2009, U.S. sprinter Maurice Greene set a world record of 9.79.

The steady improvement in records of all sporting events may, at first glance, look like biological evolution, but this couldn't be further from the truth. Evolution might still have played a role shaping us back in the Ice Ages, when we were fragmented into small isolated populations, regularly dropping dead due to athletic deficiencies and other forms of bad luck. No more. Living as we now do, in large, increasingly homog-enized populations, any mutation that might crop up and that could be of value for athletic performance (e.g., an enormously large lung capacity for marathoners) would quickly be diffused in the gene pool.

That's not to say changes can't happen. Could a species stuck with our bipedal design evolve and someday run as fast as ostriches? Maybe we're still so unspecialized for the task of running that selective breeding could accomplish this. But even if we attempted that unthinkable experiment—if we bred humans like, say, racehorses, along lines of pedigree—the project would probably have to continue uninterrupted for hundreds or thousands of years. We have no idea what makes a Secretariat different from an also-ran, but if we want to beat a Secretariat, we begin with Secretariat genes. Still, if we did create human thoroughbreds, there's good reason to believe the physical "improvement" would eventually stop; despite selective breeding, thoroughbreds haven't gotten any faster in the last one hundred years. Why should it be any different with us?

Genetically we're pretty much the same as we've been for hundreds of thousands of years; the basic changes for running, throwing, jumping, and the like were made long ago, and the trajectory, and eventual endpoint, were determined then as well. Physiologically speaking, on average we may well be *devolving*, so to speak. If we picked one of our six billion brethren at random and had that person run against a fit-for-survival Pleistocene man or woman, there's a good chance we'd come out the loser.

Don't tell that to Michael Johnson. To understand performances like his, it's important to recognize that, in terms of genetics, training, and nutrition, a world-record performance is the far, far end of the normal distribution. Olympians don't represent typical physiology. Far from it. World-class athletes are generally off the scale according to every parameter one can think of—physiological systems for muscles, enzymes, hormones, bone structure, and body build. Moreover, all of these superlatives have been bolstered by the best knowledge and execution of diet, rest, training, and stress management. In an Olympic athlete, more and more we're looking at a freak, an elite specimen who is not like you or me and who is fit to do one thing well—likely at the expense of other things.

Each event has circumscribed specifications. For instance, the very best sprinters don't need much aerobic capacity because they rely on a preponderance of fast-twitch muscle fibers, which contract quickly and anaerobically, meaning they don't require oxygen to burn fuel. Those same athletes could not successfully run distance, because long-distance runners rely on a huge aerobic capacity and a larger percentage of slow-twitch fibers, which contract at a slower rate but can work for long periods, so long as they're being continually supplied with oxygen. These traits are largely inherited: If your muscles are made up mostly of slow-twitch fibers, you'll simply never be explosive. We might be able to do a lot to change the basic design we're born with, but not to the point of achieving a world-beating performance.

In the early days of Olympic and world competition, the athletes were probably closer in ability to the average population. Nevertheless, they came from a very small pool out of the total population, and that pool came largely from the privileged class or those who, for one odd reason or another, decided to throw the javelin, long jump, sprint, or run the marathon. Such is not the case now. First, talent is actively solicited: Individuals are identified, nurtured, and encouraged to pursue their dreams to the near-exclusion of more distracting concerns, like milking the cows or otherwise making a living. A second and perhaps much more significant phenomenon is that the pool from which the talented are selected has expanded dramatically. Since 1896, when the first modern Olympics were held, the world population has quadrupled. What's more, while Olympians were previously drawn only from Europe, Australia, and North America, now they also come from Asia, Africa, and South America. Statistically, by simply increasing the sample size, you increase the likelihood of having some individual runner who is faster than ever before in history (as well as one who is slower than ever).

The only real evolution has been in realms not directly related to biology. The most obvious factor in athletic improvement has been better technology. Running shoes are infinitely better. Vaulting poles morphed from ash to bamboo to aluminum to fiberglass, nearly doubling the record heights in the event. And of course, swimsuits have undergone all manner of makeovers, from wool trunks and tops in the early 1900s to skimpy Lycra numbers in the disco years to full-body suits debuting in Sydney called fastskins, which have a dimpled surface, much like golf balls, to reduce drag.

Mirroring technological breakthroughs have been changes in technique, such as Dick Fosbury's now-standard backward flop over the high-jump bar and swimmer David Berkoff's dolphin kick in the backstroke. Training methods have also evolved. Germany's Waldemar Gersheler used interval training to help his protégé, Rudolf Harbig, nab the world record of 1:46.60 in the 800-meter run in 1939. Arthur Lydiard of New Zealand helped Peter Snell take Olympic gold in the same event in 1960 and 1964 by advocating long, slow running to build endurance, and brutal hill work to build strength. And Britain's Sebastian Coe, who in 1981 set an 800-meter world record that held for sixteen years, used weight lifting in addition to Gersheler's and Lydiard's methods.

Such a multitude of factors makes it nigh impossible to predict limits, but physical limits must exist. In just one century the law of diminishing returns has already set in; in certain track events, decades pass in which records improve by no more than hundredths of a second. Take the 200-meter run: In 1968, the world record stood at 19.83 seconds; in 1996 Michael Johnson lowered it to 19.32 seconds—about a half a second in twenty-eight years.

None of this is good news for the human spirit. We need to keep desire alive. We depend on faith; records will fall only to those who believe it is possible. The heroes of my boyhood—Jim Ryun, Peter Snell, Herb Elliott, Steve Prefontaine, Billy Mills—achieved their status and success through sheer guts and work. They aspired to be gods—and to my high school cross-country mates and me, they *were* gods on some level. Yet the real reason we saw Pre and the others as heroes was that we secretly believed we were elementally equal. We were convinced that, if we only tried, if we did what they did, then we too could rank among the gods. To think that if they lived and ran today they would all be left in the dust by a herd of modern runners is devastating to my psyche. At our core we are endurance predators driven by dreams, spurred on by the antelope that we can't see but know is out there, somewhere, up ahead. To continue pushing, though, we must believe it's catchable—if only we apply ourselves.

Like the North American antelope's residual ability to outrun a cheetah—a cat that became extinct on the continent some 10,000 years ago—our abilities to run, throw, and jump are leftovers in our survival tool kits. As such, we use them in play because they are instinctually important to us. I'm not as athletically capable as an antelope or a bird or an Olympic athlete, but I enjoy my own capacities and I'm inspired to stretch them by seeing what others can do. I'm humbled by what is routine to the songbird or sandpiper, awed by their ability to fly unbelievably long distances to and from specific pinpoints on the globe.

Some might argue that, if I were a bird, I would not be able to enjoy my fantastic annual journeys, following the sun from perpetual daylight on the Arctic tundra to the pampas in Argentina and back again. But I think they are wrong. What makes the blackpoll warbler strike out south in the fall after a cold front is probably not fundamentally different from what motivates me to jog down a country road on a warm and sunny day. We're both responding to ancient urges. Proof that, in our case, it's impossible to extinguish our primal enthusiasm for the chase.

5

Thermoregulation and Hydrating Strategies in Human Evolution

Timothy Noakes

Nothing in nature is wasted; everything has a purpose, forged by the relentless pressures of selection of the fittest as originally conceived by Charles Darwin and Alfred Russell Wallace (Darwin and Wallace 1858). So it is that every human characteristic makes us more competitive as individuals and as a species, better able to cope with the unsafe and hostile environment from which we escaped perhaps as recently as 50,000–100,000 years ago. Man and our fossil ancestors, collectively known as the hominids, differ from our nearest biological relative, the chimpanzees, in a number of important ways. The common feature of many of these physiological differences is that each improves our species' ability (1) to run long distances at a moderate pace and (2) to maintain a safe body temperature when exercising in dry heat. So just as the entire biology of the lion is designed for stalking, sprinting, and dispatching large prey (Hart and Sussman 2005), it seems that evolution has directed humans to become, of all our planet's species, the best hot weather distance runners.

This unexpected conclusion invites the intriguing question: What competitive survival advantage did humans derive from this evolutionary choice? To answer this question we need to study those specific anatomical and biological features that differentiate humans from our nearest living biological peers, the great apes.

HUMANS STAND ERECT AND
WALK ON TWO LEGS (BIPEDALISM)

Our earliest human ancestors began to stand erect and to walk upright (bipedalism) at least six to seven million years ago (Wheeler 1993; Guy et al. 2005). This adaptation is considered to be the first crucial event in the divergence of our species, *Homo sapiens*, from the common ancestor (the fossil example of which has yet to be unearthed) that we share with those species of great apes like the chimpanzee and gorilla that survive today.

A popular explanation used to be that bipedalism freed our hands, which could then fashion stone tools for use as offensive weapons. Such tools then allowed early hominids to successfully hunt other mammals. But primitive stone tools were first used by early hominids about 2.5 million years ago (Tobias 1985) and it appears that the hominid diet may have included animal protein procured perhaps by scavenging or hunting of small animals approximately three million years ago (Peters and Vogel 2005; Sponheimer et al. 2005; Sponheimer and Lee-Thorp 1999). Thus, both postdate evidence for bipedalism by at least two to three million years.

Another theory holds that bipedalism occurred in response to a period of marked climate change, which caused the replacement of tropical rainforests with open grasslands in East and Southern Africa to the east of the Great Rift Valley beginning about sixteen million years ago. One explanation is that the uplifting of the Rift Valley highlands produced a rain shadow to its east with preservation of heavily wooded areas to the west and the progressive development of grasslands mixed with shrubs and some trees to the east (Hanna and Brown 1983). This change was well established two to four million years ago.

As a result, over a period of perhaps 200,000 years, our human ancestors quite suddenly (in geological time) found themselves on the edge of "the widest possible expanse of open plain devoid of forests, fruits, and nuts but abounding in a greater degree with dangerous beasts than any other country in the world" (Dart 1953). Gradually, the very bravest of our tiny ancestors must have ventured from the safety of the trees in the tropical rainforests onto the verge of those dangerous plains teeming with both terrifying risk (predators) and abundant opportunity (high protein, high fat meals on four legs). The brave choice to move onto those plains, away from the security of the forest, appears to be the singular event that produced *Homo sapiens* from our tiny early hominid ancestors including *Australopithecus africanus*, none of which appeared to have even the remotest prospect of becoming Earth's dominant creatures within the next few million years. Rather, a disinterested observer would have concluded that the tiny 1.2m tall *Australopithecus africanus,* weighing about 35kg, was headed for a rapid extinction at the claws and teeth of the terrifying group of predators (Hart and Sussman 2005) with which he shared the African savannah two to three million years ago.

Professor Raymond Dart, who discovered the first *Australopithecus africanus* fossil, described the evolutionary value of this choice:

> For the production of man a different apprenticeship [from that provided by the forest or jungle] was needed to sharpen the wits and quicken the higher manifestation of intellect—a more open veld country where competition was keener between swiftness and stealth, and where adrointess of thinking and movement played a preponderating role in the preservation of the species. Darwin has said "no country in the world abounds in a greater degree with dangerous beasts than Southern Africa" and, in my opinion, Southern Africa, by providing a vast open country with occasional wooded belts and a relative scarcity of water, together with a fierce and bitter mammalian competition, furnished a laboratory such as was essential to this penultimate phase of human evolution (1959: 207; 1925: 199).

The savannah is also much hotter than the tropical rainforests, especially at midday when the sun shines directly overhead and bakes everything it touches. Without the shady protection of the forest trees, the most effective way to reduce the radiant heat load carried in the sun's rays is to stand and walk upright.

Bipedalism reduces the surface area exposed to direct solar radiation. In addition, it raises the body into a cooler microclimate where there is an increased air flow. Here, it is possible to lose more heat by convection, the process by which the cooler air coursing over the skin is heated up, thereby removing heat from the body.

Wheeler (1988) has calculated that at typical savannah air temperatures of between 35–40°C, our early human ancestors would have been able to forage for food at all times of the day without needing to cool down by resting in the shade. Had these early hominids remained on four legs (quadripedal), in order to cool down they would have been forced to seek shade in the midday heat. Bipedalism thus opened a window of opportunity when only hominids would have been able to collect food at midday. Dangerous quadripedal predators including leopards, lions, and extinct giant hyenas (Hart and Sussman 2005) that were co-habiting with our hominid ancestors between one and four million years ago did not hunt in the heat of the midday. Rather, their inferior capacity to regulate their body temperatures (thermoregulation) forces these large, non-sweating predators to seek shade and to avoid exercise (hunting) in the midday heat.

Bipedalism would also have allowed early hominids, like the 35kg *Australopithecus africanus,* to walk up to 15km a day while losing about 1.5L of fluid as sweat. Whereas a quadripedal "human" of the same mass would have had to lose about 2.5L of sweat to cover the same distance (Wheeler 1991a; Wheeler 1993).

According to this theory bipedalism developed not because it freed our hands for offensive and creative purposes but because it provided a significant thermoregulatory advantage, first for exploring and scavenging and later for running on the African savannah in scorching midday heat. Thus evolution favored bipedalism because it alleviated "the most stressing problem of open equatorial environments: heat gain from direct solar radiation" (Wheeler 1984: 97).

So the evidence is clear that our early human ancestors stood upright and walked on two legs long before they developed either a large brain or adapted their teeth for meat eating (Wheeler 1988). Thus, at least four to six million years ago, our predominantly plant-eating, small-brained ancestors were already walking upright. But what really drove the adoption of bipedalism is unclear (Hart and Sussman 2005) since it antedated by millions of years the period of climate change that opened up the African savannah. In addition, early hominids living west of the Rift Valley where the tropical rainforests had not been replaced by open grasslands were already bipedal at that time (Guy et al. 2005). Although the factors driving the adoption of bipedalism by early hominids remains uncertain, the choice clearly antedated by some considerable time the adoption of a diet that regularly included meat (Wheeler 1988).

But if bipedalism was the first critical evolutionary adaptation, what else was needed to direct us to becoming predominantly meat-eating *Homo sapiens*?

HUMANS SWEAT MORE PROFUSELY
THAN ANY OTHER LIVING CREATURE

Relatively few mammals sweat. Those that do include the horse, the donkey, the camel, and certain large African antelope such as the Eland and the Oryx (gemsbok). Sweat removes body heat and can maintain a safe body temperature in these larger mammals, either when they are resting in a hot or humid environment or when they exercise, especially in dry heat.

But no mammal sweats as much as humans. Thus comparative studies show that horses can sweat at a rate of $100gm/m^2/hr$; camels at $250gm/m^2/hr$ but humans at rates in excess of $500gm/m^2/hr$ (Folk 1966). This requires that the concentration of sweat glands in human skin must be substantially greater than in any other sweating mammal.

Sweating allows humans to survive without distress in conditions that are fatal for apes. For example, chimpanzees cannot survive in air temperatures greater than 38°C (Hanna and Brown 1983), whereas humans are able to exercise moderately vigorously for many hours under these conditions provided the air humidity is low.

The cost of sweating is that it removes water from the body, promoting fluid loss, causing what has been termed "voluntary dehydration" (Greenleaf and Sargent 1965; Rothstein et al. 1947). For each individual there is a level of dehydration that causes physical incapacitation and ultimately death. In a very hot sunny environment typical of the desert in which there is also little shade, humans can usually survive usefully for twenty-four hours, becoming increasingly disabled thereafter with death usually occurring on the third day.

Thus our species' capacity to sweat profusely when exposed to desert heat prevents us from being true desert-dwelling mammals like the Oryx or the kangaroo rat, both of which can survive in the desert without access to free-standing water (Schmidt-Nielsen 1964). On exposure to heat humans sweat in order to maintain a whole body but specifically a brain temperature below ~40°C; sweating progressively reduces our body water stores reducing the duration that we can survive without water.

In contrast, if it has no access to water, the desert-dwelling Oryx does not sweat when exposed to midday heat. Rather it allows its body temperature to rise to 46°C (Taylor 1969). In this way the Oryx conserves water which it replaces at night by eating the leaves of the acacia, which concentrate water during the night (Taylor 1969). By delaying its need to drink until the evening, the biology of the Oryx has evolved to take advantage of this unusual physiological feature of the acacia tree. In contrast, when it has access to free-standing water, the Oryx sweats in the heat and maintains a lower body temperature.

Since human sweating severely limits our ability to survive without water in hot conditions, our species' great capacity to sweat profusely must have provided us with some decisive survival advantage. Furthermore, since no other mammal has the same capacity to sweat as profusely as do we, it is probable that sweating was the most important factor determining our evolutionary path after our earliest hominid ancestors had already become bipedal at least seven million years ago.

Perhaps R. W. Newman (1970) was one of the first finally to suggest a link between the change in habitat populated by early hominids, the change in their body habitus toward that of the modern human but with a small brain, and an evolving capacity to sweat profusely. So he concluded that the extra heat load resulting from exposure to the large radiant heat load on the hot, shadeless African savannah required that humans both stand upright (to reduce the radiant heat load) and develop an effective sweating mechanism. He understood that the loss of hair was a disadvantage that could be offset if humans evolved sweating as an additional and more effective method of heat loss. But Newman's insight stopped short of explaining why humans evolved a sweating capacity that exceeded by far that required just to offset the thermoregulatory disadvantage of the loss of hair.

COMPARED TO THE GREAT APES
HUMANS ARE ESSENTIALLY HAIRLESS

Like clothing, hair traps a thin layer of air next to the skin. The body soon heats that trapped air layer to the temperature of the skin. This insulating air layer prevents a continual heat loss from the body when the skin temperature is higher than the surrounding air temperature. The optimum skin temperature that allows humans to maintain thermal balance at rest is about 33°C compared to the usual core body temperature at rest of 37°C.

The absence of human hair indicates either that humans evolved in an environment in which hair was not required to conserve body heat, or else that by losing body hair humans gained some other more important evolutionary advantage. Since, like sweating, the main function of body hair is thermoregulatory, this loss of body hair must have produced a decisive thermoregulatory advantage. This poses the question: What factors selected for a superior thermoregulatory capacity in our early ancestors as they evolved in sub-Saharan African over the past seven or more million years?

One possibility was the opportunity for our hominid ancestors to explore the changing habitat when the equatorial rainforests were replaced with woodlands and savannah east of the Great Rift Valley.

The tropical rainforest that the savannah replaced has the following characteristics—a daily maximum temperature of about 28–32°C, very little air movement, and a very high humidity of up to 100 percent caused by the water expired by plants. But in the tropical forest there is little exposure to radiant heat from the sun since the leaves of the jungle absorb that energy.

Provided they do not exercise too vigorously, the large primates—the gorillas and chimpanzees—can comfortably exist in the tropical rainforest under these conditions since their skin temperatures (~34°C) are always higher than the air temperature in the forest. As a result, their bodies are able to transfer heat by convection from the skin surface to the cooler surrounding air, thereby cooling the primate.

However, solar radiation is much more intense on the savannah than in the tropical forest. The direct sun's rays add a substantial amount of radiant heat to creatures that venture beyond the shade provided by the forest canopy. This added heat load is the equivalent of an effective 7°C increase in air temperature.

But air moves more freely on the savannah across open spaces, unimpeded by forest vegetation. This increases the rate at which heat can be convected away from the (hotter) skin by the (cooler) air passing over it. This effect increases as an exponential function of the wind speed. Convection cools the body very effectively, even during vigorous exercise (Saunders et al. 2005).

In addition, the air on the savannah has a much lower water content (humidity) because there is limited vegetation to add water to the air. The efficiency of heat loss by sweating is greatly increased at low humidities but falls steeply as the humidity rises. Thus sweating is a more effective method for heat loss on the savannah than in the more humid jungle environment.

A coat of hair that reflects most of this radiant heat is the best protection against solar radiation, better even than an upright body posture. Thus the coats of the African antelopes, the Eland and the hartebeest reflect 70 percent of the radiant heat carried in the sun's rays (Finch 1972). The light-colored coat of the Oryx, the only true desert-dwelling antelope, is so reflective that the Oryx does not need to seek shade at midday but can continue grazing. Those Oryx with the lightest-colored coats have penetrated the farthest into the desert (Taylor 1969). Camels with a full coat sweat less in desert heat than when they are shorn (Schmidt-Nielsen 1959), proving the efficacy of the camel's coat for reflecting radiant heat.

Thus when evolution favored those of our early hominid ancestors who had lost their fur coats it can only have been because the thermoregulatory disadvantage of a reduced capacity to reflect radiant heat from the sun caused by the loss of hair must have been offset by some other more valuable thermoregulatory advantage.

The key advantage was probably the ability to lose heat more effectively by sweating since profuse sweating provides humans with the greatest heat-losing capacity of any mammal. And this advantage becomes greatest in hot dry conditions—the exact conditions present on the African savannah east of the Rift Valley beginning about 1.8 million years ago.

The disadvantage of a coat of hair is that it traps a layer of (warm) air within the fur, a few millimeters from the skin surface. This reduces the efficiency of sweating since sweat is evaporated from the surface of the fur, not from the skin itself. Sweating from a hairy surface fails to cool the skin directly while drawing some of the heat needed to evaporate the sweat from the air itself, not from the skin surface. Loss of hair increases the efficiency of heat loss by sweating, reducing the sweat losses needed to cool the body (Wheeler 1992a). Provided humans can sweat profusely from the entire skin surface area, the amount of heat they can lose by sweating far exceeds that needed to offset the extra radiant heat gain resulting from the loss of a reflective fur coat (Wheeler 1985).

Calculations show that this trade-off makes biological sense. Thus, because they have a much inferior sweating capacity than do humans, primates are unable to regulate their body temperatures when exercising in a savannah-type environment and cannot survive in air temperatures greater than 38°C. In addition, their coat of hair provides a significantly greater barrier to heat loss by convection than does the hairless skin of humans (Johnson and Elizondo 1979).

The result is that the loss of hair and a much superior capacity to lose heat by sweating would have allowed early hominids to maintain their body (and brain) temperatures safely below ~ 40°C even while they performed vigorous physical activity in air temperatures of 29–35°C—precisely the conditions that our human ancestors faced on the African savannah.

Newman (1970: 13) concludes that our primate ancestors "probably did not step from tropical forest to sun-baked grasslands in one short bound." He proposes that it would have been the least disadvantageous for our ancestors to lose their hair while they were still in the ancient forest, protected from the sun's rays by the jungle canopy. But the evolutionary pressure to lose our fur coats would have occurred only *after* we had already ventured onto the savannah to be exposed for the first time to the direct rays of the midday sun. According to this logic, human sweating likely evolved to offset the increased radiant heat load that befell already hairless hominids when they first ventured onto the savannah.

Or else, once on the savannah, our hominid ancestors developed this unmatched sweating capacity, not just to offset this increased radiant heat load but perhaps because sweating provided an even greater advantage— the ability to maintain a safe body temperature not just when walking in the midday heat but also perhaps when exercising more vigorously on the open savannah.

HUMANS DO NOT SELECTIVELY COOL THEIR BRAINS TO THE SAME EXTENT AS DO SOME MAMMALS

Some mammals, but not primates or hominids, have developed methods to maintain their brains at cooler temperatures than the rest of their bodies (Wheeler 1988, 1993, 1984). They achieve this by panting, which cools the nasal passages and the blood present in an extensive network of veins in the muzzle. This acts as a radiator, cooling the venous blood draining from the face as its returns to the heart. The arterial blood vessels taking blood to the brain form a plexus or network surrounding these veins near the base of the brain. In this way the hotter (arterial) blood traveling to the brain from the center of the body is cooled by a transfer of heat to the (cooler) venous blood draining from the face. As a result, the temperature of the blood perfusing the brain of an antelope running to escape, for example, a chasing cheetah may be only 41°C when its body temperature, increased by the heat produced by the vigorous muscular activity of an all-out sprint, may be 45–46°C (Taylor and Lyman 1972).

Another advantage of this brain-cooling adaptation is that when exposed to direct sunlight on the African savannah, many antelope allow their body temperatures to rise unchecked to temperatures well above 42°C while this special anatomical design maintains their brain temperatures at a safe level below 42°C. Thus the Oryx and the camel allow their body temperatures to rise to 45°C at midday while maintaining their brain temperatures below 41°C (Schmidt-Nielsen 1964; Taylor 1969). The Oryx appears unique in its ability to sustain a core body temperature in excess of 46°C when the environmental temperature is 45°C, thereby allowing heat loss by convection without the need to sweat (when the Oryx has no access to free-standing water).

Humans chose a different solution, the development of a larger "radiator" in the form of an overwhelming sweating response able to maintain a safe brain temperature by keeping the whole body temperature below that at which brain damage occurs. The advantage of this choice is that it allows humans to maintain the body (and brain) temperatures within a safe range even when exercising vigorously in midday heat.

Quite recently it has been shown that humans (White 2006) and horses (McConaghy et al. 1995), both of which lack a carotid rete, do indeed cool at least some parts of their brains, including the hypothalamic temperature sensors, especially during exercise in the heat. An important effect of selective brain cooling may be water conservation, since it reduces sweating and water loss from the respiratory tract during exercise that produces a rise in the whole body temperature (hyperthermia) (Robertshaw 2006; White 2006).

Further, to insure that we do not exercise too vigorously in the heat, humans have also developed a subconscious controller which insures that we slow down (Tucker et al. 2004; Tucker et al. 2006) when the environmental conditions are excessively hot and in which uncontrolled exercise might overwhelm even the human's superior cooling ability, causing dangerously high brain temperatures.

HUMANS HAVE AN INSULATING LAYER OF FAT IMMEDIATELY BELOW THE SKIN—THE SUBCUTANEOUS FAT LAYER

The loss of body hair in humans increases both radiant heat gain during the day but also heat loss from the body when the environment cools at night. However, a thin layer of fat below the skin increases insulation, reducing heat loss. Clothing, the use of fire, and behavioral changes like huddling together further improve cold tolerance at night.

During exercise the insulating effect of the subcutaneous fat layer can be bypassed by sweating and by an increased blood flow to the skin. The increased blood flow raises the skin temperature, increasing heat loss by convection. The presence of an insulating subcutaneous fat layer does not alter the efficiency of either of these mechanisms.

HUMANS HAVE A MORE LINEAR DESIGN THAN PRIMATES AND ARE TALLER THAN 1M

Whereas bipedalism minimizes the surface area of the body that is exposed to radiant heat from the sun, a greater vertical height (linearity) increases the total skin surface area, enhancing the capacity to lose heat by convection, reducing the need to lose heat by sweating. Thus, bipedalism and increased vertical height maximize the total skin surface area for evaporation and convection but minimize the area exposed to direct solar radiation. Importantly, increased linearity, like bipedalism, is a water-conserving adaptation for humans living in a hot dry environment.

But in extreme heat (>35°C) when the environmental temperature exceeds that at the skin surface (~33°C), this benefit is lost as heat is transferred to the body from the surrounding air.

Compared to a smaller (1.5m), less linear *Australopithecus africanus*, a 1.9m *Homo sapiens* of the same mass (for purposes of comparison) would have a 50 percent greater capacity to lose heat by convection (Wheeler 1993) while still exposing less of his total skin surface to the sun's rays.

The result is that when compared to a less linear, shorter (1.21m) and lighter (37kg) *Australopithecus africanus*, a 70kg *Homo sapiens* would expose the same absolute area of skin to the sun's rays at midday. But *Homo sapiens* would have two distinct advantages: First a greater body mass associated with this increased height increases the total body water (TBW) content. The benefits of this adaptation are discussed subsequently. Second, a greater total skin surface area increases the capacity for convective and evaporative heat losses (Wheeler 1993). As a result, if both performed the same activities, compared to the smaller 37kg *Australopithecus africanus,* a 70kg *Homo sapiens* would save about 800ml of water every twenty-four hours.

The vegetation on the African savannah is between 25 to 150 cm tall (Wheeler 1991a; Wheeler 1991b). Thus, an important benefit of being taller than 1.21m—the height of *Australopithecus africanus*—is that air movement is greater and the air temperatures lower ~150cm above the ground.

The transition to a larger body size, especially an increased vertical height, occurred about 1.6 million years ago with the appearance of *Homo erectus,* whose body dimensions were more similar to modern sub-Saharan Africans. This was also the time when the savannah had begun to develop east of the Great Rift Valley.

HUMANS ARE HEAVIER THAN
OUR NEAREST (PRIMATE) RELATIVES

The chimpanzee and the bonobo are the living primates that most closely resemble those early hominids that led ultimately to man. The weights of female and male chimpanzees and bonobos are 30 and 40kg respectively, somewhat smaller than modern sub-Saharan Africans. Thus somewhere in our evolutionary past, perhaps between one and two million years ago, our hominid ancestors increased their size. This too must have provided an evolutionary advantage.

Wheeler (1992b) has proposed that their greater size would have allowed early hominids to scavenge further from their home base without becoming debilitated by dehydration. Thus a greater body mass would have allowed a 60kg *Australopithecus africanus* male to scavenge for about 35km on a hot day of 35–40°C before becoming dehydrated by 5 percent. In contrast, a 30kg hominid would have been restricted to a range of only about 25km.

Interestingly, early hominid males were much larger than females, a phenomenon known as sexual dimorphism. This too would have resulted from evolutionary selection. Since larger males would have been able to carry more food more efficiently than smaller males or females, a division of labor in which males were the hunters while the females stayed at home, would explain this difference.

The larger size of the males would also have increased their total skin surface area increasing their capacity to lose heat by convection and sweating, allowing them to scavenge more widely without becoming dehydrated by more than 5 percent.

HUMANS HAVE SHORTER ARMS THAN THE APES AND OUR ARMS ARE SHORTER THAN OUR LEGS; THE REVERSE APPLIES IN THE GREAT APES

Their relatively longer arms and fingers would have allowed *Australo-pithecus africanus* to climb more effectively than later hominids. This would have been a valuable survival technique for those tiny hominids when forced to escape from large feline predators in search of an evening meal (Hart and Sussman 2005). The time period during which hominids exchanged their longer arms and shorter legs for shorter arms and longer legs defines when our early hominid ancestors gave up tree climbing as a method of avoiding predation.

Early hominids dispensed with the obvious advantage of tree climbing because some other more valuable advantage was achieved by having longer legs but shorter arms and fingers.

HUMANS HAVE LONG LEGS WITH BUILT-IN SPRINGS THAT INCREASE OUR EFFICIENCY WHEN WE RUN

Relative to our body weight, humans have the longest legs of any species. We also have in-built springs in our lower limbs that conserve energy when we run. In addition, we have a subconsciously controlled brain mechanism that activates our leg muscles immediately before the foot touches the ground (Nummela et al. 2006; Nummela et al. 2008). This further increases and regulates the "springiness" of our legs. Humans also have thinner legs than other greater apes and the most successful distance runners in the world usually have extremely thin legs.

The increased springiness of our lower limbs allows energy to be stored when our feet land on the ground as we run. As the foot leaves the ground the spring stretches, releasing this temporarily stored energy. This adapta-tion is of no value in walking as little energy can be stored and returned during the walking stride.

Rather this adaptation must have developed specifically to improve our efficiency as long distance runners (Carrier 1984; Bramble and Li-eberman 2004; Lieberman and Bramble 2007). This is the first piece of compelling evidence suggesting that long distance running ability was a critically important outcome in the evolution of *Homo sapiens*.

HUMANS HAVE LARGE BUTTOCK MUSCLES
(GLUTEUS MAXIMUS)

Compared to all the primates, "being endowed with prominent rounded buttocks is the unique privilege of humans" (Jouffroy and Médina, 2007: 135). Interestingly, the gluteus maximus muscle is essentially inactive when standing or when walking on a level surface: Humans in whom the gluteus maximus is paralyzed are able to walk on the flat without any obvious difficulty. Thus, those activities that require the action of the gluteus maximus muscle "should have been of paramount importance during the course of human evolution" (Jouffroy and Médina 2007: 141).

Those activities include jogging, running, sprint-starting, leaping, climbing stairs or walking up a slope. In these activities, the muscle acts to extend the hip and to control the side-to-side balance of the trunk. Contraction of the muscle also slows the rotation of the trunk in the throwing motion, transferring angular momentum to the arm and increasing the speed at which an object can be thrown. Thus the gluteus maximus muscle is highly active in baseball pitching (Watkins et al. 1989). In addition, the muscle is active when straightening up from a stooping, squatting, or crouching position.

Jouffroy and Médina (2007) propose that the biomechanical demands of jogging and running, including the stabilization of the side-to-side movements during faster running, the capacity to throw objects with force, and to straighten up from the crouching position when living at ground level, would all have directed the evolutionary development of the gluteus maximus muscle in humans.

HUMANS ARE ABLE TO COUNTER-ROTATE THE UPPER
BODY ON THE PELVIS WHILE KEEPING THE HEAD STILL

This adaptation is essential to maintain balance when running and is perhaps the second piece of compelling evidence suggesting that some critical selective factors in our evolutionary past directed *Homo sapiens* on the road to becoming superior long distance runners.

When running, but not when walking, the center of gravity transfers from one side of the body to the other as we land on alternate feet with each stride. It is not possible to balance when only one foot is on the ground (as occurs in running but not in walking) other than by rotating the upper body and arm in the opposite direction while keeping the head still. Chimpanzees and other great apes are unable to run for any extended period because they lack this ability to rotate their upper bodies while keeping the head still.

This ability to rotate the upper body while keeping the head still also provides humans with an ability to throw an object and to strike with an implement; these skills are the basis for human sporting ability in all hitting sports, including golf, tennis, and hockey, and in combined throwing and hitting sports like cricket and baseball.

As Raymond Dart wrote:

This accuracy in hitting and hurling which apes lack but which men universally possess is an inherited instinct. It demands no greater intelligence than human microcephalic idiots, with less than australopithecine endocranical capacities, can command. . . .

What it does depend upon is the short and enlarged pelvis of basin form, such as human beings and also Australopithecinae possessed, which is capable of rotating during the body swing on the top ends of two columnar lower limbs. These in their turn move about powerful ankles above feet that have planted heels and big and little toes capable of gripping the ground firmly. With this stable type of double-columned understructure the elongated human flanks can bend laterally or rotate upon the pelvis, as well as flex and extend, while the arms swing; and the poised head can move freely and co-ordinatedly upon its lengthened neck in any direction on this fantastically flexible torso. . . .

All these co-ordinated movements of the slender up-right human type of body, head, neck, and arms are required for the performance of accurate hitting or dextrous hurling. Above all the divergence in accuracy or skill between apes and man in hitting and hurling depends upon the acquisition by human beings of a brain capable of co-ordinating with the movements of the hands and the eyes a series of postural body reflexes (1959: 204).

HUMANS HAVE LARGER BRAINS AND SMALLER INTESTINES THAN PRIMATES

The size of the human brain has increased dramatically in the last million years. Thus between three and four million years ago the brain size of fossilized hominids increased by only a few hundred milliliters. But within the last one million years the brain nearly trebled in size.

Aiello and Wheeler (1995) argue that the maintenance of this much larger brain is metabolically expensive since, relative to its weight, the brain is the most metabolically active organ in the human body. They suggest that another important step in human evolution could have been the simultaneous reduction in the size of other metabolically expensive organs as the size of the brain increased, demanding an increasingly larger proportion of the daily energy intake.

Primates need very long intestines to digest the food they ingest, the predominant constituents of which are plants with low energy content. Thus, the size of the metabolically expensive intestine can be reduced only after the diet has become more energy-dense because it contains proteins and fats of animal origin.

Once the hominid diet changed to include more energy-dense food-stuffs, allowing the size of the human intestine to be reduced, so the human abdomen also became smaller. As a result, the barrel-shaped chest and the protruding belly of the apes gave way to the more compact funnel-shaped chest and the appearance of the waist in *Homo erectus,* leading to the present-day anatomical shape of *Homo sapiens.*

Evolution could have chosen to reduce the size of any energy-expensive organ but, once the diet changed, the intestine became the most expendable. A reduction in muscle mass would have been an unwise choice since muscle has a relatively low energy requirement only at rest; during exercise muscle consumes as much as 80 percent of the energy that is produced. Conservation of an adequate muscle mass was essential to provide our ancestors with the strength and endurance to acquire the high-energy diet necessary to sustain the health of the brain through either hunting or scavenging.

The kidneys are also metabolically expensive; thus a reduction in their size was a possibility. That the human kidneys remain relatively large indicates that evolution did not favor this choice. A reduction in the size of the kidneys would have left early *Homo sapiens* with a reduced capacity to excrete a concentrated urine. As a result, daily water losses would have been increased requiring a greater daily water intake. This would have been feasible if early humans had evolved in an environment in which water was plentiful. That humans have retained large, metabolically expensive kidneys suggests that we must have evolved in a relatively dry environment in which water was not always freely available.

As a result, human kidneys can excrete a moderately concentrated urine but not as concentrated as the urine of desert-dwelling animals like the kangaroo rat, the camel and the Oryx, all of which can survive for either prolonged periods (camel) or indeed indefinitely (Oryx) without the need to ingest free-standing water. All these mammals excrete a urine that is many times more concentrated than is the maximally concentrated human urine.

The functional capacity of the human intestine and kidney has been described as "enough, but not too much" (Diamond 1991). Within the constraints imposed by a dietary energy supply that was also "enough but not too much," evolution determined our biology by selecting the most efficient physiology that would perform those functions that provided us with the selective biological advantage to insure our survival as a successful species.

Had our ancestors enjoyed access to an unlimited food and water supply, human physiology would have been quite different. In particular, we would have retained a larger intestine but not so large that it interfered with our ability as long distance runners. A larger intestine would have allowed humans to drink larger volumes of fluid before satiation. As a result, we would have been able to drink more during exercise and so minimize the extent to which any water deficit (caused by sweating) would develop during exercise.

Instead, to survive as a species forced to exercise in the heat in order to secure food, humans must have undergone a series of parallel physiological adaptations which insured that the reduced intestinal absorptive capacity (resulting from the necessity to reduce the size of the intestine once our brains began to enlarge) would not interfere with our ability to exercise in dry heat when we also sweated profusely.

What is the nature of these adaptations?

HUMANS DRINK FREQUENTLY IN SMALL AMOUNTS (USUALLY BY OURSELVES) AND DELAY THE FULL CORRECTION OF ANY FLUID DEFICITS GENERATED BY EXERCISE

The reduced size of the human gut, including the small size of the holding chamber leading into the intestine, the stomach, means that humans are unable to ingest very large volumes of fluid quickly. Rather we tend to drink enough to fill our stomachs (~500ml); we then wait until the stomach has emptied that volume (requiring fifteen to twenty minutes) before we are again able to drink another large volume. Alternatively, we can ingest small volumes more frequently (sipping). The result, however, is the same: Humans are less able to drink large volumes of fluid quickly than are most other mammals of equivalent size.

Thus the camel can ingest 100 liters of fluid in ten minutes, the donkey 20 liters in three minutes; the dog 5 liters in ten minutes (Schmidt-Nielsen 1964) whereas humans usually stop drinking once they have ingest 1 liter in about ten minutes (Newman 1970).

One consequence of this biological adaptation is the existence of public houses, which usually close at midnight or later, and not before. For if humans had the intestinal design of camels, donkeys or dogs, those who so wished would be able to ingest all the alcohol they desired in a few minutes and then go elsewhere to await the consequences. Instead, humans wishing to become inebriated must expend many hours imbibing small amounts of alcohol frequently. That humans seem to have a special need to drink in the evening or at night is indeed significant, as will be argued subsequently.

If our hominid ancestors chose to collect their food by exercising daily on the hot African savannah, where water was relatively scarce, a logical biological adaptation would be, as first proposed by Hanna and Brown (1983: 262), to uncouple thirst from the actual fluid loss that developed when our ancestors were away from their home base during the day. This would delay the desire and indeed the need to drink until evening when they returned to their home base where stored fluid would have been more freely available. Some believe that this development of the "home base with daily foraging" was a major factor influencing subsequent human social evolution (Hanna and Brown 1983: 263).

So specifically, to maximize their ability to exercise in the heat, our hominid ancestors would have needed to delay the need to drink until they returned to their home base where water was more abundant. Or else they would have spent their days searching for water, not for edible foods.

Furthermore, other bodily mechanisms would have had to develop simultaneously to allow early hominids to continue exercising with an undiminished performance even though their sweating was causing a progressive water deficit to develop. Or else our ancestors would have disappeared as a species just as, it seems, did a large number of other early hominids.

Thus, our hominid ancestors must also have developed the capacity to continue exercising, often quite vigorously, even as they developed a progressive and significant water deficit as they went about their daily business collecting food on the hot African savannah.

What is more, those of our ancestors who were best able to continue exercising without either impairment or without becoming thirsty while they developed the highest levels of fluid loss ("dehydration") would have been the most successful gatherers of food. The family groupings, which included the best food gatherers, would also have been more likely to raise more offspring and so to pass their genes on to subsequent generations. The most successful gatherers would also have been best able regularly to acquire the high-energy diets necessary to maximize brain growth in the infants in their band.

The reduction in the size of the human intestine would also have produced a behavior change so that humans could begin drinking frequently but were freed from always drinking as a group with other hominids. In contrast, most large mammals drink as groups or herds, usually only once a day. They too have developed the ability to delay the need to drink but for a different reason. Drinking only once a day reduces the risk of predation, which occurs with increased probability at watering holes.

Our species' inability to drink large fluid volumes rapidly, forced upon us by our large brains and small intestines, has promoted the pejorative concept that humans are poorly adapted for exercise in the heat because we are "reluctant drinkers" who develop an undesirable condition termed "voluntary dehydration" (Rothstein et al. 1947, Greenleaf and Sargent 1965).

Thus, it is argued that human physiology is inferior, indeed fatally flawed, since we are unable completely to replace a fluid deficit as it develops whereas camels, donkeys and dogs do. Since "voluntary dehydration" develops only in humans, this proves that humans are incapable of safely managing their fluid balances during prolonged exercise in the heat. As a result, humans can exercise safely only if they are told exactly when and how much to drink during exercise, especially if it is in the heat. When left to their own devices humans will not drink enough during exercise, becoming "dehydrated" with potentially fatal consequences. This conclusion conveniently ignores the fact that dogs especially and to a somewhat lesser extent donkeys and camels (since both sweat) are quite unable to match the human's exceptional capacity for exercising in the heat.

Thus, whereas dogs can match the performance of humans in cool conditions, because they do not sweat, when exercising in the heat (~40°C) dogs are unable to cool their skin temperatures below that of the environment. As a result, they continuously absorb heat from the environment and are unable to maintain as low a body temperature as humans exercising in the same conditions (Dill et al. 1932), leading to a marked impairment in exercise performance. In one study, a dog's endurance in the heat was one-third that in cooler conditions and significantly inferior to that of an athletic human, stated the legendary U.S. exercise physiologist Dr. David Dill (Dill et al. 1932).

Since dogs fully replace their fluid losses during exercise, this impairment in performance and elevation of rectal temperature occurred even though the dog did not lose any weight during exercise. In contrast, David B. Dill, whose performance was unimpaired when he exercised with the dog in the same conditions, lost a total of 3.1kg during seven hours of exercise in which he walked 32km; the dog stopped after covering 26km.

So the truth is that even though we are less able to replace our water deficits (larger because we sweat) as they develop during exercise, humans are better adapted for prolonged exercise in the heat than are those mammals who do not develop "voluntary dehydration."

Hence, in my view, the human tendency to develop "voluntary dehydration" during exercise would have developed as an essential and advantageous biological adaptation, necessary to allow humans to exercise effectively in hot, dry, waterless conditions without developing an overpowering thirst that would have forced a premature and unsuccessful conclusion to their exercise.

According to this explanation, "voluntary dehydration" is nothing more than evolution's elegant solution to a complex biological challenge in which humans needed to exercise vigorously in hot dry conditions with limited water availability in order to acquire a sufficiently energy rich diet on a regular basis to support the development of a larger brain. To do so, our exercising ancestors had to sweat vigorously. But as they became better able to secure a consistently high-energy diet that allowed their brains to enlarge and their intestines to become smaller, so our hominid ancestors had to delay the correction of the fluid deficit incurred by sweating during exercise until they had returned to their water store at their home base, presumably in the afternoon or early evening. But this would have been without benefit if any water lost during exercise in the heat produced a marked impairment in exercise performance, causing a premature return home to replace the water deficit incurred by sweating.

For all the reasons subsequently described, the spectacular commercial success of the world's first sports drink in the late 1990s was driven at least in part by the development of the "zero dehydration rule" (American College of Sports Medicine 1996), which holds that any level of "voluntary dehydration" that develops during exercise is dangerous and could be fatal. Instead, in order to prevent this novel and potentially catastrophic "disease," exercising humans must be taught to replace their sweat losses as they develop.

But this advice ignores all the evolutionary evidence that humans evolved this unmatched capacity to sweat profusely specifically so that they could better regulate their body temperatures during exercise. This did however produce the potential that high levels of fluid loss ("dehydration") would also develop especially (1) if the size of the intestine had also to be reduced so that fluid could never be ingested as rapidly as it was being lost and (2) if water was relatively scarce on the savannah and could not be carried to any great extent when either foraging or hunting, being freely available only at the home base. As a result, only at night would our hominid ancestors have been able to correct the fluid deficit that they developed during the day. Hence, the need to develop a physiology that favored delayed drinking.

Newman concludes that since humans do not show any of the water conserving adaptations observed in true desert-dwelling mammals, we must have evolved in a "well-watered tropical habitat, or, at least certainly not a tropical desert" (1970: 23). Such an environment would have been the tropical parklands or grasslands of the African savannah where free-standing water was scarce, especially in the dry seasons, but could be stored at the home base.

So humans may not have been designed to live in deserts; yet as a result of our unequalled ability to sweat and to resist the physiological effects of dehydration, we did evolve an unmatched capacity to exercise in conditions of dry heat typical of those found in arid environments. Thus, Hanna and Brown (1983: 280) conclude:

> Humans are remarkably well adapted to tolerate heat whether derived from environmental or from metabolic sources. This adaptation apparently developed early in hominid evolution and permitted successful colonization of savannah and other hot environments. Apparently the selective pressures were very strong and included a behavioral component with high levels of physical activity. The major adaptation was a high sweating response. The adaptation came with a price; however, the necessity for a reliable daily water supply. We have speculated that the necessity for water may have contributed to the establishment of a home base for hominid social groups.

HUMANS CAN ADAPT ("ACCLIMATIZE") SO THAT THEY ARE BETTER ABLE TO EXERCISE IN THE HEAT

Repeated exposures to heat, especially when exercising, further improves the human's unmatched capacity to exercise in the heat (Wyndham 1973). The key adaptations are the ability to increase further our already generous sweat rates and to maintain lower body temperatures while placing less demand on the heart and circulation (Wyndham 1973). It would stand to reason that we also become more economical so that after acclimatization, we produce less heat when performing the same task.

Other features of acclimatization are that it occurs rapidly and is easily accomplished, even in those who have lived all their lives in temperate environments (Hanna and Brown 1983). Heat acclimatization is also associated with an improved sodium chloride (salt) economy as it reduces the amounts of salt lost in sweat and urine.

HUMANS ACTIVELY REGULATE THE AMOUNT OF SODIUM CHLORIDE (SALT) THEY LOSE IN SWEAT AND URINE TO EQUAL THE AMOUNT THEY INGEST IN THE DIET

These mechanisms evolved in early hominids to insure that they were able to sweat profusely during exercise without becoming sodium-deficient even though their diet contained little sodium. Salt was first harvested from the surface of salt lakes in China about eight thousand years ago. Thus, four to seven million years ago early hominids probably did not have the opportunity to add salt to their diets.

Once humans began to sweat, they increased their capacity to lose salt in sweat, since sweat contains variable concentrations of salt. Humans eating a high salt western diet excrete large amounts of salt in both their sweat and urine in order to remain in sodium balance and avoid developing a sodium overload. Had our hominid ancestors lost equivalent amounts of salt in their sweat (and urine), they could not have survived since they would have become sodium deficient whenever they exercised. Since their diet was low in sodium, our hominid ancestors must have developed very powerful sodium-conserving mechanisms that were active at rest but even more so during exercise.

SUMMARY

The evidence presented here clearly establishes that evolution directed our species, *Homo sapiens*, to develop a superior capacity to regulate our body temperatures when exercising in hot conditions. The capacity to sweat profusely combined with the loss of body hair and a greater body size were the three most important adaptations that produced a species better able to exercise more vigorously and for longer periods in dry heat than any other species, even when access to water was limited.

Importantly, these adaptations must have developed for some crucial evolutionary purpose; they did not happen perchance.

But for what possible purpose could that have been?

The development of a novel hypothesis: The key selective factor driving the subsequent evolution of humans was the need to run long distances in the heat to hunt and capture energy-dense mammals, including fleet-footed antelope.

In his book first published in 1900, Charles Morris concluded that humans must have given up the benefit provided by long arms for something that provided an even more substantial advantage.

Morris next asked the questions: "Why did the man ape gain a length of arm not the best suited to its arboreal habitat? Why, in fact, do changes in physical structures ever take place? How does an animal succeed in passing from one mode of life to another, when during the transition period it is imperfectly adapted to either, and therefore at a seeming disadvantage in the struggle for existence?" (1900: 58). He concluded that any advantage resulting from such a risky experiment had to be substantial. "Such changes are usually the result of some change of habit in the animal, frequently one that has to do with food. Change of diet *or of the mode of obtaining food* (my emphasis) is the most potent influencing cause of change of habit in animals" (1900: 60).

He concluded that our human ancestors changed their diets from vegetable to animal food and this change "would certainly demand a more active employment of the arms as agents in capture" (1900: 61). Thus: "In short, the pursuit and capture of any of the larger animals for prey could not fail to modify to a greater degree the use of the arms" (Ibid).

Morris believed that once the arms had been freed, they could be employed to use weapons for the capture of prey. He envisaged an early human ancestor "probably much smaller than existing man, little if anything more than four feet in height and not more than half the weight of man" (1900: 67) walking "upright on the earth, pursuing the larger animals and capturing them for food" (Ibid). Morris believed that it was the clever use of artificial weapons that allowed humans to dominate all other species (1900: 122).

Unexplained by this original theory are the other differentiating features of humans, specifically our long springy legs, hairless bodies, and our capacity to sweat more effectively than any other surviving mammal. Nor could Morris's theory explain how our early human ancestors were able to capture, kill and eat large mammals long before they developed effective killing weapons like spears and arrows, which make their first appearance on earth only more recently. Somehow, if early hominids were indeed able to kill these animals with nothing more than "a sharp wooden stick" (Conniff 2008) they must have developed some other effective technique, especially since they had to cope with the real risk of a fatal injury: "It's incredibly dangerous. You have to move close to the animal, which means the animal can kick you or gore you" (Conniff 2008).

Twenty-four years later Professor Carveth Read advanced a similar hypothesis that "Man was Differentiated from the Anthropods by Becoming a Hunter" (Read 1920: 1). He too concluded that the determining factor directing human evolution away from the primates was "the adoption of a flesh diet and the habits of a hunter in order to obtain it. Without the adoption of a flesh diet there could have been no hunting; but a flesh diet obtained without hunting (supposing it possible) could have done nothing for [the distinctive biological differentiation of] our family" (1920: 2).

Read concluded that man became a two-footed hunter: "Why is man a running animal? Is it for the advantage of running away? To run away is sometimes useful, but it is not characteristic of man: Rather to run to the attack and to pursue. Accordingly, though fairly swift, he is not amongst the swiftest animals; but he is very long-winded and indefatigable, and in that, as in many other things, he resembles the dogs and wolves" (1920: 20).

Like Morris, Read was so certain that early hominids used weapons to kill prey that he too overlooked the possible implications of the other defining characteristics of humans—our ability to thermoregulate more effectively than any other mammal of similar size.

In 1965, Brace and Montagu proposed that the superior thermoregulatory capacity provided by man's hairlessness and superior sweating response could have provided humans with the ability to track animals in the heat when other carnivores were incapacitated.

In 1968, Grover Krantz suggested that the increase in brain size in *Homo erectus* came about because that hominid was "a successful big game hunter as well as a gatherer." He proposed that Homo evolved as a successful "persistence hunter" and that this method of capturing animals has since been replaced by the use of "projectile weapons" including arrows and spears. He noted that the Tarahumara of Mexico were known to chase deer for up to two days and never less than a day: "The Indian chases the deer until the creature falls from exhaustion, often with its hooves completely worn away." He noted that the Bushmen use the same tactic in part because the absence of vegetation in the semi-desert makes stealth and concealment difficult. But, he argued, that hunting required that the brain should increase in size since hunting requires "the ability to keep the task constantly in mind for several days and to anticipate the results well into the future" (1968: 450).

Thus, Krantz conceived that human hunting produced the high-energy diet that allowed the size of the brain to increase. This in turn produced the intellectual capacity to become increasingly more adept at hunting, acquiring more food and thus allowing the clever brain to become even bigger and cleverer: "At first, *Australopithecus* could run down only those animals most quickly exhausted, and must have been in keen competition with many other carnivores. As the reward in food for successful pursuit of the game tended, on the average, to go to those individuals with the greater mental time spans [due to their larger brain sizes], selective pressure would favor larger brains with better memories" (1968: 451).

In the same year, a monograph (Lee and DeVore 1968) on human hunting was published, the result of a conference held at the University of Chicago in April 1966. In their presentation, Sherwood Washburn and C. S. Lancaster noted that when protected, modern elephants soon multiply to the point where they threaten the environment. Since *Homo sapiens* and not the elephant became the dominant mammal, "it is tempting to think that man replaced the saber-toothed tiger as the major predator of large game, both controlling the numbers of the game and causing the extinction of the Old World saber-tooths" (Washburn and Lancaster 2008: 2950). They concluded that *Homo erectus* had developed the tools to become a successful hunter 500,000 years ago and that this produced a change in the relationship between man and animals: "But with the origin of human hunting, the peaceful relationship was destroyed and for at least half a million years man has been the enemy of even the largest mammals. In this way the whole human view of what is normal and natural in the relation of man to animals is a product of hunting, and the world of flight and fear is the result of the efficiency of the [early human] hunters" (Ibid: 299). Thus, according to this interpretation, animals flee from man not because of an inherited instinct, but because of the long history of human predation on many animals both large and small.

In 1972 Stern proposed that the development of the upper part of the human gluteus maximus muscle which functions principally to control the side-to-side balance of the trunk during fast locomotion, including jogging and running, might have developed as the result of persistence hunting similar to that undertaken by the !Kung Bushmen. The resulting changes in the site of the insertion of that muscle into the pelvic bone, the ilium, shown in the fossil hominid record "may be important osteological evidence of well established hunting behavior" (Stern 1972: 329).

While a doctoral student at the University of Michigan, David R. Carrier began where Darwin, Morris and Read had left off. He re-affirmed that the feature differentiating early hominids from the primates from which we evolved is not a large brain size but "the set of characteristics associated with erect bipedal posture and a striding gait" (Carrier 1984: 483). These characteristics were already present at least 3.5 million years ago in the small-brained Australopithecines living in East and South Africa. Thus, he again proposed that the ability to walk and run, not brain size, is the defining difference between humans and primates. But Carrier's innovative idea was his realization that the energy cost of human walking and running is about twice as high as that of other running mammals and birds. He concludes that there must have been a very worthwhile incentive for humans to have evolved into an animal whose sole modes of transport, walking and running, are relatively inefficient compared to other, especially four-legged, mammals.

Carrier also noted the energy cost of traveling a certain distance is independent of the speed of travel in humans but not in other mammals that have been studied, including horses. Thus, it matters not how fast a human finishes a footrace of any distance. Since the distance run by all finishers is the same, the total energy cost is the same whether the athlete finishes first or last.

In contrast, horses (Hoyt and Taylor 1981) have a specific speed at each locomotory pattern (walking, trotting, cantering and galloping) at which their energy cost is least and about 50 percent lower than that of humans ($100ml$ versus $200mlO_2.kg^{-1}.min^{-1}.km^{-1}$). Thus, Carrier wondered: "What is it about humans that detaches the cost of running from speed?"; and "What advantages or disadvantages does this unusual situation create for running humans?" (Carrier 1984: 486). His key conclusion was that humans are not constrained to run at only one or two optimal speeds; rather they can run at many different speeds depending on requirement.

Carrier argues that quadripedal mammals are constrained to breathe only once with every stride as they must alternatively inhale when the body is in flight and exhale when landing. In contrast, smaller bipedal humans can breathe once, twice or even three times with each stride, depending on how fast they run. Since the demand to breathe is set by the muscles' metabolic activity, by breathing either more or less frequently per stride, humans can run with a much wider range of metabolic rates, that is, running speeds, without changing their basic locomotor pattern of walking or running. In contrast, quadripedal mammals can run only as fast as their one-breath-per-stride breathing will allow within each locomotory pattern.

The end result is that while quadripedal animals must run at a restricted range of running speeds for each locomotory pattern, bipedal humans can run at a wide range of speeds without changing to a different form of locomotion other than changing to running from walking when their speed rises above about 6km per hour.

Furthermore, non-sweating running mammals, like most medium-sized antelopes that modern humans still hunt, lose heat through their respiratory tracts as the air they expire has a higher temperature than does the inspired (ambient) air. This is analogous to panting. Their capacity to lose heat in this way is also constrained by the same factors that limit their breathing rate to one breath per stride.

In contrast, running humans can increase their capacity to lose heat from the respiratory tract by running faster and breathing more frequently. But humans are better equipped to lose heat by sweating and so to match rates of heat loss and heat production across a much wider range of running speeds in more severe environmental conditions.

Persistence or endurance hunting is the one activity in which these differences in thermoregulatory capacity between sweaters and panters could clearly become important. For compared to the non-sweating antelope that they hunt, sweating humans have a greater capacity to adapt to a wider range of environmental conditions and running speeds at which they can remain in thermal balance. In contrast, panting antelope have two distinct disadvantages.

First, they are constrained to canter or to gallop at speeds greatly in excess of the pursuing humans. But they are not "trained" to sustain those speeds for prolonged periods.

For all predators other than man that hunt African antelope, they do so at high speeds, but usually over short distances. Even the African hunting dog, known for its endurance, can sustain speeds of up to 40km/hr for prolonged periods. In contrast, hunting humans use much slower running speeds, seldom faster than 10km/hr.

As a result, the hunted antelope must adopt a different strategy when chased by either sprinters like cheetahs, lions or wild dogs or persistence hunters like humans. When chased by the former, the antelope must run as fast as it can for just long enough to evade capture; against humans, it must perform repeated short bouts of high intensity exercise. This form of intermittent exercise is inefficient.

Second, as they become progressively hotter as the hunt progresses, the antelope chased by humans must pant continuously in both the rest periods between exercise bouts and ultimately during the exercise itself. This must either progressively slow the speed they can maintain when cantering or galloping (since their breathing must serve two functions—fueling activity and regulating their body temperatures) or they must reduce the distance they can cover in each exercise bout.

Humans, on the other hand, can choose a running speed that their prey finds the most inefficient.

Thus, a clever hunter would chase a horse at a speed of 16–17km/hr as this speed falls midway between the optimal speeds of the trot and the gallop, a speed at which no horse wishes to run. As a result the hunted animal would be forced either to run at its less optimal speed or to sprint ahead intermittently and then to rest. Interestingly 16–17km/hr is the optimum running speed that the world's best athletes can sustain during competitive races lasting five to seven hours. Lieberman and Bramble (2007) conclude that a horse can sustain a maximal gallop of 32km/hr for about 10km; a gallop of 28km/hr for only ten to fifteen minutes; and a canter at 21km/hr for approximately 20km. None of these would allow a horse to escape a determined human hunter.

The crucial challenge for the hunter is that when the pursued animal sprints intermittently to escape capture, it will be out of sight for most of the hunt. To be successful, pursuing hunters have to track the unseen animal at a distance. Some contend that learning this skill may have been the source of human intelligence and the origin of the scientific method (Liebenberg 1990).

Carrier (1984) also describes other biological advantages enjoyed by sweating humans. First, the human sweat glands are under nervous control. This allows a very wide range of sweating rates to be achieved by humans during exercise—from as little as 200ml.hr^{-1} in marathon runners competing in ice-cold Arctic conditions (Stuempfle et al. 2003) to about 3000ml.hr^{-1} in large (~160kg) American football players (Fowkes Godek et al. 2005). This represents a fifteen-fold range in the capacity of humans to lose heat by controlled sweating. This exceeds by a wide margin the sweat rates required to maintain a safe body temperature during hunting in the dry heat conditions on the African savannah.

In addition, humans have the capacity to store carbohydrates in the form of glycogen in their muscles. Glycogen is the optimum fuel for endurance exercise but requires a carbohydrate-rich diet to maximize storage. In addition, when glycogen is stored in liver and muscle, it attracts water molecules which are released as the glycogen is used during exercise. In this way, additional water is released as that fuel is used during exercise. This water can offset some of the sweat losses.

Thus by 1984, Carrier had proposed that humans evolved as diurnal predators who "depended upon an exceptional endurance in hot (mid-day) temperatures to disable swifter prey animals" (Carrier 1984: 489). In support of his hypothesis, he referred to studies showing that kangaroos, even though they lose heat by both panting and sweating in approximately equal proportions, are unable to lose all the heat they produce when hopping at speeds in the range from 4–22km.hr^{-1} in moderately warm conditions (24°C) (Dawson et al. 1974). As a result, kangaroos overheat within one to two hours when forced to run under those conditions. The Aborigines of northwestern Australia are known to chase kangaroos to their exhaustion in the heat in the same way as the !Kung San hunt antelope in the Kalahari desert.

Carrier therefore concluded that "man is a primate that has become specialized for . . . endurance running" (1984: 489). He hypothesized that our superior ability to lose heat, especially by sweating from individually innervated sweat glands, drove the evolution of *Homo sapiens* by providing the opportunity to occupy a novel predatory role. This hypothetical niche was that of a diurnal predator able to capture swifter non-sweating prey chased in midday heat. This is the hunting technique still followed by modern !Kung San hunters (Liebenberg 2006).

THE PARALYSIS OF PROFOUND HYPERTHERMIA

Even if the evolution of the *Homo sapiens* was indeed directed by our superior ability to thermoregulate when hunting in extreme dry heat, the intellectual challenge that remains is to explain how early hominid hunters killed their prey, given their small size, relatively weak arms, and likely absence of offensive weapons other than perhaps a crude hand tool that assisted in opening the skin and dissecting the carcass. Exercise physiologists happened upon the solution relatively recently.

In 1993 a group of Danish scientists (Nielsen et al. 1993) showed that when humans exercise at a work rate fixed by the experimenter, they choose to terminate the exercise when their body temperatures reach a temperature predictable for each individual (Nielsen et al. 1993). This research has concluded that an elevated body temperature acts on those brain centers (the motor region of the cerebral cortex) which normally activate the limb muscles during exercise. Inhibition of those centers caused a motor paralysis, terminating exercise when the body temperature reaches the critical body temperature.

For example, animal biologists have known for decades that antelope have the special brain-cooling mechanism described earlier. During exercise, for example, the Thomson's gazelle, a favorite staple of the cheetah's diet, and which must run at >80kph in order to stay ahead of the chasing cheetah, stores all the heat it produces when running at high speeds. However, by cooling the blood entering its brain, it produces a difference of 4–5°C between the body and brain temperatures. As a result, this gazelle will not develop the paralysis of hyperthermia; rather if chased for sufficiently long it will die from an uncontrolled elevation of its body temperature (heat stroke) as occurred to one of the gazelles studied by Taylor and Lyman (1972).

The point is that this mechanism allows antelope to keep their brains cool while allowing the body temperature to rise without control presumably until heat stroke develops. This provides an evolutionary advantage that the cheetah does not enjoy. Thus, the gazelle must just run fast enough for just long enough until the cheetah becomes paralyzed when its brain temperature reaches its maximum allowable value.

The cheetah, perhaps for good reason, lacks this protective brain mechanism. Instead, during exercise it too stores all the heat it produces. This causes a very rapid elevation in its body temperature, probably reaching the critical brain temperatures of ~41°C before it has run 1000m. In the laboratory, cheetahs refused to run when their body temperatures reached ~40.5°C (Taylor and Rowntree 1973). The cheetah must then pant for about an hour in order to lower its body temperature before it can again exercise.

Hyperthermic paralysis makes it relatively easy to capture a cheetah. A cheetah followed in a car for about 1–2km reaches its critical brain temperature and becomes relatively docile and defenseless. Early hominids could have exploited this weakness by following the cheetah's hunt and then chasing the overheated, panting and relatively defenseless cheetah from its dead prey. Hyenas and lions frequently adopt this strategy.

Animals that are not as fast as the cheetah have adopted a different hunting strategy. African hunting dogs hunt in a pack and tirelessly run down their prey in much the same way that early humans might have. While hunting, the African hunting dog has little access to water, as was almost certainly the case for early hominid hunters. Thus, the hunting dog needs to maintain its brain temperature below the critical temperature without losing too much water.

Studies by the iconic physiologists C. R. Taylor and Knut Schmidt-Nielsen (Taylor et al. 1971) revealed that hunting dogs store about 20 percent of the heat they generate during exercise; they exercise at higher body temperatures than do domestic dogs; and they lose heat mainly through the respiratory tract with some (minor) sweating. But the hunting dog restricts the amount of heat it loses by respiratory evaporation (panting) to about one-half that lost by the domestic dog under similar exercise conditions. It achieves this by maintaining a higher body temperature. This increases heat loss by convection from the skin surface. Convection does not require the evaporation of water. This water-conserving technique increases the ability of these hunting dogs to chase their prey for longer distances before they need to drink.

Thus, it has been suggested that at some time in our evolutionary past early hominids learned that certain mammals chased for a short distance would soon overheat and could be caught relatively easily. With experience, they would soon begin to chase even larger mammals. To catch these larger prey, early hominids needed to improve further their thermoregulation, by developing a greater sweating capacity and an even better endurance running ability.

FURTHER DEVELOPMENT OF THE HUNTING HYPOTHESIS

Bramble and Lieberman (2004) have recently extended the scientific argument, first proposed by Carrier, that humans evolved for endurance running. The specific question they wished to answer was: Was running a form of locomotion that influenced human evolution?

So they began with the question: "Why would early Homo run long distances when walking is easier, safer and less costly? One possibility is that endurance running played a role in helping hominids exploit, protein-rich resources such as meat, [liver], marrow and brain, first evident in the archaeological record at approximately 2.6 million years ago, co-incident with the first appearance of Homo" (2004: 351).

Their conclusion was that humans evolved to run, not to walk, since humans show a multitude of traits in the human body that are essential for running but not for walking. These include, among others (Lieberman and Bramble 2007): springs in the legs that allow energy to be alternatively stored and released when running; the ability to maintain the center of mass stable by rotating the upper body while stabilizing the head and neck when both feet are off the ground—as occurs in running but not in walking; enlarged sensory organs in the ear (the semi-circular canals) to improve the sensitivity of the reflexes that control rapid pitching movements that occur in running but not in walking; and a superior capacity for thermoregulation when exercising vigorously in dry heat.

The human leg is designed as a spring with long spring-like tendons attached to short muscles that can generate force most economically. This arrangement allows energy to be conserved when the foot lands on the ground, stretching these tendons, which then release that energy as the calf muscle contracts, the ankle extends and the foot leaves the ground. This form of energy return can save approximately 50 percent of the metabolic cost of running (Alexander 1991). Bramble and Lieberman argue that the Achilles tendon elongated and evolved some time after the appearance of *Australopithecus africanus* about three million years ago.

The second spring is the plantar ligament that spans the arch of the foot and which was probably present in *Homo habilis* who first appeared about two million years ago. To maximize this spring effect requires a rigid foot with a stiff, stable arch and a big toe aligned next to the second toe. These features are present in *Homo habilis* but not in *Australopithecus*.

Long legs first appeared unequivocally 1.8 million years ago in *Homo habilis*. Long legs increase the stride length and reduce the time that the foot is in contact with the ground when running. But long legs increase the energy cost of running. Reducing the weight of the foot relative to the weight of the leg saves energy and is apparent in humans compared to chimpanzees.

Running exposes the joints to greater loading stresses when landing. This is reduced by pliable, spring-like legs, and by increasing the joint surfaces: humans have substantially larger joint surface areas than do chimpanzees or did *Australopithecus africanus*.

When running, the body is less stable and pitches slightly forward. This requires additional muscular stabilization including well-developed back muscles, the action of the uniquely human gluteus maximus muscle, and the necessary brain controls to maintain balance and prevent falling.

There is also the need to maintain balance when one leg is off the ground as occurs in running but not during walking. This is achieved by swinging the opposite arm independently of the pectoral girdle while keeping the head still. This movement also allows throwing and hitting to occur.

Daniel Lieberman and his colleagues (2006) have performed the first modern review of the role of the gluteus maximus in human evolution. They suggest that there are three possible reasons for the unique development of this muscle in humans: Either it evolved to assist climbing in early hominids; or to control flexion of the trunk when performing foraging activities such as digging, throwing or clubbing; or else to support long distance running. By measuring the electrical activity in gluteus maximus during running and walking, they were able to show that the gluteus maximus muscle is considerably more active when running than when walking on a flat surface and that two important functions of the muscle appear to be the control of trunk flexion when the foot is on the ground and to decelerate the leg swinging forward prior to heel strike. The fossil evidence suggests that the gluteus maximus muscle had not yet achieved the fully developed human form in *Australopithecus*. They conclude that the expansion of the gluteus maximus muscle in humans would have benefitted all activities requiring trunk stabilization. An obvious such activity is long distance running.

On the basis of this anatomical evidence, Bramble and Lieberman conclude that running directed the biological evolution of *Homo* but not of *Australopithecus*, who lacked the skeletal evidence that they were runners. *Homo habilis* must have been adapted for running and not walking since many of the adaptations present in *Homo habilis* are specific to running and not walking. In particular, the springing motion of running is not required for the pendular movements of walking. Hence lower limb springs in leg and foot; large gluteus maximus muscle and extensor spine muscles, both of which stabilize the trunk in running but not in walking; narrow elongated waist combined with a low, wide, decoupled shoulder girdle that has an essential stabilizing function only in running. Then eating a high-energy diet that developed the brain.

There is clear evidence that running fashioned human evolution, giving us specialized ankles and lower limbs, long legs, thin waist, and shoulders able to move independently of the pelvis. But was this just to allow us to scavenge over long distances? Or did humans develop as cursorial hunters, that is hunters that chase down their prey as do wild dogs for example?

CONCLUSION

The biological record appears to give a consistent answer. Humans evolved as long distance runners especially well adapted to running in the heat because of a superior thermoregulatory capacity. The most likely explanation was that this ability developed to allow the persistence hunting of other mammals with a lesser ability to thermoregulate during prolonged exercise in the heat.

If this is indeed so, it means that many modern concepts of how humans should conduct themselves during exercise are wrong. These include the theory that humans should drink enough during exercise to insure that they do not lose any weight and that they need also to ingest sodium during exercise.

In fact, the human has evolved as a delayed drinker with an inordinate ability to exercise without impairment, despite the development of high levels of dehydration (Sharwood et al. 2002; Sharwood et al. 2004). In addition, humans are able to live on a very low sodium diet (Conn 1962; Conn and Johnston 1944) because of the intense sodium-conserving mechanisms that developed in the course of our evolution as hot weather runners living in an arid, salt-free environment.

BIBLIOGRAPHY

Aiello, L. C. and P. Wheeler. "The Expensive-Tissue Hypothesis: The Brain and the Digestive System in Human and Primate Evolution." *Current Anthropology* 36 (1995): 199–221.

Alexander, R. M. "Energy-Saving Mechanisms in Walking and Running." *Journal of Experimental Biology* 160 (1991): 55–69.

American College of Sports Medicine. "Position Stand: Heat and Cold Illnesses During Distance Running." *Medicine and Science in Sport and Exercise* 28 (1996): i–x.

Brace, D. L. and M. F. A. Montagu. *Man's Evolution*. New York: Macmillan, 1965.

Bramble, D. M. and D. E. Lieberman. "Endurance Running and the Evolution of Homo." *Nature* 432 (2004): 345–52.

Carrier, D. R. "The Energetic Paradox of Human Running and Hominid Evolution." *Current Anthropology* 25 (1984): 483–95.

Conn, J. W. "Some Clinical and Climatological Aspects of Aldosteronism in Man." *Transactions of the American Clinical and Climatological Association* 74 (1962): 61–91.

Conn, J. W. and M. W. Johnston. "The Function of the Sweat Glands in the Economy of NaCl Under Conditions of Hard Work in a Tropical Climate." *Journal of Clinical Investigations* 23 (1944): 933.

Conniff, R. "Yes, You Were Born to Run." *Men's Health*, 1–2. 2008. www.menshealth. com/run/yes-you-were-born-to-run.php (accessed July 12, 2010).

Dart, R. "The Predatory Transition from Ape to Man." *International Anthropological Linguist Review* 1 (1953): 201–19.

Dart, R. A. "Australopithecus Africanus: The Man-Ape of South Africa." *Nature* 2884 (1925): 195–99.

——. *Adventures with the Missing Link*. London: Hamish Hamilton Ltd., 1959.

Darwin, C. and A. R. Wallace. "On the Tendency of Species to Form Varieties; and on the Perpetuation of Varieties and Species by Natural Means of Selection." *Journal of the Linnean Society of London* (Zoology) 3 (1858): 45–62.

Dawson, T. J., D. Robertshaw, and C. R. Taylor. "Sweating in the Kangaroo: A Cooling Mechanism During Exercise, but not in the Heat." *American Journal of Physiology* 227 (1974): 494–98.

Diamond, J. "Evolutionary Design of Intestinal Nutrient Absorption Enough but not too Much." *News in Physiological Science* 6 (1991): 92–96.

Dill, D. B., A. V. Bock, and H. T. Edwards. "Mechanisms for Dissipating Heat in Man and Dog." *TBA* (1932): 36–43.

Finch, V. A. "Thermoregulation and Heat Balance of the East African Eland and Hartebeest." *American Journal of Physiology* 222 (1972): 1374–79.

Folk, G. E. *Introduction to Environmental Physiology*. London: Henry Kimpton, 1966.

Fowkes Godek, S., A. R. Bartolozzi, and J. J. Godek. "Sweat Rate and Fluid Turnover in American Football Players Compared with Runners in a Hot and Humid Environment." *British Journal of Sports Medicine* 39 (2005): 205–11.

Greenleaf, J. E. and F. Sargent. "Voluntary Dehydration in Man." *Journal of Applied Physiology* 20 (1965): 719–24.

Guy, F., D. E. Lieberman, D. Pilbeam, M. P. de Leon, A. Likius, H. T. Mackaye, P. Vignaud, C. Zollikofer, and M. Brunet. "Morphological Affinities of the Sahelanthropus tchadensis (Late Miocene Hominid from Chad) Cranium." *Proceedings of the National Academy of Science* 102 (2005): 18836–41.

Hanna, J. M. and D. E. Brown. "Human Heat Tolerance: An Anthropological Perspective." *Annual Review of Anthropology* 12 (1983): 259–84.

Hart, D. and R. W. Sussman. *Man the Hunted*. Boulder, Colo.: Westview Press, 2005.

Hoyt, D. F. and C. R. Taylor. "Letter to the Editor: Gait and Energetics of Locomotion in Horses." *Nature* 292 (1981): 239–40.

Johnson, G. S. and R. S. Elizondo. "Thermoregulation in *Macaca mulatta*: A Thermal Balance Study." *Journal of Applied Physiology* 46 (1979): 268–77.

Jouffroy, F. K. and M. F. Médina. "A Hallmark of Humankind: The Gluteus Maximus Muscle: Its Form, Action and Function." *Human Origins and Environmental Backgrounds*, edited by H. Ishida. New York: Springer, 2007: 135–48.

Krantz, G. S. "Brain Size and Hunting Ability in Earliest Man." *Current Anthropology* 9 (1968): 450–51.

Lee, R. B. and I. DeVore. *Man the Hunter*. New York: Aldine de Gruyter, 1968.

Liebenberg, L. *The Art of Tracking: The Origin of Science*. Claremont, South Africa: David Philip Publishers (Pty.) Ltd., 1990.

———. "Persistence Hunting by Modern Hunter-Gatherers." *Current Anthropology* 47 (2006): 1017–25.

Lieberman, D. E. and D. M. Bramble. "The Evolution of Marathon Running: Capabilities in Humans." *Sports Medicine* 37 (2007): 288–90.

Lieberman, D. E., D. A. Raichlen, H. Pontzer, D. M. Bramble, and E. Cutright-Smith. "The Human Gluteus Maximus and its Role in Running." *Journal of Experimental Biology* 209 (2006): 2143–55.

McConaghy, F. F., J. R. Hales, R. J. Rose, and D. R. Hodgson. "Selective Brain Cooling in the Horse During Exercise and Environmental Heat Stress." *Journal of Applied Physiology* 79 (1995): 1849–54.

Morris, C. *Man and His Ancestor*. New York: Macmillan and Co., 1900.

Newman, R. W. "Why Man is Such a Sweaty and Thirsty Naked Animal: A Speculative Review." *Human Biology* 42 (1970): 12–27.

Nielsen, B., J. R. Hales, S. Strange, N. J. Christensen, J. Warberg, and B. Saltin. "Human Circulatory and Thermoregulatory Adaptations with Heat Acclimation and Exercise in a Hot, Dry Environment." *Journal of Physiology* 460 (1993): 467–85.

Nummela, A. T., K. A. Heath, L. M. Paavolainen, M. I. Lambert, G. A. St Clair, H. K. Rusko, and T. D. Noakes. "Fatigue During a 5-km Running Time Trial." *International Journal of Sports Medicine* 29, no. 4 (2008): 738–45.

Nummela, A. T., L. M. Paavolainen, K. A. Sharwood, M. I. Lambert, T. D. Noakes, and H. K. Rusko. "Neuromuscular Factors Determining 5 km Running Performance and Running Economy in Well-trained Athletes." *European Journal of Applied Physiology* 97 (2006): 1–8.

Peters, C. R. and J. C. Vogel. "Africa's Wild C4 Plant Foods and Possible Early Hominid Diets." *Journal of Human Evolution* 48 (2005): 219–36.

Read, C. *The Origin of Man of His Superstitions*. Cambridge: University Press, 1925.

Robertshaw, D. "Mechanisms for the Control of Respiratory Evaporative Heat Loss in Panting Animals." *Journal of Applied Physiology* 101 (2006): 664–68.

Rothstein, A., E. F. Adolph, and J. H. Wills. "Voluntary Dehydration." *Physiology of Man in the Desert*, edited by E. F. Adolph. New York: Interscience Publishers, 1947: 254–70.

Saunders, A. G., J. P. Dugas, R. Tucker, M. I. Lambert, and T. D. Noakes. "The Effects of Different Air Velocities on Heat Storage and Body Temperature in Humans Cycling in a Hot, Humid Environment." *Acta Physiologica Scandinavica* 183 (2005): 241–55.

Schmidt-Nielsen, K. "The Physiology of the Camel." *Scientific American* 201 (1959): 140–51.

———. *Desert Animals*. London: Oxford University Press, 1964.

Sharwood, K., M. Collins, J. Goedecke, G. Wilson, and T. D. Noakes. "Weight Changes, Sodium Levels, and Performance in the South African Ironman Triathlon." *Clinical Journal of Sports Medicine* 12 (2002): 391–99.

———. "Weight Changes, Medical Complications, and Performance During an Ironman Triathlon." *British Journal of Sports Medicine* 38 (2004): 718–24.

Sponheimer, M. and J. A. Lee-Thorp. "Isotopic Evidence for the Diet of an Early Hominid, Australopithecus africanus." *Science* 283 (1999): 368–70.

Sponheimer, M., J. Lee-Thorp, D. de Ruiter, D. Codron, J. Codron, A. T. Baugh, and F. Thackeray. "Hominins, Sedges, and Termites: New Carbon Isotope Data from the Sterkfontein Valley and Kruger National Park." *Journal of Human Evolution* 48 (2005): 301–12.

Stern Jr., J. T. "Anatomical and Functional Specializations of the Human Gluteus Maximus." *American Journal of Physical Anthropology* 36 (1972): 315–39.

Stuempfle, K. J., D. R. Lehmann, H. S. Case, S. L. Hughes, and D. Evans. "Change in Serum Sodium Concentration During a Cold Weather Ultradistance Race." *Clinical Journal of Sport Medicine* 13 (2003): 171–75.

Taylor, C. R. "The Eland and the Oryx." *Scientific American* 220 (1969): 88–95.

Taylor, C. R. and C. P. Lyman. "Heat Storage in Running Antelopes: Independence of Brain and Body Temperatures." *American Journal of Physiology* 222 (1972): 114–17.

Taylor, C. R. and V. J. Rowntree. "Temperature Regulation and Heat Balance in Running Cheetahs: A Strategy for Sprinters?" *American Journal of Physiology* 224 (1973): 848–51.

Taylor, C. R., K. Schmidt-Nielsen, R. Dmi'el, and M. Fedak. "Effect of Hyperthermia on Heat Balance During Running in the African Hunting Dog." *American Journal of Physiology* 220 (1971): 823–27.

Tobias, P. V. "Ten Climacteric Events in Hominid Evolution." *South African Journal of Science* 81 (1985): 271–72.

Tucker, R., T. Marle, E. V. Lambert, and T. D. Noakes. "The Rate of Heat Storage Mediates an Anticipatory Reduction in Exercise Intensity During Cycling at a Fixed Rating of Perceived Exertion." *Journal of Physiology* 574 (2006): 905–15.

Tucker, R., L. Rauch, Y. X. Harley, T. D. Noakes. "Impaired Exercise Performance in the Heat is Associated with an Anticipatory Reduction in Skeletal Muscle Recruitment." *Pflugers Archiv* 448 (2004): 422–30.

Washburn, S. L. and C. S. Lancaster. "The Evolution of Hunting." *Hunting and Human Evolution*, edited by R. B. Lee and I. DeVore. New York: Aldine de Gruyter, 1968: 293–303.

Watkins, R. G., S. Dennis, W. H. Dillin, B. Schnebel, G. Schneiderman, F. Jobe, H. Farfan, J. Perry, and M. Pink. "Dynamic EMG Analysis of Torque Transfer in Professional Baseball Pitchers." *Spine* 14 (1989): 404–8.

Wheeler, P. "The Evolution of Bipedality and Loss of Functional Body Hair in Hominids." *Journal of Human Evolution* 13 (1984): 91–98.

———. "The Loss of Functional Body Hair in Man: The Influence of Thermal Environment, Body Form and Bipedality." *Journal of Human Evolution* 14 (1985): 23–28.

———. "Stand Tall and Stay Cool." *New Scientist* (May 12, 1988): 62–65.

———. "The Influence of Bipedalism on the Energy and Water Budgets of Early Hominids." *Journal of Human Evolution* 21 (1991a): 117–36.

———. "The Thermoregulatory Advantages of Hominid Bipedalism in Open Equatorial Environments: The Contribution of Increased Convective Heat Loss and Cutaneous Evaporative Cooling." *Journal of Human Evolution* 21 (1991b): 107–15.

———. "The Influence of the Loss of Functional Body Hair on the Water Budgets of Early Hominids." *Journal of Human Evolution* 23 (1992a): 379–88.

————. "The Thermoregulatory Advantages of Large Body Size for Hominids Foraging in Savannah Environments." *Journal of Human Evolution* 23 (1992b): 351–62.

————. "The Influence of Stature and Body Form on Hominid Energy and Water Budgets; A Comparison of Australopithecus and Early Homo Physiques." *Journal of Human Evolution* 24 (1993): 13–28.

White, M. D. "Components and Mechanisms of Thermal Hyperpnea." *Journal of Applied Physiology* 101 (2006): 655–63.

Wyndham, C. H. "The Physiology of Exercise Under Heat Stress." *Annual Review of Physiology* 35 (1973): 193–220.

6

Homo cursor: Running into the Pleistocene

Robert R. Sands

The adage "you have to be able to walk before you run" can easily be applied to the evolution of human movement patterns. The role of movement in human evolution has centered, until recently, on the development of bipedalism, which over time has become the defining and signature attribute distinguishing what is and what is not a hominin. In fact, the first hominins are routinely characterized as "bipedal apes" (Johanson and Edey 1981, Lovejoy 1981). Significant fossil discoveries in the last four decades, starting with *Australopithecus afarensis*, have become associated with movement and have become benchmarks in pushing the dates of appearance of bipeds further back in time.

There are several theories on the origins of bipedalism that feature as a significant variable the changing East African Pliocene paleoenvironment; starting with the iconic "savanna" theory, as well as theories that center around behavioral and resultant anatomical adaptations to feeding, reproduction, thermoregulation, locomotion across an increasingly terrestrial and arid landscape. Lovejoy (1981) and others distinguish early hominins as functional bipeds anatomically built for upright, bipedal locomotion. Current research indicates the origins of bipedalism to date back to the early Pliocene and to be consistent with a more mosaic environment featuring a range of habitats from savanna to woodland or gallery forests. It is certain that movement patterns as an adaptation to a changing environment was crucial in and sustaining the evolution of early hominids.

Recent speculation on the evolution of human running also features similar relationships between the environment and adaptive behavior with changes in anatomy and the emergence of a "functional" runner. Research has progressed in a variety of areas, which, not surprisingly, are similar to those in reconstructing bipedalism: thermoregulation, subsistence (to include scavenging and hunting), and bioenergetics. As in the development of bipedalism, the development of running is suggested to have had far-reaching impacts on the lifeways of hominins, to include subsistence (e.g., hunting). This chapter will inventory research that has been accomplished to date regarding the development of running in human evolution. It will be suggested that running as a movement pattern would have had been featured in many facets of hominin lifeways such as subsistence, play, transport, communication, even the development of spirituality, and thus running would have been *culturally* selected as an important movement pattern in addition to the selection pressures for running in response to a changing paleoenvironment. In essence, the importance of running in human evolution can be reflected in the designation for humans as *Homo cursor*: "*man the runner*."

FROM BIPED TO STRIDER

Biomechanics and the Cost of Running

The significance of endurance running in hominin evolution has recently been explored (Bramble and Lieberman 2004, Liebenberg 2006, Lieberman et al. 2006, Lieberman and Bramble 2007, Steudal-Numbers et al. 2007, Sands and Sands 2009). The position advanced by Bramble and Lieberman (2004), following Carrier (1984) and Heinrich (2001), is that humans are uniquely adapted for long distance running, in addition to bipedal striding, and there are unique skeletal and significant physiological features that can be traced to fossil remains of *Homo*. Long distance running, referred to as endurance running (ER) by Lieberman and Bramble, is defined as "running many kilometers over extended time periods using aerobic metabolism" (Lieberman and Bramble 2004: 1). The focus on distances and extended time periods is an important distinction as gait (or speed) and the ability to sustain this gait over time can be translated into an optimal energetic efficiency and energetic cost to the individual. Lieberman and Bramble (2004) suggest that endurance running is a derived feature of the genus *Homo* and speculate that it originated around two million years ago, although the suggestion in this paper is that running became anatomically reflected in *Homo erectus*.

Energetics

The biomechanical foundation for ER rests on a bipedal structure and features developed or advanced by bipeds would have been essential for developing ER. Carrier's (1984) research looked at the paradox of the high energy costs of running and outlined potential reasons for an adaptation for such a behavior, "energetically inefficient transport and endurance running would seem to be incompatible" (1984: 483). To Carrier, humans excel among cursorial mammals in long distance running, yet there were certain physiological and morphological obstacles presented by ER that needed to be solved as the paradox of energy and transport played out in human evolution. Obstacles that seem to have been overcome include dissipation of metabolic heat incurred by such a high energy sustained movement activity; the actual cost of transport incurred when running versus walking; and storage and utilization of energy (Carrier 1984). Humans have the most advanced evaporative (surface) thermoregulation system of all mammals, aided by loss of body hair and an upright posture developed in response to the earlier evolution of bipedalism (Wheeler 1993). Humans expend over twice the amount of energy than other similarly sized mammals that seem to be adept at running long distances, but savings are incurred when frequency of gait (speed) is factored in—humans seem to be able to optimize and balance out energy costs for differential speeds of transport. Bipedal walking in humans is at least economical, or more so than other walking mammalian quadrupeds based on a four million year refinement of storing and recovering energy in each motion within each stride—"energy savings due to transfer between potential and kinetic energy are substantial" (Carrier 1984: 485). When gait increases (frequency of stride and stride length) in non-human mammals with regard to walking and running, there seems to be muscular and contractile limits assigned to optimal gait increases. In other words, in energetic cost and biomechanical constraints, mammals such as horses are dialed into almost pre-selected windows or gears of optimal speeds and seem to only exhibit these "preferred" speeds, deviating rarely for any sustained speeds outside these "gears." Human locomotion speeds are not tied exclusively to these gears. Carrier hypothesizes that upright, bipedal posture overcomes the mammalian restriction of one breath per stride due to shock of impact on forelimbs of quadrupeds. Thus, humans can employ a larger number of breathing patterns (one, two or three breaths per stride), allowing a greater flexibility in stride frequency. In addition, meeting the running mammal's need for oxygen is tied to the structure of the compartment where the lungs sit.

Increasing running speed requires greater amounts of oxygen and mammalian anatomy can allow only a certain volume of ventilation efficiency. Stride length and frequency, matching metabolic demand for oxygen via lung ventilation, matching breath frequency and volume, and synchronizing breathing with locomotor movement, all combine to create a gait that is energetically optimal for breathing. Outside of this gait, the energetic cost of running increases while efficiency decreases. In humans, speed is variable with motion and the range of speed is tied to one basic energy cost. This presents humans with a disadvantage of maintaining a higher cost of running, but with adaptations in physiology for thermoregulation and energy consumption, and consistent costs, the advantage of variable speeds could prove to be beneficial to human runners, especially when running after prey.

Anatomy of Running

Bramble and Lieberman (2004) and Lieberman and colleagues (2006) extend Carrier's treatise in terms of biomechanics, while agreeing with Carrier's assessment of the more efficient thermoregulatory system in human runners. They advanced a running legacy visible in living humans: maintaining skull and upper body stability while running; the enhanced and advanced arrangements of the gluteus muscles, especially gluteus maximus, to aid in a running gait; a larger body size and a longer hind limb; an increase and complexity of tendons in and around the ankle and foot to act as absorbers and springs; and as discussed earlier, a more efficient thermoregulatory or sweat system. Areas such as the longer limb lengths have been proposed to confer greater running efficiency and hence lower energetic cost in not only individuals but species as well.

Further delineation includes:

- the development or appearance of a nuchal ligament that aids in keeping the head steady while running (a trademark of all great animal runners), and associated nuchal crest on the inside of the skull (Bramble and Lieberman 2004). Bramble and Lieberman also highlight mechanisms to aid in stabilization and balance, such as expanded areas on the sacrum and iliac spine for muscle attachment allowing for counterbalancing rotations within the trunk;
- well-developed gluteus muscles, especially gluteus maximus and its wrapped around forward placement that acts to brake the forward lean of the body during running and balance the center of gravity—the quadrupedal great runners have a tail, in effect so do humans (Bramble and Lierberman 2004, Lieberman et al. 2006). Following kinematic analysis on effects of running on the gluteus maximus Lieberman and colleagues found that the muscle has reorganized in humans as compared to non-human primates and that, plus the enlargement of the muscle, improves running performance and has little influence on increased performance in bipedal walking. The gluteus muscle is in fact "quiescent in . . . level and uphill walking" (Lieberman et al. 2006: 2152) but is actively engaged during running. Other results indicate gluteal activity is similar in running and vertical climbing, suggesting a potential explanation for the "derived configuration of human GM (gluteus muscle) anatomy in terms of the reorganization of the human pelvis for bipedalism" (Lieberman et al. 2006: 2152);
- the array of tendons found in and around the arch and foot—especially the Achilles tendon)—the ankle and lower limb bones that act both as springs for absorbing the stress of impact as well as storing and releasing kinetic energy necessary for the gait (Bramble and Lieberman 2004);
- a longer hindlimb in relation to stride coverage and energetic cost. The rationale used by several paleoanthropologists, according to Stuedal-Numbers and colleagues (2007) is that energetic efficiency is gained by increasing stride length utilizing the increase in lower limb length. Pontzer (2005) and Liebenberg (2006), following the Sokhol and colleagues (2006) study on the lower energetic cost of bipedal walking, suggest that a longer hindlimb confers greater energetic efficiency in running. Steudal-Numbers and Tilkens (2004) posited the increasing lower limb lengths in hominid evolution

would track to greater locomotion efficiency, not specific to running. A later study by Steudal-Numbers and colleagues (2006) involving running and lower limb length found that relatively longer hind limbs generated lower locomotor costs than those with shorter hindlimbs, similar to costs associated with bipedal walking, yet a "linear relationship between stride length and lower limb length was not found" (Steudal-Numbers et al. 2007: 191). In other words, the locomotor efficiency, the authors suggest, is more along the lines of what one would expect to find in bipedal walking—hence a hypothesis that posits a lower limb length selected by the evolution of running is not supported by their initial findings;

- increased body size, Carrier (1984); and
- a well-developed thermoregulatory system of sweat glands. Carrier advanced the theory that a loss of body hair and the advanced performance of heat dissipation through the hyper development of the human sweat glands (humans secrete the highest amount of sweat per surface area of all cursorial mammals). Liebenberg (2006) allows for a higher level of performance activity in the heat of the day based on a higher thermal conductance. Wheeler (1991) advanced the hypothesis of erect posture, larger body size, and increased heat dissipation was the genesis for the evolution of bipedalism. Bramble and Lieberman (2004), Liebenberg (2006), and Lieberman and Bramble (2007) all cite the human propensity for sweating as a unique feature to hominids, and one advantageous to endurance running.

Runner's High: The Neurobiology of Running

Until recently, there have been few studies reconstructing the paleoneurology of running. Long distance differs from sprinting, and as such, long distance running incorporates different neurobiological pathways. As any distance runner is intimately aware, there are high amounts of stress and pain associated with prolonged aerobic physical exercise. In sprinting, anaerobic movement produces a shutdown of the body, due to lactic acid buildup in muscles. In distance running, due to our evolution of associated anatomical systems and depending on pace (discussed above), muscle fatigue leading to body shutdown can be delayed hours, even days. Obviating and/or minimizing pain and stress, however, would be critical to running performance in duration and distance. The suggestion here is that the popular conception of euphoric sensations experienced during running is actually a legacy of a Paleolithic runner's high seen in the neurobiological reward system that evolved in distance running in Pliocene-Pleistocene *Homo* and developed as a means to minimize pain and stress (Sands and Sands 2009).

Evidence of a running in *Homo* can also be inferred from recent work in neurobiology, specifically centering on the neural reward system of mammals. In humans, prolonged periods of running generate an elevation or enhancement of neurobiologically based rewards (runner's high). Endogenous neurochemicals, in the form of pain-inhibiting endorphins and other neurotransmitters, are released during rhythmic and repetitive activities that occur longer than forty-five minutes (Dietrich 2004), such as long distance running. The neurotransmitter dopamine is responsible for regulating the motivational aspect of the reward system by stimulating certain brain regions and providing pleasurable effects. Other neurotransmitters, such as serotonin and endogenous opioids and endocannibinoids, are also involved in this complex reward system by regulating dopamine release and reuptake, promoting a cumulative effect on the dopamine reward pathway. Endorphins contribute to the overall reward system by partnering with an array of pleasure-inducing neurotransmitters by blocking pain and producing euphoria and other related experiences such as transcendence.

Modulation of the reward system during endurance running represents an evolutionary strategy to ensure that running was maintained as a critical behavior to *Homo* lifeways (a collective suite of behaviors), just as the perception of pleasure is tied to play, eating and sexual activity. As evolution is so adept at doing, running would have hijacked the existing neural hardware and associated releases and engineered the development of a Paleolithic runner's high.

A plethora of anecdotal and personal narratives, and even some scholarly work, suggest that ultra running or even a prolonged period of running in a workout, generates a "runner's high"—"euphoric sensation experienced during running, usually unexpected, in which the runner feels a heightened sense of well-being, enhanced appreciation of nature, and transcendence of barriers of time and space" (Pargman et al. as cited in Dietrich and McDaniel 2004: 3), and in more than a few runners, equates into what many would call spiritual feelings and even altered states (Dietrich and McDaniel 2004, Colmant 2005, Dietrich 2003, Jones 2006, Cooper 2004, Ackerman 2000, Battista 2004). For obvious reasons, due to the private and ephemeral nature of not only defining a runner's high, but also constructing reasonable and testable experimentation, research on this subject has been less than rigorous and highly subjective.

A long-held view of "runner's high" was based on the "endorphin hypothesis," a direct consequence of alterations in endogenous opioid release due to induced exercise. Candau and colleagues in Jones (2006) and James and Doust (2000) characterize the high as primarily the result of "the release of endorphins, the first stage of activation of the sympathetic nervous system and adrenal glands." Endorphins respond to episodes of stress or pain and are generated in the pituitary gland. Upon release, endorphins bind to specific neural receptor sites (also the sites that exogenous opioids such as morphine bind) thereby blocking the release of neurotransmitters sending pain signals to the brain. There seems to be a time delay (perhaps as much as thirty minutes or more, depending on context, location, reason for exercise and perhaps goal attainment) in endorphin release (Dietrich and McDaniel 2004), which in recent studies, has been related to blood pressure. This association of exercise with endorphin release has been suggested to produce feelings other than pain reduction, which includes feelings of euphoria and transcendence. This view replaced the commonly held perspective that exercise activated analgesic and euphoric mental states brought on by alterations in adrenaline (epinephrine) and noradrenalin (norepinephrine).

Extreme athletic activity, such as rock climbing and ultra distance trail running has shaped a popular perception that ties prolonged intense activity to psychological states of calm, transcendence, and heightened awareness. Publications such as Battista's (2004) *The Runner's High: Illumination and Ecstasy in Motion*, a popular "ethnographic" collection of runners' tales of their experience with the high, Diane Ackerman's (2000) *Deep Play*, and Andrew Cooper's (2004) *Playing in the Zone* create and reinforce a public construction of this emotive state.

Recent work has indicated that perhaps the endorphin hypothesis may not account for all biochemical inconsistencies "between the endorphin hypothesis and the physiological and biomechanical responses to endurance exercise" (Dietrich and McDaniel 2004: 2). Dietrich points out that prominent endorphin researchers have found fault with the hypothesis as being too simplistic, not supportable and built on a myth perpetrated by popular culture. Huda Akil, the president-elect of the Society for Neuroscience said to a *New York Times* reporter, "This endorphin-in-runners is a total fantasy in the pop culture" (Kotler 2006: 209).

Extreme states of activity and/or stress—which more than few would classify endurance running into that category of activity—releases endorphins, but also has been found to flood the brain with mood-enhancing and performance-enhancing serotonin and dopamine. Recent studies on mammals such as mice, rats, horses, non-human primates and humans, have greatly increased our knowledge of the reward pathway and the inter-species genetic variability that results in varying levels of individual reward experiences. This large body of work can be extrapolated to show the interaction between nuerochemicals in the reward pathway and the potential addictive properties of human running.

Research on Fisher and Lewis rats (Werme et al. 1999) has shed light on not only the reward system, but also the varying levels of reward experience. Lewis rats are both addictive-prone and chronic runners. In lab tests, Lewis rats ran markedly longer when having free access to running wheels, engaging the same neural monoamine pathways in the brain as those engaged by morphine, cocaine, amphetamine, and so forth; in effect, by running, the Lewis rat activated the same neurological circuits as those activated by drugs of abuse. The authors posit chronic running and addictive drugs increase endorphins and "modulates turnover" of central brain monoamines (where dopamine is suggested to be the mediator of central reward mechanism) resulting in less aggressive behavior and less "hyperexplorative" behavior when allowed to run. Forced withdrawal from running in Lewis rats leads to aggressive behavior that is similar to forced withdrawal from addictive drugs (Kanarek et al. 1998, Mathes and Kanarek 2006).

When looking at pain minimization in running, even low intensity exercise has been found to activate the opioid system (Li et al. 2004, Bement and Sluka 2005), but with slightly different effects. Interestingly, when horses were put through their paces on a treadmill, an additional source of opioid peptides were released into the circulatory system from the exercise-induced lysis of red blood cells during high intensity running, but not low intensity running (Collinder et al. 2005). Over time, as exercise increases in intensity, the number of opioid receptors on a cell's surface are reduced, therefore more running (hence activation) is needed to produce the same reward (Smith and Yancey 2003). Work by Koltyn and Umeda (2006) indicates that activation of the endogenous opioid system occurs when blood pressure is elevated during extended physical exercise, which in turn decreases the perception of pain.

Dietrich and McDaniel, testing both endurance runners and bicyclists on treadmills and stationary exercise bikes, found an appreciable increase of anandamide, one of the endocannabinoids, in blood plasma taken from the subjects (2004: 2). Endocannibinoids are endogenous small fatty acids that seem to act as an analgesic as well as altering emotional and cognitive processes by mediating certain physiological responses to exercise (2004: 3). Basically, endocannibinoids moderate or reduce pain sensations for both the peripheral and central nervous systems and produce similar psychoactive effects to THC, a constituent of marijuana (THC binds to the same CB1 receptor as endocannibinoids). These effects include time distortion, enhanced euphoria, transcendence, reduced anxiety, and sensory perception, and for some "touching" the sacred and divine. There is additional evidence to suggest that anandamide mediates vasodilation and bronchodilation, which contribute to the body's response to exercise. Endocannibinoids along with their exogenous counterpart, THC, further regulate the dopamine system by inhibiting the effects of GABA and glutamic acid, thereby enhancing dopamine expression (Gardner 2005). More recent work by Raichlen and colleagues (2008) seems to corroborate the importance of endocannibinoids in the neural pathways engaged during running. He has done preliminary studies on mice bred to run and found elevated amounts of endocannibinoids in the runners versus nonrunning mice after exercise.

In summary, dopamine is responsible for regulating the motivational aspect of the reward system (Rhodes et al. 2005). Dopamine neurons extending through the ventral tegmental area, nucleus accumbens, and the medial forebrain bundle form the core of this reward pathway. When it comes to the reward (and motivation) system, dopamine stimulates certain brain regions, providing pleasurable effects. Other neurotransmitters such as serotonin, GABA, glutamic acid, and the endogenous opioids (Kelly and Berridge 2002) are also involved in this complex reward system by regulating dopamine release and act to promote a cumulative effect on the dopamine reward pathway.

In all this research, what can be agreed upon is that a few or several endogenous neurochemicals, in the form of pain inhibiting endorphins, and a number of other neurotransmitters are released during rhythmic and repetitive activities such as long distance running. These same neurochemicals play an important role in play engagement and high stress situations and have been documented to produce psychological and physiological states in rats, mice, other mammals, humans, and non-human primates that benefit performance, either by acting upon the reward system which enforces the desire to seek the activity to produce pleasure, euphoria, and so on, or allowing enhanced and/or extended performance. It may be the case that endorphins contribute to the overall reward system by partnering with an array of pleasure-inducing neurotransmitters such as serotonin, dopamine, or endocannibinoids, blocking pain so the effects of dopamine, serotonin, and endocannibinoids that produce euphoria, transcendence, or pleasure are more apparent.

Integration of the pain and reward system with endurance running certainly would seem to represent an evolutionary strategy to ensure that running, as a critical behavior to *Homo* lifeways, was expressed. Perceptions of pleasure tied to eating and sexual activity also seem to follow that strategy (Rhodes et al. 2005, Wise 2002). As we further explore manifestations of behaviors, this theme of essential behavior modulated by simple pleasure or more intensive states of awareness will be revisited.

PALEOCLIMATE AND FOSSIL EVIDENCE OF ENDURANCE RUNNING IN *HOMO*

Climatic fluctuations in the late Pliocene and early Pleistocene, starting at three million years ago (mya), created a large degree of environmental variability (Potts 1998, Bobe and Behrensmeyer 2004, Stanford 2006, Stanford et al. 2008) or "climate deterioration" (Richerson and Boyd 1998). Glacial cycles became more severe around 2.5 mya, causing many environmental changes, which included lowering the sea level, allowing land connections between mainland Asia and the islands of Southeast Asia. Stanford and colleagues (2008) suggest three periods of "climate instability," each coinciding with major periods of great variability in the fossil record. The first coincided with species diversity in the mammalian fossil record and occurred at the time of the emergence of *Homo*, the other two are linked to the first appearance of stone tools and then the extinction of australopithecines.

Just as an array of late Miocene apes produced the first hominids, the array of bipedal apes found in the Pliocene produced an early species of the genus *Homo* around 2.5 mya in the form of what many, not all, label as *Homo habilis*. Found in East Africa, *H. habilis* was distinguishable from the contemporary East and South African robust australopithecines/paranthropines and South African *A. africanus* by their larger brain (550–600 cc) and body size and the first indisputable evidence of stone tool making, characterized by the primitive Olduwan industry. *H. habilis* also seems to represent a mosaic of australopithecine and later *Homo* traits. Although there seems to be an increase in overall body size, there is a qualitative increase in cranial capacity beyond expected increase tied to body size increase. Postcranial *H. habilis* remains, however, indicate ape-like features, such as longer forelimbs, in relation to hind limbs, suggesting a non-human-like bipedal movement pattern and related anatomical structure.

Lieberman and colleagues (2006) suggest that australopithecines had an intermediate gluteal configuration between apes and human and that similarity between australopithecines and humans was more a result of the continued dependence on climbing as well as walking. Following Marzke and colleagues (1988), the configuration could have also been beneficial in foraging tasks, such as digging, that require trunk flexion, but the features associated with trunk flexion and rotation so necessary in running were minimally present. It does seem to be clear that australopithecines did not habitually run long distances and tree climbing played a major role in their locomotion.

Nariokotome Boy (KNM-WT 15000)

If we are to look for the first long distance runners, it seems as if the first clear and demonstrable evidence in terms of post-cranial anatomy and physiology is found in *Homo erectus*, as exemplified by the KNM-WT 15000 (The Nariokotome Boy) remarkably complete skeleton. Found by Alan Walker and Richard Leakey in the vicinity of Lake Turkana, the 1.6-million-year-old specimen is generally regarded to be from a twelve-year-old male. Given maturation development, the specimen represents a very robustly built population and that the adolescent male would have reached close to 6 feet in height, exhibiting a very long and linear build (Ruff and Walker 1993). The reconstructed paleoclimate offers a mosaic of features to include the seasonally active and variable floodplain fed by the Omo River (at times, with heavy rains in the Ethiopian highlands to the west, the river basin would have jumped the basin boundaries and flooded the floodplain to make a lake); seasonal shallow lakes or ponds and further shallow marshes would have filled in the topographically lower spots in the basin that would have existed in bordering regions; and due to the seasonal variability, a thin belt of riparian vegetation, including trees and thornbush, that would have provided a yearly supply of fresh water to local inhabitants. Much of the flood basin, however, would have been carpeted by grasslands with ample growth following the flood season, giving way to gradual browning through the remainder of the year.

Ruff and Walker's detailed reconstruction of WT-15000 reveals many of the running features discussed above. The male was tall, thin, possessing long limbs that are proportioned much like that of modern African tropical and savannah inhabitants, reaching 6'1" and 150 pounds when fully matured. Even though he would have been the largest hominid known if lived to maturity, he is not much larger than contemporaneous reconstructed *H. erectus* fossil individuals. The pelvic bones in reconstruction indicated a linear and narrow shape and, according to Ruff and Walker, testament to bipedal locomotion. The robustness of WT-15000 indicates a wider shoulder carriage, contrary to australopithecines and perhaps early *Homo*, indicating stability in the upper body was a possible counterforce to the running motion of the lower body.

Gruss and Schmidt (2004) analyzed the limbs of KNM-WT-15000 (the length of the lower limbs and distal limb elements) and although the body proportions have limb lengths approximate to living Nilotic Africans, 15000 lies at the extreme end even of this linear and gracile population. Through experimental modeling, Gruss and Schmidt suggest the extreme length of the distal limb bones—reflected in a cural index (tibia length relative to femur length)—in WT-15000 would lead to higher bending forces along the leg and knee. Modern humans with a similar crural index compensate for this bending by postural adaptations, such as stooping. Given the extreme nature of the limb proportions, the authors postulate that KNM-WT-15000 would have exhibited a modified locomotion pattern in comparison to modern humans to diffuse the stresses at the knee.

To Ruff and Walker, the dimensions of hind limbs and body size are a result of environment, "KNM-15000's tall, thin body and long limbs were adaptive for diurnal activity in a hot, relatively dry climate, in an environment that was probably more open than closed" (1993: 262). Further, the similarity to modern African tropical populations is not so much a phylogenetic relationship, but a "hypertropical" adaptation in terms of body proportions to thermoregulation principles. However, as discussed above, lower intralimb proportions and shape could have been under selection for increasing speed and cost-efficiency for locomotion, especially running.

Given the paleoenvironment and the dimensions, size, and linearity of KNM-WT-15000, the explanation that KNM-WT-15000's locomotion abilities reflect an already established and efficient running package is based on inferred human-like thermoregulation adaptation, to include longer lower limbs, shorter upper limbs and the unique cylindrical-shaped torso and trunk compared to hominids prior to *Homo* (Hilton and Meldrum 2004, McHenry and Coffing 2000, Richmond et al. 2002, Ruff and Walker 1993) and the ability to dissipate heat during intense physical activities in the ever-encroaching savannah (Hilton and Meldrum 2004, Aiello and Wheeler 1995, Ruff and Walker 1993, McHenry and Coffing 2000). These adaptations refined this running package in terms of the high inter- and intramembral indices. These indices "may both have acted to maximize the efficiency of bipedal walking, by increasing stride length and decreasing the energy required to swing the limb, respectively" (Gruss and Schmidt 2004: 119). Research by Steudal-Numbers and colleagues (2007) and Lieberman and colleagues (2006) does indicate continued energetic efficiency of running. Gruss and Schmidt's suggestion of a modified *H. erectus/ergaster* locomotion based on these indices poses the possibility that there may have been different biomechanical variations of running as there was walking in early *Homo* and that this trend of variation can be found in the extreme inverse intramembral indice (shorter tibia relative to femur) of later "hyperarctic" Neanderthals, which echo that of living populations of Lapps (Trinkaus 1981).

From a locomotion perspective, *H. habilis* in terms of morphology can be considered an extension of the more generalized australopithecine package, still with a legacy of arboreal and/or male-male aggression behaviors manifested in sexual dimorphism of forelimbs as well as a general higher intermembral index of forelimb to hind limb. Certainly a biped, yet without those features that have been highlighted to provide an endurance running platform. Whether *H. habilis* anatomy reflects a continued adaptation to a more mosaic environment or legacy features yet selected out is still unanswered, or perhaps an alternative yet advanced.

SCAVENGING AND HUNTING HYPOTHESES
FOR RUNNING SELECTION

Potential hypotheses advanced for selection of long distance running are centered on subsistence, most notably scavenging and hunting. Underlying both sets of hypotheses is the notion that one of the defining behaviors of the evolution of *Homo* was, among other things, the more consistent intake of animal-based food into their diet, either through the remnants (sinew, marrow, ligaments) of carcasses or through actual hunting of and consuming prey. Carrier (1984) first suggested running capability in hominids was due to the ability to run mammals into exhaustion. Heinrich (2001) further advanced this hypothesis adding that being "endurance predators" rather than the sprint champions of the savannah, such as cheetahs, requires having and maintaining a clear goal (vision to Heinrich) over extended periods of time, "to reach into the future" (2001: 164). However, Bramble and Lieberman argue that initially this type of subsistence strategy would have been "too energetically expensive and low-yield for the benefits to have outweighed the costs" (2004: 11–12) due to the lack of developed hunting tools, such as bows and arrows and spears, which would have minimized the effort in the chase. Instead, they posit that endurance running developed in early *Homo* as a means to effectively scavenge protein-rich carcasses in an increasing open and "semi-arid" late Pliocene East African environment. Successful scavenging requires the ability to cover distance to the kill when olfactory or visual cues, including the presence of avian scavengers, are identified.

PERSISTENCE HUNTING

Recently, Liebenberg (2006), based on two decades of ethnography of hunting in the Kalahari by the !Xo, among others, suggests that what he labels as "persistence hunting," to include running prey into exhaustion and thereby unable to escape killing, in the hottest part of the day, was, under certain conditions (and prior to the relatively recent domestication of dogs, 12,000–14,000 years ago, and the subsequent evolution of dogs as "working dogs" to include hunting aids [Case 2005: 10]), the most efficient form of hunting and therefore crucial in human evolution. Although hunting with

bows and arrows, spears and clubs, Liebenberg found under certain conditions (based on local traditional knowledge of the !Xo hunters of the ecology and the related biology of the prey), persistence hunting offered a more
reliable and effective method of hunting. He also discovered that all forms
of hunting were opportunistic and even fortuitous in nature and that strategy
was fluid and dynamic. A bow and arrow may initially engage a hunting
session, although Liebenberg discovered that even though this method generated many attempts, actual success rate was low due to missed targets, or
targets hit and then finished off by other predators before the hunters could
locate and kill it themselves. Locating and killing prey hiding or in sleeping
burrows was effective, but engaged a different kind of hunting technique.
However, it was when conditions presented good opportunity that persistence hunting was more successful and afforded a much higher margin of
error than other means.

Based on his ethnography and observations, Liebenberg advances
persistence hunting as a critical behavior in human evolution and that,
along with Bramble and Lieberman and Heinrich, posits that endurance
running was first selected for in scavenging by the earliest *Homo* and
that increased protein yield in the form of meat would have selected for
and refined running abilities in terms of speed and greater coverage of
landscapes. Increasingly over time, this movement pattern would have
"preadapted" the users for persistence hunting and as a greater yield
would have resulted from "getting there first" and even more beneficial, being the killer and the consumer, persistence hunting would have
developed.

Most recently, Bunn and Pickering (2007) and Lieberman and colleagues (2007) have exchanged replies that discuss the importance of
persistence hunting in the lower Pleistocene African environment. The
suggestion by Bunn and Pickering was that the paleoecology of East Africa 2 mya was not a savanna as much as it was a "savanna-woodlands"
ecosystem which possessed a "mix of open and closed components . . .
and tend to be more compacted than the loose sands found in deserts and
are certainly more obscured by groundcover than desert sands" (2007:
234–35). Thus, the mix of environments would have included "true mosaic" systems, riparian forests and wooded thickets, as well as open areas
of savanna. For activities such as scavenging and hunting that require
open space with little groundcover, persistence hunting would have been

difficult. In addition, Lieberberg's ethnographic analogy of Kalahari "persistence hunting" offers little evidence to advance that type of subsistence patterns to early Pleistocene *Homo.*

Carrier (2004) advances a hypothesis that endurance running in *Homo* was made possible by defying the trade-offs expected between specializations for a bipedal and, hence, further advanced running locomotion and specialization for fighting. Carrier's analysis of the australopithecine skeletal system, including sexual dimorphism in body and forelimb size, suggests male-male aggression was implicit in their behavior and adapting to a terrestrial habitat and a structural bipedal posture theoretically enhanced their fighting ability, but as well, through forelimb strength, short stature, wide hips, and so on, provided structural limits on their terrestrial locomotion, including running efficiency. Potentially, as a legacy from Miocene apes, the fighting ability in australopithecines promoted the switch to a terrestrial hominid.

In *Homo*, however, after only perhaps 500,000 years, we see a fully developed endurance runner, lacking the structural constraints found in australopithecines, but according to Carrier, still a hominid with behavioral legacy of *male-male* aggression. The development and enhancement of weapon systems, such as stone tools, not tied directly to the physiology of *Homo*, removed the anatomical necessity of maintaining an internally based weapon system. Following Carrier's theory, the scenario already advanced to explain endurance running would incorporate the combined environmental shift to more savanna and the development of weapons that could easily be used to facilitate scavenging and promote hunting.

Hart and Sussman (2005) argue differently; the legacy of hominin behavioral patterns were a result of human not as the hunter nor the fighter, but the human as the hunted. Fossil evidence suggests that early humans were much more vulnerable to predation than traditional anthropology dogma that casts the genus as the predator. Escape from predators on an increasingly open horizontal landscape selected for many adaptations that promoted survival from increased brain size and speech to human appreciation for scenic vistas as a legacy of watching for danger on a more open landscape. It would seem that the ability to locomote away from danger would have also been crucial to survival, and as the authors suggest, the adaptations were critical to allowing a very rapid evolution of human-like traits not seen in other primates and non-primate mammals.

PALEODIET

It seems as if there is some consensus that scavenging and then hunting were behaviors practiced by *Homo*. However, the role of animal protein in the evolution of *Homo* has been advanced to account for brain growth and the higher cost (energetics) of living on an expanding savanna.

Underlying these subsistence scenarios is the proposed need for early Pleistocene *Homo* to increase meat protein consumption. Much has been written on the increased intake of meat protein as a defining characteristic of *Homo*. In fact one could consider publications such as *Meat Eating and Human Evolution* (Stanford and Bunn 2001) and *Evolution of the Human Diet* (Ungar 2006) or individual articles such as *Meat Made Us Human* (Bunn 2006) as signatures of the *Meat First Movement* that stretches back to Raymond Dart. Authors suggest that meat was essential to "growing the brain," fueling a more active lifeways through adaptation to the horizontal landscape, developing the need for a reduced gut size, and creating a procurement pattern that has been identified in the opportunistic hunting behavior of extant primates. Certainly animal remains in the archaeological record are favorable to the suggestion of an increase of meat consumption in Pleistocene *Homo* over time, yet generally *erectus/ergaster* and contemporaneous lithic industries reflect gradual, if little technological advances till late in the middle Pleistocene.

One of the lynchpins of *Homo* evolution is the infatuation with the "need" of increased quantities of meat to fuel not only increased energetics, but as well to spur on brain growth (Milton 1999). The combined paleoanatomy and paleoenvironment of the Plio/Pleistocene suggests, due to a radical shift in the environment and vegetation, a scenario of marked change in subsistence behavior and the importance of increased protein and caloric intake in the diet derived from available resources. Many consider the inclusion of a markedly larger amount of meat in the diet of early *Homo* to be an important factor in adapting to the paleoecology. As discussed earlier, the strategies given create a scenario, more or less, involving a mix of scavenging and opportunistic hunting. There is no need to exclude opportunistic hunting, even hunting that involves a controlled and cooperative effort, from the early subsistence strategies employed by early *Homo*. As most mammals, and non-human primates, due to anatomy, physiology and ecology/environment, are poor endurance runners, *Homo* would have commandeered a unique spatially determined horizontal environmental niche.

PRIMATE HUNTERS

Chimpanzees have been well documented hunting colobus monkeys as a secondary and opportunistic supplement to their diet. Stanford (1998, 1999) documented chimpanzees hunting through 20 percent of the colobus monkey population at Gombe. Heinrich (2001) reported observing olive baboons corner a hare and dispatch it with "gusto." Systematic hunting and meat eating is not uncommon in primates. Baboons have been observed to catch flamingos and turtles (K. Lewis, personal communication September 28, 2008). Boesch (2005) indicates that chimpanzees in the wild also exhibit a coordinated effort in hunting involving multiple roles as *driver*, *blockers*, and *ambusher*, with hunting success increasing with the number involved. "During . . . a collaborative hunt, each hunter synchronizes and spatially coordinates his movements to those performed by others, and sometimes anticipates their future actions" (Boesch 2005: 692). It is not a stretch to extrapolate the carryover of these behaviors in early hominid evolution and certainly not a stretch to suggest an active, opportunistic, and, at times, predatory scavenging subsistence for early *Homo*, if not already established for australopithecines. In short, as the environment fragmented into first mosaic and later savannah-like conditions, meat, derived from kill remains or opportunistic or ad hoc coordinated hunting, became more readily available for inclusion into the hominin diet.

Boesch's commentary of chimpanzee hunting behavior certainly lends credence to including this strategy as well in the subsistence activities of early *Homo*. While the australopithicine diet, especially prior to the emergence of *Homo*, would have been similar to the omnivorous selections of chimpanzees—fruits, leaves, and more than occasional meat obtained through opportunistic hunting (Stanford et al. 2008)—it is possible that a generalist diet strategy would continue with the emergence of early *Homo*, inferring the greatest of flexibility as the climate provided a very uncertain and dynamic backdrop. Venturing onto a growing savanna would have given early *Homo* more access to scavenging opportunities.

However, we cannot ignore the absence or minimal amounts of meat in the diets of both the Kalenjin and the Tarahumara when it comes to inferring diet in *Homo*, especially the running *Homo erectus*. Even though both groups have been subsistence farmers for hundreds of years, as well as livestock herders, and the time or resources needed for hunting are reduced, meat still assumes a less important dietary focus. Running continues to be central to cultural existence. Intense physical activity requires certain nutritional needs which can be satisfied in any number of ways; it is problematic to narrow choices to specific resources, such as meat, to fulfill these needs. Studies of extant foraging groups, such as the !Kung (Marshall 1976, Shostack 1976, Draper 1997, Zilman 1997, Heinrich 2001) and Puma of Venezula (Hilton and Greaves 2004) reflect the importance of non-meat resources to the diet (and females for actively aiding in providing that resource, more below) and there is no reason not to infer that a similar pattern was maintained as *Homo* moved out on the savanna.

Milton (1999) suggests that, based on analysis of extant apes and humans, and constraints placed on early *Homo* due to the pattern of gut anatomy and digestive kinetics characteristics, inferred from ancestral *Hominoidea* and the environment and fostered by climate change, meat eating became a central part of the human lineage. Extant apes and humans seem to share similar gut anatomy and digestive kinetics, with some minor differences, even though all but humans share an herbivore gut and digestive system. In an elegant thesis, Milton identifies three hominoid evolutionary models based on diet: gut anatomy, body size, energy and sociability. One model is exemplified by extant *Pongo* and *Gorilla*, where increased body size and a lower dietary quality of food, mature foliage, bark and unripe fruit has led to a low metabolism and passive sociality. The second model is characteristic of *Pan* and to an extent *Hylobatidae*, where a high energy diet, consisting of mostly ripe fruit (and some instances of meat and other non-meat food stuffs) has supported a relatively large body size with a highly social and active lifestyle. Chimpanzees have much larger home ranges where extensive travel is necessary to procure food.

Milton suggests a third alternative which represents the early *Homo* model. Faced with a more arid and seasonally variable environment, different from the continued evolutionary trajectory of *Hominoidea* ancestors, *Homo* "routinely" included animal protein in their diet while still maintaining the "basic physiological design" of the hominoid gut and digestive system. This high in essential amino acids and micronutrients food allowed the hominins nutritional advantages similar to carnivores while retaining the "basic physiological design" of the herbivorous gut and digestive system of its hominoid ancestors. Meat takes up less space in the gut, and because basic dietary requirements are being met through animal protein, opens up opportunity to be more selective of plant choices, opting for high energy kinds. This strategy allowed for an increase in body size without losing the "mobility, agility or sociality" necessitated by the changing environment and potential energy for "cerebral expansion."

Milton's overall thrust of animal protein—with just a few modifications to a phylogentically herbivorous gut and digestive systems—became a part of the human lineage in *Homo* well before modern *sapiens* is well supported in archaeological sites and, given the past trajectory of a "generalist" omnivore from the emerging hominid biped, supportable. Yet, acquisition of animal protein by at least *erectus* was along the lines of the hypothesized generalized omnivorous strategy of its hominid predecessors. Save for adaptation to extreme environments, such as arid desert or arctic climes (made possible by advanced cultural technology not yet present in *Homo* 1.6 mya), human ancestors would have maintained a finely tuned balance between animal protein and plant resources, exploiting what the environment provided during its annual seasonal fluctuations as well fluctuations fueled by climate change over generations of *erectus*. Animal protein was certainly an added dietary benefit and one that seemed to require little physiological adaptation. The inclusion of meat itself was not the sole dietary reason that *Homo* had sufficient energy to adapt to a growing horizontal space, to promote the sociability that is inferred with that ecological shift, and the driving force for a healthy cerebral expansion.

The reasons Milton and others have provided for meat inclusion, that of a more arid and seasonally limiting environment constraining the necessary high-energy plant foods leading to a greater reliance on meat (remember, animal protein was already a featured part of the omnivorous strategy) are possible, yet from analogies to living and recent African foraging cultures and the examples of Tarahumara and the Nandi, meat is not featured as a primary dietary resource, and energy demands for subsistence and other cultural behaviors are more than adequately met.

From our dentition and mastication patterns of chewing (reminiscent of plant eaters), with variable movement, side to side, up and down, forward to backward, which is very different from carnivores (McDougal 2003) that have little side-to-side motion, to the shape and length of the gut (see above and McDougal 2003), humans have more similarity with a plant-eating ancestry than that of meat-eating. In addition, the bane of modern humans—high cholesterol—is testament to a plant-eating ancestry. Humans lack the evolved cholesterol-removing system (including the liver) found in carnivores, plant foods don't contain cholesterol and humans process just enough required for normal embryonic development and daily cell maintenance. Eating meat creates excessive surpluses of cholesterol, which only slowly vacates the body without an efficient removal system. Finally, humans, as most plant-eaters, do not produce some of the necessary vitamins, such as A and C, and have developed systems that synthesize vitamins from elements found in their diet. "Because humans have lived throughout most of their evolution on diets with very little animal matter, they have had to develop or retain the ability to synthesize some substances they need that are abundantly found in meat" (McDougal 2003). Carnivores in contrast have the enzymes required to convert directly raw materials into the essential vitamins required, thereby not having to augment the process through synthesizing.

Studies of Tarahumara runners and personal narratives point to diets of vegetables, fruits and whole grains as deriving maximum nutrition from minimal calories so as to reduce processing extraneous bulk. As carbohydrates process faster than proteins, their running is affected less than having to clear proteins. In addition, in the right quantity and variety, vegetables, grains and legumes provide the necessary amino acids that are essential to building and sustaining muscle from scratch; "plant resources can be as powerful as meat sources" (Nancy Clark, nutritionist in McDougal and McClintock 2006).

In fact the amount of meat found in the Tarhumara diets reflects the more omnivorous strategies of extant apes and inferred early *Homo* diet. The reconstruction of WT-15000's environment was not one of an arid and dry savanna, but one that would have provided a smorgasbord of plant resources sufficient for exploiting without having to increase meat consumption. In addition, endurance running, and more efficient striding would have provided *Homo* a means to range over much greater distances in shorter periods of time, allowing a greater potential to allow the continuation of their generalist diet.

In the Kenyan and Tarahumara examples, both groups live at altitudes between 5,000 and 8, 000 feet, both have integrated running into all aspects of their culture, both are subsistence farmers, but as well have herding as an element of their subsistence, and both exist on a diet that features meat as just one of many resources, and in quantities far less than has been hypothesized for emerging *Homo*. Both feature a diet heavy in corn, which has in its current form only been available in the last 4,000–6,000 years; however, the suggestion is that comparable non-meat food stuffs that could have provided the necessary protein and calories could have been found on the expanding savanna. It is also the suggestion that running would have factored in exploiting resources that would have matched the seasonal changes. In contemporary foraging groups, estimates up to 85 percent of the diet is non-meat and provided by females. Several studies suggest that the diet of Paleolithic *H. sapiens* would have been less meat-centric and more reflective of a foraging diet to include nuts and other available resources (Eaton et al. 1998, Eaton et al. 1997, Cordain 2006).

There does not seem to be one prime selective agent for development of endurance running; although scavenging and opportunistic hunting, and later hunting, would have greatly benefitted from such a movement pattern. It will be suggested that the changing environment and the hypertropicality associated with equatorial Africa, selected for endurance running and this behavior was expressed in a variety of cultural activities such as subsistence, transport, ritual and awareness and play (Sands 2008a, 2008b; Sands and Sands, 2009). Running would have enhanced each of these behaviors and related activities, thereby operating as selective agents to reinforce and fine-tune the running skeletal and muscle platform along with the associated physiology and neurobiology.

A SWISS ARMY KNIFE MOVEMENT PATTERN

It is the suggestion in this paper that running emerged not so much as a behavior based on subsistence activities, focused on scavenging and hunting and the increase of meat in the diet of *Homo erectus*, although it certainly is probable that running allowed a greater opportunity to exploit this resource, but instead endurance running was a behavior that was tied more to the increase in the expanse of landscape, both spatially in a localized setting and also in a sense of greater flexibility to migrate over larger areas of geographical space. In the changing environment, there would have been selection toward a more efficient and rapid movement pattern beyond walking or short distance running, allowing for a synthesis of greater coverage of the landscape and relative speed in moving across the landscape (McHenry and Coffing 2000). Bramble has suggested (1991) shorter upper limb length would have reduced energy expenditure of upper limb arm swing occurring with each stride. In addition, Carrier and Lieberman and colleagues suggest that human-running ability allows for the relative ease of changing gaits, as opposed to the running capability of quadrupeds. As such, this would have allowed an extended range of running speeds and greater control of energy expenditure. Certainly, endurance running would have conferred on *Homo* any number of benefits related to scavenging and hunting, such as predator avoidance, timeliness in travel, and speed to potential scavenging sites. However, the proposed passive and opportunistic hunting pattern cannot be the sole selection for this anatomical running chassis.

The Tarahumara provide a cultural tapestry with running as an essential thread in transport, movement, games, sport, play, and building and maintaining social alliances; acquisition of meat is only a peripheral concern. Even before Kenyan's Nandi became the planet's most dominant distance runners in the organized sport of running, their culture was, as well, an ode to running. Now, the cultural benefits of running in terms of status, wealth and recognition is turning the Rift into a training ground for *über* runners, and with the ideal conditions of moderate temperatures, altitude, and a cultural emphasis along with a past of running prowess that extends back in time for hundreds, if not thousands of years that has certainly acted to select contemporary distance running machines.

The below are just a few examples of *Homo* lifeways attributes that would have featured running and reinforced the importance of that movement and as such would have been culturally selected for throughout *Homo* ontogeny.

PLAY

One element of emerging hominids that has received scant attention is that of play and its role in human evolution (see Kerrie P. Lewis in this volume). Much theoretical work exists that ties animal play to the evolution of human play; however, little work has been done that focuses on what kind of play forms would have been involved in hominid evolution (Bateson 2005; Lewis 2000; Lewis and Barton 2004; Bekoff and Byers 1998; Burghardt 1998, 2001, 2005; Byers and Walker 1995; Siviy 1998). Extant work on apes produces a picture of play that spans all play types; solitary locomotor, object, and social. Featured in all categories are movement patterns that incorporate running. For those mammals who are "career" runners, such as ungulates, running, as locomotor play, is an integral and critical component to each of these categories. These movements include chasing, avoiding, play hunting, which incorporates object play, to running as movement it seems solely for the sake of running.

Play provides unique evolutionary advantages and acts as training for the unexpected through kinematic and emotional responses as stress relief and an aid to learning. Play behaviors trigger the reward pathway and modify neuronal connections within the developing brain, with juvenile play peaking during this critical period of neural wiring. Specific neurochemical releases found in running are linked to the engagement of play in mammals. By activating the reward system, play behavior brings pleasurable responses to the participants while being an important ingredient in facilitating cognition and social development, as well as initiating the process of environmental awareness. Inhabiting a more horizontal landscape would have offered a greater playground for juvenile play, rich with an array of environmental stimuli with potential danger that would have generated a never-ending continuum of unique play situations and high-stress interactions with the environment.

One of the most important elements of running as play was a direct and *sensuous* way to develop an intimate familiarity with the landscape and its inhabitants. Animals familiarize themselves with the environment during play, thereby decreasing the risk of later becoming prey. Play offers the developing brain a smorgasbord of activity to learn from while influencing neural growth and rewiring. In *Homo*, running during play would have "trained" the juvenile body and brain for adult running.

Theories advanced on the evolution of play consider play as a means to learn and enhance skills later necessary as an adult and as a means to build and maintain physical stamina and strength. Recent work on play advances theories based on neurobiology that speaks to play being a critical component in providing new and necessary stimulation to the brain during a critical period of brain growth and development, where synapse generation and neural wiring is at its most flexible (Iwaniuk et al. 2001). Lewis (2000 and this volume) suggests that due to a slowdown in brain cell growth and the fact that play seems to reach its intensity during terminal synaptogenesis, this may correlate to play's influence on brain structure (Lewis in Furlow 2004). Other theories include play as training for the unexpected through "kinemetic and emotional responses" (Spinka et al. 2001), and play as stress relief and a partner in learning (Siviy 1998). Not only would the stimulation from play provide a greater intensity to each play experience, but the menu of available situations that play patterns can provide is infinite.

Spinka and colleagues (2001) suggest that locomotor play, which would include running, should be common to species that inhabit variable environments, where training for the unexpected in such a variable setting would include a safe venue for rehearsing (although recent play theory seems to discount play as the only selection agent for play development), and play itself would be beneficial to those species adapting to a dynamic environment. Heinrich alludes to hunting, as in the movement activity and the process of the hunt, providing a necessary "long term vision that both rewarded us by the chase itself and that held the prize in our imagination even when it was out of sight, smell and hearing" (2001: 178). Simply, it is the "pull" of the hunt that propels the hunter into the future. Yet, play theorists suggest that play, in all of its unpredictability of action derived from novel activity in an a ever-changing environment, offers a maturing brain a smorgasbord of activity to learn from while potentially influencing a period of neural growth and rewiring.

Play serves to create, strengthen and preserve social ties and a hominid such as *erectus*, faced with a large array of environmental stimuli, and in such a risk-filled setting would have found cooperation included in social play to be adaptive. Everyone has memories of how much running was integrated into childhood games and sport. For most of us, running was to race friends, integrated into social games like tag and hide-and-seek, and was an important element found in sports such as soccer and baseball. The older one became, the more formalized and rule-governed play and games became. Although theories advancing building stamina and physical strength as the primary function for play origins are suspect, running during play would have maintained a certain level of conditioning and muscle development that would be necessary for further play, but as well, to train the body and mind for running into adulthood. One of the most important elements of running as play was that running was a direct and sensuous way to develop an intimate familiarity with the environment, including the landscape and its inhabitants.

Running as play would have also been an element of intergenerational play and, as well, adult play. As the savanna horizons opened up, endurance running would have been critical for both juveniles, as well as adults, to survey and build a mental compendium of the nature of their universe. Heinrich suggests at some point during hominids necessity to traverse through and on the landscape, there would have grown a trust and enjoyment (even pleasure) for the "allure" of the relationship between runner and environment (more on this below). This pleasure would be present in play and other facets of cultural lifeways, especially subsistence, providing reinforcement of behavior.

TRANSPORT—OF MESSAGES, IDEAS, AND MATERIALS

An opening landscape in many facets selected for a running physiology that shaped the development of more obvious lifestyle facets as subsistence and even play, yet running in other less obvious ways impacted the development of an emerging Pleistocene culture to include spanning and connecting *H. erectus* across an ever-increasing open horizontal landscape. Not to suggest that it is possible to parse what would have been a bioculturally complex evolution of behaviors and capabilities that resulted from adapting to a much larger and more arid environment, but running would have facilitated the development and maintenance of *Homo* social and cultural networks that would have been unique in kind and structure from earlier hominins. It is true that the development of bipedalism would have facilitated in similar ways the same behaviors and capabilities; however, the simple fact of increasing the ability to traverse longer distances in shorter time would have profound impacts on the development of *H. erectus* and later *Homo* culture. The concept of transport—not so much a singular notion of transportation, but a larger concept of moving not just bodies but also more cultural elements such as physical materials as well as mental "materials" such as messages and ideas—would have promoted a more efficient use of the landscape and its resources.

Mammals communicate through a variety of mechanisms, from olfactory to verbal. Those arboreal such as most primates communicate sound and smell and non-verbal signals. Most terrestrial species such as canids and felids communicate through the same mechanisms; however, the mobility of a species defines the range of territory those terrestrial animals inhabit. Following this, an effective communication system is based on how far and perhaps how fast an individual can travel. Running can also be a form of communication in animals as different gaits and pace can express a wide variety of environmental situations such as danger or feeding or even social situations such as play or mating; this would be no different in runners, leisurely gaits versus frantic sprints. However, forelimbs not directly involved in gait (no longer involved in quadrupedal locomotion) become both mechanisms of transport as well as communication signals during running. Most generally, however, with few exceptions such as elephants or dolphins that can travel long distance in search of food, communication mechanisms are defined by composition and size of home range.

As *Homo* evolved to survive within an expanding and changing landscape, to include first a mosaic environment and then later a more savanna-type ecology, the communication mechanisms that fit specific environments either became delayed in transmittal or due to the environmental shift not as useful in the form taken by either arboreal or terrestrial species, such as olfactory or sound. Immediacy of communication became at times less significant, and the increased distance (and time) traveled would have selected for those with a greater ability to retain the message.

Running provided a means for urgency of communication over distance and allowed a means of establishing and maintaining social networks that would have otherwise been out of sight and out of mind. Increased and rapid coverage of land, as discussed in play, would have supported a similar and more complex "awareness" of the environment, extending the periphery of what was known from less frequent visits, including an increased compendium of natural resources (this is discussed more in the following section).

RITUAL IN RUNNING

Of the behaviors altered, modified or developed from the evolution of running, the ability to move further and more quickly through the horizontal landscape, coupled with a more responsive neurbiological pathway to obviate the pain of extended aerobic exertion and the need to "mentally" catalog more of the natural resource environment, would have produced a heightened state of awareness (Sands and Sands 2009). It is not difficult to extend this reward system to a foundation for the development of ritual in human running. Utilizing the same neural reward pathways, biomechanical platform, and intimate environmental relationships as play, running would have promoted the development of an incipient "spirituality" based on ritual. The suggestion here is that endurance running featured prominently in the formation of a *Homo*-specific *"Paleolithic horizontal consciousness"* that included exploration and cataloging of the natural environment and the establishment of an intimate environmental "trust," elsewhere referred to as *biophilia* (Wilson 1984, 1993; Kellert 1993, 1997, 2007), an intimate and biologically based bond between humans and the environment, and the effect of the Paleolithic runner's high. This horizontal consciousness is similar to Berman's (2000) comparison of hunting and gathering awareness defining early *Homo sapiens* from a more vertical spirituality and religion best corresponding to humanity after the adoption of a more sedentary lifestyle about 10,000 years ago. It is suggested here that Berman's notion of a horizontal awareness applies with little difficulty to earlier *Homo* as well. Early humans submerged the conflict of an emerging ego apart from nature, sustaining conflict by dispersing the "tension" horizontally through trust in the environmental present.

Development of a relationship between the environment and the runner matches well with the development of a more advanced neural reward system, providing interludes of experience that would always be experienced as the runner moved through the horizontal landscape. The more running was integrated into the cultural behaviors of *Homo*, and the more the reward pathway adapted to this behavior, the more efficient the runners would have become. This would have been a kinetic experience, encoded in the genes and culturally translated into traditions and ritual, where movement would have provided the entrance and continued participation in a state of heightened reality and the continual sensitization of the reward system. This paradox can be seen as the Paleolithic runner's high, where the ritual of movement was interwoven with the necessity of survival. In essence, running, along with physical movement patterns of play, developed into ritual infused with awareness or heightened consciousness that reinforced *Homo*'s need to capture the essence of its natural resources for adapting and surviving in a changing environment. This heightened awareness would have hardwired the mechanism and expression of ritual into *Homo*.

A biological artifact or legacy of running in early *Homo* can be found in the *runner's high* of contemporary endurance runners, including ancient Indian (Nabokov 1981) and contemporary ultra runners. This runner's high is often characterized as spirituality that seems to engage when movement, neurochemical release, and nature provide a *perfect storm* of experience.

RUNNING INTO THE PLEISTOCENE

By the time KNM WT 15000 lived, *H. erectus* had already migrated out of Africa and was living in other regions of the planet, in what is known today as the Republic of Georgia and as well in Java. This early adaptive success of *H. erectus* can in part be attributed to the development of movement patterns that would have facilitated survival in a changing horizontal landscape. In many activities, running episodes in East African *Homo* were mostly over long distances. In terms of food acquisition, through scavenging, opportunistic hunting, and bouts of foraging, moving across the landscape would have necessitated intense periods of running, thereby selecting for efficient runners in human evolution. As the expanding savanna selected for those individuals most efficient at running, the play forms that were already present would have ontologically reinforced the running movement patterns and incorporated running-specific activity echoing patterns seen in adults. The sheer intensity that much of their running would have commanded would have triggered the existing reward system minimizing pain while producing sensations of euphoria and, for some runners, altered states.

The neurochemicals and associated receptor sites within the brain would have already been a part of the neurobiology of early *Homo*, a legacy of mammalian evolution. The benefits to refining and fine-tuning the neurochemical releases and neural circuitry over time would have selected for faster (in endurance speed), stronger, and more efficient runners. Running would have been a frequent and essential movement pattern in daily activity for not only subsistence, but also featured in other cultural and social behaviors as well, to include travel, communication, ritual, and play. The more endurance running bouts, the more the release system was sensitized and engaged. In essence, it is suggested that *Homo* was experiencing some of the same kinds of neural rewards, if not more intense due to more frequent and extended bouts of running, that are seen in runners today.

In fact, it is reasonable to suggest that as the environment fluctuated and opened up, running became a critical component of the successful physical and cultural adaptation both in East Africa as well as the initial pulse out of Africa. It might be said that running was a manifestation of both physical and cultural adaptations to the environment. The early and middle Pleistocene seems to be bereft of cultural signifiers, save a gradual development of stone tools and evidence of hunting. However, a dramatic African exodus occurred from the tropical and subtropical climates of Africa into the more temperate and seasonal regions of the Northern Hemisphere, such as Eurasia and the Far East. Success of the species for more than a million years indicates an intelligence that is more than adept at the process of social learning and the necessary development and passing on of cultural traditions. These migrating groups of *Homo* were foragers, a lifestyle well suited for movement and adaptive to differing environments. Running would have been instrumental in moving through a foreign landscape and developing new environmental "almanacs" of plant and animal life.

By the time Nariokotime Boy was living, running and dying on the shores of Lake Turkana, *erectus*-like forms were residing in regions from Georgia in the now defunct Soviet Union to Java. Recent investigations into the 1.8 mya Georgian Dmansi *erectus* from newly discovered individuals, reveal primitive traits such as tree-climbing that are noticeably different from later populations of the same species elsewhere (Owen 2007). Dmansi *erectus* has been described as small-brained, tree-climbing, meat-eating and very short, was both apelike and human in appearance. The new fossils also reveal apelike arms and hands. However, the species also had modern human features, including long legs and a spine suited for long-distance running and walking. Although it is likely that East African *H. erectus* represented a more environmentally adapted and refined running platform, running was a critical component of the migration of *H. erectus* to environments not particularly reminiscent of African savannas.

In summary, from the physiological reconstruction of Pleistocene *Homo*, the environmental reconstruction that suggests influences that support *Homo* running, including the advantage running presents to opportunistic subsistence and foraging, the understanding of the role play and neural reward system contribute to evolutionary encouragement of long distance running, and the importance running would have been to the initial populations out of Africa, long distance running has been posed as a critical behavior to the evolutionary success of Pleistocene *Homo*.

To shed more light on how running would have been integrated in *Homo* lifeways, ethnohistory and ethnography of recent and contemporary running cultures such as the East Africans, most notably the Nandi of the Great Rift and the Tarahumara of the Sierra Madres of Northwest Mexico, might benefit elaboration. There is a plethora of work on both cultures that is applicable in some ways to advancing knowledge on the relationship of running to human evolution, both to selection of running in early Pleistocene as well as development of running in recent human history. The research done on East African runners focuses on Kenyan running and performance (see Jon Entine, Yannis Pistalidis, and Dirk Christensen this volume), specifically the Kalejin and the Nandi in particular, while work on the Tarahumara explores how running is an important cultural feature of Tarahumara society.[1] The local environments share some similarity, altitude, periods of extended summer heat, and a low humidity; however the runners reflect different biokinetic platforms, perhaps testament to a host of factors: ancestry, diet, subtle environmental differences, and so on. This area of exploration offers exciting possibilities to understanding the role of running in recent, and not so recent, human evolution.

NOTES

I would like to acknowledge Kerrie P. Lewis and Linda R. Sands for reviewing drafts of this manuscript and contributing meaningful and significant commentary.

1. For research on Kenyan running, see the following sample of research: J. Bale and J. Sang, *Kenyan Running: Movement Culture, Geography and Global Change* (London: Frank Cass & Co. Ltd.), 1996; J. Manners, "Kenya's Running Tribe," *The Sports Historian* 17, no. 2 (1997): 14–27; R. E. Mayes, *The Cybernetics of Kenyan Running: Hurry, Hurry Has No Blessing* (Durham, N.C.: Carolina Academic Press), 2005; T. Tanser, *Train Hard, Win Easy: The Kenyan Way* (Mountain View, Calif.: Tafnews Press), 1997;

A. Burfoot, "African Speed, African Endurance," in *Anthropology, Sport, and Culture*, edited by R. R. Sands (Westport, Conn.: Bergin & Garvey) 1999: 53–63. For research on the Tarahumara, see the following sample of research: W. C. Bennet and R. M. Zingg, *The Tarahumara, an Indian Tribe of Northern Mexico* (Chicago: The University of Chicago Press), 1935; C. W. Pennington. *The Tarahumara of Mexico: Their Environment and Material Culture* (Salt Lake City: University of Utah Press), 1963; J. G. Kennedy, *Tarahumara of the Sierra Madre: Beer, Ecology, and Social Organization* (Arlington Heights, Ill.: AHM Publishing), 1978; W. L. Merrill, *Raramuri Souls: Knowledge and Social Process in Northern Mexico* (Washington, D.C.: Smithsonian Institution Press), 1988; D. L. Christensen, "From Tradition to the Olympics: Running Cultures in Mexico and Kenya," *Play the Game*, 2002, www.playthegame.org/Knowledge%20Bank/Articles/From%20 Tradition%20to%20the%20Olympics%20Running%20Cultures%20in%20Mexico%20 and%20Kenya.aspx (accessed September 23, 2007); C. McDougall and B. McClintock, "The Men Who Live Forever," *Men's Health* 21, no. 6 (2006): 180–91.

BIBLIOGRAPHY

Ackerman, D. *Deep Play*. New York: Vintage Press, 2000.

Aiello, L. C. and C. Key. "Energetic Consequences of Being a *Homo erectus* Female." *American Journal of Human Biology* 14, no. 5 (2002): 551–65.

Aiello, L. C. and P. Wheeler. "The Expensive Tissue Hypothesis: The Brain and the Digestive System in Human and Primate Evolution." *Current Anthropology* 37 (1995): 199–222.

Anton, S. C., W. R. Leonard, and M. L. Robertson. "An Ecomorphological Model of the Initial Hominid Dispersal from Africa." *Journal of Human Evolution* 43, no. 6 (2002): 773–85.

Atran, S. *In Gods We Trust: The Evolutionary Landscape of Religion*. Oxford: Oxford University Press, 2002.

Bateson, P. "The Role of Play in the Evolution of Great Apes and Humans." *The Nature of Play: Great Apes and Humans*, edited by A. D. Pelligrini and P. K. Smith. New York: Guilford Press, 2005: 13–24.

Battista, G. *The Runner's High: Illumination and Ecstasy in Motion*. Halcottsville, N.Y.: Breakaway Books, 2004.

Bekoff, M. and J. A. Byers. *Animal Play: Evolutionary, Comparative and Ecological Perspectives*. Cambridge: Cambridge University Press, 1998.

Bement, M. K. and K. A. Sluka. "Low-Intensity Exercise Reverses Chronic Muscle Pain in the Rat in a Naloxone-Dependent Manner." *Archives of Physical Medicine and Rehabilitation* 86, no. 9 (2005): 1736–40.

Bennet, W. C. and R. M. Zingg. *The Tarahumara: An Indian Tribe of Northern Mexico*. Chicago: The University of Chicago Press, 1935.

Berman, M. *Wandering God: A Study in Nomadic Spirituality*. Albany: State University of New York Press, 2000.

Bobe, R. and A. K. Behrensmeyer. "The Expansion of Grassland Ecosystems in Africa in Relation to Mammalian Evolution and the Origin of the Genus *Homo.*" *Palaeogeography, Palaeoclimatology, Palaeoecology* 207 (2004): 399–420.

Bramble, D. M. "Functional and Evolutionary Significance of the Occipital Torus in *Homo.*" *American Journal of Physical Anthropology* (Supplement) 12 (1991): 52–53.

Bramble, D. M and D. E. Lieberman. "Endurance Running and the Evolution of Homo." *Nature* 432 (2004): 345–52.

Bunn, H. T. "Hunting, Power Scavenging and Butchering by Hadza Foragers and by Plio-Pleistocene *Homo.*" *Meat-Eating and Human Evolution*, edited by C. Stanford and H. T. Bunn. Oxford: Oxford University Press, 2001: 199–218.

Bunn, H. T. "Meat Made Us Human." *Evolution of the Human Diet: The Known, the Unknown and the Unknowable,* edited by P. Ungar. New York: Oxford University Press, 2006: 191–211.

Burghardt, G. "The Evolutionary Origins of Play Revisited: Lessons from Turtles." *Animal Play: Evolutionary, Comparative, and Ecological Perspectives,* edited by M. Berkoff and J. A. Byers. Cambridge: Cambridge University Press, 1998: 1–26.

———. "Play: Attributes and Neural Substrates." *Developmental Psychobiology: Vol. 13 Handbook of Behavioral Neurobiology,* edited by E. Bass. New York: Kluwer Academic/Plenum Press, 2001: 327–66.

———. *The Genesis of Animal Play.* Cambridge, Mass.: MIT Press, 2005.

Byers, J. and C. Walker. "Refining the Motor Training Hypothesis for the Evolution of Play." *American Nature* 146, no. 1 (1995): 25–40.

Candau, R., A. Belli, G. Y. Millet, D. Georges, B. Barbier, and J. D. Rouillon. "Energy Cost and Running Mechanics During a Treadmill Run to Voluntary Exhaustion in Humans." *European Journal of Physiology and Occupational Physiology* 77, no. 6 (1998): 479–85.

Carrier, D. R. "The Energetic Paradox of Human Running and Hominid Evolution." *Current Anthropology* 25, no. 4 (1984): 483–95.

———. "The Running/Fighting Dichotomy and the Evolution of Aggression in Hominids." *From Biped to Strider: The Emergence of Modern Human Walking, Running and Resource Transport,* edited by D. Meldrum, J. Hilton, and C. E. Hilton. New York: Kluwar Academic/Plenium Publishers, 2004: 135–62.

Case, Linda P. *The Dog: Its Behavior, Nutrition and Health.* New York: Wiley-Blackwell, 2005.

Collinder, E., F. Nyberg, K. Sanderson-Nydahl, M. Gottlieb-Vedi, and A. Lindholm. "The Opioid Haemorphin-7 in Horses During Low-Speed and High-Speed Treadmill Exercise to Fatigue." *Journal of Veterinary Medicine* 52, no. 4 (2005): 162–65.

Colmant, S. "Interview with Arne Dietrich: Altered States of Consciousness, Creativity, and the Brain." *PsychSymposium.com,* 2005. psychsymposium.com/32 (accessed September 26, 2007).

Cooper, A. *Playing in the Zone: Exploring the Spiritual Dimensions of Sports.* Boston: Shambhala, 2004.

Cordain, L. "Implications of Plio-Pleistocene Hominin Diets for Modern Humans." *Evolution of the Human Diet: The Known, the Unknown and the Unknowable*, edited by P. S. Ungar. Oxford: Oxford University Press, 2006: 363–83.

Dietrich, A. "Functional Neuroanatomy of Altered States of Consciousness: The Transient Hypofrontality Hypothesis." *Consciousness and Cognition* 12, no. 2 (2003): 231–56.

Dietrich, A. and W. F. McDaniel. "Endocannabinoids and Exercise." *British Journal of Sports Medicine* 38, no. 5 (2004): 536–41.

Draper, P. "Institutional, Evolutionary, and Demographic Contexts of Gender Roles: A Case Study of !Kung Bushman." *The Evolving Female: A Life History Perspective*, edited by M. E. Moreback, A. Galloway, and A. Zilman. Princeton, N.J.: Princeton University Press, 1997: 220–32.

Eaton, S. B., M. Konner and M. Shostak. "Stone Agers in the Fast Lane: Chronic Degenerative Diseases in Evolutionary Perspective." *American Journal of Medicine* 84, no. 4 (1988): 739–49.

Eaton, S. B., S. B. Eaton III, and M. J. Konner. "Paleolithic Nutrition Revisited: A Twelve-Year Retrospective on its Nature and Implications." *European Journal of Clinical Nutrition* 51, no. 4 (1997): 207–16.

Furlow, Bryant. "Play's the Thing." *New Scientist* 2294 (June 9, 2001): 28–31.

Gardner, E. L. "Endocannabinoid Signaling System and Brain Reward: Emphasis on Dopamine." *Pharmacology, Biochemistry and Behavior* 81, no. 2 (2005): 263–84.

Gruss, L. T. and D. Schmitt. "Bipedalism in *Homo Ergaster*: An Experimental Study of the Effects of Tibial Proportions and Locomotor Biomechanics." *From Biped to Strider: The Emergence of Modern Human Walking, Running and Resource Transport*, edited by D. Meldrum, J. Hilton, and C. E. Hilton. New York: Kluwar Academic/Plenium Publishers, 2004: 117–34.

Hart, D. and R. W. Sussman. *Man the Hunted: Primates, Predators and Human Evolution.* New York: Basic Books, 2005.

Heinrich, B. *Why We Run: A Natural History.* New York: HarperCollins Publishers, 2001.

Hilton, C. E. and R. D. Greaves. "Age, Sex and Resource Transport in Venezuelan Foragers." *From Biped to Strider: The Emergence of Modern Human Walking, Running and Resource Transport*, edited by D. Meldrum, J. Hilton and C. E. Hilton. New York: Kluwar Academic/Plenium Publishers, 2004: 163–83.

Hilton, C. E. and D. Meldrum. "Striders, Runners and Transporters." *From Biped to Strider: The Emergence of Modern Human Walking, Running and Resource Transport*, edited by D. Meldrum, J. Hilton and C. E. Hilton. New York: Kluwar Academic/Plenium Publishers, 2004: 1–8.

Iwaniuk, A., J. Nelson, and S. Pellis. "Do Big-Brained Animals Play More?" *Journal of Comparative Psychology*, 115 (2001): 29.

James, D. V. P. and J. H. Doust. "Time to Exhaustion During Severe Intensity Running: Response Following a Single Bout of Interval Training." *European Journal of Applied Physiology and Occupational Physiology* 81, no. 4 (2000): 337–45.

Johanson, D. and M. Edey. *Lucy, the Beginnings of Humankind.* New York: Simon and Schuster, 1981.

Jones, P. "Ultrarunners and Chance Encounters with 'Absolute Unitary Being.'" *Journal of Anthropology of Consciousness* 15, no. 2 (2006): 39–49.

Kanarek, R. B, A. V. Gerstein, R. P. Wildman, W. Foulds Mathes, and K. E. D'Anci. "Chronic Running-Wheel Activity Decreases Sensitivity to Morphine-Induced Analgesia in Male and Female Rats." *Pharmacology, Biochemistry, and Behavior* 61, no. 1 (1998): 19–27.

Kellert, S. R. "The Biological Basis for Human Values of Nature." *The Biophilia Hypothesis*, edited by S. R. Kellert and E. O. Wilson. Washington, D.C.: Island Press, 1993: 42–69.

———. *Kinship to Mastery: Biophilia in Human Evolution and Development*. Washington, D.C.: Island Press, 1997.

———. *Building for Life: Designing and Understanding the Human-Nature Connection*. Washington, D.C.: Island Press, 2005.

———. "Connecting with Creation: The Convergence of Nature, Religion, Science and Culture." *Journal for the Study of Religion, Nature and Culture* 1, no. 1 (2007): 25–37.

Kellert, S. R. and E. O. Wilson, editors. *The Biophilia Hypothesis.* Washington, D.C.: Island Press, 1993.

Kelly, A. E. and K. C. Berridge. "The Neuroscience of Natural Rewards: Relevance to Addictive Drugs." *Journal of Neuroscience* 22, no. 9 (2002): 3306–311.

Koltyn, K. F. and M. Umeda. "Exercise, Hypoalgesia and Blood Pressure." *Sports Medicine* 36, no. 3 (2006): 207–14.

Kotler, S. *West of Jesus: Surfing, Science and the Origins of Belief.* New York: Bloomsbury, 2006.

Lewis, K. P. "A Comparative Study of Primate Play Behavior: Implications for the Study of Cognition." *Folia Primatologica* 71 (2000): 417–21.

Lewis, K. P. and R. A. Barton. "Playing for Keeps: Evolutionary Relationship between Social Play and the Cerebellum in Nonhuman Primates." *Human Nature* 15, no. 1 (2004): 5–21.

Li, G., J. S. Rhodes, I. Girard, S. C. Gammie, and T. Garland, Jr. "Opioid-mediated Pain Sensitivity in Mice Bred for High Voluntary Wheel Running." *Physiology and Behavior* 83, no. 3 (2004): 515–24.

Liebenberg, L. "Persistence Hunting by Modern Hunter-Gatherers." *Current Anthropology* 47, no. 5 (2006): 1017–26.

Lieberman, D. E., D. A. Raichlen, H. Pontzer, D. M. Bramble, and E. Cutright-Smith. "The Human Gluteus Maximus and its Role in Running." *The Journal of Experimental Biology* 209, no 11 (2006): 2143–55.

Lieberman, D. E. and D. M. Bramble. "The Evolution of Marathon Running Capabilities in Humans." *Sports Medicine* 37, no. 5 (2007): 288–90.

Lieberman, D. E., D. M. Bramble, D. A. Raichlen, and J. J. Shea. "The Evolution of Endurance Running and the Tyranny of Ethnography: A Reply to Pickering and Bunn." *Journal of Human Evolution* 53, no. 4 (2007): 434–37.

Lovejoy, C. O. "The Origin of Man." *Science* 211 (1981): 341–50.

Marzke, M. W., J. M. Longhill, and S. A. Rasmussen. "Gluteus Maximus Muscle Function and the Origin of Hominid Bipedality." *American Journal of Physical Anthropology* 77 (1988): 519–28.

Marshall, L. *The !Kung of Nyae Nyae.* Cambridge, Mass.: Harvard University Press, 1976.

Mathes, W. F. and R. B. Kanarek. "Chronic Running Wheel Activity Attenuates the Antinocicpetive Actions of Morphine and Morphine-6-glucouronide Administration into the Periaqueductal Gray in Rats." *Pharmacology, Biochemistry and Behavior* 83, no. 4 (2006): 578–84.

McDougal, J. "Meat in the Human Diet." *The McDougal Newsletter* 2, no. 7 (2003): 1–10. www.nealhendrickson.com/mcdougall/030700MeatinthehumandietPF.htm (accessed October 8, 2008).

McDougall, C. and B. McClintock. "The Men Who Live Forever." *Men's Health* 21, no. 6 (2006): 180–91.

McHenry, H. and K. Coffing. "*Australopithecus* to *Homo*: Transformation in Body and Mind." *Annual Review of Anthropology* 29 (2000): 125–46.

Milton, K. "A Hypothesis to Explain the Role of Meat-Eating in Human Evolution." *Evolutionary Anthropology: Issues, News and Reviews* 8, no. 1 (1999): 11–21.

Nabakov, P. *Indian Running: Native American History and Tradition.* Santa Fe: Ancient City Press, 1981.

Owen, J. "Odd Fossil Skeletons Show both Apelike and Human Traits." *National Geographic News,* September 19, 2007. news.nationalgeographic.com/news/2007/09/070919-human-fossil.html (accessed March 6, 2008).

Pickering, T. R. and H. T. Bunn. 'The Endurance Running Hypothesis and Hunting and Scavenging in Savanna-Woodlands." *Journal of Human Evolution* 53, no. 4 (2007): 438–42.

Pontzer, H. "A New Model Predicting Locomotor Cost from Limb Length via Force Production." *Journal of Experimental Biology* 208 (2005): 1513–24.

Potts, R. "Environmental Hypotheses of Hominin Evolution." *Yearbook of Physical Anthropology* 41 (1998): 93–136.

Raichlen, D. A., B. K. Keeney, G. Gerdeman, T. H. Meek, R. S. Wijeratne, and T. Garland. "Wired to run? The Evolution of Novel Locomotor Behaviors in Hominins." Paper presented at the Seventy-Seventh Annual Meeting of the American Association of Physical Anthropologists, Columbus, Ohio, April 2008, 176.

Rhodes, J. S., S. C. Gmmie, and T. Garland. "Neurobiology of Mice Selected for High Voluntary Wheel-running Activity." *Integrative and Comparative Biology* 45, no. 3 (2005): 438–55.

Richerson, P. J. and R. Boyd. "The Pleistocene and the Origins of Human Culture: Built for Speed." *Perspectives in Ethology* 13 (2000): 1–45.

Ruff, C. B. and A. Walker. "Body Size and Body Shape." *The Nariokotome Homo Erectus Skeleton,* edited by A. Walker and R. Leakey. Cambridge, Mass.: Harvard University Press, 1993: 234–65.

Sands, R. R. "Play Deep: Speculations on the Evolutionary Relationship Between Nature, Spirituality and Deep Play." Paper given at the International Society for the Study of Religion, Nature, and Culture in Morelia, Mexico, January 2008a.

———. "*Homo cursor*: Running into the Pleistocene." Paper given at the 2008 Central States Anthropological Association meetings, Indianapolis: March, 2008b.

Sands, R. R. and L. R. Sands. "Running Deep: Speculations on the Evolution of Running and Spirituality in The Genus *Homo*." *Journal for the Study of Religion, Nature and Culture* 3, no. 4 (2009): 552–77.

Shostak, M. *Nisa: The Life and Words of a! Kung Woman.* Cambridge, Mass.: Harvard University Press, 1976.

Siviy, S. M. "Neurobiological Substrates of Play Behavior: Glimpses into the Structure and Function of Mammalian Playfulness." *Animal Play: Evolutionary, Comparative, and Ecological Perspectives,* edited by M. Bekoff and J. A. Byers. Cambridge, Mass.: Cambridge University Press), 1998: 221–42.

Smith, M. A. and D. L. Yancey. "Sensitivity to the Effects of Opioids in Rats with Free Access to Exercise Wheels: μ-opioid Tolerance and Physical Dependence." *Psychopharmacology* 168, no. 4 (2003): 426–34.

Sockol, M.D., D.A. Raichlen, and H. Pontzer. "Chimpanzee Locomotor Energetics and the Origin of Human Bipedalism." *Proceedings of the National Academy of Sciences* 30 (2007): 12265–69.

Spinka, M., R. Newberry and M. Bekoff. "Mammalian Play: Training for the Unexpected." *The Quarterly Review of Biology* 76, no. 2 (2001): 141–67

Stanford, C. B. *Chimpanzee and Red Colobus: The Ecology of Predator and Prey.* Cambridge, Mass.: Harvard University Press, 1998.

———. *The Hunting Apes.* Princeton, N.J.: Princeton University Press, 1999.

———. "The Behavioral Ecology of Sympatric African Apes: Implications for Understanding Fossil Hominoid Ecology." *Primates* 47 (2006): 91–101.

Stanford, C. B., J. S. Allen, and S. C. Anton. *Biological Anthropology* (2nd edition). New York: Prentice Hall, 2008.

Stanford, C. and H. T. Bunn. *Meating Eating and Human Evolution.* New York: Oxford University Press, 2001.

Steudel-Numbers, K. L. "Energetics in *Homo erectus* and Other Early Hominins: The Consequences of Increased Lower-limb Length." *Journal of Human Evolution* 51 (2006): 445–53.

Steudel-Numbers, K. L and M. J. Tilkens, "The Effect of Lower Limb Length on the Energetic Cost of Locomotion: Implications for Fossil Hominins." *Journal of. Human Evolution* 47 (2004): 95–109.

Steudel-Numbers, K. L., T. D. Weaver and C. M. Wall-Scheffler. "The Evolution of Human Running: Effects of Changes in Lower-limb Length on Locomotor Economy." *Journal of Human Evolution* 53, no 2 (2007): 191–96.

Trinkaus, E. "Neanderthal Limb Proportions and Cold Adaptation." *Aspects of Human Evolution,* edited by C. Stringer. London: Taylor & Francis, 1981: 187–224.

Ungar, P. S. *Evolution of the Human Diet: The Known, the Unknown and the Unknowable.* New York: Oxford University Press, 2006.

Ungar, P. S., F. E. Grine, M. F. Teaford and S. El Zaatari. 2006. "Dental Microwear and Diets of African Early Homo," *Journal of Human Evolution* 50.1: 78–95.

Werme, M., P. Thoren, L. Olson and S. Brene. "Addiction-Prone Lewis but Not Fischer Rats Develop Compulsive Running that Coincides with Downregulation of Nerve Growth Factor Inducible-B and Neuron-Derived Orphan Receptor 1." *The Journal of Neuroscience* 19, no. 14 (1999): 6169–74.

Wheeler, P. E. "The Influence of Bipedalism on the Energy and Water Buckets of Early Hominids." *Journal of Human Evolution* 21 (1991) 117–36.

Wheeler, P. E. "The Influence of Stature and Body Form on Hominid Energy and Water Buckets; A Comparison of *Australopithecus* and Early *Homo* Physiques." *Journal of Human Evolution* 24 (1993): 13–28.

Wilson, E. O. *Biophilia.* Cambridge, Mass.: Harvard University Press, 1984.

———. "Biophilia and the Conservation Ethic." *The Biophilia Hypothesis,* edited by S. R. Kellert and E. O. Wilson. Washington, D.C.: Island Press, 1993: 31–41.

Wise, R. A. "Brain Reward Circuitry: Insights from Unsensed Incentives." *Neuron* 36, no. 2 (2002): 229–40.

Part 3

CULTURE, GENES, RACE, AND PERFORMANCE

One of the most controversial and polarizing issues for those who conduct research in the area of sport and culture is the effect of genes and race on performance. For some, the consistent performances at elite national and international levels produces a visual argument for the segmentation of the human condition when it comes to sport. Authors and researchers such as Entine that stress the influence of genes on performance use the track, pitch, court, and trail in combination with genomic and physiological research to produce scientifically valid evidence.

On the other side of the debate are those that argue that to use science to unravel the mystery of performance is just an excuse to advance, subtly or not so subtly, racist agendas that have been perpetrated for over a century by "scientific" exploration. Mediating this divide are those who suggest that science is nowhere near being able to capture the right kind of data to advance any rigorous hypotheses concerning the engine of human performance. To further complicate matters, there are many aspects of elite performance that are social and cultural in nature. Economic opportunity as well as cultural and social selection for different sport forms, either through cultural or national identity with a sport (Jamaican sprinters, Kenyan runners) or the antecedent history of sport within a cultural group that would promote contemporary sport participation (colonialism). There are also other factors such as personality that engender certain types of sport participation, as well as the singular motivation to excel.

Underlying the discussion of human performance is the more pervasive argument that there are no "biological" categories that correspond to human race. It has been suggested that using phenotypic manifestations such as skin color to posit human differences is socially dangerous and leads to creating artificial categories of humankind that promote "racism." This discussion ranges far beyond the science of human variation and includes both cultural and social implications. There are those who mediate this argument by advocating that there are many variables that should be folded into the discussion of elite performance, such as the role of environment and culture, along with the biological propensity supplied by the individual's genotype. The tone of this argument has also been softened by positing that the specific details behind the suite of variables required for elite performance is yet unknown. And finally there are those who stand firmly convinced that genes (and ancestry) hold the key to performance. Recent work on the human genome has greatly contributed to our understanding of the complexity of gene regulation and expression. This work has provided some evidence to support the logic of biologically based performance and, in some cases, has provided venues for further investigation on the genetic basis of performance.

To reorient the discussion on sport performance as an aspect of human movement, elite performances are brought into context through an evaluation of running cultures. This evaluation equates performance to a biocultural evolutionary journey, incorporating contemporary movements, such as running. These running cultures are the result of many different variables that are part of natural and cultural selection, including genotype, and processes that affect genetic makeup, such as genetic drift (founder's effect) and migration, the prehistory and history of location, subsistence patterns, environment, how running was integrated in ritual and lifeways, and other culture-specific domains. In addition to human prehistory, historic and contemporary cultural selection in the form of national and international competitions that feature economic gain, reinforcement of national and ethnic identity and pride, and individual accomplishments are also viewed as variables that influence performance.

The equation that yields elite performance, according to different perspectives and authors, can be written surprisingly simple or in varying degrees of complexity. If you do not possess the necessary genes that code for the optimal biomechanical anatomy and physiology, you will not be an elite performer—this is true in all types of running, from sprinting through ultrarunning, as it is true in individual sports such as swimming.

The equation becomes more complex when beginning to parse out the effect of environmental and socio-cultural variables.

This section features three chapters that reflect the differing perspectives of the makeup of this equation. Each author has written extensively on this subject and the chapters included here approach the construction of the equation from perspectives of historic cultural domains (Christensen), evolutionary genetics (Entine), and along with Entine, Ptisladis and colleagues inventory recent genetic advances that bear on parsing out the performance equation.

Dirk Christensen approaches the phenomenon of Kenyan running from both a historical and cultural perspective. Cattle raiding was an integral part of the cultural fabric of the Kalenjin ancestry. Within this culture, the cattle served as both status and economic indicators of successful Kenyan males and the act of cattle raiding served as a measure of masculinity that was surrounded by ritual. As Sands (chapter 4, this volume) postulates, running was an integral behavior to evolutionary success and continues to be been a selective force through cultural adaptation. Christensen follows this integration of running in contemporary Kenyan society as a continuation of culturally selective behaviors.

The highly controversial author of *Taboo*, Jon Entine updates that book with more recent advances in identifying genetic indicators of performance, while maintaining his perspective that genes and ancestry are the overriding architects of elite performance. Moving beyond the notion of race, Entine suggests that phenotypic expression is but a crude reminder of the genotypic certainty that influences performance. Entine continues to fault prominent researchers, such as Gould and Lewontin, for delaying, or worse yet, redirecting research. To Entine, the search for the underlying mechanisms of elite performance is not a racist endeavor. Understanding the physiological processes of the human body should be viewed as an academic endeavor, with implications for advancement in many fields, such as medical research and drug therapy.

Exercise physiologist Yannis Pistaldis (coauthor of *East African Running*) along with fellow coauthors Rachel Irving, Vilma Charleston, and Robert Scott do agree that genes play an important role in performance. Although mediating Entine's position, Pistaldis points out that single gene variants probably are advantageous to "fine tuning" performance; however, these gene variants are not by themselves determinants of success or failure. The author suggests that genetic advantages are not due to unique genes, but instead to populations that maintain the right genetic mix of those advantageous gene variants. He goes on to stress that even with the "right" genetic material, social and cultural pressures still contribute greatly to the outcome of individual performance.

However, the explanation or theory put forward, even before Jon Entine's controversial book, *Taboo*, was published in 2000, the thorny issue of race, genes, and performance continues to be a spirited academic and popular discussion.

7

Traditional and Modern Running Culture among the Kalenjin of Kenya: A Historical and Anthropological Perspective

Dirk Lund Christensen and Søren Damkjaer

ABSTRACT

The success of Kenyan runners connects different anthropological themes such as the background to their success and the historical background of the running techniques and cultures. An interesting and unique aspect of the Kenyan success in running is the fact that a single ethnic group, the Kalenjin, numbering only three million, has "produced" most of the athletes. This has created a long-lasting interest in this particular phenomenon. The ancestors of the Kalenjin were emigrants from Ethiopia, Cushites, and the Sudan, Nilotes, as well as hunter-gatherers from present-day Kenya. When the British officially colonized Kenya in 1895, Kalenjin society was rooted in all three cultures. The Kalenjin were assiduous cattle thieves and prowess in running was crucial for success in cattle raids. European sport gradually substituted cattle raiding for athletics. The Kalenjin, however, did not achieve a dominant role domestically until the late 1940s, and internationally from the 1960s onward. The complex running culture of the Kalenjin eventually became part of the institutionalized global sporting system.

When French anthropologist Marcel Mauss (1979) wrote his article about body techniques during the late 1930s, its impact was not immediate. Mauss put forward the notion of body techniques which has since become central to the sociology and anthropology of the body. The notion of body techniques describes all the different ways of walking, running, and sleeping that exist in distinct cultures. In the 1930s, the sociology and anthropology of the body were primarily a philosophical program that attempted to emphasize embodiment as a condition for human existence into a phenomenological theme. No sociological, historical, or anthropological specification or concretization existed. From its beginning, western anthropology had, to some extent, dealt with the embodiment of non-western cultures by only describing the strange ways in which they treated the body. Body painting, tattooing and scarification were exotic themes of otherness and not subjected to profound analysis. The main emphasis was on the otherness of social structure, that is, economy, religion and kinship. At the theoretical level, the main emphasis was placed on pinning down otherness as primitive and underdeveloped as opposed to modern and developed. This was paradoxical as the omnipresent embodiment was only noted as a peripheral phenomenon. Anthropologists also noted otherness within forms of dance and movement. These observations, bar a few exceptions, were, however, not profoundly analysed either. Just as other body phenomena, they were treated as exotic body forms and, ultimately, as proof of how primitive they were. The fact of the matter is that sociology did not deal with the body even though it dealt with modernity within the social sciences. Two paradoxes are apparent here: anthropology ignored embodiment although anthropologists were exposed to body culture and technique on a daily basis, and sociology was blind to embodiment as a central element in western societies.

As mentioned earlier, this also applies to forms of movement including different sports within non-European cultures. Some do not exist any more or do so within entirely different social contexts. This is also true of body culture in Africa. Many African dance forms have either disappeared or been transformed into folkloristic features of the tourist industry. Other forms of movement have been reconstructed from photographs and unsystematic observations made by colonial administrators and military personnel who only noted those elements that were exotic from a European point of view. These observations were made without the necessary understanding of the culture and social context in which the activities took place (Bale, personal communication).

The success of African runners on the global scene combines different themes. There is the mystery of the background to their success. There is the historical background to their running technique and culture, the importance of which has been decisive. There are the historical themes in Mauss's sense of running forms as well as of body techniques.

African running culture and African runners have provided a unique theme of the relationship between otherness and modernity, the local or regional and the global sports market. Running and walking are very basic body techniques in Mauss's sense. Running, however, is incorporated in many different contexts ranging from mode of transport to top-level sport. Mauss made body techniques into a notion though not running, movement or body cultures. Mauss failed, however, to make a theme out of his notion when it came to specific body techniques and their incorporation into movement and body cultures. In other words, specific body techniques are incorporated into a systematic relationship and form part of the combined social structures of a culture and its significance.

Running, along with walking, is a simple body technique; there are, however, many ways in which one can run. A given technique is part of a running style. The running style is part of a running culture. Running is a body technique for transport and for sport as well as being part of an economic and cultural way of life. As will be made clear, running was part of a special form of terms of trade and will be shown through the running culture of pre-colonial and colonial Kenya. All this stemmed from the simple fact that running was a necessary part of cattle theft in Kenya, especially during the pre-colonial era. In other words, body techniques are part of a complex cultural pattern.

KENYA: A POWERHOUSE IN RUNNING

Kenyan runners have arguably been the single greatest phenomenon within athletics in the twentieth century. There is no indication that this will change in the twenty-first century. Their success in the 1980s at middle and long distances—including cross-country and road racing—has reached heights hitherto unseen in the world of athletics, maybe even in the world of sport in general. One only needs a little factual information to put the results of the Kenyan runners into perspective. Since their international breakthrough in the 1960s there has been an unusual recruitment pattern for the elite runners in that about 70 percent of them have emerged from a small ethnic group called the Kalenjin who number about 3.5 million people. The remaining 30 percent come from various ethnic groups, that is, Kisii (or Gusii), Kikuyu (or Gikuyu), Akamba, Maasai and Turkana. The fact that such a small ethnic group as the Kalenjin has contributed so overwhelmingly to the talent pool of Kenyan runners more or less continuously for a period of forty years makes the Kenyan running phenomenon all the more interesting. These facts alone make it no surprise that numerous researchers, journalists and laymen have over the years asked the following question: what lies behind this phenomenon?

Our intention with this paper is not to contribute to the discussion of whether the Kenyan or, more specifically, the Kalenjin running phenomenon is based primarily on physiological or sociological factors or a mixture of the two. Such a discussion would be inappropriate in this context. We wish instead to look at the historical development of this phenomenon and examine this development from an anthropological perspective. Our aim is to present historical facts with an emphasis on matters of sport, from the history of migration with its mixed culture to the present-day global culture of nomadic sportsmen, in such a way that makes the historical development comprehensible within the correct context and perspective. We want to show with this model the distinct connection between the developmental history of Kalenjin sports culture with its emphasis on running and the success they have subsequently achieved in international athletics as a part of global sport.

METHODOLOGICAL CONSIDERATIONS

There are certain methodological limitations for researchers wanting to contribute to the history of Kenya in general and to the history of Kenyan sport in particular. This is due to several factors. First of all, there are only a few written sources from the pre-colonial era since Kenya, like other sub-Saharan African nations, consisted of societies and cultures based on oral traditions as opposed to the written sources introduced at the time of colonization. The written sources that do exist concerning the so-called traditional societies of Kenya and Africa as such, bar a few exceptions, do not deal with the conditions of traditional movement culture, including running, prior to 1960 where sport, including traditional movement culture, was acknowledged as a legitimate part of anthropological research. The reason for the limited inclusion of sports matters in most previous books and papers was due to the anthropologists' lack of interest in the study of sport in foreign cultures (Blacking 1987). A classic article considered by many as pioneering within anthropological sports research was

"Games in Culture" by Roberts and collaborators (1959). In this work, sport was analysed and discussed as a serious cultural phenomenon. The following year, German sports scientist Carl Diem published his voluminous work *Weltgeschichte des Sports und der Leibeserziehung* (Diem 1960), and African sports culture was specifically discussed here, among others. The first French book on sports culture in Africa was not published until a decade later (Mélik-Chakhnaarov 1970), and the importance of sport in French West Africa was only thoroughly analysed more recently by Deville-Danthu (1997).

When dealing with research into pre-colonial sport cultures, problems arise in that only a few written references concerning sport in Kenya and Africa in general prior to 1960 actually exist. This means that researchers have to rely on two sources, traditional running culture as it appeared in colonial and post-colonial times and oral tradition.

Both of these sources have their limitations. As for traditional running culture, that is, cattle theft, during and after colonial times, the possibility could not be excluded that development had occurred, which meant that pre-colonial running culture was, in fact, different to that on which we had based our judgement. We have based our judgement on a close relationship with the early period of European colonization in Kenya when the British administration brought about drastic change in large parts of traditional society while recording the cultures of African peoples. The problem of interpreting the cultural history of the past, even within a span of a little over a hundred years, can be illuminated by drawing a parallel to our understanding of pre-historic hunter-gatherer societies based on studies of present-day hunter-gatherer societies (Gosden 1999). When two cultures meet, especially in an unequal power relationship, as was the case in Kenya and the rest of Africa, it is easy to imagine rapid change in the culture of the weaker party. The degree of this change is naturally hard to establish, especially when there are only very few written sources extant as documentation. These written sources were furthermore made by Europeans, which could mean problems in interpretation when passing on information about cultural matters that they most likely did not fully understand.

We have thereby indirectly touched upon the problem posed by oral tradition. It cannot act as historical evidence for more than a couple of hundred years and, most likely, only for a shorter period of time. It has been suggested that oral tradition should not be treated as a source of evidence in a historical perspective. Oral tradition is to be regarded instead as *part of an overall cultural system, which emerges out of a people's historical experience* (Spear 1981). We have decided, in the present text, to use oral tradition as a supplement to more established scientific sources in only one instance, this in order to support the written references.

Two other academic disciplines normally regarded as important in historical studies, archaeology and linguistics, have only been used indirectly in the present context. The reason being that while the two disciplines do provide general information about migratory history and the peoples and cultures that eventually were to make up the Kalenjin, they do not tell us anything specific about the traditional movement culture. We are thus dependent on socio-anthropological studies, despite the already-mentioned shortcomings, in order to be able to piece together a picture of the running culture along with the remaining traditional sports culture of the Kalenjin.

This paper has been framed chronologically, beginning with a short review of the history of Kalenjin migration, in order to understand the origin of the mixed cultures that were to shape them. We shall then discuss traditional running culture prior to British colonization in more detail. The next item of discussion will be the relatively short though, from a sports cultural point of view, intense and revolutionary colonial period and, finally, we shall examine modern running culture, the trademark of the contemporary Kalenjin.

KALENJIN—TERMINOLOGY AND CULTURAL BACKGROUND

The term "Kalenjin" is of recent origin. The term, which in English means something like "I tell you" or "I told you," first became the common name for a total of eight small ethnic groups in the late 1940s. They spoke a common language, albeit with distinct dialects, that was termed "Nandi" by the British. Since ethnic unification, however, it has been known as Kalenjin. The eight ethnic groups who decided to join forces in order to obtain greater cultural and political visibility and influence consisted, and still do, of Kipsigis, Nandi, Terik, Marakwet, Keiyo, Tugen, Saboat, and Pokot (Kipkorir 1985). Prior to British colonization, some of these Kalenjin sub-groups were further sub-divided. Administrative and political reasons or just the plain need to maintain control, however, made the British decide to create larger units, also known as tribes.

Approximately 3,000 years ago the first agriculturalists and pastoralists migrated to present-day Kenya from Ethiopia (Sutton 1976). Many continued their migration to present-day Tanzania. The migrants belonged to the Cushite linguistic group, formerly known as Hamites. The Cushites mixed with and assimilated large groups of hunter-gatherers, jointly known as the Okiek and Dorobo, who already lived in Kenya. The migrating Cushites became the dominant culture in western and central Kenya for a period of 1,000 years. New groups of people subsequently migrated to Kenya, some to Uganda; this time round they were Nilotes from the Sudan. They were pastoralists first and agriculturalists second. They assumed the dominant role from the Cushites over a period of 1,000 to 1,500 years in western Kenya through cultural assimilation and intermarriage (Fedders and Salvadori 1979). It is probable that, at the end of the latter period, the Nilotes began to form groups and undertake separate migrations within the borders of what would become Kenya; it was not until that time that they began to settle down in the area of Kenya where the majority of the Kalenjin live today.

Prior to the arbitrary classification of the so-called tribes by the British, the Nandi most probably was the only one of the eight Kalenjin subgroups that had a true group identity. The Nandi had a distinct mentality and lifestyle which was expressed through their running culture, among other things. The different Kalenjin peoples were, nonetheless, aware of common cultural traits which acted as a unifying factor prior to British colonization. They would also unite against an outside foe in times of war as they did when, for instance, the Maasai decided to attack one of the Kalenjin sub-groups (Sutton 1976).

The mixed culture which resulted in the integrated lifestyle of the Kalenjin consisted of a number of traits that were to prove important for movement, body culture in general, and running culture in particular. The Cushites brought to Kalenjin culture such important traits as the ritual circumcision of adolescent boys and girls between the ages of ten and eighteen, the so-called *rite de passage* (Ehret 1974). The Cushites as well as the Nilotes also brought cattle and other domesticated animals such as sheep and goats with them to Kenya. It was the Nilotes, however, who infused Kalenjin culture with semi-religious feelings toward cattle that have characterized their relationship with the bovine livestock ever since. Since Cushites and Nilotes brought grain products along with them to Kenya besides their domesticated animals, the Kalenjin were thus from the very outset both agriculturalists and pastoralists (Sutton 1974). Hunting culture seems to have been a contribution from the Okiek and the Dorobo who were, by and large, assimilated by the waves of migration from the north. This brief review of the important cultural characteristics of the Kalenjins' ancestors clearly demonstrates that cultural contributions of major significance did not come exclusively from the Cushites, although this misconception had otherwise prevailed in anthropological theory for many decades. Until about 1970, anthropologists thought that the more sophisticated Kalenjin cultural traits stemmed solely from the Cushites. This was primarily due to the *Hamitic myth* propagated by the British anthropologist C. G. Seligman who was, among others, very active during the 1920s and 1930s. In essence, the Hamitic myth claims that the Cushites came all the way from Egypt, bringing with them a cultural background that made them superior to the black African peoples. It has since, however, become evident that all the peoples who made up the Kalenjin have all contributed something to the overall culture with traits from their own initial cultures. All the cultural aspects outlined above became central elements in Kalenjin everyday life. These aspects were either necessary in order to survive—domesticated animals, agriculture, hunting and warfare—or they possessed profound symbolic value in rites of initiation when boys and girls left childhood behind for adulthood through circumcision.

CATTLE THIEVES

Cattle raiding was the most prestigious of all Kalenjin sports within the traditional culture. It was an important part of a young man's identity. The most popular movement culture, however, was dance. This was due to the fact that a cattle raiding was an exclusively male activity, whereas members of both sexes could participate in dance. It is important to point out that, among the Kalenjin, cattle raiding could be interpreted in two ways: positively and negatively. It was regarded as positive if, for example, Nandi warriors raided cattle from the Terik or the Maasai. In that case it was not regarded as theft by the Nandi so much as a way of regaining divine property. Should, however, Nandi warriors steal cattle from fellow Nandis, this was regarded as pure theft and the thieves were then liable to be publicly cursed and socially ostracized (Snell 1954). The reason for cattle being the object of both positive and negative raiding was due to the fact that they were of very high social and economic value. Cattle were used, among other things, as a means of payment of bride wealth. This meant that a man who owned many cows was able to buy many wives and, thereby, father many children. Ownership of cattle was a sign of wealth, in practical as well as symbolic terms.

For a more profound understanding of this essential part of Kalenjin culture, E. E. Evans-Pritchard's comprehensive work on the Sudanese Nuer is required reading, especially the volume *Nuer Religion* (1956). The Nuer along with the Kalenjin belongs to the Nilotic Cluster and the ancestors of the Nuer were among the people who migrated to Kenya, becoming the dominant part of the Kalenjin. Evans-Pritchard's thorough description of the Nuers' religious relationship with their cattle, therefore, provides a good illustration of the relationship between the Kalenjin and their cattle in historical terms and for most of the twentieth century.

A cattle raiding was essentially a war game in which young warriors risked their lives in order to obtain social prestige and economic prosperity. They had to, on occasion, run up to 150 kilometers in order to reach inhabited areas with plenty of cattle and then return with their spoil. A cattle raid was carried out by groups that varied considerably in numbers, from a mere handful to as many as five hundred warriors. Most cattle raids, however, were probably small scale affairs only involving a handful of warriors (Ng'eny 1970). The raids required careful planning and tough discipline as the element of surprise had to be obtained vis-à-vis the enemy in order to optimize the gains. This meant that warriors had to be capable of sustained effort as only small rations of food were allowed during the long return trips on foot. It was regarded as an unnecessary expenditure of energy, besides being impractical and time consuming, to bring along food rations in excess of the required minimum. The raid itself took place at dawn while most of the enemy were still asleep. This was mainly a Nandi tradition as most of the other sub-groups of the Kalenjin carried out their raids during the day. It was important to get the stolen cattle back home as quickly as possible, preferably before the victims of the raid could take up the pursuit (Matson 1970). Once the stolen cattle were brought safely home by their now "legitimate" owners, they were then distributed according to a carefully established pattern (Hollis 1909).

A cattle raid was carried out in one of the three following situations: when cattle died due to drought or rinderpest, when new land became available, and in order to forestall boredom among newly initiated warriors.

The first reason was practical in nature and besides the securing of food supplies there was also an urgent social necessity, the payment of bride wealth for instance (Snell 1954). The Nandi looked upon raiding as a routine occupation that helped maintain the tribal economy (Matson 1970).

The second reason for cattle raiding was to take advantage of abandoned geographical areas. Again it was the Nandi who were the ones to take advantage of such a situation. An instance of this was when the Maasai chose to abandon the Uasin Gishu plateau around 1880 after fighting with the Nandi and among themselves. The new land and grazing areas for cattle that thus became available to the Nandi expanded their scope for raiding activity as they moved closer to potential victims. It is important to stress that the Nandi, as well as the other Kalenjin sub-groups, seldom went cattle raiding with an eye to conquering new territory (Sutton 1976).

The third reason was rooted in the desire of the young Kalenjin warriors to go on raids as some kind of sport; in this way a warrior could have some excitement in his life (Matson 1970) even if it was at the risk of life and limb. Raiding also offered a young warrior a way out of poverty, possibly even to expand any eventual personal fortune.

The capacity for sustained effort was an important prerequisite for becoming a successful cattle thief. Running in itself was seen merely as a means for achieving the final goal: expanding the cattle herd. In theory running skills, as the most important tool in cattle raiding, could just as well have been respected and admired characteristics of Kalenjin culture. The running abilities of the warriors could, however, have been overshadowed by the fact that stolen cattle were *the* manifestation of success. One could theorize that running per se was buried under the large quantity of other criteria for success inherent in cattle raiding—elements, for instance, such as courage, when a warrior killed an enemy or saved the life of a fellow warrior; endurance, physical as well as mental; the ability to cover long distances at night as did the Nandi on limited rations, indicative of strict discipline.

In light of the above, it could be theorized that the praise of successful cattle raiders in Kalenjin societies was an indirect appreciation of the warriors' running abilities. According to Samuel K. arap Ng'eny, a Nandi historian, the fact of the matter was that "no warrior was worthy of the name unless he distinguished himself in one of the raids" (Ng'eny 1970).

War and cattle raiding were inextricably bound up with one another in Kalenjin culture. As war also played an important part in the lives of young men in pre-colonial Kalenjin culture, running must have played a central role in different aspects of culture, such as social prestige, economy and the expression of manliness, besides providing an outlet for aggression. Competition was an important aspect in its own right—who was the bravest? Then there was the semi-religious character of cattle raiding enshrining the divine right of property over all cattle.

Participation in cattle raiding, at least among the most feared of all cattle thieves, the Nandi, was often arranged through personal invitation. This is indicated by Ng'eny in 1970 when he wrote "[b]ut not all raids were undertaken haphazardly." This would have given the more skilled cattle thieves more opportunities to acquire cattle than the less skilful cattle thieves.

In summary, in the days of pre-colonial Kalenjin culture there are strong indications that good running abilities were regarded as a necessity for becoming a good cattle thief. A cattle raiding where running was the principal tool was regarded as "sport," at least amongst the young warriors.

There was another more informal and unstructured manifestation of traditional Kalenjin running culture. It took the form of running contests between the young herdsmen during the long tedious hours spent tending herds of cattle or other domesticated animals. To the best of our knowledge, however, specific details about such informal competition have not been recorded in the historical literature.

The question of whether it was children, as in contemporary Kalenjin society, or whether it was young warriors in the pre-colonial period that looked after the herds of cattle has been the subject of controversy. Several authors claim that children tended cattle in pre-colonial Kalenjin society (Kipkorir 1985; Godia 1989; Mählmann 1992). Other authors, however, repudiate this and claim that tending cattle was mainly the duty of young warriors (Huntingford 1951; Langley 1979; Oboler 1985). A. C. Hollis (1909) in his work on Nandi culture lends support to the latter school of thought by writing "cattle herding is the chief occupation of the men and the big boys." The position of the latter group is, in our opinion, the most plausible in view of the constant danger of cattle raids from other groups. It seems fair to suggest that young warriors at the very least tended the cattle in the early hours of the day, a time when the danger of a cattle raid taking place was at its highest. This did not apply to the Nandi themselves. They were, however, the cause of the early morning danger to everyone else to whom it most definitely applied. The young warriors would take over again when the cattle returned from grazing and count them.

The importance of cattle raiding to pre-colonial Kalenjin society was clearly reflected in the oral tradition, in this case a song praising the Kalenjin in their prime as cattle thieves (Chesaina 1991). In the last two verses of the song translated from the original Kalenjin, the connection between cattle raiding and war becomes very obvious indeed:

> Colobus monkey
> When you are on top of a tree
> Only your skin can kill you
> Oiyoho, only your skin can kill you
>
> Long time ago, our men raided
> Places like Kipnyorei
> Men of the generations of
> Kaplelach and Kipnyigei
> The generation of Nyangi
> Raided when they were initiates
> Oiyoho, they went to Sison
> They took with them shields and clubs
> They tied on themselves knives and spears
> The Kipsigis, Nandi, Tugen and Keiyo
> Were men who tied war feathers on themselves
> But today this sounds like a story

When the British came across the Kalenjin in the fertile and hilly highlands of western Kenya in the nineteenth century, they were confronted with cattle thieves who were capable of exceptional levels of sustained effort, physical as well as mental.

WHITE MAN'S SPORT

Kenya was officially colonized by the British in 1895. Even then the British administration had to use military force in order to quell the tough

Nandi warriors intermittently over a period of eleven years. So it was not until 1906 that they were able to inhabit and cultivate this part of the Great Rift Valley known as *the White Highlands* during the colonial era (Ogot 1970).

Many of the colonists who went to Kenya either as farmers or as employees of the colonial administration were keen sportsmen. Documentation exists which shows that those chosen by the Foreign and Colonial Office to work in the colonial administration were favored if they themselves were sportsmen. This applied not only to Kenya but to all British colonies. In Great Britain, the authorities held that sporting abilities were important in potential candidates. They were seen as a sign of fitness as well as implying good personal characteristics such as initiative, sound judgement and the ability to keep inferior types under control (Holt 1989).

The cult of athleticism was an integral part of the "moral curriculum" imported from the major English public schools such Eton, Harrow, Winchester and Rugby, and it was adopted with alacrity by schools in British tropical Africa. There was an overarching idea that, by means of sport and games, the African could be shaped to conform to Victorian gentlemanly ideals and Christian values then pertaining, such as perseverance, stamina, honesty, godliness, purity and courage. The means to that ideal end were often implemented by enthusiastic and well-meaning albeit paternalistic and ethnocentric individuals. The combination of this strict physical regimen and an equally strict moral code has since been termed "muscular Christianity." The main advocate of this philosophy in Kenya was, arguably, Francis Carey, Second Headmaster of the Alliance High School in Nairobi (Mangan 1987).

The British busied themselves with sports such as golf, tennis, polo, horseracing, squash, croquet and cricket, all so-called country club sports, in order to stave off boredom when abroad and strengthen social ties with other Britons stationed in the colonies. Sports among the British served a double function in that there was a culture of participants along with one of spectators; sports comprised both competition and recreation (Naibei 1989; Bale and Sang 1996).

The Kalenjin, along with all the other African peoples of Kenya, were banned from participation in country club sports. These were, with very few exceptions, the exclusive preserve of the Europeans. Africans, however, were allowed to take part in athletics, football and, later on, boxing.

Athletics became the most popular sport among the Kalenjin. The main reason for this is most probably to be found in the fact that thanks to their cattle-raiding tradition, or running tradition, they were well prepared to take on the European way of running, that is to say, *a sports-oriented* way. Athletics also required fewer resources than did either football or boxing. Athletics were, in theory at least, immediately open to most Kalenjin.

The first officially recorded athletics meeting in Kenya did not, however, take place in the Kalenjin residential area but at the coastal town of Mombasa on November 9, 1901. There were several different competitions at the athletics meeting open to Africans, Asians and Europeans; the last ethnic group, the Arabs, were not represented. Athletics meetings at that time were often a mixture of classic athletic disciplines and competitions in a category best described as traditional games. An annual sports and games meeting was, from the earliest years of the colonization of Kenya held on Boxing Day, alternately in Nairobi and Mombasa, the two largest towns of the colony. The various events at such a meeting in Nairobi in 1906 comprised a hundred yards dash as well as an egg race for women only, a donkey race and pole climbing for Africans only. These meetings had enormous popular appeal (Wortberg 1994).

There were few officially arranged athletics meetings until the mid-1920s. The traditional meetings mentioned above were probably the only common meetings in the early years of the colony. An Athletics Department was established in 1924 under the National African and Arabic Sports Association. The Arabians formed their own national sports associations while the Europeans continued with their exclusive country-club sporting activities. The bureaucratization of athletics in Kenya started with the formation of the National Athletics Association; this led to the spread of athletics to schools, the police force, the army (King's African Rifles) as well as the employees of the prison administration. The founding of ethnically based sports associations meant that the athletics meetings in Kenya were also held on a basis of ethnic separation. This had not been the case in the very early years of colonization in Kenya when Africans and Europeans did take part in the same meeting albeit in ethnically segregated events. In other words, de facto apartheid had been introduced to Kenya by the mid-1920s. This was at a time when the colonial authorities had finally overcome the initial difficulties in terms of administrative and political control of Kenya. In 1920, Kenya changed status from being the East African Protectorate to that of the Colony of Kenya. The time had come to administer and control sports from above. The British colonial authorities had an overall political purpose with the new organization of sport that was the political and social control of the African peoples in particular.

The schools were important institutions when it came to introducing athletics to the Africans and the British teachers and missionaries, often one and the same person, placed the emphasis squarely on British-style games within a team context. The school system as an institution, however, seems to have been overestimated in the years up to 1945. A good case in point is the number of physical education lessons, athletics included, that numbered only five per week in 1932 (Harris 1932). The relatively small number of lessons makes it hard to forward the claim that the colonial authorities, that is, the central administration, placed much emphasis on physical education and sports activities among the Africans at this time during the colonial years—this in spite of the amply documented concern, sometimes even obsession, with character training through sports. Two further factors underline this state of affairs—poor quality of facilities and education along with the small number of relatively privileged African pupils who went to school prior to the Second World War. According to Hardman and Nteere (1994) "the imposed system . . . was a poor replica of the British system, being under resourced and subject to poor quality teaching."

We should like to lie to rest the persistent myth that the Kenyan dominance in running is due to their running to and from school as children. To start with there were no schools to run to until after Kenya was colonized and then, few children, mainly boys, went to school at all before 1945, which afforded only the smallest of minorities the opportunity to run to school. In other words, Kalenjin pupils have only been running to and from school to any significant extent for about sixty years. This period represents about six generations of runners of around ten years each. The extent—that is to say, the frequency, quantity and intensity—of this type of running as well as how many may have run thus remains unknown to us. We can only venture an educated guess based on a few more recent questionnaires in which running activity varies greatly as a mode of transport for individuals (Saltin et al. 1995). Running as a mode of transport has probably had a positive effect on the results of competitive runners over the years in the form of fewer injuries and a large base from which to recruit talented runners. Well-trained pupils would have had an opportunity sooner or later to display their running abilities during physical education lessons. The assertion, however, that the predominance of Kalenjin runners is directly due to their having run to and from school for the past six generations has no scientific basis whatsoever.

The army played an important part in the propagation of athletics throughout the school system during the colonial era. The National Archives have records of a Rift Valley district commissioner's proposal "that an army physical training instructor should be attached to all Rift Valley schools" (KNA/PC/PVP 2/3/2).

It should be evident at this point that Africans, including the Kalenjin, participated in athletics in different institutions throughout Kenya. The fact that the first permanent running track in Nandi was built as early as the 1950s at the Government African School in Kapsabet, the main town in Nandi, attests to the popularity of athletics among the Kalenjin (Bale and Sang 1996). Very few running tracks existed elsewhere at that time in Kenya. The first proper athletics stadium was built in Nyeri north of Nairobi in 1960 (Velzian, personal communication).

The first national athletics championships for men were held in 1925, the first for women in 1961. Kalenjin runners, however, did not show their strength in the middle and long distances until the mid-1940s, although the first national victory for a Kalenjin was obtained for the three mile race in 1938 by a runner called Kiptume. However, the national athletics championships were subsequently cancelled for the duration of the Second World War (Wortberg 1994).

It is difficult to answer the question why did the male Kalenjin, who were used to running in their traditional society, not fare better in athletics at this stage. One obvious answer could have been a strong aversion to the European way of running, round and round a track without the possibility for gaining riches, social prestige and the excitement of cattle raiding. There is another plausible theory, however, namely that the lack of early success for Kalenjin runners was due to the fact that organized athletics training was first introduced in schools in the Nairobi area which few if any Kalenjin attended (Bale and Sang 1996). For this reason, athletes from other ethnic groups gained an early advantage in track running, which they exploited to the full. We assume that athletes of Kalenjin origin participated in national athletics championships before 1938. We do not, however, know to what extent if any.

The Kalenjin should, in theory, have had a more dominant role in athletics through their training in the King's African Rifles (K.A.R.) as they were over-represented by comparison with their percentage of the population. Africans in the K.A.R. were, however, generally uninterested in sporting activities although these became a permanent part of K.A.R. activities in the 1930s. It was not until the outbreak of the Second World War that there was any significant increase in the African interest in sports when they became an integrated part of the army welfare program. American author Timothy H. Parsons (1999), in his book on the history of the K.A.R., says "the African rank-and-file" uses the word "athletics," which we assume to imply sports in general since athletics is specifically termed "track and field" in American English. Since athletics provided an inexpensive, easy and physically efficient way of engaging in sport, particularly in terms of the track disciplines, it is fair to suppose that athletic events were part of the K.A.R. sports curriculum. The army's success in several post-war running, jumping and throwing events at the national Kenyan athletics championships supports our supposition.

DIFFERENT FORMS OF CATTLE RAIDING

One of the first legal measures to be taken by the colonial authorities was to outlaw cattle raiding (Manners 1975). This, however, did not stop cattle raiding during the colonial period. Instead, cattle raiding had a further dimension added to it. This meant that two distinct varieties of cattle raiding existed for most of the colonial period; traditional cattle raids executed by warriors of the same sub-group, the Nandi for instance; and then, the new variety whereby warriors from the different ethnic groups, including non-Kalenjin such as the Luo, all worked together (Anderson 1986).

A. C. Hollis (1909) might have been the first to document the fact that cattle raiding continued after the colonization of Kenya. As the colonial authorities extended their control over the White Highlands from 1900 to 1920, large-scale cattle raiding did, however, become an ever rarer occurrence. This was due to the British practice of punishing cattle theft severely, irrespective of whether the offence had taken place in an African residential area or on a European farm. The traditional pattern of Kalenjin cattle theft in general did not exist after 1920, that is, Kalenjin sub-groups stealing from other Kalenjin sub-groups or other African ethnic groups, all in accordance with traditional moral standards, although there was the occasional grand cattle raid carried out at the extreme northern or southern boundaries of Kalenjin territory. This shift reflected the changing circumstances that the colonial administration had imposed upon traditional African societies along with the fact that Europeans had taken over large parts of the fertile land of the White Highlands (Anderson 1986).

The changed circumstances brought about a response that led to the decline of traditional cattle raids and an increasing professionalism of cattle theft undertaken by specialized cattle thieves from several ethnic groups. There were, however, some inter-tribal gangs at this time who did respect elements of the traditional moral codes in that they took into account the economic value of the cattle to their original owners. The Keiyo, for instance, would steal cattle from the Nandi or European farmers who employed non-Keiyo farmhands. They would, however, never steal cattle from within the Elegyo reservation where the Keiyos lived (Anderson 1986).

There were two reasons for the gradual shift toward cattle raiding undertaken by multi-ethnic gangs who operated without reference to the traditional moral economic values connected with cattle as an economic asset. First of all, the possibilities for the Kalenjin to engage in their favorite "sport" were drastically reduced after the Europeans took control of the fertile Rift Valley area and introduced legal restrictions on cattle raiding. Second, the introduction of money as the basis of economic transactions in the East African region encouraged young warriors to retain their cattle until a good business opportunity arose (Anderson 1986).

The development of organized crime placed the elders in a dilemma as they were the authority whose advice was sought by the young warriors who usually respected it in traditional society. Those young men who joined the multi-ethnic gangs were beyond the control of the elders. Interestingly, as late as 1959, the Provincial Commissioner of the Rift Valley made the following statement; "After all, stock theft is the traditional sport of the young men of many tribes and the elders cannot be expected to act as kill-joys and stamp it out unless they themselves are liable to suffer" (KAN PC/NKU/2/15/9). It is doubtful, however, that the commissioner had any knowledge of the changed nature of cattle raiding that had become the predominant way of stealing cattle for over three decades by the time he made his statement.

DIFFERENT WAYS OF RUNNING

The dominance of the Kalenjin on the Kenyan running track began in the mid-1940s as mentioned above. The question is why did this dominance come about? Two interwoven reasons can be put forward. As cattle raiding was outlawed and thus limited, this signaled change in living conditions that might have gradually motivated young men to channel their energy and restlessness into organized athletics after slowly overcoming their aversion toward the European way of running, that is, racing on a track. Over time the heroes of Kalenjin society changed character, from being successful cattle thieves they became winners on the track. The young men would now receive awards, though not yet fortunes, for running against the clock instead of bringing home cattle. This was how the most important way for a Kalenjin male to climb the social ladder was gradually changed.

The underlying reason for the promotion of sports by the colonial administration is quite obvious. It was done in order to avoid cattle raiding. Sports meetings were organized at regional and local levels with many Africans taking part as both competitors and spectators. The winner of an event was rewarded with, among other things, carpets and lamps. The colonial administration sought to provide a substitute for cattle raiding through sports meetings where warriors could win awards while competing against other warriors. An example of the eagerness with which the British tried to put an end to cattle raids is the following sentence used in the late 1930s as part of a campaign to stop cattle raiding among the Kipsigis: Show your valour in sports and games, not in war (Manners 1975).

The successful emergence of the male Kalenjin as competitive runners on domestic tracks was most noticeable from the mid-1940s to the mid-1950s. It happened at a time when there was very little organized training and the athletics season only lasted a few weeks (Nortberg 1994). Then, in 1949, an Englishman called Archie Evans arrived in Kenya. Appointed as a colony sports officer, he became responsible for the formation of the national Kenyan Amateur Athletics Association, KAAA (recently re-named Athletics Kenya), in 1951. Training and meetings were subsequently better organized and, for the first time, Kenyan athletes began to compete outside the African continent with some degree of success. This was especially true for the British Empire and Commonwealth Games of

1954 and 1958. The best Kalenjin runners of this period, however, were overshadowed by a strong group of Gusii runners, the most prominent being Nyandika Maiyoro, who became Kenya's first internationally renowned runner (Bentsen 1983).

GLOBAL NOMADS

When Kenya gained independence in 1963, the country's athletes were ready to be part of the modern sports world and globalization. This was a globalization that had already begun when the British introduced European sport to Kenyans as well as to other colonies of the British Empire. In 1964, Kipsigis runner Wilson Kiprugut Chuma won Kenya's first Olympic medal, a bronze in the 800 meters. This particular event marked the international breakthrough of the Kalenjin that was to be of a magnitude no one dreamt of at the time.

The final breakthrough for Kenyan runners came in the years 1965–1968 when Kipchoge Keino, a Nandi, the father of running, broke world records in the 3,000 and 5,000 meter events and won medals at international championships such as the 1,500 meters gold at the Mexico City Olympics of 1968. Several Kalenjin runners followed up on this success at this time. A Gusii runner, Naftali Temu, also won an Olympic gold medal for Kenya when he took advantage of the thin air to win the 10,000 meters final in Mexico City (Amin and Moll 1972).

The enormous success that Kenyan, especially Kalenjin, runners achieved quickly led to the recruiting of the talented for American universities. The steady flow of Kenyan runners to America, especially from the mid-1970s on, did thus become the first *muscle industry* in which Kenyan runners were involved. A university scholarship in the United States afforded the runners the opportunity of achieving an academic degree paid for by their results on the track. The recruiting of athletes abroad led to the recruiting of runners in Kenya proper. This meant that coaches at secondary schools in Kenya started to recruit runners from primary schools. The majority of this recruiting took place, and still does, in the Rift Valley Province where the Kalenjin live and from where most of the running talent emerges (Christensen 2000).

The introduction of money into international athletics in the mid-1980s resulted in the increased interest of European athletics agents in Kenyan runners as part of a lucrative business; this, in turn, led to the intensified domestic recruiting of running talent. More and more permanent training camps sponsored by international sports-goods manufacturing companies pop up in the Rift Valley Province where young, hopeful, runners train and live. The most suitable term for these training camps is *muscle facto-ries* where the runners, with only a few exceptions, are offered anything besides organized training, food and shelter. Talent and hope motivate the runners but only luck and perseverance in training will lead to an op-portunity of obtaining a starting license for the desired athletics meetings in Europe. The worship of the golden calf has thus been intensified over the past fifteen years (Christensen 2000).

The whole business has become self-sustaining. The enormous poverty and rate of unemployment in Kenya, along with the arrival of serious money in international athletics and energetic athletics agents have all conspired to pave the way for the intensive recruiting of young Kenyan running talent. This effect, quite naturally, is especially profound among the young Kalenjin, male and female, as they possess the most significant and proudest tradition within running, the formidable combination of feared cattle raiders of yore and today's gold medalists at international athletics championships. It must be pointed out, however, that all Kenyan peoples living in the Highlands such as the Kikuyu or the Gusii have a cattle-raiding tradition, so cattle raiding alone does not explain the athlet-ics success of the Kalenjin (Christensen 2000).

By using the model of "typology of sport labour migration" introduced by Joseph Maguire (1999), it becomes possible to gauge the role of the Kalenjin runners by comparison with their participation in international athletics since independence in 1963. In the first phase of their inter-national success from the mid-1960s to the mid-1980s, the pre-money era of athletics, the Kalenjin runners were, first and foremost, "nomadic cosmopolitans." During this phase, they used their sports careers to go traveling; furthermore, good results in running events abroad could re-sult in admission to an American university that, in turn, could lead to a first-class education and the possibility of a good job. In reality, however, many runners of this period ended up as de facto full-time athletes and only de jure students (Bale and Sang 1996).

From the mid-1980 onward the Kalenjin runners have shifted to the categories of either "mercenaries" or "returnees." Those in the former category are characterized by being motivated by short-term gain and by being employed as hired guns. As migrants, they have "little or no attachment to the local, no sense of place in relation to the space where they currently reside or do their body-work" (Maguire 1999). The profusion of running talent among the Kalenjin and the stiff competition for money makes the mercenary lifestyle understandable. The overall aim of the athletes seems to stem from the possibility of earning as much money as possible in a single athletics season since, come the next season, they might no longer be good enough even to be invited to international athletics meetings.

Those in the latter category will, more often than not, be experienced athletes. They are best characterized as persons for whom "the lure of "home soil" can prove too strong" (Maguire 1999). Such characterization might—in the case of returnee Kalenjin runners—have a more practical source. When the athletics or cross season is over, there is no reason to stay abroad from a sports', that is, economic, point of view. Besides, the weather outside the athletics season is, in most parts of Europe and America, too dreadful and impractical from a training point of view, by comparison with Kenya.

Whichever category they might belong to, Kalenjin runners belong to a group that can be termed "global nomads."

CATTLE RAIDING STILL A FACTOR

Cattle raiding remained an important factor in Kalenjin culture after independence in both the traditional inter-tribal form and the newer multiethnic form (Hall 1973). The reasons behind modern-day cattle raids seem to be eminently practical such as shortage of cattle due to drought and/or epidemics. This means that the more cattle people own, the less likely it is they will organize cattle raids. Modern weapons have, moreover, replaced traditional weapons to a certain extent, which has undoubtedly tempted some to engage in cattle raiding; although it has become an extremely dangerous "sport," or enterprise for want of a better term.

The Pokot, the most traditional of all the Kalenjin sub-groups, provide a good case in point. From 1979 to 1981 there was a devastating drought in their home area which resulted in the outbreak of livestock epidemics. The number of cattle, goats and sheep declined dramatically and ever since the total number of domesticated animals has fluctuated without ever reaching pre-1979 levels. The Pokot area is still drought-stricken and population increase is high, so there is little chance of livestock numbers reaching pre-1979 levels (Zaal and Dietz 1999). There is, in other words, still considerable incentive for the Pokot to continue cattle raiding.

One of the authors (DLC) obtained verification during a stay in Kenya in 1999 that the Pokot were still active cattle raiders. This verification came about through interviews and a travel restriction to the northern boundaries of the Kalenjin home area. The travel restriction had been imposed due to heavy fighting between the Pokot, Marakwet and Sabaot sub-groups of the Kalenjin.

Another factor to be considered when evaluating the reasons for the extent of cattle-raiding activity is the state of general economic development and the possibilities for alternative occupational activities for the people in question. As far as the Pokot are concerned, their dire economic conditions and long travel distances to the closest urban area with sports facilities have resulted in far fewer opportunities to excel in running by comparison with, for instance, the Nandi among others. Of all the Kalenjin sub-groups, it is precisely the Pokot, with only a few exceptions, who have not contributed to any significant extent to the "talent factory" of the Kalenjin in middle- and long-distance running disciplines. It is for this reason that it does not come as a surprise that cattle raiding remains a significant cultural and economic factor in this remote area of the Kalenjin homeland.

TRADITIONAL MOVEMENT CULTURE AND GLOBAL SPORT

It should be evident by now that the traditional East African running culture did not solely consist of running techniques in Marcel Mauss's sense, that it was, in fact, a complex running culture in relation to cattle raiding and the initiation rites of the young males. The fact that such a specifically local and traditional running culture has been able to contribute so much to modern and global running culture would, most probably, have exceeded Mauss's wildest imagination. He created a methodological program for the analysis of body techniques, thus contributing a central notion to the sociology and anthropology of the body. Mauss created in the 1930s a methodological program for the study of body and movement. The limitations of his notions and methodological programs lie in the fact that they were not reflected upon or taken to a higher level. Mauss never created a theory of body anthropology and his observations concerning movement techniques remained firmly at program level. Although he did not propose the notion of movement culture, he did nonetheless create a number of crucial concepts, not least of which was that of body techniques.

African-style running demonstrates how running, as a body technique, is part of a complex pattern of movement culture pertaining to central elements of the overall culture as such. It is, of course, no simple matter to reconstruct this part of African history. The global success of African running culture reveals a highly specialized version of the connection between the historical, local and global. African running culture in its historical guise acts as a mirror to both sports sociology and sports anthropology. Every body technique forms part of a movement culture which, in turn, forms part of different sub-cultures, such as cattle raiding, as a special variant of barter economy and male initiation rites, in other words, the culture of a traditional African society. Within just a few decades, this venerable movement and running culture even became part of a totally different body cultural context; in this case, contemporary global sport.

NOTES

We are indebted to American author and freelance journalist, John Manners of Montclair, New Jersey, for his help with suggestions and providing us with literature on the cattle-raiding culture of the Kalenjin. The content of the article is an elaboration on themes presented earlier by Dirk Lund Christensen in print as a book in Danish and as a thesis, supervised by Associate Professor Søren Damkjær. The latter was submitted to the Centre of African Studies at the University of Copenhagen, Denmark. This manuscript has previously been published in Danish in the journal *Idrætshistorisk Årbog* (Yearbook of Sports History) in 2002.

BIBLIOGRAPHY

Amin, M. and P. Moll. *Kenya's World-Beating Athletes*. Nairobi: East African Publishing House, 1972.

Anderson, D. "Stock Theft and Moral Economy in Colonial Kenya." *Africa* 56 (1986): 399–416.

Bale, J. and J. Sang. *Kenyan Running: Movement Culture, Geography and Global Change.* London: Frank Cass & Co., Ltd., 1996.

Bentsen, C. "Kenya I." *The Runner* 5 (1983): 52–70.

Blacking, J. "Games and Sport in Pre-colonial African Societies." *Sport in Africa: Essays in Social History*, edited by W. J. Baker and J. A. Mangan. New York: Africana Publishing Company, 1987: 3–22.

Chesaina, C. *Oral Literature of the Kalenjin.* Nairobi: Heinemann Kenya, Ltd., 1991.

Christensen, D. L. *Washindi: Løberne fra Kenya.* Copenhagen: Frydenlund grafisk, 2000.

Deville-Danthu, B. *Le sport en noir et blanc.* Paris/Montreal: L'Harmattan, 1997.

Diem, C. *Weltgeschichte des Sports und der Leibeserziehung.* Stuttgart: Cotta-Verlag, 1960.

Ehret, C. "Cushites and the Highland and Plains Nilotes to A.D. 1800." *Zamani: A Survey of East African History*, 2nd edition, edited by B. A. Ogot. Nairobi: East African Publishing House, 1974: 150–69.

Evans-Pritchard, E. E. *Nuer religion.* London: Oxford at Clarendon, 1956.

Fedders A. and C. Salvadori. *Peoples and Cultures of Kenya.* Nairobi/London: Transafrica/Rex Collings, 1979.

Godia, G. "Sport in Kenya." *Sport in Asia and Africa: A Comparative Handbook*, edited by E. A. Wagner. New York: Greenwood Press, 1989: 267–81.

Gosden, C. *Anthropology & Archaeology: A Changing Relationship.* London/New York: Routledge, 1999.

Hall, S. "The Role of Physical Education and Sports in the Nation Building Process of Kenya." Non-published PhD thesis, The Ohio State University, 1973.

Hardmann, K. and J. S. Nteere. "Politics in Physical Education and Sport in England and Kenya." *Sport in the Global Village*, edited by R. C. Wilcox. Morgantown, W.Va.: Fitness Information Technology, Inc., 1994: 413–24.

Harris, P. W. Syllabus Revision African-schools 1932, Education 1/1/25.

Hollis, A. C. *The Nandi: Their Language and Folk-lore.* London: Oxford University Press, 1909.

Holt, R. *Sport and the British: A Modern History.* Oxford: Oxford University Press, 1989.

Huntingford, G. W. B. *Nandi Work and Culture.* London: His Majesty's Stationery Office for the Colonial Office, 1950.

Huntingford, G. W. B. *The Nandi of Kenya: Tribal Control in a Pastoral Society.* London: Routledge & Kegan Paul, Ltd., 1953.

Kenya National Archieves/PC/NKU/2/15/9.

Kenya National Archives /PC/PVP 2/3/2.

Kipkorir, B. *Kenya's People: People of the Rift Valley— Kalenjin*, 2nd ed. Nairobi: Evans Brothers, Ltd., 1985.

Langley, M. S. *The Nandi of Kenya: Life Crisis Rituals in a Period of Change.* New York: St. Martin's Press, 1979.

Maguire, J. *Global Sport: Identities, Societies, Civilisations.* Cambridge, Mass.: Polity Press, 1999.

Mählmann, P. "The Role of Sport in the Process of Modernisation: The Kenyan Case." *Journal of Eastern African Research & Development* 22 (1992): 120–31.

Mangan J. A. "Ethics and Ethnocentricity: Imperial Education in British Tropical Africa." *Sport in Africa: Essays in Social History*, edited by W. J. Baker and J. A. Mangan. New York: Africana Publishing Company, 1987: 3–22.

Manners, J. "In Search of an Explanation." *The African Running Revolution*, edited by D. Prokop. Mountain View, Calif.: World Publications, 1975: 26–39.

Matson, A. T. "Nandi Traditions on Raiding." *Hadith 2: Proceedings of the 1968 Conference of the Historical Association of Kenya*, edited by B. A. Ogot. Nairobi: East African Publishing House, 1970: 61–78.

Mauss, M. *Sociology and Psychology: Essays*. London: Routledge and Kegan Paul, 1979.

Mélik-Chakhnaarov, A. *Le Sport en Afrique*. Paris: Présence africaine, 1970.

Naibei, W. C. "The Development of Sports in Kenya." *Geschichte der Leibesübungen: Perspektiven des Weltsports, vol. 6H*, edited by Ueberhorst. Berlin: Bartels & Wernitz, 1989: 537–51.

Ng'eny, S. K. A. "Nandi Resistance to the Establishment of British Administration 1893–1906." *Hadith 2: Proceedings of the 1968 Conference of the Historical Association of Kenya*, edited by B. A. Ogot. Nairobi: East African Publishing House, 1970: 104–29.

Oboler, R. S. *Women, Power, and Economic Change: The Nandi of Kenya*. Stanford, Calif.: Stanford University Press, 1985.

Ochieng W. R. *An Outline History of the Rift Valley of Kenya*. Nairobi: East African Literature Bureau, 1975.

Ogot, B. A., ed. *Hadith 2: Proceedings of the 1968 Conference of the Historical Association of Kenya*. Nairobi: East African Publishing House, 1970: 104–29.

Parsons, T. H. *The African Rank-and-File: Social Implications of Colonial Military Service in the King's African Rifles, 1902–1964*. Oxford: James Currey, Ltd., 1999.

Roberts, J. M., M. J. Arth, and R. R. Bush. "Games in Culture." *American Anthropologist* 61 (1959): 597–605.

Saltin, B. et al. "Aerobic Exercise Capacity at Sea Level and at Altitude in Kenyan Boys, Junior and Senior Runners Compared with Scandinavian Runners." *Scandinavian Journal of Medicine and Science in Sports* 5 (1995): 209–21.

Snell, G. S. *Nandi Customary Law*. Nairobi: Literature Bureau, 1954.

Spear, T. T. "Oral Traditions: Whose History?" *History in Africa* 8 (1981): 165–81.

Sutton, J. E. G. "The Settlement of East Africa." *Zamani: A Survey of East African History*, edited by B. A. Ogot. Nairobi/London: East African Publishing House/Longman Group, Ltd., 1974: 70–97.

Sutton, J. E. G. "The Kalenjin." *Kenya Before 1900*, edited by B. A. Ogot. Nairobi: East African Publishing House, 1976: 21–52.

Wortberg, N. "Die Geschichte der Leichtathletik in Kenia." Non-published masters thesis, University of Cologne, 1994.

Zaal, F. and T. Dietz. "Of Markets, Meats, Maize and Milk." *The Poor are not Us: Poverty and Pastoralism in Eastern Africa*, edited by D. M. Anderson and V. Broch-Due. Oxford: James Currey, 1999: 163–98.

8

Black Like Me: The Shared Origins of Humanity and Why We Are Different

Jon Entine

Jamaica's Usian Bolt's world-record-breaking 9.69-second sprint for the Olympic gold in the 100-meters at the Beijing Olympics was a spectacular individual achievement, but in another way it was entirely ordinary. Bolt traces his primary ancestry to West Africa, as has almost every man who has held the title "world's fastest human." The last time a non-black claimed the 100-meter title was back in 1920, when Charles Paddock ran a now pokey 10.4 seconds. In fact, no white, Asian or, tellingly, a North or East African black has ever broken ten seconds in the 100 meters. When it came to the 100-meter finals in Beijing, the 2008 Olympics played out much as the previous six. All of the qualifying sprinters were black and of West African ancestry. Considering the fractional size of the West African population in the world—less than 5 percent—the odds of this occurring by chance is roughly the equivalent of a meteor landing in your bedroom—and you surviving. Something a lot more than serendipity is going on.

There are population-based disparities in other sports as well. West African–descended blacks are dramatically over-represented based on their tiny population footprint in other sports that place a premium on running and jumping, such as football, soccer, and basketball, and East Africans and North Africans dominate distance running. Although there are a handful of elite black weightlifters and field event stars, Eurasian whites and Asians are far more common. Blacks are virtually absent in the swimming events, which are dominated by whites and Asians. East

Asians are premier divers and shine in sports in which flexibility is essential, such as certain gymnastic and ice skating events.

What explains this? The fear of being accused of racism has made it almost taboo to suggest that anything but culture explains these patterns. Yet, we are faced with the striking phenomenon that as equality of opportunity on the athletic fields of the world has increased over the last fifty years, the results on the playing field has become increasingly segregated by population ancestry. Is this just cultural serendipity or is something more fundamental at work?

The scientists have spoken, loudly and with one voice. "Differences among athletes of elite caliber are so small," noted Robert Malina, the retired Michigan State anthropologist and former editor of the *American Journal of Human Biology*, in summarizing more than fifty years of studies, "that if you have a physique or the ability to fire muscle fibers more efficiently, that might be genetically based . . . it might be very, very significant. The fraction of a second is the difference between the gold medal and fourth place" (Malina 1998).

TABOO AND THE REACTION

I explored these staggering patterns in 2000 with the publication of *Taboo: Why Black Athletes Dominate Sports and Why We're Afraid to Talk About It* (Entine 2000). My intention was to answer questions and debunk myths about human biodiversity in the context of the unfolding genetic revolution. Genetically linked, highly heritable characteristics such as skeletal structure, the distribution of muscle fiber types, reflex capabilities, metabolic efficiency, lung capacity and the ability to use energy more efficiently are not evenly distributed among populations. What impact does that have in athletics, particularly at the elite level of competition?

Scientists are just beginning to isolate the specific genes or gene constellations linked to biologically based differences, the fact that the human phenotype is grounded in genetics is unequivocal. For the most part, the science community welcomed the honest discussion of issues touched off by *Taboo,* subjects frequently addressed only in the most circumspect or politicized ways. "Entine has put together a well-researched . . . and lucidly written case," noted *Scientific American* in its review. "[His] proposed bio-cultural theory offers an attractive explanation, suggesting that cultural conditions can amplify small but meaningful differences in performance related to heredity" (DiPietro 2000: 112).

While *Taboo* was received respectfully in the science community, it came under sharp attack among social scientists of the post-modernist bent. Many argued that "race," the popular proxy for genetic populations, is no more than a "social construction," using the jargon of post-modernism. "Differentiating species into biologically defined 'races' has proven meaningless and unscientific as a way of explaining variation," the American Anthropological Association has proclaimed in one of numerous widely publicized encyclicals on race (1996). Social construction theorists were further emboldened in 2000 when Francis Collins, head of the National Human Genome Research Project, and Craig Venter, then chief scientist at the private firm Celera Genomics, unveiled their crude early maps of the human genome. "Americans, regardless of ethnic group, are 99.9 percent genetically identical," said Collins (Collins 2000). Race has no genetic or scientific basis," added Venter (Olsen 2001). There was no mention of the uncomfortable fact that the genome project and disease research rest on the premise of finding distinguishable differences between individuals and populations.

Predictably, the media burst with stories that the nation's most famous geneticists had declared that racial differences do not exist. "As it turns out, the human species is so evolutionarily young, and its migratory patterns so wide, restless and rococo, that it has simply not had a chance to divide itself into separate biological groups or 'races' in any but the most superficial ways," concluded an article in the *New York Times* titled, "Do Races Differ? Not Really, DNA Shows." The supposed proof touted in the article and hundreds like it published around the world: people can't be very different because humans are genetically 99.9 percent alike; our differences, while superficially significant, are "biologically meaningless" (Angier 2000:C1).

Those assertions assumed great moral power. After all, if we only differ by 0.1 percent, or even as much as 0.4 percent according to the latest estimates, it seems intuitively improbable to conclude that racial and ethnic differences are more than skin deep. No population could be inherently superior or inferior to another in any meaningful way. Population and ancestry or its crude proxy, race, would seem to be little more than social inventions—race is "socially constructed" goes the post-modernist claim.

99 PERCENT PURE?

The paradox over the notion of "race" revolves around a common misunderstanding about what it means to say that humans are 99.9 percent genetically the same, or to claim any differences based on percentages. Geneticists are now convinced that using such percentage claims paints a misleading picture of group differences. After all, bone marrow extracted from Neanderthal skeletons indicates that our extinct hominid relative was more than 99.5 percent genetically identical to us, yet they were remarkably primitive and lost out to more modern humans in the battle of evolution.

Although DNA has the historical advantage of having been deciphered at Cambridge University in 1953 instead of in Hitler's Berlin a few years earlier, it has nonetheless carried uncomfortable associations with notions of racism. The nature-nurture debate tipped decidedly in the early 1970s, when Harvard University zoologist Richard Lewontin provided what appeared to be a genetic basis for the nurturists' argument. He examined classic genetic markers, like blood groups, across many populations. His eye-opening conclusion: 85 percent of all human variation is randomly found between individuals within a nation or tribe. He found 8 percent between populations within races and only 6 percent between the races (defined in Lewontin's parlance as Caucasoid, Negroid, and Mongoloid).

By his measure, the differences separating races was little more than what distinguishes two random fans at a World Cup match—almost nothing, genetically speaking, he claimed. "In other words, two individuals are different because they are individuals, not because they belong to different races," he wrote. Lewontin, widely respected as a geneticist but controversial for his avowed Marxist political leanings, crowed over the findings as they coincided with his revulsion over the concept of race. "Since . . . racial classification is now seen to be of virtually no genetic or taxonomic significance . . . no justification can be offered for its continuance (Lewontin 1972:398). Genome studies a quarter century later by Luca Cavalli-Sforza and others would confirm Lewontin's technical findings on genetic diversity, setting racial differences at about 10 percent (Barbujani et al. 1997:4516).

Coming from a geneticist, Lewontin's views had enormous influence and he was making a valid argument at the time. As Laval University anthropologist Peter Frost has pointed out, Lewontin was referring to classic genetic markers such as blood types, serum proteins, and enzymes, which do show much more variability within races than between them. But his comments are widely misinterpreted even today to extend beyond that limited conclusion. Further research has shown this pattern of variability cannot reliably be extrapolated to all traits with higher adaptive value.

The 99.9 percent figure represents the identical sequences of base pairs (the combinations of nucleotides known as single nucleotide polymorphisms or SNPs) that geneticists would expect to find if they compare the same portions of the genome of two living creatures. Because living things share many functions (for example, respiration) going back millions, or even billions, of years, much of human DNA is remarkably similar to reptiles, invertebrates, and in some cases even plants. University of Wisconsin geneticist James Crow estimates that in our mammalian ancestry "an average base has changed . . . at the almost unbelievably slow rate of about one change per billion years" (2002:81).

As a result, as Jared Diamond, UCLA physiologist has noted, if an alien were to arrive on our planet and analyze our DNA, humans would appear as a third race of chimpanzees, who share 98.4 percent of our DNA (1992:111). Human beings share roughly 90 percent of DNA with mice and only slightly less with dogs, cattle, and elephants. The tiny roundworm, barely visible to the naked eye, shares about 74 percent of its gene sequences with humans. Using crude percentages, even daffodils share about 35 percent of their SNPs with us. Those suggestive statistics certainly don't mean that we harbor an instinct to bury ourselves into rotten apples or that daffodils are one-third human (Marks 2003: 28–29).

A large-scale study of the variability in the human genome by Genaissance Pharmaceuticals, a biotechnology company in Connecticut, has convincingly shown the fallaciousness of arguments tied to the 99.9 percent figure. The real programming information is in the gene sequences. Humans carry between 400,000 and 500,000 gene versions, which is where differences are rooted. Consequently, even a small difference can turn on the tiniest sliver of DNA. In 1975 at Berkeley, Mary-Claire King and Allan Wilson were the first scientists to show how the variation separating humans from chimpanzees was not in itself enough to account for the dramatic physical and mental differences between the two species. They speculated that the way key genes are organized and "expressed," sometimes by environmental triggers, determines behavioral and physical differences, not the percentage of differences in SNPs (King and Wilson 1975:108).

That view is now widely embraced by geneticists. A change in the sequence of only one base in a gene can have catastrophic effects on an organism or a population, including leading to a killer disease found more commonly in a specific ethnic group. The small variation in a single gene, FOXP2, may explain why humans can talk and chimps cannot. Just 50 out of the 2,200 genes that humans and chimps are thought to possess, or approximately 0.15 percent, may account for all of the cognitive differences between man and ape. Although SNP studies have shown that humans and chimps are 98.7 percent identical, a chimp brain is one-third the size of a human's. It makes no more sense to say that chimps are one-third as smart as humans than to say they are 98.7 percent human—or that humankind is 99.9 percent alike across all ethnicities.

To look at it another way, there are more than three billion nucleotide pairs in the human genome, about as many genetic letters as there are bits of code instruction in Windows NT. Try changing 1 percent or even just 0.1 percent of that code—that's equivalent to three million base pairs in a human—and dare suggest that these differences are insignificant. It's the 0.1 percent of the genome that contains the record of human evolution and existence on our planet. It's the 0.1 percent that separates Albert Pujols or Lebron James from a weekend warrior or Luciano Pavarotti from a high school choral teacher—and leaves us with a kaleidoscope of human populations. Without more context, percentage comparisons are little more than statistical mumbo jumbo. To use them to bolster the argument that there are no meaningful differences between populations is scientifically and intellectually dishonest.

More specifically, scientists have discovered that different versions of many genes and gene sequences are more common in a group of people from one geographical region, compared with people from another. "We need to stop thinking about people as being so genetically similar," concluded Charles Lee, at Brigham and Women's Hospital and Harvard Medical School in Boston, commenting on his far-reaching study, "Global Variation in Copy Number in the Human Genome," published in *Nature* in 2006. The genetic researchers from the United States and Canada screened hundreds of Africans, Asians, and North Americans but looked instead at whole sentences, paragraphs, and pages of their DNA— blocks of gene sequences known as haplotypes. Some 2,900 genes and regions—12 percent or more of the genome—can differ between people and in some cases between ethnic groups. The greatest differences show up in complex organs, like the brain. They also estimated that using the now archaic measure developed by Lewontin, human gene sequences differed by three times as much: 0.3 percent (Redon et al. 2006).

CRITICISMS OF THE RACE CONCEPT

Another line of argument advanced by critics of population genetics goes like this: The genetic variation among European, African and Asian populations is minuscule compared to differences between individuals within those populations. This factoid, which is a variation on the misleading 99.9 percent figure, has been elevated to the level of revealed truth. According to Lewontin, "Based on randomly chosen genetic differences, human races and populations are remarkably similar to each other, with the largest part by far of human variation being accounted for by the differences between individuals" (1972:397).

What does that mean? Not much by today's nuanced understanding of genetics, it turns out. Consider the cichlid fish found in Africa's Lake Nyas. The cichlid, which has differentiated from one species to hundreds over a mere 11,500 years, "differ among themselves as much as do tigers and cows," noted Diamond. "Some graze on algae, others catch other fish, and still others variously crush snails, feed on plankton, catch insects, nibble the scales off other fish, or specialize in grabbing fish embryos from brooding mother fish." The kicker: these variations are the result of infinitesimal genetic differences—about 0.4 percent of their DNA studied (Diamond 1992:111). As retired University of California molecular biologist Vincent Sarich has often commented, there are no clear differences at the level of genes between a wild wolf, a Labrador, a pit pull and a cocker spaniel, but there are certainly differences in gene frequencies and therefore biologically based functional differences between these within-species breeds.

There are other more fundamental problems resulting from misinterpretations of Lewontin's original studies about gene variability. Numerous scientists since have generalized from his conclusions to the entire human genome, yet no such study has been done, by Lewontin or anyone else. Today, it is believed that such an inference is dicey at best. The trouble with genetic markers is that they display "junk" variability that sends a signal that variability within populations exceeds variability between populations.

Most mammalian genes, as much as 70 percent, are "junk" that have accumulated over the course of evolution with almost no remaining function; whether they are similar or different is meaningless. The "junk" DNA that has not been weeded out by natural selection accounts for a larger proportion of within-population variability. Genetic makers may therefore be sending an exaggerated and maybe false signal.

The entire issue of gene variability is widely misunderstood. "In almost any single African population or tribe, there is more genetic variation than in all the rest of the world put together," Kenneth Kidd told me in an interview. "Africans have the broadest spectrum of variability, with rarer versions at either end [of the bell curve distribution]. If everyone in the world was wiped out except Africans, almost all human genetic variability would be preserved" (Kidd 1999).

Many journalists and even some scientists have taken Kidd's findings to mean that genetic variability equates with phenotypic variability. Since Africans have about 10–15 percent more genetic differences than people from anywhere else in the world, the argument goes, Africans and their Diaspora descendents should show more variability across a range of phenotypic characteristics including body type, behavior, and intelligence. This "fact" is often invoked to explain why athletes of African ancestry dominate elite running: it's a product of variability, not inherent population differences.

This is a spurious interpretation of Kidd's data. Chimpanzees display more genetic diversity than do humans. That's because genetic variability is a marker of evolutionary time, not phenotypic variability. Each time an organism, human or otherwise, propagates, genetic "mistakes" occur as genes are mixed. The slightly increased variability in Africans reflects the accumulation of junk DNA as mutations have occurred over time. Such data "prove" little more than the fact that Africa is the likely home of modern humans—and it may not even signify that.

University of Utah anthropologist and geneticist Henry Harpending and John Relethford, a biological anthropologist from the State University of New York at Oneonta, have found that this genetic variation results from the fact that there were more people in Africa than everywhere else combined during most of the period of human evolution. In other words, greater African genetic variability may be the result of nothing more than fast population growth (Relethford and Harpending 1995:672).

When I asked Kidd directly whether his findings of genetic variability, which showed that Africans were most likely to show the most phenotypic variability in humans—the tallest and shortest, the fastest and slowest, the most intelligent and most retarded—he laughed at first. "Wouldn't that be mud in the eye for the bigots," he said, not eager to puncture the politically correct balloon. Finally, he turned more serious. "Genes are the blueprint and the blueprint is identifiable in local populations. No matter what the environmental influences, you can't deviate too far from it."

Part of the confusion stems from the fact that some scientists, and certainly the general public, have embraced the popular shorthand that discrete genes have specific effects. Journalists sometimes write that there is a "gene for illness X." Lewontin himself has expressed scorn for what he calls the "religion" of molecular biology and their "prophets," geneticists, who make grandiose statements about what genes prove or disprove. Genes only specify the sequence of amino acids that are linked together in the manufacture of a molecule called a polypeptide, which must then fold up to make a protein, a process that may be different in different organisms and depends in part on the presence of yet other proteins. "[A] gene is divided up into several stretches of DNA, each of which specifies only part of the complete sequence in a polypeptide," Lewontin has written. "Each of these partial sequences can then combine with parts specified by other genes, so that, from only a few genes, each made up of a few subsections, a very large number of combinations of different amino acid sequences could be made by mixing and matching" (2001:191). Lewontin's reasonable conclusion: the mere sequencing of the human genome doesn't tell us very much about what distinguishes a human from a weed, let alone a Kenyan from a Korean.

Significant between group differences have been identified in the harder-to-study regulatory genes. This tiny fraction of the human genome controls the order and makeup of proteins, and may be activated by obscure environmental triggers. For instance, the presence of an abnormal form of hemoglobin (hemoglobin S) can lead to sickle-cell anemia, which disproportionately afflicts families of African descent. But the genetic factors that actually lead to the disease operate at a much finer level. Just one change in the base pair for hemoglobin can trigger the disease. However, the genetic factors involved are even subtler in part because of gene-gene and gene-environment interactions. For example, a separate set of genes in the genome—genes that code for fetal hemoglobin—can counteract some of the ill effects of the adult hemoglobin S genes if they continue to produce into adulthood. This range of possibilities, encoded in the genome, is found disproportionately in certain populations, but do not show up in the gross calculations of human differences that go into the misleading 99.9 percent figure.

Francois Jacob and Jacques Monod, who shared the Nobel Prize for Medicine in 1965 for their work on the regulator sequences in genes, have identified modules, each consisting of twenty to thirty genes, which act as an Erector Set for the mosaics that characterize each of us (Jacob 1998:158). Small changes in regulatory genes make large changes in organisms, perhaps by shifting entire blocks of genes on and off or by changing activation sequences. But, whether flea or fly, cocker spaniel or coyote, Hannah Montana or Oprah Winfrey, the genetic sequences are different but the basic materials are the same. Minute differences can and do have profound effects on how living beings look and behave, while huge apparent variations between species may be almost insignificant in genetic terms.

POPULATION DIFFERENTIATION

According to another oft-heard criticism of categorizing people by population or ancestry, human differences are superficial because populations have not had enough evolutionary time to differentiate. "*Homo sapiens* is a young species, its division into races even more recent," wrote the late Stephen Jay Gould wrote years ago. "This historical context has not supplied enough time for the evolution of substantial differences. . . . Human equality is a contingent fact of history" (Gould 1987:198). In other words, our relatively recent common heritage—differentiation into modern humans may have occurred as recently as 50,000 years ago, an eye blink of evolutionary time—renders the possibility of "races" absurd.

Despite massive evidence to the contrary, "there are no significant differences" view, first proffered a quarter century ago in the pre-genetic era, has made its way into the popular media as fact. It's difficult to believe that even Gould believed his own moral rhetoric, for his own theory of punctuated equilibrium, which argues that swift genetic change occurs all the time, demolishes this assertion. Gould and American Museum of

Natural History curator Niles Eldredge long ago addressed the controversial issue of why the fossil records appeared to show that plants and animals undergo little change for long periods of time and then experience sudden, dramatic mutations. They argued that new species do not evolve slowly so much as erupt, the result of a chain reaction set off by regulatory genes. Their theory, though controversial and still widely debated, helps explain the limited number of bridge, or intermediary, species in the fossil record (as Creationists never fail to point out). Either as a mutation or in response to an environmental shock, these regulators could have triggered a chain reaction with cascading consequences, creating new species in just a few generations.

Much of this debate turns on the issue of what constitutes significant genetic differences. In one of many examples, De Code Genetics has found dramatic population differences in each of the eleven districts in Iceland, which was settled only in the ninth century. They emerged because there was so little intermarriage between villages for centuries. The evolutionary record is filled with such examples. A breakthrough study by University of Maryland population geneticist Sarah Tishkoff and colleagues of the gene that confers malarial resistance (one known as the G6PD gene) has concluded that malaria, which is very population specific, is not an ancient disease, but a relatively recent affliction dating to roughly 4,000–8,000 years ago. When a variant gene that promotes its owner's survival is at issue, substantial differences can occur very rapidly (Tishkoff 2001). The dating of the G6PD gene's variants, done by a method worked out by a colleague of Tishkoff, Andrew G. Clark of Pennsylvania State University, showed how rapidly a life-protecting variant of a gene could become widespread. The finding is of interest to biologists trying to understand the pace of human evolution because it shows how quickly a variant gene that promotes its owner's survival can spread through a population. Genes that have changed under the pressure of natural selection determine the track of human evolution and are likely to specify the differences between humans and their close cousin the chimpanzee.

These findings reinforce those of Vince Sarich. "The shorter the period of time required to produce a given amount of morphological difference, the more selectively important the differences become," he has written (1995:84). Sarich figures that since the gene flow as a result of intermingling on the fringes of population pockets was only a trickle, relatively

distinct core races would likely have been preserved even where inter-
breeding was common.

Stanford University geneticist Luigi Cavalli-Sforza has calculated the
time it could take for a version of a gene that leads to more offspring to
spread from one to 99 percent of the population. If a rare variant of a gene
produces just 1 percent more surviving offspring, it could become nearly
universal in a human group in 11,500 years. But, if it provides 10 percent
more "reproductive fitness," it could come to dominate in just 1,150 years
(Cavalli-Sforza, 1994:182).

Natural selection, punctuated equilibrium, and even catastrophic events
have all contributed to what might loosely be called racial differences. For
example, University of Illinois archaeologist Stanley Ambrose has offered
the hypothesis that the earth was plunged into a horrific volcanic winter
after a titanic volcanic blow-off of Mount Toba in Sumatra some 71,000
years ago (Ambrose 2005). The eruption, the largest in 400 million years,
spewed 4,000 times as much ash as Mount St. Helens, darkening the skies
over one-third of the world and dropping temperatures by more than 20
degrees. The catastrophe touched off a six-year global winter, which was
magnified by the coldest thousand years of the last ice age, which ended
some fourteen thousand years ago. It is believed to have resulted in the
death of most of the Northern Hemisphere's plants, bringing widespread
famine and death to hominid populations. If geneticists are correct, some
early humans may have been wiped out entirely, leaving no more than
15,000 to 40,000 survivors around the world.

What might have been the effect on evolution? "Humans were suddenly thrown into the freezer," said Ambrose. Only a few thousand people
in Africa and a few pockets of populations that had migrated to Europe
and Asia could have survived. That caused an abrupt "bottleneck," or
decrease, in the ancestral populations. After the climate warmed, the survivors resumed multiplying in what can only be described as a population
explosion, bringing about the rapid genetic divergence or "differentiation"
of the population pockets.

This hypothesis addresses the paradox of the out-of-Africa origin
model: Why do we look so different if all humankind recently migrated
out of Africa? "When our African recent ancestors passed through the
prism of Toba's volcanic winter, a rainbow of differences appeared," Ambrose has said. The genetic evidence is in line with such a scenario. Anna
DiRienzo, a post-doctoral fellow working out of Wilson's lab at Berkeley

in the early 1990s, found evidence in the mitochondrial DNA data of a major population spurt as recently as 30,000 years ago.

What's clear is that little is clear. Human differences can be ascribed to any number of genetic, cultural, and environmental forces, including economic ravages, natural disasters, genocidal pogroms, mutations, chromosomal rearrangement, natural selection, geographical isolation, random genetic drift, mating patterns, and gene admixture. Taboos such as not marrying outside one's faith or ethnic group exaggerate genetic differences, reinforcing the loop between nature and nurture. Henry Harpending and John Relethford have concluded "human populations are derived from separate ancestral populations that were relatively isolated from each other before 50,000 years ago" (Wolpoff and Caspari 1997:32).

Clearly, there are significant genetically based population differences, although it is certainly true that dividing humans into discrete categories based on geography and visible characteristics reflecting social classifications, while not wholly arbitrary, is crude. That does not mean, however, that local populations do not show evidence of patterns. The critical factor in genetics is the arrangement of gene allele frequencies, how genes interact with each other and the environment, and what traits they influence. This inalterable but frequently overlooked fact undermines the notion that gene flow and racial mixing on the edges of population sets automatically renders all categories of "race" meaningless. Human characteristics can and do cluster and clump even without reproductive isolation. Many so-called species are still linked by some ongoing gene flow. Population genetics can help us realize patterns in such things as the proclivity to diseases and the ability to sprint fast.

Although the shared blueprint of our humanity has not changed much over the past 50,000 years, populations in different parts of the world have had to adapt to profoundly different evolutionary challenges. Genetic and physical differences are far more pronounced in populations that have been geographically and culturally separated. Pick up any Anthropology 101 book and you will find a picture of a beanpole Masai standing next to short and stout Eskimo to illustrate how body types evolved to fit exacting climates. These are, for lack of a better term, "racial differences." It's believed that many racial differences became fixed as a result of the population explosions in Africa, Australia, East Asia, and Europe during the Holocene period that succeeded the last great ice age 10,000 years ago. "This is perhaps particularly clear for eastern Asia (the present day hearth of the 'Mongoloids'), but it also applies to Europe (the homeland of the 'Caucasoids')," wrote Stanford University genetic paleoanthropologist Richard Klein (1999:502).

"The fact that monolithic racial categories do not show up consistently in the genotype does not mean there are no group differences between pockets of populations," stressed Farleigh Dickinson University biological anthropologist Joseph Graves, Jr., who is African American. "There are many genetic variants that are only found in certain Asian populations, only in sub-populations in Africa, only in certain European populations. If research on disease or drugs is limited to certain sub-groups of whites or Asians or blacks then you may develop drugs for, say, Alzheimer's or Parkinson's, that work best only in those populations. Group differences do not necessarily correlate with skin color but with geography. Such patterns are the result of migratory waves and are reflected in gene frequencies" (Graves 2000).

Intense evolutionary pressures have shaped identifiable if fuzzy population groupings. In his monumental 1994 book *The History and Geography of Genes*, Cavalli-Sforza, using classic markers like blood proteins, identified 491 world populations. Although he and his coauthors noted that "the concept of race has failed to obtain any consensus," they nonetheless broke the world populations into what amounts to racial groupings: nine major clusters consisting of sub-Saharan Africans, Caucasians from Europe, Caucasians from outside Europe, Northern Mongoloids (excluding Arctic populations), Northeast Asian Arctic populations, Southern Mongoloids (mainland and insular Southeast Asians), New Guineans (plus Australians), Pacific islanders, and Native Americans (Cavalli-Sforza et al. 1994).

THE HAPMAP, RACE AND SPORTS

More recent advances in genomic research have led geneticists to identify human groups based on genotypic patterns. Populations—some large, such as people of West African descent, and some small, such as Jews— have sizable regions of their genome that have evolved distinctively over time. These blocks are being assembled into a picture known as a Haplotype Map. The International Haplotype Map Project, or "HapMap," aims at a short-term cost of $138 million to provide an index to the genomic

Book of Life by using patterns of variation to break the genome into more manageable pieces, allowing for rapid identification of the genes passed from parent to child that could play a role in specific diseases. Because humans have evolved so differently in different parts of the world, not one but three major HapMaps are currently under construction: for individuals of African ancestry, Asians, and Europeans (Gabriel et al. 2002).

There have been a slew of studies since the publication of *Taboo* and the release of the first map of the human genome that incorporates the insights of HapMap analysis. In 2002, Stanford University geneticist Neil Risch and Esteban Burchard, director of the DNA bank at the University of California at San Francisco and a lung disease specialist at San Francisco General Hospital who studies how different groups respond to asthma medicines, identified five races as proxies for populations— Africans, Caucasians, Pacific Islanders, East Asians, and Native Americans. Each "race and even ethnic groups within the races" have their own collection of diseases and specific reactions to drugs. They believe that environmental triggers for many common disorders, from cancer to asthma, that have no effect on one population group could devastate another. That's the explanation for many "Jewish diseases."

"We provide an epidemiological perspective on the issue of human categorization in biomedical and genetic research that strongly supports the continued use of self-identified race and ethnicity," they have concluded. "Ignoring racial and ethnic differences in medical and biomedical research does not make them disappear" (Rish et al. 2002:1).

Another comprehensive study, released that same year, scanned the whole human genome in what geneticists say was the most thorough look ever at the genetics of race. The authors did not analyze individual genes but segments of DNA in more than 1,000 people from 52 ethnic groups. They concluded that 95 percent of the genetic variations in the human genome is found in people all over the world, as might be expected for the small African population that dispersed as recently as 50,000 years ago. But like Risch and his colleagues, they found that humans eventually formed relatively distinct, if overlapping racial groups. Using haplotype markings, they sorted people into five principal groups corresponding to the major geographical regions of the world: Africa, Europe, Asia, Melanesia and the Americas (Rosenberg et al. 2001:2381).

"What this study says is that if you look at enough markers you can identify the geographic region a person comes from," said Kenneth Kidd, professor of genetics at Yale University and a coauthor of the study. "Self-reported population ancestry likely provides a suitable proxy for genetic ancestry"—the way people categorized themselves—whether black, white, or Asian—matched closely with DNA categories. It is often "less expensive and less intrusive" for a doctor to ask patients about their race or continent of origin than to authorize extensive genetic tests to gain useful information about their genetic makeup, added Marcus Feldman of Stanford University, the senior author (Wade 2002).

These findings have escalated the classic war between those who see race as a reasonable proxy for population and an important tool in diagnosing disease and those who fear the consequences of resurrecting the race concept. The use of the term "race" with all of its social baggage remains taboo in most social and some scientific circles. It's difficult to even raise this issue without being branded a bigot. As UCLA physiologist and Pulitzer Prize–winning author Jared Diamond has noted, "[F]ew scientists dare to study racial origins, lest they be branded racists just for being interested in the subject" (1992:111). As recently as 2001, two prestigious science magazines ran editorials railing against the notion of race. An editorialist writing for The *New England Journal of Medicine* asserted that "'race' is biologically meaningless" while *Nature Genetics* warned of the "confusion and potential harmful effects of using 'race' as a variable in medical research" (Schwartz 2001:239).

But the tide of acceptable discourse has begun to turn. Geneticists are breaking with the old orthodoxy to endorse the utility of race, while being careful to acknowledge all its limitations. DNA from person to person is indeed somewhat similar because of human intermixing, but the way our genetic information is organized—the gene variants—differs measurably, by millions of nucleotides, from gene pool to gene pool, ethnic group to ethnic group—or race to race. Physical qualities like skin color, stature, or cranium size and shape are crude markers, but they provide key information for forensic science and medical researchers trying to identify population-specific diseases.

The challenge for scientists has been how to refer to the descendants of ancient ethnic groups without resurrecting the noxious assumptions of the nineteenth century. They have begun developing a lexicon to discuss race without using the word, substituting "population group." "Continent of ancestry" has also emerged as a socially acceptable, if awkward, proxy. Geneticists don't ask, "Can people be divided into groups?" Richard Lewontin, Mary-Claire King, and Marcus Feldman, all well known for their anti-race sentiments, jointly wrote in *Nature*. Rather, they ask: "Is it possible to find DNA sequences that differ sufficiently between populations to allow correct assignment of major geographical origin with high probability? The answer to this question is 'Yes'" (Feldman et al. 2003:374).

HUMAN DIFFERENCES AND SPORTS

Science does require a theory to be predictive and supported by empirical evidence even when laboratory tests remain elusive. So, how do we test the theory that there are some patterned group differences? Certainly, we cannot automatically infer innate abilities from observed performances. As I noted in *Taboo*, Jews dominated basketball in the 1920s and 1930s. One of the era's great sports journalists, *New York Daily News* sports editor Paul Gallico, ascribed this to the "alert, scheming mind, flash trickiness, artful dodging and general smart aleckness" of Jews. Whatever reality there may have been to such a stereotype, the fact that many Protestants avoided the sport in its infancy and blacks were banned from the white semi-pro leagues undermines the biological explanation. Today, however, the playing field is a lot flatter, which means that the empirical, on-the-field evidence actually means something.

What distinguishes today's assertions of racial or population-based differences from the wrongheaded, and racist, claims that Jews had some "natural" advantage in basketball or that blacks are an inferior race? An increase in alternatives for Jews and more opportunity in basketball for other ethnic groups has demonstrated the absurdity of Gallico's assertions. In the 1930s, blacks were banned from participation in the all-white semi-pro leagues dominated by inner city athletes. As the game became more popular, it attracted a more competitive athlete.

The twenty-year reign of Jews in basketball does underscore the importance of cultural factors and the danger of post hoc reasoning when nature and nurture are being discussed. After all, there are no Texans, white, black or Latin, starring in the National Hockey League or great American cricketers. The success of each individual is a product of that person's ambition, creativity, and intelligence matched with the serendipity of life—the X factors that make sports so compelling. But opportunity alone doesn't guarantee success. The national sport of Mexico is baseball, yet they are not generally good enough to make much of a mark in the Major Leagues: their ancestral body type works against them. If the roulette wheel of genetics does not land on an athlete's number, hard work alone will not turn clay into marble. Though individual success is about fire in the belly and opportunity, the pattern of success in many sports are somewhat circumscribed by population genetics.

Some skeptics claim that any genetic differences that may exist between population groups are, in the end, utterly swamped by environmental influences. That statement reflects the enduring legacy of Cartesian dualism that sees environment and genes as polar opposite forces. "As scientists continue to study the complex interactions between genes and the environment, population-based genetic differences will continue to surface," noted Michael Crawford, University of Kansas professor of biological anthropology and genetics, president of the Human Biology Association, and former editor of the journal *Human Biology*. "We need to dispense with the notion that athleticism is entirely due only to biology or only to culture. Biological variation in complex traits is always a result of their interaction" (Crawford 2000).

Today, with basketball played throughout the world, there is a far more level playing field. Although opportunities remain meager for poverty-riddled Africa, there are more elite basketball players from Nigeria than from Nebraska. In running, the trends are even more startling: athletes of African ancestry hold every major running record, from the 100 meters to the marathon. What is the driving force behind this phenomenon? Competitive running is nature's laboratory. "A scientist interested in exploring physical and performance differences couldn't invent a better sport than running," wrote Amby Burfoot, executive editor of *Runner's World*.

It's a true world-wide sport, practiced and enjoyed in almost every country around the globe. Also, it doesn't require any special equipment, coaching or facilities. Ethiopia's Abebe Bikila proved this dramatically in the 1960 Olympic Games when—shoeless, little coached, and inexperienced—he won the marathon. Given the universality of running, it's reasonable to expect that the best runners should come from a wide range of countries and racial groups. This isn't, however, what happens. Runners of West African descent win nearly all the sprints. Nearly all the distance races are won, remarkably, by runners from just one small corner of one small African country, Kenya (Burfoot 1992:89).

Running provides the most persuasive prima facie case suggesting that sports success cannot be explained by cultural and environmental factors alone. Kenya, a Texas-sized nation with a population of approximately 16 million people, is the world epicenter of distance running. East African runners almost exclusively come from the Nandi Hills, the 6,000–8,000 foot highlands that snake along the western edge of the Great Rift Valley of Kenya, Ethiopia, and Tanzania. Home to roughly 1.5 million people, this region has produced more than 50 percent of the best times ever run in distance races. Kenyans, almost all of them Kalenjin, win 25 percent of top international events.

The Kalenjin represent roughly half of Kenya's world-class runners. Hundreds of years ago, what African historians refer to as a proto-Kalenjin population migrated from the Nilotic core area northwest of Lake Turkana to the Mt. Elgon area, where the group fragmented and moved to its present locations in the highlands. This is the home of the Nandi district of 500,000 people. One-twelve-thousandth of Earth's population sweeps an unfathomable 20 percent, marking it as the greatest concentration of raw athletic talent in the history of sports.

According to socially acceptable wisdom, the sure explanation for Kenya's success can be found in Kenyan culture. After all, the country's national sport is the passion of the masses. Little boys dream that one day, they might soak up the cheers of the adoring fans that regularly crowd the stands at the National Stadium in Nairobi. Coaches comb the countryside for the rising generation of stars, who are showered with special training and government perks. It's no exaggeration to call Kenya's national sport a national religion.

There's only one problem: The national sport, the hero worship, the adoring fans, the social channeling—that all speaks to Kenya's enduring love affair with soccer, not running. Despite the enormous success of Kenyan runners in the past fifteen years, running remains a relative afterthought in this soccer-crazed nation. Unfortunately, Kenyans are among the world's worst soccer players. They are just terrible. In fact, there is no such thing as an East African soccer powerhouse. Clearly, cultural channeling, the lure of privilege, and hero worship, bedrock components of the environmentalist argument, have not done much to make East Africa competitive in soccer.

The East African edge, if you will, reflects the impact of evolution on body type and physiology. "Africans are naturally, genetically, more likely to have less body fat, which is a critical edge in elite running," noted Joseph Graves, Jr., an evolutionary biologist at Arizona State University and author of *The Emperor's New Clothes: Biological Theories of Race at the Millenium*. "Evolution has shaped body types and in part athletic possibilities. Don't expect an Eskimo to show up on an NBA court or a Watusi to win the world weightlifting championship," added Graves "Differences don't necessarily correlate with skin color, but rather with geography and climate. Endurance runners are more likely to come from East Africa. That's a fact. Genes play a major role in this" (Graves 2000).

Neither science nor the empirical evidence supports the default myth widely peddled by the media that Kenyans dominate because of social factors. "I lived right next door to school," laughed Kenyan-born Wilson Kipketer, formerly the world 800-meter record holder, dismissing such cookie-cutter explanations. "I walked, nice and slow" (Kipketer 1988). Some kids ran to school, some didn't, he says, but it's not why we succeed. And for every Kenyan monster-miler, there are others, like Kipketer, who get along on less than thirty.

"Training regimens are as varied in Kenya as anywhere in the world," noted Colm O'Connell, coach at St. Patrick's Iten, the famous private school and running factory in the Great Rift Valley that turned out Kipketer and other Kenyan greats (O'Connell 1988). O'Connell eschews the mega-training so common among runners in Europe and North America who have failed so miserably in bottling the Kenyan running miracle.

"Very many in sports physiology would like to believe that it is training, the environment, what you eat that plays the most important role in sports. But based on the data, the genes are what counts most," stated the top scientist in human performance research, Bengt Saltin, director of the Copenhagen Muscle Research Center. "The extent of the environment can always be discussed but it's less than 20, 25 percent. It is 'in your genes' whether or not you are talented or whether you will become talented" (Saltin 1998).

BIO-CULTURAL ATHLETIC HOTSPOTS

Sport success is a bio-social phenomenon, with cultural factors such as opportunity amplifying small but meaningful differences in performance related to heredity. Genetically linked, highly heritable characteristics such as skeletal structure, the distribution of muscle-fiber types, reflex capabilities, metabolic efficiency, lung capacity, and the ability to use energy more efficiently are not evenly distributed among populations and cannot be explained by known environmental factors. Scientists are just beginning to isolate the genetic links to those biologically based differences (though the fact that this patterned biology is grounded in genetics is unequivocal).

A glance at a world map of athletic pockets or hothouses highlights places where evolution and accidents of culture play a key role in the patterns of excellence we see in sports: the domination of endurance running by East Africans, sprinting by blacks of primarily West African ancestry, Eurasian white supremacy in weightlifting and power events, and so on, are explained, in part, by patterned anatomical differences.

East Africans have a near perfect biomechanical package for endurance: lean, ectomorphic physiques, huge natural lung capacity, and a high proportion of slow twitch muscle fibers. It's also a poor combination for sprinting, which undoubtedly helps explain East Africa's dismal sprinting history. Kenya has tried desperately over the past decade to replicate its wondrous success in distance running at the sprints, but to no avail. The best Kenyan time ever in the 100 meters–10.28 seconds—ranks somewhere near 5,000th on the all-time list.

The pool of potential great sprinters (and athletes with fast burst, anaerobic skills) is deepest among athletes of West African descent. Claude Bouchard, geneticist at the Pennington Biomedical Research Center at Louisiana State University, found that such populations have a higher percentage of "energy efficient" fast twitch muscle fibers to complement their naturally more mesomorphic physiques (Bouchard 1999). "West Africans have 70 percent of the fast type muscle fibers when they are born," added Saltin. "And that's needed for a 100-meter race around 9.9 seconds."

Some critics have noted that there have been a few great white sprinters, such as Valery Borzov, the Russian who won Olympic gold in 1972. Borzov's moment of glory, although an Olympic win, was pedestrian in historical terms. It doesn't even rank in the top 500 sprints of all time. Athletes of primarily West African origin, including African Americans, hold the top 200 and 497 of the top 500 times. There are more elite sprinters from any one of the many West African or black Caribbean countries—Jamaica, St. Kitts and Nevis, Senegal, Cameroon, Ivory

Coast, Nigeria, Ghana—than from all of Asia and the white populations of the world combined.

The old Eastern bloc countries provided a unique laboratory to evaluate the radical environmentalist's canard that humans are infinitely plastic. The world's most elaborate sports factory combined with state-supervised illegal drug supplements still could not turn even one East German or Soviet sprinter into the world's fastest human. The vaunted Eastern European sporting machines lavished much of their efforts, which included sophisticated use of performance-enhancing drugs, on its female athletes, where the drug cocktails had the most impact.

This is not evidence that blacks are "superior" athletes. Genetics does not confer rank. There are no Master Races. Populations with naturally less body fat, such as Africans, who are the world's best runners, quickly find that advantage a huge negative when attempting a cross channel swim or the Iditarod. And for all their achievements in running, athletes of African ancestry are notable underperformers in strength events, from weightlifting to the shot putt.

Eurasian whites are more likely to have the endomorphic physique of the best strength athletes. The world's top weightlifters and wrestlers live in or trace their ancestry from a swath of Eurasia, from Bulgaria through upper Mongolia. The original inhabitants of this mostly northern region likely arrived no more than 25,000 years ago. Evolutionary forces shaped a population that is large and muscular, particularly in the upper body, with relatively short arms and legs and thick torsos.

Where flexibility is key, East Asians shine, such as in diving and some skating and gymnastic events. Their body types tend to be small with relatively short extremities, long torsos, and a thicker layer of fat—a scaled down mixture of mesomorphic and endomorphic characteristics. As a result, athletes from this region are somewhat slower and less strong than whites or blacks, but more flexible on average. "Chinese splits," a rare maneuver demanding extraordinary flexibility, has roots in this anthropometric reality. It's a key skill set for martial arts, which of course also are rooted in Asian traditions. Those anthropometric realities circumscribe Asian possibilities in jumping: not one Asian male or female high jumper makes the top 50 all-time. Many scientists believe this distinctive body type evolved as adaptations to harsh climes encountered by bands of *Homo sapiens* who migrated to Northeast Asia about 40,000 years ago. The excavation of an abundance of precise tools in Asia, including needles for sewing clothes to survive cold winters, has led scientists to speculate that Asians were "programmed" over time to be more dexterous. Studies indicate that East Asians do have the quickest reaction time, which some have speculated may play a role in Asian domination of Ping-Pong.

CONSEQUENCES OF DISINGENUOUSNESS

Some race realists seduce themselves into believing that they are being intellectually honest in pointing out the "natural" advantages of certain "races," but they reach beyond limited data to speculative and sweeping conclusions. Anti-race ideologues, on the other hand, posture that the public cannot grasp the nuances of population differences so they deny them altogether. Darwin has enemies on the right and the left. Unfortunately, the leftwing demagogues have long gotten a pass in the media and in some corners of the academic world. The consequences of such intellectual tap dancing are serious and mounting.

Such hypocrisy was on display a few years ago in New York at a conference on race and sports attended by Stephen Jay Gould, shortly before his death. Renowned for his political correctness as much as for his scientific acumen, Gould declared that there was no "running gene," as if that somehow resolved the debate over the causes of black domination of running. Such bluster is a classic straw man. No scientist claims there is a "running gene." That's a dodge of the real question: Do genes proscribe possibility in some sports, running most specifically, and are there some population-based patterns?

The answer is an indisputable yes. Scientists have already identified specific genes linked to athletic performance. In one of numerous such studies, Steven Rudich, a transplant surgeon then at the University of California at Davis, has demonstrated that a single injection of the EPO gene (the gene that codes for the production of erythropoietin, which regulates red blood cell production) into the leg muscles of monkeys produced significantly elevated red blood cell levels for 20 to 30 weeks (Rudich 200: 102). EPO is a key factor in endurance. Although all humans have the EPO gene, different alleles of the EPO gene are found in greater numbers in certain populations.

Researchers isolating a gene responsible for muscle weakness caused by the debilitating effects of muscular dystrophy may even have stumbled upon a "smoking gun" that bolsters the genetic case for population-linked differences in sprinting capacity. While researchers at the Institute for Neuromuscular Research in Sydney, Australia, found that 20 percent of people of Caucasian and Asian background have what they called a "wimp gene," a defective gene that blocks the body from producing α-actinin-3, which provides the explosive power in fast-twitch muscles. Samples drawn from African Bantus, specifically Zulu tribal members, showed that only 3 percent had the wimp gene. Kathryn North, head of the Neurogenetics Research Unit at the New Children's Hospital speculate that the need for a "speed gene" is dying out because the speed to hunt animals or flee from enemies is no longer necessary for our survival—although it certainly helps in sprinting (North et al. 1999).

Caricaturing the rhetorical use of folk categories of race is not going to make the patterned biological variation on which some differences are based disappear. "We may believe that most differences between races are superficial, but the differences are there, and they are informative about the origins and migrations of our species," said Alan Rogers, a population geneticist and professor of anthropology at the University of Utah in Salt Lake City. "To do my work, I have to get genetic data from different parts of the world, and look at differences within groups and between groups, so it helps to have labels for groups" (Angier 2000:C1).

"I believe that we need to look at the causes of differences in diseases between the various races," agreed Claude Bouchard, who is also one the world's leading experts in obesity, in the *American Journal of Human Biology*. "In human biology . . . it is important to understand if age, gender, and race, and other population characteristics contribute to phenotype variation. Only by confronting these enormous issues head-on, and not by circumventing them in the guise of political correctness, do we stand a chance to evaluate the discriminating agendas and devise appropriate interventions" (Bouchard 1998: 279–80).

A case might be made that the ideologically driven perspectives of Gould and others make some sense as a tactical response to the adaptionist, genetic-centered arguments that looms in the background in evolutionary theory. Indeed, the environment and the complex interrelationship of genes, individuals, and groups of populations can explain much in life. But they have staked out the most extreme and least credible position with *ad hominem* attacks on even those who articulate a nuanced understanding of the inseparability of genes and culture.

As Barbara Ehrenreich and Janet McIntosh wrote in the liberal weekly *The Nation*, "What began as a healthy skepticism about misuses of biology [has become] a new form of dogma," they wrote. "Like the religious fundamentalists, the new academic Creationists defend their stance as if all of human dignity—and all hope for the future—were at stake. [But] in portraying human beings as pure products of cultural context, the secular Creationist standpoint not only commits biological errors but defies common sense" (1997).

This unrelenting assault on the straw man of race has been directed at some of the most respected researchers in the world. Cavalli-Sforza, who helped establish the Human Genome Diversity Project (HGDP) in 1991, came under relentless attack by University of North Carolina at Charlotte geneticist Jonathan Marks and others for "encouraging racist thinking," "stealing" the genes of developing countries, "destroying" their culture and even "contributing to genocide." At a symposium on the HGDP, Marks and Debra Harry, a Northern Paiute Indian, co-authored an attack that combined misleading statements about genetics with a blatant agenda. "The vast majority of human genetic variation is known to be within-group variation," they wrote. "Thus the value of such a project would appear to be quite minimal, especially given the ill will it has managed to generate" (Connor 2001).

Their analysis was scientifically nonsense but politically potent. To underscore their point, Marks and Harry cleverly mocked the disingenuousness of the HGDP scientists, who waffle about the existence of "race" to protect their left flank (and to keep the research dollars flowing) while publishing research that clearly shows population differences. "We learn, on the one hand, that races do not exist," he writes citing public statements by HGDP scientists, "and on the other hand, we learn in widely publicized color-coded maps [of genetic variation] in which Africans are yellow, Australians red, [Mongoloids blue] and Caucasoids green. . . . Perhaps, then, the project ought to be sandbagged," he jibes, "until the people writing about it have thought more clearly about the actual nature of the diversity they wish to study." And Marks is right, if for the wrong reasons.

Splitting rhetorical hairs to preserve ideological purity (and head off a potential public backlash) has serious consequences. "Here we have the black community accepting the concept that African-Americans need to be studied as a group, and then we have the scientific community claiming that race is dead," said Jay Cohn, a professor of medicine at the University of Minnesota. "It seems to me absolutely ludicrous to suggest that this prominent characteristic that we all recognize when we look at people should not be looked at" (Stolberg 2008).

The irony in this soft-censorship is immense, since a taboo on open discussion on the grounds that it encourages racism is the exact and entirely cynical position proffered by Creationists who oppose the teaching of Darwin. It's at this point that the views of the far right and demagogic left become virtually indistinguishable. The consequences of following their radical prescription is enforced ignorance, which will only fracture even more the fragile support for genetics research. As Jared Diamond has noted, "Even today, few scientists dare to study racial origins, lest they be branded racists just for being interested in the subject" (1992:9). Moreover, by encouraging censorship for fear that this data will be misused, righteous social thinkers unwittingly legitimize the taboo that traditional races can be ranked from superior to inferior ("if we shouldn't talk about racial differences for fear of causing offense, maybe there is some truth to it").

Folkloric notions of race have come into being because a host of phenotypes are correlated. That does not mean that the folkloric categories (whichever ones are used) are distinct and discrete. They are not and their explanatory powers are limited. That understood, it's without question that some population groups do resemble ethnic or "racial" groups. The radical cant that groupings based on relatively isolated phenotypic traits such as fingerprint markings are as "equally valid" as population clusters based on genetic alleles is totally fallacious. Some fuzzy-edged population groups do resemble folkloric groupings; pretending that they do not defies logic and undermines the credibility of those whose motives otherwise appear noble.

It might be nice if there were no innate differences of any kind among population groups, at least besides the obvious cosmetic ones. But genes do not confer equality, for without differences, evolution would be impossible. Humans are different, the consequence of thousands of years of evolution in varying terrains. Society, and science in particular, pay a huge price for not discussing this openly, if carefully. We are within a decade of perfecting tools that could make humans run faster, jump higher and throw farther—and most important—live longer and healthier lives, as the result of gene therapy for diseases.

As the focus of genome research continues to shift from our shared humanity to human differences, tensions and misunderstandings are bound to escalate. Considering the historical abuse of race studies, there needs to be caution, without shying away from the vast bounty of knowledge that the study of populations yields. Yes, DNA findings can be exaggerated or misleading. Yes, we are in perilous waters when we talk about inherited traits, especially intelligence. But the potential misuse of ancestral research should not be allowed to scare us away from its promise.

Defying the dire warnings of those who helped scuttle the HGDP DNA is shedding light on pre-historic human migrations and has fired the study of ethnic minorities often ignored by history, especially in Africa and Asia. Humanity is in the early stages of a biotechnological revolution that is transforming our understanding of the nature of human nature—the commonalities that bind us, but also the differences that confer uniqueness in individuals and often distinguish one group from another. We are far from understanding either the genetic makeup or the origins of complex traits, from behavior to intelligence to athletic performance. Because of the blur of culture and the environment, we may never be able to do so completely. But we are getting closer, and this is not just fanciful speculation.

The acknowledgement of identifiable human races and ethnic groups is not an endorsement of simplistic racist stereotyping. "The billion or so of the world's people of largely European descent have a set of genetic variants in common that are collectively rare in everyone else; they are a race," has noted Armand Marie Leroi, the respected evolutionary developmental biologist at Imperial College in London. "Race is merely a shorthand to enable us to speak sensibly, though with no great precision, about genetic rather than cultural or political differences. But it is shorthand that seems to be needed. One of the more painful spectacles of modern science is that of human geneticists piously disavowing the existence of races even as they investigate the genetic relationships between 'ethnic groups'" (Leroi 2005:A23). Those of us, scientists included, who have long embraced the orthodoxy that racial differences are "skin deep" are having a difficult time adjusting to this new and provocative—but ultimately informative and sensible—reality.

DNA is at once an atlas, time machine, and microscope. Caricaturing population genetics as pseudo-science just devalues legitimate concerns about how this information will be put to use. Science is not an assertion of inalterable facts but a method of interrogating reality. The question is no longer whether these inquiries will continue but in what manner and to what end. Our collective challenge is what we do with these nuanced notions of race and racial stereotypes.

The thorny reality is that if all of us were alike, the entire Human Genome Project would be fruitless. Our DNA tells contrasting stories: the crude map revealed in 2000 suggests that we are individuals with a shared past, while a magnified look at our genes finds patterns of small but meaningful population differences—in some cases, racial differences, to use the popular, if imprecise and socially unacceptable term. While we often posture that we are all the same, human differences provide each of us, and our families and extended communities, rootedness in the world. The challenge is to harmonize these competing narratives of unity and separation. The great paradox of human biodiversity research is that the only way to understand how similar humans are is to learn how we differ. If we do not welcome the flowering of this more complex appreciation of human nature with open minds, if we are scared to ask and to answer difficult questions, if we lose faith in science, then there is no winner; we all lose.

BIBLIOGRAPHY

Ambrose, Stanley H. "Late Pleistocene Human Population Bottlenecks, Volcanic Winter, and Differentiation of Modern Humans." *Journal of Human Evolution* 34 (2005): 623–51.

American Anthropological Association. "AAPA Statement on Biological Aspects of Race." *American Journal of Physical Anthropology* 101 (1996): 569–70.

Angier, Natalie. "Do Races Differ? Not Really, DNA Shows." *New York Times*, August 22, 2000, C1.

Barbujani G. et al. "An Apportionment of Human DNA Diversity." *Proceedings of the National Academy of Sciences USA* 94, (April 29, 1997): 4516–19.

Bouchard, Claude. "Response." *American Journal of Human Biology* 10, 3 (1998), 279–80.

Bouchard, Claude. Interview with author, February 2, 1999.

Bowman, Lee. "We're More Genetically Diverse Than Previously Thought." Scripps Howard News Service, November 27, 2006.

Burfoot, Amby. "White Men Can't Run." *Runner's World* (August 1992): 89–95.

Cavalli-Sforza, Luigi L., Menozzi, Paolo, and Piazza, Alberto. *The History and Geography of Human Genes*. Princeton, N.J.: Princeton University, 1994.

Collins, Francis. "Director of NHGRI Applauds President Clinton's Action to Protect Federal Workers From Genetic Discrimination." *National Human Genome Research Institute,* February 2000, accessed September 19, 2008. www.genome.gov/10002345.

Connor, Steve. "How Accusations of Racism Ended the Plan to Map the Genetic Diversity of Mankind." *The Independent* (September 10, 2001): 47.

Crawford, Michael. Letter to author, March 4, 2000.

Crow, James F. "Unequal by Nature: A Geneticist's Perspective on Human Differences." *Dædalus* (Winter 2002): 81–88.

Diamond, Jared. *The Third Chimpanzee: Evolution and the Future of the Human Animal.* New York: HarperCollins, 1992.

DiPietro, Loretta. "Tackling Race and Sports: A Review of *Taboo,* by Jon Entine." *Scientific American* (May 2000): 112–13.

Editorial. "Genes, Drugs and Race." *Nature Genetics* 29 (2001): 239–40.

Ehrenreich, Barbara and McIntosh, Janet. "The New Creationism: Biology Under Attack." *The Nation* (June 9, 1997): 29.

Entine, Jon. *Taboo: Why Black Athletes Dominate Sports and Why We're Afraid to Talk About It.* New York: Public Affairs, 2000.

Feldman, Marcus W., Lewontin, Richard C., and King, Mary-Claire. "A Genetic Melting-Pot." *Nature* 424 (July 24, 2003): 374.

Gabrieal, Stacey B. et al. "The Structure of Haplotype Blocks in the Human Genome." *Science* 296 (June 21, 2002): 2225–29.

Gould, Stephen Jay. *The Flamingo's Smile: Reflections in Natural History.* New York: Norton, 1987.

Graves, Joseph. Interview with author, June 17, 2000.

Jacob, Francois. *Of Flies, Mice, and Men* (trans. G. Weiss). Cambridge, Mass.: Harvard University Press, 1998.

Kidd, Kenneth. Interview with author, January 9, 1999.

King, Mary-Claire and Wilson, Allan C. "Evolution at Two Levels in Humans and Chimpanzees." *Science* 189 (1975): 107–116.

Kipketer, Wilson. Interview with author, November 14, 1988.

Klein, Richard G. *The Human Career: Human Biological and Cultural Origins.* Chicago: University of Chicago Press, 1999.

Lewontin, Richard C. "The Apportionment of Human Diversity." *Journal of Evolutionary Biology* 6 (1972): 381–98.

Lewontin, Richard C. *It Ain't Necessarily So: The Dream of the Human Genome and Other Illusions.* New York: New York Review Books: 2001.

Leroi, Armand Marie. "A Family Tree in Every Gene." *New York Times,* March 14, 2005, A23.

Malina, Robert. Interview with author, June 3, 1998.

Marks, Jonathan. *What it Means to be 98% Chimpanzee.* Berkeley: University of California Press, 2003.

North, Kathryn N. et al. "A Common Nonsense Mutation Results in -actinin-3 Deficiency in the General Population." *Nature Genetics* 21 (April 1999): 353–54.

O'Connell, Colm. Interview with author, November 8, 1988.

Olson, Steve. "The Genetic Archaeology of Race." *Atlantic*, April 2001. www.theatlantic. com/doc/200104/olson (accessed July 12, 2010).

Redon, Richard et al. "Global Variation in Copy Number in the Human Genome." *Nature* 444 (November 23, 2006): 444–54.

Relethford John H. and Harpending, Henry C. "Ancient Differences in Population Size Can Mimic a Recent African Origin of Modern Humans." *Current Anthropology* 36 (1995): 667–74.

Risch, Neil et al. "Categorization of Humans in Bio-Medical Research: Genes, Race and Disease." *Genome Biology* 3 (2002): 1–12.

Rosenberg, Noah A. et al. "Genetic Structure of Human Populations." *Science* 298 (2001): 2381–85.

Rudich, Steven M. et al. "Dose Response to a Single Intramuscular Injection of Recombinant Adeno-associated Virus-Erythropoietin in Monkeys." *Journal of Surgical Research* 90 (May 15, 2000): 102–8.

Saltin, Bengt. Interview with author, March 21, 1998.

Sarich, Vincent. "In Defense of the Bell Curve." *Skeptic* 3 (1995): 84–93.

Schwartz, Robert S. "Racial Profiling in Medical Research." *New England Journal of Medicine* 344:18 (May 3, 2001): 1392–93.

Stolberg, Sheryl Gay. "The World: Skin Deep: Shouldn't a Pill Be Colorblind?" *New York Times*, August 17, 2008, D1.

Tishkoff, Sarah A. et al. "Haplotype Diversity and Linkage Disequilibrium at Human G6PD." *Science* 293 (July 20, 2001): 455–62.

Wade, Nicholas. "Gene Study Identifies Five Main Human Populations." *New York Times*, December 20, 2002, D1.

Wolpoff. M. and Caspari, R. *Race and Human Evolution: A Fatal Attraction*. New York: Simon & Schuster, 1997.

9

"White" Men Can't Run: Where is the Scientific Evidence?

*Yannis P. Pitsiladis, Rachael Irving,
Vilma Charlton, and Robert Scott*

A look at the final medal tally at the XXIX Olympiad in Beijing reveals that certain countries enjoy particular success on the running track. Two compelling examples are that of East African runners from Kenya and Ethiopia and their domination of middle- and long-distance running, and athletes from the Caribbean island of Jamaica and their domination of the sprint events. The Beijing results further augment the idea of "black" athletic supremacy and the suggestion that these athletes possess some inherent genetic advantage predisposing them to superior athletic performance. Despite the speculation that these athletes have a genetic advantage, there is no genetic evidence to date to suggest that this is the case, although research is ongoing. The only available genetic studies of elite African athletes do not find that they possess a unique genetic makeup; rather they serve to highlight a high degree of genetic diversity among these athletes. Although genetic contributions to the phenomenal success of African athletes in distance running and Jamaican athletes in sprinting cannot be excluded, results to date predominantly implicate environmental factors.

The athletic events at the XXIX Olympiad in Beijing may be remembered most for the achievements of sprinters from Jamaica and middle- and long-distance runners from Kenya and Ethiopia. Collectively, these three nations won 23 percent of all the track and field medals. The sporting achievement of these nations is more impressive when only the track events are considered; Ethiopia, Kenya, and Jamaica won 36 percent of all track medals. The success of East African athletes in distance running and the concurrent success of athletes from Jamaica in the sprint events will undoubtedly augment the idea of "black" athletic supremacy. This idea is not new and has emerged from simplistic interpretations of performances such as those illustrated in table 9.1, combined with the belief that similar skin color indicates similar genetics. As such, a number of studies have compared the physiological characteristics of "black" and "white" athletes. They compared characteristics such as maximal aerobic capacity ($\dot{V}O_2$ max), lactate accumulation and running economy between groups of "black" and "white" athletes. "Black" South African athletes were found to have lower lactate levels than "white" athletes for given exercise intensities (Coetzer et al. 1993). "Black" athletes also had better running economy (Weston et al. 2000) and higher fractional utilization of $\dot{V}O_2$ max at race pace (Coetzer et al. 1993, Noakes et al. 1999, Weston et al. 2000). It has been suggested that "if the physiological characteristics of sub-elite black African distance runners are present in elite African runners, this may help to explain the success of this racial group in distance running" (Weston et al. 2000). However, this assertion is difficult to reconcile with earlier studies concluding that their findings were compatible with the idea that "Black male individuals are well endowed to perform in sport events of short duration" (Ama et al. 1986). This area of genetics is clearly confusing when studies comparing subjects of differing skin color can conclude on the one hand that the results can explain the success of this "racial" group (i.e., "blacks") in distance running (Weston et al. 2000), and on the other hand that results are compatible with "black" athletes being suited to events of short duration (Ama et al. 1986). Such

Table 9.1.   Male World Records from 100m to marathon. Ancestral origin is derived from geographical and ethnic status

Distance	Athlete	Time	Ancestral Origin
100m	Usain Bolt (JAM)	9.69s	West Africa
110m Hurdles	Dayron Robles (CUB)	12.87s	West Africa
200m	Usain Bolt (JAM)	19.30s	West Africa
400m	Michael Johnson (USA)	43.18s	West Africa
400m Hurdles	Kevin Young (USA)	46.78s	West Africa
800m	Wilson Kipketer (KEN)	1:41.11	East Africa
1000m	Noah Ngeny (KEN)	2:11.96	East Africa
1500m	Hicham El Guerrouj (MOR)	3:26.00	North Africa
Mile	Hicham El Guerrouj (MOR)	3:43.13	North Africa
3,000m	Daniel Komen(KEN)	7:20.67	East Africa
5,000m	Kenenisa Bekele (ETH)	12:37.35	East Africa
10,000m	Kenenisa Bekele (ETH)	26:17.53	East Africa
Marathon	Haile Gebrselassie (ETH)	2:04:26	East Africa

contradictions highlight the problem associated with grouping athletes based simply on skin color.

Evidence that many of the world's best middle- and distance-runners originate from distinct regions of Ethiopia and Kenya, rather than being evenly distributed throughout their respective countries (Onywera et al. 2006, Scott et al. 2005a), appears to further sustain the idea that the success of East African runners is genetically mediated. Interestingly, a similar phenomenon can be observed in Jamaica where the vast majority of successful sprinters can trace their origins to the northwest region of Jamaica: the parish of Trelawny (Robinson 2007). It has been proposed that geographical disparities in athlete production may reflect a genetic similarity among those populating these regions for an athletic genotype and phenotype (Manners 1997). In isolated populations, genetic drift can cause certain alleles to increase or decrease in frequency and, if the variants are beneficial to sprint/power or endurance ability, may predispose the population to that type of performance.

Alternatively, there may be selection for a particular phenotype such as sprint/power or endurance, if it offers a selective advantage in that environment. Indeed, some believe that certain East African tribes (e.g., the Nandi tribe in Kenya) have been genetically selected for endurance performance through cultural practices such as cattle raiding (Manners 1997, Entine 2000). It is not surprising, therefore, that there are assertions in the literature that East Africans have the "proper genes" for distance running (Larsen 2003). Similarly, it has been postulated that the superior sprint performances of African Americans was due to a favorable biology (e.g., muscle-fiber characteristics, metabolic pathways, and pulmonary physiology) hypothesized to have been concentrated by natural selection over the centuries in the Afrocentric peoples displaced from West Africa to the New World during the slave trade (Morrison and Cooper 2006).

Morrison and Cooper (2006) proposed that biochemical differences between West African and West African–descended populations and all other groups, including other black Africans, began but did not end with the sickling of the haemoglobin molecule. The authors advocate that individuals with the sickle cell trait possessed a significant selective advantage in the uniquely lethal West African malarial environment that triggered a series of physiological adjustments and compensatory mechanisms that had favorable consequences for sprint/power performance (2006). While this intriguing hypothesis remains to be tested, another untested hypothesis that also warrants investigation is the idea that the favorable West African biology referred to by Morrison and Cooper (2006) may have been concentrated as a consequence of the displacement process and the harsh living conditions where mainly the "fittest" survived. During the whole period of the slave trade, ~10 million West Africans were enslaved and some 10 million more died during the process of capture and transportation. The transportation across the Atlantic was extremely brutal, lasting many weeks and at least 1 in 4 people who were transported from Africa died before reaching their destination (Scottish Executive). Despite these untested hypotheses having potential theoretical underpinnings, it is unjustified to regard the phenomenal athletic success of East Africans or indeed the Jamaicans as genetically mediated; to justify doing so one must identify the genes that are responsible for that success. Many scientists advocating a biological or genetic explanation typically ignore the socio-economic and cultural factors that appear to better explain these phenomena (Scott and Pitsiladis 2006, 2007). This chapter aims to address these and other beliefs in the context of the limited amount of scientific evidence available.

GENETIC EXPLANATIONS

Despite the idea being perpetuated that "black" athletes are genetically adapted for athletic performance (Hamilton and Weston 2000), until recently, no studies had attempted to assess and quantify this genetic effect (Moran et al. 2004, Scott el al. 2005a, Scott et al. 2005b). The concept of "black" athletic superiority is based on a preconception that each "race" constitutes a genetically homogeneous group, with "race" defined simply by skin color. This belief is contrary to the assertion that there is more genetic variation among Africans than between African and Eurasian populations (Yu et al. 2002). The genetics of "race" is controversial and gives rise to a number of contrasting viewpoints with particular emphasis on the use of "race" as a tool in the diagnosis and treatment of disease. Some argue that there is a role for "race" in biomedical research and that the potential benefits to be gained in terms of diagnosis, treatment and research of disease outweigh the potential social costs of linking "race" or ethnicity with genetics (Burchard et al. 2003).

Others, however, advocate that "race" should be abandoned as a tool for assessing the prevalence of disease genotypes and that "race" is not an acceptable surrogate for genetics in assessing the risk of disease and efficacy of treatment in human populations (Cooper et al. 2003). Arguments for the inclusion of "race" in biomedical research often focus on its use to identify single gene disorders and their medical outcome. The genetic basis of complex phenotypes such as athletic performance is poorly understood and more difficult to study. It is estimated that most human genetic variation is shared by all humans and that a marginal proportion (normally less than 10 percent) is specific to major continental groups (Cavalli-Sforza and Feldman 2003). Estimates from the human genome project and analysis of haplotype frequencies show that most haplotypes (i.e., linked segments of genetic variation, rarely subject to re-assortment by recombination) are shared between two of the three major geographic populations: Europe, Asia, and Africa (A Haplotype Map of the Human Genome. 2005). It is currently estimated that the level of genetic diversity between human populations is not large enough to justify the use of the term "race" (see Jobling et al. 2004 for a review). Consequently, any differences in physiology, biochemistry and/or anatomy between groups defined solely by skin color (e.g., comparing "black" with "white") are not directly applicable to their source populations, even if the differences found are indeed genetically determined.

The approach of comparing physiological characteristics between groups defined solely by skin color does not offer much insight into why some groups are more successful than others in certain sporting events. Even within groups of individuals with similar skin color, many ethnic and tribal groups exist. For example, more than seventy languages are in everyday use in Ethiopia, while in Kenya, more than fifty distinct ethnic communities speak close to eighty different dialects. Similarly, the Jamaican population, currently estimated to be ~2.8 million, trace their origins primarily to West Africa as a result of the transatlantic slave trade that began during the early sixteenth century and persisted until the passing of the Abolition of the Slave Trade Act in 1807 (Scottish Executive 2007). During this period, slaves were captured from a large number of geographical areas. In particular, slaves were captured from Senegal, Genegambia, Guinea, Sierra Leone, Ivory Coast, Ghana, Benin (Dahamey), Nigeria, Cameroon, and Angola (Alleyne 1988). The ethnic makeup of the slaves transported to the Caribbean was therefore extremely diverse, comprising more than eighteen main ethnic groups (e.g., Mandinka, Fulani, Wolof, Dyula (Jola), Mande, Dan, Kru, Asante (Cromanti), Fante, Ewe, Ga (dialect of Ewe), Yoruba, Igbo, Nziani, Agni, Fula, and Bantu (Alleyne 1988).

Furthermore, it was often the case during the slave trade period that slave owners (primarily "white" British men) would father children of their slaves, thus further influencing the resulting gene pool (the indigenous people of the island, the Arawak and Taino, can be discounted from any significant influence as they were almost completely wiped out by disease). This admixture is fittingly reflected in the motto of Jamaica "Out of many, one people." Consequently, the inadequate classification of subjects into groups based on characteristics such as skin color in the scientific literature will undoubtedly lead to equivocal results and serve only to augment existing stereotypes of genetically advantaged black athletes. Studies comparing "black" and "white" athletes (e.g., Jobling 2004, Saltin et al. 1995b, Kohn et al. 2007) offer some insight into the physiological determinants of elite performance but little, if any, insight into any genetic influences on the disproportionate success of African/"black" runners.

The capacity of *Homo sapiens* for endurance running (defined as the ability to sustain running for extended periods of time using primarily aerobic metabolism), although not comparable to other mammalian endurance specialists, is unique among the primates. This has led to the belief that endurance capabilities have been central to the recent evolutionary history of modern humans (Saltin et al. 1995a). The unique endurance capacity of humans relative to the other primates is purported to be due to a number of traceable adaptations beneficial to endurance running in the *Homo* genus (Saltin et al. 1995a). Although anatomically modern humans are young in evolutionary terms (~150,000 years) relative to the age of the *Homo* genus (~2 million years), human populations began to diverge into new environments outside Africa some 70,000 years ago (Bramble and Lieberman 2004). It is possible, therefore, that divergent human populations (in different continents for a significant portion of the age of the species) have accrued varying degrees of these adaptations due to different selection pressures, further specializing them for an endurance phenotype or otherwise.

The varying adaptation to hypobaric hypoxia by geographically isolated populations represents a well-studied example of this, which may relate to endurance performance. Andean highlanders display higher levels of hae-moglobin and saturation than Tibetans at similar altitude, while Ethiopian highlanders maintain oxygen delivery despite having haemoglobin levels and saturation typical of sea level ranges (Macaulay et al. 2005). There has been much conjecture surrounding such adaptations to altitude and their role in the evolution of human physiological responses (Beall et al. 2002, Beall 2003). Given the origin of modern humans in East Africa—a higher, drier and cooler environment than our more distant ancestors may have inhabited—the ancestral form of modern humans would have been well adapted for altitude tolerance and, presumably, endurance per-formance, since the altitude tolerance phenotype is similar to the endur-ance performance phenotype (Beall et al. 2002).

If the ancestral form developed in the highlands of East Africa was indeed an altitude-endurance phenotype, East Africans may have further developed an up-regulated, high capacity version (Beall et al. 2002), thus favoring them further for endurance performance. Other populations may have "diluted" the ancestral phenotype, or developed down-regulated, low capacity versions through selection for other phenotypes during migration to different environments (e.g., Andean and Tibetan populations) (Beall et al. 2002).

The genetic ancestry of elite East African runners was first tested us-ing uni-parentally inherited genetic markers such as mitochondrial DNA (mtDNA). Polymorphisms in mtDNA have been suggested to influence the variation in human physical performance as mtDNA encodes various subunits of enzyme complexes of oxidative phosphorylation, as well as components of the mitochondrial protein synthesis system (Beall 2003). Mitochondrial DNA is inherited in its entirety from mother to child, only changing as new mutations arise, resulting in the accumulation of linked complexes of mutations down different branches of descent from a single ancestor: "Mitochondrial Eve" (figure 9.1). This linear pattern of inheritance can also be used to trace the ancestral origins of individu-als or populations (Hochachka et al. 1998) and to construct phylogenetic trees back to "Mitochondrial Eve" (each branch of the tree is known as a haplogroup). The frequency of these haplogroups can be used to trace population movements and expansions and as such, different haplogroups are at widely varying frequencies in different regions of the world and even different regions of the same continent (Anderson et al. 1981). A simplified version of an mtDNA phylogeny is shown in figure 9.1. Mitochondrial DNA analysis was previously applied to the cohort of elite Ethiopian distance runners (Scott et al. 2005). Rather than the elite Ethiopian runners being restricted to one area of the tree, results revealed a wide distribution, similar to the general Ethiopian population (Scott et al. 2005, Salas et al. 2002, Rando et al. 1998, Passarino et al. 1998, Kivisild et al. 2004) (figure 9.1) and in contrast to the concept that these elite runners are a genetically distinct group as defined by mtDNA.

Furthermore, the diversity of mtDNA haplogroups found in the elite runners does not support a role for mtDNA polymorphisms in their success. It can be seen from figure 9.1 that some of the athletes share a more recent common mtDNA ancestor with many Europeans. This finding does not support the hypothesis that the Ethiopian population from which the athletes are drawn have remained genetically isolated in East Africa but shows that they have undergone migration events during the age of the species. This is in contrast to the possibility that Ethiopian athletes have maintained and further developed the ancestral endurance phenotype through having remained isolated in the East African highlands. It is likely that population movements within Africa as recently as a few thousand years ago have contributed to the peopling of East Africa, through the eastern path of the Bantu migrations (Salas et al. 2002, Kivisild et al. 2004). However, linguistic data show that Bantu languages are absent in Ethiopia (Scott et al. 2003), but frequent in Kenya (Onywera et al. 2006), showing that the neighboring regions may have been subject to widely different patterns of migration. Recent data on the mtDNA haplogroup frequencies of the Kenyan population (Brandstatter et al. 2004) and elite Kenyan runners (Scott el al. 2005b) reveal that the mtDNA haplogroups found in Kenya are very different to those found in Ethiopia and show a higher frequency of African specific haplogroups.

The idea that the elite East African runners studied to date do not arise from a limited genetic isolate is further supported by the analysis of the Y chromosome haplogroup distribution of elite Ethiopian athletes (Moran et al. 2004). The Y chromosome can be considered as the male equivalent of mtDNA. The distribution of Y chromosome haplogroups of the Ethiopian athletes relative to the general population is shown in figure

9.2. Elite Ethiopian athletes differed significantly in their Y chromosome distribution from both the general population and that of the Arsi region (Moran et al. 2004) (which produces an excess of elite runners, Scott et al. 2003). The finding that Y chromosome haplogroups were associated with elite athlete status in Ethiopians suggests that either an element of the Y chromosome genetics is influencing athletic performance, or that the Y chromosome haplogroup distributions were affected by population stratification (i.e., the population from which the athletes originate has a distinct Y chromosome distribution). However, the haplogroup distribution of the Arsi region did not differ from the rest of Ethiopia (Moran et al. 2004, Underhill et al. 2000, Semino et al. 2002), suggesting that the observed associations were less likely to be a result of simple population stratification.

Currently, these haplogroup frequencies are being assessed in a larger Kenyan cohort (Onywera et al. 2006, Scott et al. 2005a). If the same haplogroups are found to be under- or over-represented, this would provide strong evidence for a biological effect of Y chromosome on running performance. However, despite the finding of a potential effect of the Y chromosome on endurance performance, the Y chromosome results show similar levels of diversity to those found using mtDNA. In addition, it can be seen from figure 9.2 that a significant number of the athletes trace part of their male ancestry to outside Africa at some time during the age of our species. Studies using non-recombinant markers are concordant in their finding that the elite Ethiopian athletes show similar genetic diversity to the general population, and can trace their ancestry to diverse populations, rather than a uniquely "highland African" population. Collectively, the findings from Y chromosome and mtDNA studies imply that the phenomenon of East African running should best be considered as two distinct phenomena, that of Ethiopian and Kenyan success, at least from a genetic viewpoint.

For genetic selection to occur in a population there must be pre-existing genetic variation coding for phenotypic variation or new variants must arise in a population by mutation which confer a different level of evolutionary fitness on the bearer. A particular variant is likely to increase in frequency in the population as long as having a particular phenotype provides improved "Darwinian fitness." Given that East Africa is populated by a genetically diverse population who appear not to have been isolated

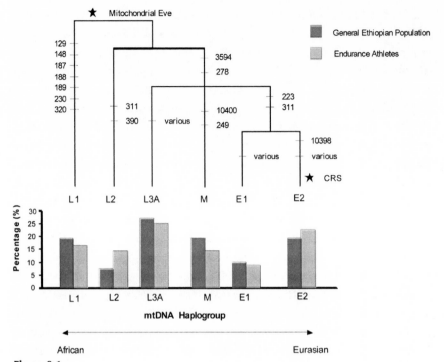

Figure 9.1.

for long periods of time (relative to the age of our species), it is less likely that genetic adaptations have occurred, as there has been less time for either selection or genetic drift to increase the frequency of hypothetical "performance alleles." However, it must be acknowledged that although the levels of genetic diversity in East Africa reduce the likelihood of such a theoretical framework for genetic selection to have occurred for endurance performance, the possibility remains. If the advantage offered by a particular genetic variant is large enough, that allele can rapidly increase in frequency within the population (Rupert and Hochachka 2001).

For example, evidence of different strategies to cope with hypobaric hypoxia (Beall 2003) used by geographically isolated indigenous populations may suggest that rather than it being an ancestral phenotype, strategies to cope with altitude may have developed separately in isolated populations (Beall 2003). Therefore, the possibility exists that environmental pressure in the form of hypobaric hypoxia has more recently (in the last few thousand years rather than the last 150,000) caused selection for variants conferring advantage in oxygen utilization and subsequently increased the frequency of these variants in moderate altitude populations. In the moderate altitude populations of Ethiopia and/or Kenya, such adaptations may have the potential to concurrently influence the endurance phenotype (Hochachka et al. 1998). Although unlikely to be isolated to East Africans, it is entirely possible that changes in the frequency of particular candidate genes for human performance would have an influence on East African success. However, this has not been shown to date.

In the case of the Jamaican sprint phenomenon, one hypothesis proposed in the scientific literature to explain the superior sprint performances of this population and of the African Americans in general, is a favorable biology hypothesized to have been concentrated by natural selection over the centuries as individuals were displaced from West Africa to the New World during the slave trade (Morrison and Cooper 2006). As such, these authors proposed that individuals with the sickle cell trait possessed a significant selective advantage in the uniquely lethal West African malarial environment that triggered a series of compensatory mechanisms that had favorable consequences for sprint/power performance (Morrison and Cooper 2006). Although this hypothesis has not been rigorously tested, this idea is subject to the same limitations as genetic explanations of the East African running phenomenon, namely diverse genetic pools of founding populations and time constraints for genetic adaptations to occur. However, in the West African case, improved "Darwinian fitness" may have resulted as a consequence of the displacement process and the harsh living conditions where mainly the "fittest" survived, as previously described, a form of rapid or accelerated Darwinian evolution. Some insight into this idea is currently being attempted as DNA from more than 120 of Jamaica's finest sprinters has been collected for gene variant analysis of the major performance candidate genes and results compared to a large representative Jamaican control group and to sprinters from other Caribbean islands, Nigeria and from the United States.

To date, only two studies have investigated the frequency of a nuclear candidate gene for human performance in East African athletes (Scott et al. 2005a) and athletes of West African ancestry (Yang et al. 2003). The gene studied in elite East African runners was the Angiotensin converting enzyme (*ACE*) gene: the most studied of the putative candidate genes for human performance, where an insertion polymorphism (I) is associated with lower levels of circulating and tissue ACE than the deletion (D) (Rigat et al. 1990, Danser et al. 1995). The *ACE* gene has been associated with a number of aspects of human performance, reviewed elsewhere (Jones et al. 2002, MacArthur and North 2005). In general, the I allele has been associated with endurance type performance and the D allele with power type performance. Intriguingly, the *ACE* I allele has also been associated with altitude tolerance (Montgomery et al. 1998) making it an ideal candidate gene to investigate in East African athletes given the suggestion that the altitude at which these athletes live and train may partially account for their success (Schmidt et al. 2002). As such, *ACE* I/D genotype frequencies were tested in elite Kenyan athletes relative to the general population (Scott et al. 2005a). Based on previous findings (Jones et al. 2002), it may have been expected that the elite runners would show an excess of the I allele. However, no significant differences were found in I/D genotype frequencies between athletes and the general population (Scott et al. 2005b). Different levels of linkage disequilibrium in Africans and Caucasians (Zhu et al. 2000, Rieder et al. 1999) meant that an additional, potentially causal variant (A22982G) was tested. However, no significant differences in A22982G genotype frequencies were found between athletes and the general population (Scott et al. 2005a). Indeed 29 percent of Kenyan controls and only 17 percent of international Kenyan athletes had the putatively advantageous "AA" genotype (always found in concert with II in Caucasians) for endurance performance. While controversy over the influence of *ACE* genotype on endurance performance continues (Montgomery et al. 1998), this study did not support a role for *ACE* gene variation in explaining the East African distance-running phenomenon.

The only gene to have been studied in elite sprinters from Nigeria and data compared to elite distance runners from Kenya and Ethiopia is alpha-actinin-3 (*ACTN3*), which has been associated with elite physical performance (Yang et al. 2003) and found at widely differing frequencies in different populations (Mills et al. 2001). In particular, a strong association has been found between the R577X polymorphism and elite athlete status in Australian Caucasian populations, with the α-actinin-3-deficient XX genotype being present at a lower frequency in sprint/power athletes, and at slightly higher frequency in elite female endurance athletes, relative to controls (Yang et al. 2003). This negative association of the XX genotype with sprint performance has subsequently been replicated in a cohort of Finnish elite track and field athletes (Niema and Majamaa 2005). Such data has helped established the link between R577X and muscle strength and sprint performance. It was therefore of interest that the α-actinin-3 deficient XX genotype was found to be almost absent in controls and sprinters from Nigeria (and currently being examined in U.S. and Jamaican sprinters), while there was no evidence for an association between the R577X polymorphism and endurance performance in East African athletes, suggesting that α-actinin-3 deficiency is not a major determinant of East African running success. Whether other nuclear variants can help explain such phenomena remains to be determined. However, the extraordinary achievements of certain populations in sprinting or endurance running must rely upon the successful integration of a number of physiological, biochemical, and biomechanical systems, which themselves are the product of a multitude of contributors. The success of these athletes is unlikely, therefore, to be the result of a single gene polymorphism; rather it is likely that elite athletes rely on the presence of a combination of advantageous genotypes at a multitude of loci. Currently, studies are underway to investigate the frequency of other candidate genes in these unique cohorts, which will certainly shed more light on this question.

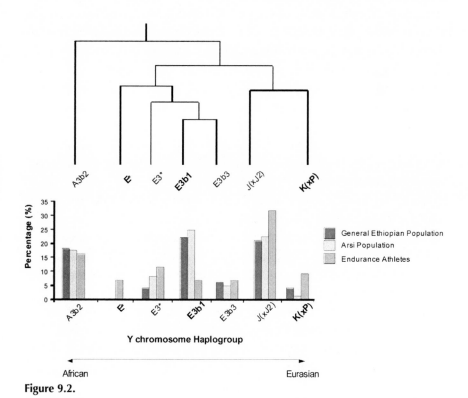

Figure 9.2.

NON-GENETIC EXPLANATIONS

Non-genetic explanations for the success of East African athletes in middle- and long-distance running include the suggestion that the distances East Africans run to school as children serve them well for subsequent athletic success. A study by Scott and colleagues (2003) found that elite distance runners had traveled further to school as children, and more had done so by running. Many of the distances traveled were incredible: some children traveling upward of 20 km each day by running to and from school. A previous study by Saltin and colleagues (1996b) has shown that East African children who had used running as a means of transport had a $\dot{V}O_2$ max some 30 percent higher than those who did not, therefore, implicating distance traveled to school as a determinant of East African success. Other studies have shown regional disparities in the production of Ethiopian and Kenyan middle- and long-distance runners (Onywera et al. 2006, Scott et al. 2003). In a study of the demographic characteristics of elite Ethiopian athletes, 38 percent of elite marathon athletes were from the region of Arsi, which accounts for less than 5 percent of the Ethiopian population (Scott et al. 2003). These findings were mirrored in Kenya, where 81 percent of international Kenyan athletes originated from the Rift Valley province, which accounts for less than 25 percent of the Kenyan population (Onywera et al. 2006). Although some believe that this geographical disparity is mediated by an underlying genetic phenomenon (Manners 1997, Entine 2000). It is worth considering that both of these regions are altitudinous (Onywera et al. 2006, Scott et al. 2003), and athletes have long used altitude training to induce further adaptations. It has been suggested that endurance training and altitude combine synergistically in those native to moderate altitude to partially account for the success of East African athletes (Schmidt et al. 2002).

The phenomenal success of Jamaicans in sprinting, especially in the recent Olympics, has also been attributed to non-genetic factors. For example, in Jamaica there exists an excellent and unique model that focuses on identifying and nurturing athletic talent throughout junior to senior level. In his recent book, *Jamaican Athletics: A Model for the World*, Patrick Robinson concludes: "The real explanation of the outstanding achievements of the system is that all of its actors are moved by a spirit that unifies them to work to ensure that Jamaican athletics lives up to its rich history and tradition of excellence" (2007). This is a theme that echoes what is found in Ethiopia and Kenya (Onywera et al. 2006, Scott et al. 2003). Given these unique circumstances, the superior performances of athletes from Kenya, Ethiopia and Jamaica seen in Beijing come as no surprise to those fortunate enough to study these amazing athletes closely.

Others have suggested that African/"black" athletes enjoy a psychological advantage, mediated through stereotype threat (Baker and Horton 2003). A consequence of strengthening the stereotypical view of the superior "black" or African athlete is the development of a self-fulfilling prophecy of "white" athletes avoiding sporting events typically considered as favoring African/"black" athletes. This self-selection has resulted in a vicious cycle where the avoidance of these athletic events by "whites" has further strengthened the aforementioned stereotypical view to the extent that the unsubstantiated idea of the biological superiority of the African/"black" athlete becomes dogma. This development is surprising given the lack of any scientific evidence to warrant such an assertion.

CONCLUSIONS

It is inevitable that the results of the Beijing Olympics will spark an even greater interest from scientists, the media, and others to identify the biological mechanisms (including genes) responsible for East African runners from Kenya and Ethiopia dominating middle- and long-distance running events, while athletes from the Caribbean island of Jamaica dominated the sprint events. However, the limited studies reviewed in this chapter constitute the only available data to date on the genetics of the African/"black" running phenomenon and demonstrate that the athletes, although arising from distinct regions of East Africa, do not arise from a limited genetic isolate. For example, the Y chromosome types found in excess in elite Ethiopian athletes are also found outside Africa. Other findings suggest that the most studied of the previously identified performance genes (i.e., *ACE*), does not appear to influence the success of East African athletes, which highlights another important point surrounding the genetics of exercise performance: it is likely that all single gene variants that offer some advantage influence the fine-tuning of performance rather than simply conferring success or failure. Any of these potentially advantageous gene variants are likely to be found in excess among elite athletes but the exact combinations needed for international success remain unknown. It is perhaps unlikely that East Africa or Jamaica is producing unique genotypes that cannot be matched by those from other areas of the world, but more likely that those in these areas with an advantageous genotype realize their advantage. It is interesting that Ethiopia and Kenya do not share a similar genetic ancestry, as defined by mtDNA, but what they do share is a similar environment: moderate altitude and high levels of physical activity. While genetic data supporting or refuting a genetic explanation for the Jamaican sprint phenomenon is imminent, the implications of the Jamaican motto "out of many, one people" that is seemingly overlooked and ignored by those arguing in favor of a genetic explanation for Jamaican sprint success, are that these islanders are potentially of even greater genetic diversity than either Kenyans or Ethiopians. It is therefore unlikely that the remarkable sprint successes of Jamaica can be attributed to genetics. However, much can be learned by studying the similarities and differences of the East African and Jamaican running phenomena. For example, few other regions of the world have such high levels of childhood physical activity combined with such cultural and financial importance being placed on running, whether sprinting or endurance running. In summary, it is unjustified at present to regard either phenomenon as genetically mediated; to justify doing so one must identify the genes that are important, which has proven elusive to date.

BIBLIOGRAPHY

"A Haplotype Map of the Human Genome." *Nature* 437, no. 7063 (October 27, 2005): 1299–320.

Alleyne, M. *Roots of Jamaican Culture*. Chicago: Frontline Distribution International, 1996.

Ama, P. F., J. A. Simoneau, M. R. Boulay, O. Serresse, G. Thériault, and C. Bouchard. "Skeletal Muscle Characteristics in Sedentary Black and Caucasian Males." *Journal of Applied Physiology* 61, no. 5 (1986): 1758–61.

Anderson, S., A. T. Bankier, B. G. Barrell, M. H. L. de Broijn, A. R. Coelsoit, J. Drouin, and I. C. Eperoit. "Sequence and Organization of the Human Mitochondrial Genome." *Nature* 290, no. 5806 (1981): 457–65.

Baker, J. and S. Horton. "East African Running Dominance Revisited: A Role for Stereotype Threat?" *British Journal of Sports Medicine* 37, no. 6 (2003): 553–55.

Beall, C. M. "High-Altitude Adaptations." *Lancet* 362 (2003) Supplemental: s14–s15.

Beall, C. M., M. J Decker, G. M. Brittenham, I. Kushner, A. Gebremedhin, and K. P. Strohl. "An Ethiopian Pattern of Human Adaptation to High-Altitude Hypoxia." *Proceedings of the National Academy of Science U.S.A.* 99, no. 26 (2002): 17215–18.

Bosch, A. N., B. R. Goslin, T. D. Noakes, and S. C. Dennis. "Physiological Differences between Black and White Runners during a Treadmill Marathon." *European Journal of Applied Physiology and Occupational Physiology* 61, no. 1–2 (1990): 68–72.

Bramble, D. M. and D. E. Lieberman. "Endurance Running and the Evolution of Homo." *Nature* 432 (2004): 345–52.

Brandstatter, A., C. T. Peterson., J. A. Irwin, S. Mpoke, D. K. Koech, W. Parson and T. J. Parsons. "Mitochondrial DNA Control Region Sequences from Nairobi (Kenya): Inferring Phylogenetic Parameters for the Establishment of a Forensic Database." *International Journal of Legal Medicine* 118, no. 5 (2004): 294–306.

Burchard, E. G., E. Ziv, N. Coyle, S. L. Gomez, H. Tang, A. J. Karter, J. L. Mountain, E. J. Perez-Stable, D. Sheppard, and N. Risch. "The Importance of Race and Ethnic Background in Biomedical Research and Clinical Practice." *New England Journal of Medicine* 348, no. 12 (2003): 1170–75.

Cavalli-Sforza, L. L. and M. W. Feldman. "The Application of Molecular Genetic Approaches to the Study of Human Evolution." *Natural Genetics* 33 (2003 Supplement): 266–75.

Coetzer, P., T. D. Noakes, and B. Sanders. "Superior Fatigue Resistance of Elite Black South African Distance Runners." *Journal of Applied Physiology* 75, no. 4 (1993): 1822–27.

Cooper, R. S., J. S. Kaufman, and R. Ward, "Race and Genomics." *New England Journal of Medicine* 348, no. 12 (2003): 1166–70.

Danser, A. H., M. A. Schalekamp, W. A. Bax, A. Maassen van den Brink, P. R. Saxena, G. A. J. Riegger, and H. Schunkert. "Angiotensin-Converting Enzyme in the Human Heart. Effect of the Deletion/Insertion Polymorphism." *Circulation* 92, no. 6 (1995): 1387–88.

Entine, J. *Taboo: Why Black Athletes Dominate Sports and Why We're Afraid To Talk About It.* New York: Public Affairs, 2000.

Hamilton, B. and A. Weston. "Perspectives on East African Middle and Long Distance Running." *Journal of Science and Medicine in Sport* 3, no. 4 (2000): vi–viii.

Hochachka, P. W., H. C. Gunga, and K. Kirsch. "Our Ancestral Physiological Phenotype: An Adaptation for Hypoxia Tolerance and for Endurance Performance?" *Proceedings of the National Academy of Science U.S.A.* 95, no. 4 (1998): 1915–20.

Jobling, M. A, M. E. Hurles and C. Tyler-Smith. *Human Evolutionary Genetics.* (Oxford: UK: Garland Publishing, 2004): 278.

Jones, A., H. E. Montgomery and D. R. Woods. "Human Performance: A Role for the ACE Genotype?" *Exercise Sport Science Review* 30, no. 4 (2002): 184–90.

Kivisild, T., M. Reidla, E. Metspalu, A. Rosa, A. Brehm, E. Pennarun, J. Parik, T. Geberhiwot, E. Usanga, and R. Villems. "Ethiopian Mitochondrial DNA Heritage: Tracking Gene Flow Across and Around the Gate of Tears." *American Journal of Human Genetics* 75, no. 5 (2004): 752–70.

Kohn, T. A., B. Essen-Gustavsson, and K. Myburgh. "Do Skeletal Muscle Phenotypic Characteristics of Xhosa and Caucasian Endurance Runners Differ When Matched for Training and Racing Distance?" *Journal of Applied Physiology* 103 (2007): 932–40.

Larsen, H. B. "Kenyan Dominance in Distance Running." *Comparative Biochemistry and Physiology Part A: Molecular & Integrative Physiology* 136, no. 1 (2003): 161–70.

Maca-Meyer, N., A. M. Gonzalez, J. M. Larruga, C. Flores and and V. M. Cabrera. "Major Genomic Mitochondrial Lineages Delineate Early Human Expansions." *BMC Genetics* 2, no. 1 (2001): 13.

MacArthur, D. G. and K. N. North. "Genes and Human Elite Athletic Performance." *Human Genetics* 116, no. 5 (2005): 331–39.

Macaulay, V., C. Hill, A. Achilli, C. Rengo, D. Clarke, W. Meehan, J. Blackburn, O. Semino, R. Scozzari, F. Cruciani, A. Taha, N. K. Shaari, J. M. Raja, P. Ismail, Z. Zainuddin, W. Goodwin, D. Bulbeck, H. J. Bandelt, S. Oppenheimer, A. Torroni, and M. Richards. "Single, Rapid Coastal Settlement of Asia Revealed by Analysis of Complete Mitochondrial Genomes." *Science* 308 (2005): 1034–36.

Manners, J. "Kenya's Running Tribe." *The Sports Historian* 17, no. 2 (1997): 14–27.

Mills, M., N. Yang, R. Weinberger, M. Mills, N. Yang, R. Weinberger, D. L. Vander Woude, A. H. Beggs, S. Easteal and K. North. "Differential Expression of the Actin-Binding Proteins, Alpha-Actinin-2 and -3, in Different Species: Implications for the Evolution of Functional Redundancy." *Human Molecular Genetics* 10, no. 13 (2001): 1335–46.

Montgomery, H. E., R. M. Marshall, H. Hemingway, S. Myerson, P. Clarkson, C. Dollery, M. Hayward, D. E. Holliman, M. Jubb, M. World, E. L. Thomas, A. E. Brynes, N. Saeed, M. Barnard, J. D. Bell, K. Prasad, M. Rayson, P. J. Talmud, and S. E. Humphries. "Human Gene for Physical Performance." *Nature* 393, no. 6682 (1998): 221–22.

Moran, C. N., R. A. Scott, S. M. Adams, S. J. Warrington, M. A. Jobling, R. H. Wilson, W. H. Goodwin, E. Georgiades, B. Wolde and Y. P. Pitsiladis. "Y Chromosome Haplogroups of Elite Ethiopian Endurance Runners." *Human Genetics* 115, no. 6 (2004): 492–97.

Morrison, E. Y. and P. D. Cooper. "Some Bio-Medical Mechanisms in Athletic Prowess." *West Indian Medical Journal* 55, no. 3 (2006): 205–9.

Niemi, A. K and K. Majamaa. "Mitochondrial DNA and ACTN3 genotypes in Finnish elite endurance and sprint athletes." *European Journal of Human Genetics* 13 (2005): 965–69.

Onywera, V. O., R. A. Scott, M. K. Boit, and Y. P. Pitsiladis. "Demographic Characteristics of Elite Kenyan Endurance Runners." *Journal of Sports Science* 24, no. 4 (2006): 415–22.

Passarino, G., O. Semino, L. Quintana-Murci, L. Excoffier, M. Hammer, and A. Santa-chiara-Benerecetti. "Different Genetic Components in the Ethiopian Population, Identified by MtDNA and Y-Chromosome Polymorphisms." *American Journal of Human Genetics* 62, no. 2 (1998): 420–34.

Patterson, O. *The Sociology of Slavery: An Analysis of the Origins, Development and Structure of the Negro Slave.* Cranbury, N.J.: Associated University Press, 1969.

Rando, J. C., F. Pinto, A. M. Gonzalez, M. Hernandez, A. M. Gonzalez, F. Pinto and H. J. Bandelt. "Mitochondrial DNA Analysis of Northwest African Populations Reveals Genetic Exchanges With European, Near-Eastern, and Sub-Saharan Populations." *Annals of Human Genetics* 62, Pt 6 (1998): 531–50.

Richards, M., V. Macaulay, E. Hickey, E. Vega, B. Sykes, V. Guida, C. Rengo, D. Sellitto, F. Cruciani, and T. Kivisild. "Tracing European Founder Lineages in the Near Eastern MtDNA Pool." *American Journal of Human Genetics* 67, no. 5 (2000): 1251–76.

Rieder, M. J., S. L. Taylor, A. G. Clark, and D. A. Nickerson. "Sequence Variation in the Human Angiotensin Converting Enzyme." *Natural Genetics* 22, no. 1 (1999): 59–62.

Rigat, B., C. Hubert, F. Alhenc-Gelas, F. Cambien P. Corvol and F. Soubrier. "An Insertion/Deletion Polymorphism in the Angiotensin I-Converting Enzyme Gene Accounting for Half the Variance of Serum Enzyme Levels." *Journal of Clinical Investigation* 86, no. 4 (1990): 1343–46.

Robinson, P. *Jamaican Athletics: A Model for the World.* Kingston, Jamaica: Marco Printers Ltd, 2007.

Rupert, J. L. and P. W. Hochachka. "Genetic Approaches to Understanding Human Adaptation to Altitude in the Andes." *Journal of Experimental Biology* 204, Pt 18 (2001): 3151–60.

Salas, A., M. Richards, T. De la Fe, M. V. Lareu, B. Sobrino, P. S´anchez-Diz, V. Macaulay, and A. Carracedo. "The Making of the African MtDNA Landscape." *American Journal of Human Genetics* 71, no. 5 (2002): 1082–111.

Saltin, B., C. K. Kim, N. Terrados, et al. "Morphology, Enzyme Activities and Buffer Capacity in Leg Muscles of Kenyan and Scandinavian Runners." *Scandinavian Journal of Medicine and Science in Sports* 5, no. 4 (1995a): 222–30.

Saltin, B., H. Larsen, N. Terrados, J. Svedenhag and C. J. Rolfe. "Aerobic Exercise Capacity at Sea Level and at Altitude in Kenyan Boys, Junior and Senior Runners Compared With Scandinavian Runners." *Scandinavian .Journal of Medicine and Science in Sports* 5, no. 4 (1995b): 209–21.

Schmidt, W., K. Heinicke, J. Rojas, J. Gomez Manuel, M. Serrato, B. Wolfarth, A. Schmid, and J. Keul. "Blood Volume and Hemoglobin Mass in Endurance Athletes From Moderate Altitude." *Medicine Science Sports Exercise* 34, no. 12 (2002): 1934–40.

Scottish Executive. Scotland and the Slave Trade. 2007 Bicentenary of the Abolition of the Slave Trade Act. Edinburgh: St. Andrews House, 2007.

Scott, R. A., E. Georgiades, R. H. Wilson, W. H. Goodwin, B. Wolde, Y. P. Pitsiladis. "Demographic Characteristics of Elite Ethiopian Endurance Runners." *Medical Science Sports Exercise* 35, no. 10 (2003): 1727–32.

Scott, R. A., Moran, C., Wilson, R. H., V. Onywera, M. K. Boit, W. H. Goodwin, P. Gohlke, J. Payne, H. Montgomery and Y. P. Pitsiladis. "No Association between Angiotensin Converting Enzyme (ACE) Gene Variation and Endurance Athlete Status in Kenyans." *Comparative Biochemistry and Physiology Part A—Molecular & Integrative Physiology* 141, no. 2 (2005a): 169–75.

Scott, R. A., R. H. Wilson, W. H. Goodwin, C. N. Moran, E. Georgiades, B. Wolde, and Y. P. Pitsiladis. "Mitochondrial DNA Lineages of Elite Ethiopian Athletes."

Comparative Biochemistry and Physiology—Part B: Biochemistry and Molecular Biology 140, no. 3 (2005b): 497–503.

Scott, R. A. and Y. P. Pitsiladis. "Genetics and the Success of East African Distance Runners." *International Sport Medicine Journal* 7, no. 3 (2006): 172–86.

Scott, R. A. and Y. P. Pitsiladis. "Genotypes and Distance Running: Clues from Africa." *Sports Medicine* 7, nos. 4–5 (2007): 1–4.

Semino, O., A. S. Santachiara-Benerecetti, F. Falaschi, L. Cavalli-Sforza, and P. Underhill. "Ethiopians and Khoisan Share the Deepest Clades of the Human Y-Chromosome Phylogeny." *American Journal of Human Genetics* 70, no. 1 (2002): 265–68.

Torroni, A., A. Achilli, V. Macaulay, M. Richards and H. J. Bandelt. "Harvesting the Fruit of the Human MtDNA Tree." *Trends in Genetics* 22, no. 6 (2006): 339–45.

Underhill, P. A., S. Peidong Shen, A. A. Lin, L. Jin, G. Passarino, Y. H. Wei, H. Yang, E. Kauffman, B. Bonné-Tamir, J. Bertranpetit, P. Francalacci, M. Ibrahim, T. Jenkins, J. R. Kidd, S. Q. Mehdi, M. T. Seielstad, R. Spencer Wells, A. Piazza, R. W. Davis, M. W. Feldman, L. Luca Cavalli-Sforza and P. J. Oefner. "Y Chromosome Sequence Variation and the History of Human Populations." *Natural Genetics* 26, no. 3 (2000): 358–61.

Weston, A. R., O. Karamizrak, and A. Smith. "African Runners Exhibit Greater Fatigue Resistance, Lower Lactate Accumulation, and Higher Oxidative Enzyme Activity." *Journal of Applied Physiology* 86, no. 3 (1999): 915–23.

Weston, A. R., Z. Mbambo and K. H. Myburgh. "Running Economy of African and Caucasian Distance Runners." *Medical Science Sports Exercise* 32, no. 6 (2000): 1130–34.

Yang, N., D. G. MacArthur, J. P Gulbin, A. Hahn, A. Beggs, S. Easteal, and K. North. "ACTN3 Genotype Is Associated With Human Elite Athletic Performance." *American Journal of Human Genetics* 73, no. 3 (2003): 627–31.

Yu, N., F. C. Chen, S. Ota, L. B. Jorde, P. Pamilo, L. Patthy, M. Ramsay, T. Jenkins, S. K. Shyue and W. H. Li. "Larger Genetic Differences Within Africans Than Between Africans and Eurasians." *Genetics* 161, no. 1 (2002): 269–74.

Zhu, X., C. A. McKenzie, T. Forrester, D. Nickerson, U. Broeckel, H. Schunkert, A. Doering, H. Jacob, R. Cooper, and M. Rieder. "Localization of a Small Genomic Region Associated With Elevated ACE." *American Journal of Human Genetics* 67, no. 5 (2000): 1144–53.

Part 4

PAST, PRESENT, AND FUTURE

The underlying assumption to this volume is that human behavior in sport and human movement is predicated on the interaction of human culture and biology. This relationship between culture and biology in distant human evolution was explored in earlier chapters. In this concluding section, examples of culture influencing, and even modifying, behavior and human biology in more recent human prehistory, history, the present, and in the future will be highlighted.

Loren Cordain and Joe Friel's chapter, "The Paleolithic Athlete: The Original Cross Trainer," begins with an evocative passage from anthropologist Ken Hill's ethnographic work, including participant observation, with South American foraging tribes. Hill, a marathoner of some repute, found it difficult to maintain the pace or even the occasional intensity of the hunts he participated in for fieldwork. In Hill's description of performance regimens, dictated by the subsistence needs of the tribe, Cordain and Friel extend the revolutionary hard-easy training agenda of Bill Bowerman and the cross-training initiated by Doc Counselman to Stone Age hunters. In essence, as the title and chapter reflect, the principles of cross-training now so accepted in long-distance running have been shown, through ethnohistorical accounts, to have been incorporated in foraging societies where hunting was an important part of the overall subsistence strategy. The foraging lifestyle determined the kinds and quantity of movement necessary, and important factors such as diet, that helped fuel the Stone Age "engine," were dependent on available resources. Foragers, then and even now, run to live. Hill discovered that the intensity of running periods were followed by down, or off, days—over the long haul, maintaining healthy bodies was paramount for individual and group survival. However, those same factors, such as diet, resource need, and conditioning, Cordain and Friel point out, would not have made them Olympic or even international-level running elite today.

Peter Mewett examines the confluence of social class with the emergence of a distinct category of athletes, amateurs, consistent with ethnocentric class values that formed and mediated nineteenth-century perspectives on the limits of human performance. In his chapter, "When Pain = Strain = No Gain: the 'Physiology of Strain' and Exercise Intensity, c.1850–1920," Mewett suggests that the new found physiological theories, and a positivistic empiricism, no longer based on humoral physiology, emerged from the enlightenment and provided a means and way to distance the gentry class from the professionalism of athletes and sport at that time. Framing the discourse between what had been "beneath" the upper class, athleticism and sport and the emerging power of "social and medical knowledge," the start of amateur athletics allowed entry into sport for those who had been in the past denied participation due to class constraint. Supporting this entry into sport and performance was a training regimen that balanced the existing class value system with the performance needs to participate in elite sport. Some of this social "shaping" of expectations, and denial of the existing professionalism of sport and trainers and resultant performance restriction played out in the award-winning film *Chariots of Fire*.

Greg Downey did ethnographic fieldwork with Afro-Brazilian capoeira dancers. The capoeira is a martial arts dance spectacle involving energetic acrobatic movements such as kicks, cartwheels, handstand and other dynamic and fluid movements. Downey discovered that what he termed extraordinary athletes in other sport movements, such as throwing and catching, lacked even approaching the skills of Downey in this regard. In "Throwing like a Brazilian: On Ineptness and Skill-Shaped Body," Downey explores the influence of both culture and biology on producing the "skill-shaped" body. Moving beyond "throwing like a girl" involves mastering a complex suite of kinesthetic adaptations inherent in moving from novice to accomplished, not solely based on gender as Downey discovered in the Brazilian dancers. Many female Americans, and not so many male Americans and accomplished capoeria dancers alike, throw like girls. Downey suggests that a process of bio-enculturation produces gifted throwers, and in effect although throwing might have been a critical movement pattern in human evolution, being able to throw is just a range of motion capable in the range of human movement patterns. Culture, in the form of skill training imprints performance on athletes, both serious and recreational and even non-athletes. The human body is not a static and unchanging biomechanical and neurobiological platform. In throwing, the application of skill training, obviously channeled by cultural beliefs, traditions and heritage, in skeletal, physiological and neurobiological development and continued practice powerfully shapes the human movement potential so visible in the feet and leg movement potential of Brazilian dancers and the throwing superiority of American baseball pitchers.

Peering into the near future, Andy Miah's chapter, "The DREAM Gene for the Posthuman Athlete: Reducing Exercise-Induced Pain Sensations Using Gene Transfer," explores the ethics of gene manipulation of the Downstream Regulatory Element Antagonistic Modulator, or DREAM, as pain management in sport. A protein that is essential for pain sensation, modulating the protein conceivably could minimize pain sensation in training and competitive performance. Competitive sport selects for continual performance enhancement. This drive for enhancement has created a culture of "doping for performance" and athletes undergo the effect of the use of those drugs on their biologies into the future. This has also created anti-doping regulations and organizations police athletes and competitions. Miah argues that potential manipulation of DREAM poses an ethical quandary for sport, is it therapy or enhancement? The values of sport include the overcoming of pain and other sensations that modulation of DREAM could minimize. Does this ability undermine the essence of sport? Does altering the biology of the athlete open the door to redefining overall performance, in ways the use of steroids and human growth hormones do not? The effects of such manipulation could have far less severe consequences on the athlete's biology. In the end, Miah takes a stand that possible gene manipulation, such as DREAM, does not really constitute performance enhancing found in the use of steroids and human growth hormones. However, Miah's chapter brings into stark reality the ethical considerations of what really constitutes enhancing athletic performance, and even more fundamental, the nature of the relationship between sport and the culture context in which it is performed—a complex cultural calculus where culture selects movement potential and ultimately defines performance.

10

The Paleolithic Athlete: The Original Cross Trainer

Loren Cordain and Joe Friel

A DAY IN THE LIFE OF A HUNTER-GATHERER

Ten thousand years sounds like a long, long time ago. But if you think about it in terms of how long the human genus (*Homo*) has existed (2.5 million years), 10,000 years is a mere blink of the eye on an evolutionary time scale. Somewhere in the Middle East about 10,000 years ago a tiny band of people threw in the towel and abandoned their hunter-gatherer lifestyle. These early renegades became the very first farmers. They had forsaken a mode of life that had sustained each and every individual within the human genus for the previous 100,000 generations. In contrast, only a paltry 500 human generations have come and gone since the first seeds of agriculture were sown. What started off as a renegade way of making a living became a revolution that would guarantee the complete and absolute eradication of every remaining hunter-gatherer on the planet. At the dawn of the twenty-first century we are now at the bitter end. Except for perhaps a half dozen un-contacted tribes in South America and a few others on the Andaman Islands in the Bay of Bengal, pure hunter-gatherers have vanished from the face of the earth.

So what difference does it make? Why should twenty-first-century endurance athletes care one iota about whether or not there are any hunter-gatherers left on earth? Because once these people are gone we will no longer be able to see how they typically exercised or what they ate. Their lifestyle holds invaluable clues to the exercise and dietary patterns that are built into our genes. When I was a track athlete in the late 1960s and early 1970s, runners rarely or never lifted weights, and back then no runner worth their Adidas or Puma flats would even think about swimming. Fast forward thirty years. What progressive coach now doesn't know the value and benefit of cross training? The idea that cross training has value probably could have been figured out much earlier had we only taken notice of clues from our hunter-gatherer ancestors.

Very few modern people have ever experienced what it is like to "run with the hunt." One of the notable exceptions is Dr. Kim Hill, an anthropologist at the University of New Mexico who has spent the last thirty years living with and studying the Ache hunter-gatherers of Paraguay and the Hiwi foragers of Southwestern Venezuela. His description of these amazing hunts represents a rare glimpse into the activity patterns that would have been required of us all, were it not for the Agricultural Revolution.

I have only spent a long time hunting with two groups, the Ache and the Hiwi. They were very different. The Ache hunted every day of the year if it didn't rain. Recent GPS data I collected with them suggests that about 10 km per day is probably closer to their average distance covered during search. They might cover another 1–2 km per day in very rapid pursuit. Sometimes pursuits can be extremely strenuous and last more than an hour. Ache hunters often take an easy day after any particularly difficult day, and rainfall forces them to take a day or two a week with only an hour or two of exercise. Basically they do moderate days most of the time, and sometimes really hard days usually followed by a very easy day. The difficulty of the terrain is really what killed me (ducking under low branches and vines about once every twenty seconds all day long, and climbing over fallen trees, moving through tangled thorns, etc.) I was often drenched in sweat within an hour of leaving camp, and usually didn't return for 7–9 hours with not more than thirty minutes rest during the day. The Ache seemed to have an easier time because they "walk better" in the forest than me (meaning the vines and branches don't bother them as much). The really hard days when they literally ran me into the ground were long distance pursuits of peccary herds when the Ache hunters move at a fast trot through thick forest for about two hours before they catch up with the herd. None of our other grad students could ever keep up with these hunts, and I only kept up because I was in very good shape back in the 1980s when I did this.

The Hiwi on the other hand only hunted about 2–3 days a week and often told me they wouldn't go out on a particular day because they were "tired." They would stay home and work on tools etc. Their travel was not as strenuous as among the Ache (they often canoed to the hunt site), and their pursuits were usually shorter. But the Hiwi sometimes did amazing long distance walks that would have really hurt the Ache. They would walk to visit another village maybe 80–100 km away and then stay for only an hour or two before returning. This often included walking all night long as well as during the day. When I hunted with Machiguenga, Yora, Yanomamo Indians in the 1980s, my focal man days were much, much easier than with the Ache. And virtually all these groups take an easy day after a particularly difficult one.

By the way, the Ache do converse and even sing during some of their search, but long distance peccary pursuits are too difficult for any talking. Basically men talk to each other until the speed gets up around 3km/hour which is a very tough pace in thick jungle. Normal search is more like about 1.5 km/hour, a pretty leisurely pace. Monkey hunts can also be very strenuous because they consist of bursts of sprints every 20–30 seconds (as the monkeys are flushed and flee to new cover), over a period of an hour or two without a rest. This feels a lot like doing a very long session of wind sprints.

Both my graduate student Rob Walker and Richard Bribiescas of Harvard were very impressed by Ache performance on the step test. Many of the guys in their mid 30s to mid 50s showed great aerobic conditioning compared to Americans of that age. (V02 max/kg body weight is very good). While hunter gatherers are generally in good physical condition if they haven't yet been exposed to modern diseases and diets that come soon after permanent outside contact, I would not want to exaggerate their abilities. They are what you would expect if you took a genetic cross section of humans and put them in lifetime physical training at moderate to hard levels. Most hunting is search time not pursuit, thus a good deal of aerobic long distance travel is often involved (over rough terrain and carrying loads if the hunt is successful). I used to train for marathons as a grad student and could run at a 6:00 per mile pace for ten miles, but the Ache would run me into the ground following peccary tracks through dense bush for a couple of hours. I did the 100-yd in 10.2 in high school (I was a fast pass catcher on my football team), and some Ache men can sprint as fast as me.

But hunter-gatherers do not generally compare to world class athletes, who are probably genetically very gifted and then undergo even more rigorous and specialized training than any forager. So the bottom line is foragers are often in good shape and they look it. They sprint, jog, climb, carry, jump, etc., all day long but are not specialists and do not compare to Olympic athletes in modern societies.

Dr. Hill's wonderful imagery and insight tells us part of the story, but not everything. In this day and age of gender equality women are just as likely as men, if not more so, to be found at the gym lifting weights or out on the trails running or riding their bikes. In stark contrast, hunter-gatherer women almost never participated in hunting large game animals. Nearly without exception, ethnographic accounts of hunter-gatherers are in agreement on this point. Does this mean that women did no hard aerobic work? Absolutely not! Women routinely gathered food every two or three days. The fruits of their labors just didn't include plant foods, but also small animals such as tortoises, small reptiles, shellfish, insects, bird eggs, and small mammals. They spent many hours walking to sources of food, water and wood. Sometimes they would help carrying butchered game back to camp. Their foraging often involved strenuous digging, climbing and then hauling heavy loads back to camp, frequently while carrying infants and young children. Other common activities, some physically taxing, included tool making, shelter construction, childcare, butchering, food preparation, and visiting. Dances were a major recreation for hunter-gatherers and could take place several nights a week and often last for hours. Table 10.1 shows some typical hunter-gatherer activities and their modern counterparts along with the associated caloric costs.

Table 10.1. Caloric Cost of Various Hunter-Gatherer and Modern Activities

Hunter-gatherer Activity	Modern equivalent Activity	Caloric cost (kilocalories/hour) for a 176 lb Male/ 132 lb. Female
Carry log	Carry logs	893/670
Run cross-country	Run cross-country	782/587
Carry meat (20 kg) back to camp	Climb hills (20 kg load)	706/529
Carry young child	Climb hills (10 kg load)	672/504
Hunt, stalk animals (carrying bows and spears)	Climb hills (5 kg load)	619/464
Dig (tubers in a field)	Dig (in the garden)	605/454
Dance (ceremonial)	Dance (aerobic)	494/371
Stack firewood	Stack firewood	422/317
Butcher large animal	Ax chopping, slow	408/306
Walk—normal pace (fields & hills)	Walk—normal pace (fields & hills)	394/295
Gather plant foods	Weed garden	346/259
Archery	Archery	312/234
Scrape a hide	Scrape paint	302/227
Shelter construction	Carpentry, general	250/187
Flint knapping	Shoe repair, general	216/162

So, the overall activity pattern of women, like men, was cyclic with days of intense physical exertion (both aerobic and resistive) alternated with days of rest and light activity. What hunter-gatherers had to do in their day-to-day activities is turning out to be good medicine for modern-day athletes. When Bill Bowerman, the famous track coach at the University of Oregon, advocated the easy/hard concept back in the 1960s it was thought to be both brilliant and revolutionary. Using his system of easy/hard, athletes recovered more easily from hard workouts, and their chances of getting injured were reduced. Ironically, Coach Bowerman's "revolutionary" training strategy was as old as humanity itself. Similarly, weight training combined with swimming was a stunning innovation at Doc Counsilman's world-famous swim program at Indiana University in the 1960s. Now, it is a rare world-class endurance coach who doesn't advocate cross training to improve performance, increase strength and reduce injury incidence. Once again, the rationale behind the success of cross training can be found in the hunter-gatherer genes in all of us.

WHY WE ARE DESIGNED TO EXERCISE

It may seem totally obvious, but sometimes the obvious is rarely considered. Do you know why the Ache and, for that matter, all hunter-gatherers exercise? Before we go down this road, let's clarify the word "exercise." No adult hunter-gatherer in their right mind would have ever set off on a run or repeatedly lifted a heavy stone simply to expend energy and "get exercise." Virtually all movement by adult hunter-gatherers resulted from the day's mandatory activities such as food and water procurement, shelter building, journeys, tool making, wood gathering, escape from dangers, child rearing, and social activities. The activities of daily life were all the "exercise" that Stone Age people would have ever taken. Hunter-gatherers had no choice but to do physical labor of all kinds, every day—day in and day out for their entire life. Every single day, there were big tasks and small tasks alike that had to be accomplished to provide for basic human needs. There were no retirements, no vacations, no job layoffs, no career changes or labor-saving devices. Except for the very young or the very old, everyone did labor of one form or another on a regular basis.

Okay, let's get back to the obvious that you may have never considered. Hunter-gatherers "exercised" because they had to. They had no other choice—period! For all humans living before the Agricultural Revolution, energy input (food) and energy expenditure (exercise) were directly linked. If Stone Age people wanted to eat, they had to hunt, gather, forage, or fish. Now you can see what may have motivated the Ache hunters as they furiously chased that herd of peccaries hour after hour through the tropical forest in Paraguay. Whether you do a long, hard workout or no workout at all, food is always there for you at the end of the day. Wouldn't it be disappointing to do your long hard workout and come home to an empty fridge? Would an empty belly motivate you even more on the next workout (hunt), if the intensity of the workout was directly related to the amount of food in the refrigerator?

In the modern world we have totally and completely obliterated the ancient evolutionary link between energy expenditure (exercise) and food intake. As you lazily stroll down the supermarket aisle and throw one item after another into the cart, you don't give a single thought to "search time" or "pursuit" of your prey, as Dr. Hill graphically portrayed for us with his descriptions of the Ache hunters. In a modern supermarket, the "search" and "pursuit" time are identical whether you toss a smoked ham into your cart or a head of lettuce.

The consequence of severing this primeval evolutionary connection between energy expenditure and energy intake are not pretty. When we eat more energy than we expend, we gain weight. And when we gain weight, our health suffers. Unless, you haven't read a newspaper or a magazine lately, most of you know that we are in the midst of an obesity epidemic in the United States. Two-thirds of all Americans are either overweight or obese. Forty million American have type-2 diabetes, and cardiovascular disease is the leading cause of death in this country. There is little doubt in my mind that none of this would be possible without the uncoupling of energy intake and expenditure that was handed to us when we deserted our ancestral hunter-gatherer way of life.

COMPARISON OF THE LIFESTYLES OF
HUNTER-GATHERERS AND MODERN ATHLETES

After reading Dr. Hill's description of the Ache hunters you've probably got a pretty good feel for how their daily workout compares to yours. Some of you may be recreational athletes; some of you may be good local and regional endurance athletes, and a very few of you may be elite athletes of national or international caliber. How would the average hunter-gatherers stack up when it comes to high level endurance performance on race day?

First, let's take a look at the advantages on the side of the hunter-gatherer. From the time of weaning until very old age hunter-gatherer athletes would have done moderate to hard aerobic activity month in and month out for their entire life. They would have regularly rotated hard days with easy days, and strength activities would always have commonly accompanied their aerobic work. This pattern of movement would have diminished their chance of injury so that they could get up morning after morning to hunt and gather again and again.

In exercise physiology there is a commonly known law stating that aerobic capacity (VO2 max) within an individual may increase based upon exercise frequency, intensity and duration. Of these three factors, intensity is the most important feature in squeezing out the last little bit of aerobic capacity from already-trained subjects. The problem is that as intensity increases, the chance of injury and illness also increase. Hunter-gatherers were in it for the long haul. Their objectives were to obtain food day in and day out, year in and year out for their entire lives. High intensity exercise on a regular basis for them would have been a liability, since injury and illness meant less food. On the other hand, modern-day endurance athletes don't have to worry about injuries or illness getting in the way of eating. Food is available no matter whether you are injured or not. Accordingly, endurance athletes can take their chances with high intensity training. As a matter of fact, high intensity workouts (>85 percent VO2 max) are not an anomaly, but rather a requisite to perform at the highest levels upon the world's stage.

As we have previously outlined, it is virtually impossible to exercise at >85 percent VO2 max for extended periods unless muscle glycogen stores are fully topped up. Without daily consumption of high glycemic load carbs, regular high intensity workouts simply are not feasible. Since high glycemic load carbs were not on the hunter-gatherer menu, they could not have eked out the last 2–5 percent of their genetic aerobic potential by doing high intensity workouts, as can modern athletes. On the other hand, because they ate more fat and fewer daily meals than we do, their intramuscular triglyceride stores would have been much higher, thereby allowing them to do aerobic work at moderate intensity for extended periods. Just what the doctor ordered if you need to go hunting daily and high glycemic carbs don't exist. For the modern-day endurance athlete who is solely interested in maximal performance, an alternative exists. Both can be done.

Because the protein content of their diet was higher than ours, the concentration of the anabolic branch chain amino acids (leucine, isoleucine and valine) would have been much higher. As we have previously pointed out, these dietary amino acids promote muscle resynthesis following exercise and may also delay the onset of fatigue. Unless you are eating lots of lean meats and fish, hunter-gatherers would have had the advantage here. The high protein content of our ancestral diet meant that another amino acid, glutamine, would have also been higher than what you are getting if you are following a vegetarian beans and brown rice diet or simply the standard American junk food diet. A classic symptom of overtraining in endurance athletes is low blood levels of glutamine.

The trick with glutamine is not just how much you are getting, but how much you are losing. Losing excess glutamine is just like not getting enough. If you are eating a high carb, low fat diet, which is pretty much the standard endurance athlete fare, it is almost certain that your body will be in a slight state of net metabolic acidosis. As we have previously shown you, a net acid-producing diet causes your body to excrete more and more of the muscle's glutamine in an attempt to restore acid-base balance. The loss of muscle glutamine from an acid-yielding diet and from insufficient intake of glutamine-rich foods (lean meats, fish and seafood) may adversely affect performance. Chalk another advantage to hunter-gatherers.

One of the most important variables leading to athletic success is staying healthy and free of illness and colds. There is little doubt that proper nutrition is absolutely essential when it comes to optimizing your immune system. Because hunter-gatherers ate no processed foods, no cereal grains, no refined sugars or oils, their trace nutrient (vitamins, minerals and phytochemicals) intake was way higher than what the average U.S. citizen gets. Also, they consumed more healthful omega 3 fats than what most of us now get. These dietary advantages would have again allowed our hunter gatherer ancestors to go out day after day and hunt and forage for food without interruption from illness and colds. For our species, natural selection had no interest in winning a 10k or marathon, but rather was more concerned with getting our daily calories. The name of the evolutionary game was adequate calories, not necessarily maximal exercise performance.

So, let's get down to the nitty gritty. Was there ever a hunter-gatherer who could have taken home the Olympic gold in any endurance event in the last thirty years? The answer is no. The average hunter-gatherer was clearly more fit than the average American couch potato as we pointed out in the prologue. Most foragers (men or women) would have also been able to run any recreational runner into the ground. At the local and regional levels, their best athletes would have been competitive. But when we compare them to elite national and international athletes, there is no comparison for two basic reasons.

First are the numbers. The primary determinant of aerobic capacity is maximal oxygen consumption or VO2 max. If you want to be a world-class endurance athlete, you better choose your parents well because VO2 max is almost entirely determined by genetics. One of the highest VO2 max values ever reliably recorded for an elite male athlete in the United States is about 84 ml/kg/min. Contrast this value to about 40 ml/kg/min for the average American male. So what happens if the 40 ml/kg/min guy wants to become world-class and sets off upon an incredibly intense training program for years and years? Does he have a chance of getting to 84 ml/kg/min? Not even close! VO2 max can increase by about 10–15 percent in the best of all worlds, but no more. In the United States we now have more than 260 million residents. Compare this to the fewer than 1,000 Ache hunter-gatherers with whom Dr. Hill hunted. If only one person out of 1,000 has a genetically determined VO2 max of greater than 70 ml/kg/min, then in the United States population there will be 26,000 people who have the genetic potential to perform at extremely high aerobic capacities. In the Ache hunter-gatherers only one person in their entire population will have this genetic capacity.

Hunter-gatherers wouldn't stand a chance against Olympian endurance athletes not only because of the numbers game, but because they were limited to low octane fuel. Intramuscular triglyceride is a great energy source for moderate to hard exercise lasting for hours and hours, but it can't hold a candle to glycogen when it comes to high-level exertion at 85 percent or greater of the VO2 required to make Olympic champions. Because hunter-gatherers ate fewer carbs and more fats, along with fewer daily meals, their intramuscular triglyceride stores would have been higher than ours. But also, they ate no high glycemic load carbs, so their muscle glycogen reserves would have always been lower than ours. They simply lacked the fuel injection of high glycemic load carbs to restore muscle glycogen concentrations following hard exercise. You now have this option. You can not only increase muscle glycogen concentrations via careful dietary manipulation, but by following a nutritional plan, you can also increase intramuscular triglycerides.

You, as a twenty-first-century endurance athlete are no longer reliant upon the current scientific status quo relating diet to performance, but have the added advantage of knowing how the wisdom of your ancestral dietary background can improve performance. By combining the best of their world with the best of ours, your performance will soar.

BIBLIOGRAPHY

Bowerman, W. J. and W. E. Harris. *Jogging the Original Book: A Medically Approved Fitness Program for All Ages.* New York: Grosset and Dunlap, 1967.

Cordain, L., R. W. Gotshall and S. B. Eaton. "Evolutionary Aspects of Exercise." *World Rev Nutr Diet* 81 (1997): 49–60.

———. "Physical Activity, Energy Expenditure and Fitness: An Evolutionary Perspective." *International Journal of Sports Medicine* 19 (1998): 328–35.

Counsilman, J. E. *The Science of Swimming.* New York: Prentice Hall, 1968.

Hill, K. and A. M. Hurtado. *Aché Life History.* New York: Aldine De Gruyter, 1966.

Kraemer, W. J., N. A. Ratamess, and D. N. French. "Resistance Training for Health and Performance." *Current Sports Medicine Report* 1, no. 3 (June 2002): 165–71.

Loy, S. F., J. J. Hoffmann, and G. J. Holland. "Benefits and Practical Use of Cross-Training in Sports." *Sports Medicine* 19, no. 1 (January 1995): 1–8.

Millet G. P., R. B. Candau, B. Barbier, T. Busso, J. D. Rouillon, and J. C. Chatard. "Modeling the Transfers of Training Effects on Performance in Elite Triathletes." *International Journal of Sports Medicine* 23, no. 1 (January 2002): 55–63.

White L. J., R. H. Dressendorfer, S. M. Muller, and M. A. Ferguson. "Effectiveness of Cycle Cross-Training between Competitive Seasons in Female Distance Runners." *Journal of Strength and Conditioning Resistance* 17, no. 2 (May 2003): 319–23.

11

When Pain = Strain = No Gain: The "Physiology of Strain" and Exercise Intensity, c. 1850–1920

Peter G. Mewett

Moderate training, without strain, "will assist in the preservation of our young men's lives, chastity, manliness, and love and appreciation of sport."

—Rippon Seymour nd (1898, 103)

[W]here young men, by a simple course of diet and repeated exercise, have fully developed their powers, they have sustained lasting benefit from indulging in tests of endurance and skill, and have stood pre-eminent as possessed of that greatest of all blessings, "a sound mind in a healthy body."

—*Sportsman*, 1889: 96

From Greco-Roman times, a judicious combination of diet, exercise and general bodily care has been recommended for good health and longevity. The humoral theories that informed physiological understandings until well into modern times prescribed food, drinks and activities as well as medicines and other interventions such as purging and bleeding, for the well-being of people and animals.[1] Although humoral theory gradually faded into historical obscurity, the combination of diet, exercise, and body care as the underpinnings of a sound lifestyle have remained to this day. The massive growth of medical and biological science in the nineteenth century heralded the end of humoral understandings and instead replaced them by ideas germinated in this period of considerable intellectual activity. Ideas that were transposed into and provided guidance on the dietary and exercise regimes required for good health and optimal physical performance. In this chapter, the connection between the growth of modern sports, forms of training designed to optimize performance, and how the growth of post-humoral medical theory was used to evaluate training practices and assess their benefits for bodily well-being is examined. The chapter centers on a form of training developed by amateur athletes in the second half of the nineteenth century, when contemporary bio-medical knowledge was used to legitimate training practices and evaluate their health effects. In particular, the focus is on the idea that exercise-enhanced health provided a certain exercise quantum, hereafter referred to as the *point of strain*, was not exceeded—if surpassed, the consequences were thought to be serious and even life-threatening.

The health advice associated with amateur training practices is sociologically interesting because of the social backgrounds of those centrally involved with these sports and their privileged access to the "correct" physiological knowledge that was used to provide scientific justification for the body culture associated with their sports. Specifically, amateurism emerged as a means for men from the higher social classes to become active competitors in sports—tainted by allegations of gambling and corrupt practices—that were otherwise associated with working-class professionals. Amateur athletics was formalized in the 1860s and rapidly gained respectability through the inclusion of aristocrats among the competitors and by the exclusion of lower-class athletes and professionals (Griffin 1891). However, the training practices in place for athletes when amateurism was established were for professional competitors, typically under the supervision of a trainer who was an ex-professional, and traced their origins to humoral physiology. Apart from the unconscionable action of a higher-class man[2] placing himself under the guidance and control of a possibly illiterate lower-class trainer, professional training practices involved a body culture that developed a somatic type in keeping with muscled plebeians, rather than with the leisured and professional higher classes. Accordingly, amateurs devised a different system of training which operated in parallel with the time-sanctioned professional practices (Mewett 1995; Park 1992). Amateur training techniques signaled a clear separation from and an often virulent rejection of the century-old professional practices.[3] Shearman, a significant figure in the early decades of athletics, wrote that professional training "chiefly applied to men of the lower classes, used to coarse food, and with no highly organized nervous system. It needs no argument to show that such a method could be beneficial, or even practicable, to an amateur" (Shearman 1901: 185).

The caste-like partition between amateur and professional training was constructed on the social and ideological grounds of class—contemporary bio-medical knowledge was *interpreted* to legitimize amateur training procedures. In establishing amateurism as a sporting field quite separate from professionalism, amateurs melded the new forms of knowledge generated in the educational and professional institutions they frequented with their undoubted social power to establish a supposedly scientifically based body culture that constituted the normative discourse on exercise and health until the mid twentieth century.

The fallacies of many of the doctrines of old trainers would long ago have been exposed had they been gauged by the elementary principles of science. Fortunately, since the pursuit of athletics has assumed a general importance, and men of education have not only devoted thought to the rules of training but also have entered personally into the practice, we have learned to disregard much that was crude and inconsistent in the old system (Beckley 1882: 19).

This chapter focuses on how the training practices of the amateurs promoted a self-limiting exercise system designed to promote both performance and health. Bio-medical theories were applied in support of this body culture, but not because this knowledge had been derived from systematic investigations of active bodies; rather it occurred from the interpretation of these theories to maintain the indicative somatic form of higher-class bodies. Whereas some medical investigations were directed at the effects on the body of prolonged exertion,[4] research directed at ways of improving performance remained some time in the future. Although the amateurs drew from contemporary scientific knowledge to support their training practices, bio-medical knowledge and understanding about the effects of exertion were derived from extrapolations of physiological theory that were treated as fact. So amateurism in being associated with the higher classes also built around it a discourse of the body which was given credence by, among other things, the authoring of training texts by medical practitioners (e.g., Abrahams 1911, 1912; Cortis 1887; Galbraith 1895; Harrisson 1869; Hoole 1895; White nd [c1906]; Abrahams 1911: 437). A prominent medical practitioner of the early twentieth century argued that medical people had an important place in training, "We as medical men should be in a position

to utilize the weight of our authority to introduce rational physiological principles [into training] in place of an absurd medley of traditional
follies and so to prevent many opportunities for abuse." Class privilege
and differentiation from the lower classes were therefore embedded in
amateur training practices. The somatic form of the higher classes was
molded through the limited intensity of their exercise regimes, which
focused on the achievement of sound health on which was predicated an
individual's best non-health-threatening athletic performance. In short,
it was imperative not to exceed the point of strain.

EXERCISE AND STRAIN

Today, it is commonly thought that each additional quantum of exercise
produces a proportionate improvement in fitness and health. This is portrayed in figure 11.1 by line AB, which suggests a linear relationship
between exercise and well-being. Summarized in the glib expression "no
pain, no gain," intense exercise is thought to promote improved strength,
vitality, and performance; so it is commonly thought that the more effort
people put into their exercise regimes, the greater the benefits. While this
overstates the contemporary association between exercise, fitness, and
health, it is outside the scope of this chapter to consider the finer points of

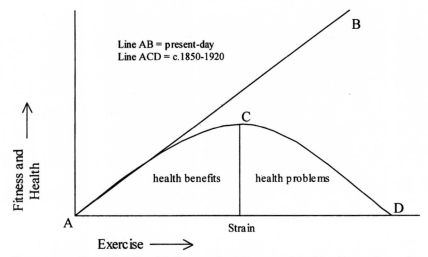

**Figure 11.1.   Representation of the perceived fitness and health effects of exercise
c.1850–1920, compared with the present day.**

this connection, and the exaggeration is heuristically useful in serving to highlight the different approach to exercise and health in the period under examination from today.

However, the amateur body culture of the second half of the nineteenth century and the early decades of the twentieth surmised differently. In that period, it was argued that exercise improved health only up to a certain level of intensity, after which fitness declined and health suffered. *Over-training* was a constant issue, especially for athletes preparing for competition, who encountered a fine line between peak condition and over-doing it. Over-training or over-doing it, as it was commonly called, came about from *too much* exertion. The line ACD in figure 11.1 represents this model. Fitness, health, and performance improve up to the point C, after which continued physical activity triggers a negative return to the possible detriment of health. The level of exercise represented by C is referred to as the *point of strain,* which, if exceeded, leads to the person becoming fatigued, strained, stale, or "over-trained."

As the optimum exercise quantum that applied to individuals at different stages in their lives, the point of strain was a relative measure. Ford (1891–1892: 424) referred to this as the "balancing point" up to which more work could be done, but going beyond it caused staleness. The exertion put in before the point of strain was reached varied from person to person. Each individual, depending on their physical condition, age, gender, constitution, type of work and lifestyle, differed in the exertion that their bodies could tolerate before triggering their point of strain and possibly causing irreparable damage. Accordingly, training programs had to be tailored to suit each individual so that a state of health was reached where every organ functioned properly (Westhall 1890: 50, 52). Unfit people could push out their point of strain (i.e., move C to the right in figure 11.1) with appropriate regular exercise. Indeed anyone, except the already highly physically trained, was thought capable of improving their level of fitness and so increase the exercise quantum that brought them to their point of strain. It was widely accepted that people were born with a finite energy store and as people aged their energy was progressively diminished so that the point of strain was reached with less exertion. When applied to women, the finite energy theory was compounded by their supposedly more nervous disposition—incurring a lessened tolerance to physical exertion—and by the effects of menstruation (Vertinsky 1990). Women were thought incapable of the same level of exertion as men and if they did engage in strenuous activities it was to the possible detriment of their children as well as to themselves (Mewett 2003). Although older people and women could not tolerate the same amount of exercise as healthy younger men, everyone had a limit. No matter a person's level of fitness, they had an exercise quantum that, if exceeded, could render them liable to impaired health and even death. Exercise was a double-edged sword: on the one hand, it was widely recognized that exercise contributed to health, but too much exertion was thought to cause strain. It was impossible to escape the point of strain. At some point, the brick wall was reached—that ultimate point of strain that a person could not push out any further. The signs that a person had reached their point of strain are discussed later.

THE PHYSIOLOGY OF STRAIN

The amateur athlete's understandings of exercise-induced strain came from contemporary bio-medical science. Central to these interpretations were the physiological theories concerning the body's cycle of waste production and excretion. Good health, fitness, and performance were associated with the efficient removal of bodily wastes. Hence, a diet that supplied the body's necessary nutriments and exercise, which improved waste excretion, were required both for living a sound, healthy life and for improving competitive performance. Several writers of the period commented that training was inseparable from good living and people who looked after their health through diet, exercise, and proper hygiene were in constant training whether or not they recognized it as such. Craven (1860: 10), for example, noted that health is maintained by "exercise and regimen; or, in other words, upon the observance of those rules which constitute the theory of training." Accordingly, training for sports should "ensure a long and active existence, and not broken health and premature death" (Hoole 1895: 4). Harrisson (1869: 17) fully supported training as a means of sustaining a healthy life:

> The general adoption of such habits of exercise and regimen as physiology and chemistry of food declare be the best for us, or in other words, a system-atic physical education based upon science and experience, would probably

extirpate that long list of diseases which arise from disorder of the nutritive processes of the body.

A point that was reiterated by Hoole (1895: 1), who claimed that the principles of training and judicious living were similar in that both required the observation of the "laws of health." Abrahams (1911: 437) added about training that there was "no mystery or fetish involved" and "that training means only clean healthy living with appropriate practice." A cycle of exercise and rest combined with an appropriate diet were required, Craven (1860) informed his readers, for the body's musculature to develop. Exercise, he averred, was crucial to health because it facilitated the removal of wastes from the body and their replacement in the cycle of the absorption and renovation of tissue characterizing biological life. In addition to the importance of exercise in developing muscles, Harrisson (1869) argued that it facilitated brain development because of the activity of the nervous system in commanding the muscles during exercise, and developed the heart and lungs because of the muscles' demand for blood. It also stimulated the stomach to "prepare the large supplies of *chyme* required to replenish the blood" (Harrisson 1869: 4, original emphasis). The stomach was thought to decoct a nutrient-rich substance from food, called chyme, which was transported by the blood to all parts of the body. Thus, the importance of diet because "physically, man is what he eats, without question. The whole purpose of eating is to make blood, which is necessary for the maintenance of life; and the power the food partaken of, the power will be the blood" (Westhall 1890: 22). The blood also collected wastes and transferred them to the sites of the body from they were removed. Moreover, good brain function hinged on the balance of all parts of the body, which were affected by poor diet, impaired respiration, problems associated with the transfer of nutritive matter from the blood, from the "accumulation of effete matters in the blood" and from hindrances to the removal of waste products from the body (Harrisson 1869: 17–18).

The cerebral substance, like all other portions of the frame, derives its nutriment from the blood, and if active exercise be neglected, this fluid, imperfectly oxygenated, and loaded with impurities from a languid action of the liver, skin, and other excreting organs, circulating the brain, and the necessary consequence is, decreased intellectual and constitutional vigor. (Harrisson 1869, 18). A balance of exercise, appropriate diet and hygiene were necessary for the good brain function required of the social elite.

Training was more than preparation for competition; it was thought to be central to a sound disciplined life.

Elements of the physiological processes discussed by Craven and Harrisson reappear in the work of Rippon Seymour (nd [1898]: 73ff), who provides a particularly useful source for the understanding of the physiology of strain. He noted that any type of movement in the body, including thinking, destroyed molecular tissue, producing the waste that was removed by the blood and replaced by new, regenerative materials. Exercise enhanced these processes because it caused "the blood to circulate quicker" (Rippon Seymour nd [1898]: 77). "Our whole frame is composed of an enormous number of minute atoms each of which is born, performs for a short period the work allotted [before] it dies, and is then removed from the system in various ways" (Rippon Seymour nd [1898]: 73–74).

The more a muscle is used, the more it decays, but it receives a correspondingly larger volume of blood to create new fibers and build muscle tissue. "It is a law of nature that the nutrition of an organ is in proportion to the quantity of blood which passes through it, and that every organ in activity draws a greater quantity of blood toward it than it does in a state of repose" (Rippon Seymour nd [1898]: 77, quoting from Lagrange—precise citation not given).

Wastes, Harrisson (1869: 60) wrote, derived from oxygen-fueled combustion in the body: "Food taken in by an animal is constantly burning away in the lungs, or in the tissues—where ever the blood yields up its combustible matters to unite with the oxygen inhaled from without." Food was divided into the two categories of nitrogenous and carbonaceous substances (Harrisson 1869: 61–64).[5] The composition of the body required the different food types, therefore, "to repair the perpetual disintegration of these parts, which constitutes the 'wear and tear' of organized life" (63). For this reason, humans required a combination of animal and vegetable foods (64).

In cleansing the blood of the carbonic acid formed from the combination of oxygen with substances stored in the muscles, the lungs formed a primary site of waste removal (Cortis 1887: 12). Other wastes were removed through the kidneys as urea, through the skin as sweat and through the bowel as feces. Good health required that each excretory organ was kept in fine condition, because one organ could not assume the work of another. Exercise, diet, and cleanliness all contributed to the efficient removal of waste and the appropriate supply of new nutritive material. Clearly, the value of good nutrition and exercise to this cycle of replenishment and excretion underpinned the reasons for recommending "training" as central to healthy living. Training removed "from the body matters which are both useless and hurtful" (Hoole 1895: 2).

Long periods of inactivity endangered health by allowing the buildup of excretory matter in the body. The distress felt from unaccustomed exercise done by the inactive occurred because the body had to cope with the accumulation of unremoved wastes in addition to the increased demands placed on it by the added exertions (Rippon Seymour nd [1898]). Inactivity encumbered the heart and lungs with wastes and so depleted them of the strength required to remove carbonic acid so that even small efforts caused breathlessness. Similarly, waste retention created carry-over fatigue, limiting further hard exercise until this matter had been removed.

So Rippon Seymour (nd [1898]: 79, original emphasis) advised that appropriate exercise was "an absolute necessity" for everyone, because "every movement and exercise taken rationally *must* have a beneficial effect throughout the whole body." The additional work placed on the heart and lungs by the increased blood flow induced by exercise strengthened these organs while facilitating waste removal and the supply of fresh nutritive material. Diet required attention for exercise to achieve its desired objective, because foods were matched with the different parts of the body to supply the appropriate nutrient to each through the digestive processes. However, "the laws which govern the attraction of those parts of food, each to their own particular place" (Rippon Seymour nd [1898]: 79) remained a mystery to late nineteenth-century physiology. Despite this, Morden (1887: 15) suggested that because human flesh and muscles most resembled that of the bullock, "the most appropriate food for the requirements of training will be a certain amount of bullock meat known as rump-steak, or beef."

Each exhalation removed body wastes, making the lungs a major organ of excretion in addition to their role of supplying the body with oxygen. Good lung function, measured by an individual's "vital capacity"—their maximum single breath inhalation—was therefore essential. Lung capacity was affected by the elasticity of its tissues, which was influenced by the flexibility and expansion of the chest. Exercises that increased chest expansion promoted elasticity, enhanced vital capacity, improved blood circulation and benefited overall fitness and health.

Harrisson (1869: 48) opined that exercise, which demanded a rapid supply of oxygen, increased the "aerating surface" of the lungs: "The available muscular force of any individual depends as much upon respiratory capacity as on the collective power of the muscles of his body." Sandlands (1903: 66) advised the addition of abdominal breathing exercises to physical training for the attainment of the best possible lung development. Conversely, a sedentary lifestyle shrunk the chest, lessened lung cell elasticity and vital capacity and made it more difficult for the lungs to cope with the waste matter produced by greater than accustomed exertion (Rippon Seymour nd [1898]: 85–86).

Given the prevalence of constipation, the removal of body wastes through defecation was an important factor in maintaining good health and athletic performance. Urination removed acids and sulphates, but an organ of excretion given considerable importance was the skin. Perspiration was divided between the insensible—the continually produced moisture that evaporates quickly—and the sensible, which collects in drops following exertion (Rippon Seymour nd [1898]: 87). The skin had to be kept clean, its pores unclogged, for it to fulfill its excretory tasks, underpinning the importance of hygiene for health and the place it was given in physical culture. Athletic exercise, according to Michod (1874: xi–xii), contributed significantly to cleanliness because it helped the body to rid itself of noxious matter that might not be excreted from the exertions of ordinary everyday life: "Perspiration *breathes* out all kinds of impurities, that, if allowed to remain in the system, would disseminate disease to an astonishing extent" (xii, original emphasis). Diet and the mastication of food affected the skin, as did internal organs, which needed to be kept in good condition to ensure the skin's good performance (Rippon Seymour nd [1898]: 109).

In applying this physiological thinking to training, Rippon Seymour (nd [1898]: 89) suggested that it involved disciplining the body so that it became accustomed to new activities. For the levels of performance then associated with amateur sport, training could create changes in the body quite quickly, within several weeks for the more active person. But the conditioning attained from this training could dissipate equally rapidly. Rigid training rules could not be set down for everyone. As temperaments and constitutions varied from person to person, so must training regimes. Individuals could judge what was best for themselves by the effects that training had on them, modifying diet, exercise or other aspects accordingly. Rippon Seymour (nd [1898]: 96) concluded from an examination of training regimes recommended by several leading sportspeople that there was general agreement over three principles: "early hours, morning bathing, and moderation in food and work." Although the physiology of strain model perhaps was best summarized in Harrisson's (1869: 6) conviction that injury was a "result of an erroneous combination of dieting and exercise, by which the waste has been made to exceed the supply."

STRAIN

Among sportspeople, over-doing it occurred from over-training or from putting in an overly sustained and intensive effort in competition. Either way, the point of strain was exceeded. The careful monitoring of exertion was very much something in the awareness of the higher social classes. The reason given for why excessive exercise—that is, going beyond the point of strain—endangered health was the effect on the body of the buildup of more wastes than it could readily excrete. While exercise promoted their excretion, wastes were produced during exertion and too much activity produced more of these toxic products than the body could remove, so instead of prolonging healthy life, training when stale was dangerous and potentially life-threatening. Continuing to exercise when fatigued served to exacerbate waste buildup, "for the removal in a natural and certain manner of these principal waste products a *sufficiency* of bodily exercise is necessary, no more, no less" (Rippon Seymour nd [1898]: 77, original emphasis). But judiciously conducted exercise up to but never beyond the point of strain promoted an improved functioning of the whole body that progressively increased the load that it could take before it became stressed. The massive exertions of working-class manual workers and their lower life expectancies were taken as evidence of the dire effects of strain.

A reason given for why excessive exercise caused such dire outcomes lay in the effects of waste buildup on the heart. Galbraith (1895: 101) explained that over-exertion caused a reduction in the flow of blood between the heart and lungs so that the "interchange of carbonic acid for oxygen does not take place with sufficient rapidity, and the blood becomes surcharged with carbonic acid." But regular exercise helped the body to adapt, increasing "the activity of the excretory glands" (92).

Gradual training, therefore, was essential to develop the muscular action of the heart, to avoid the dangerous condition known as athlete's heart and to improve the body's oxygen intake and usage, enabling it to better deal with wastes. By the 1920s, it was known that the trained person had a lower pulse rate and lower blood pressure when exercising than the untrained person. Accordingly, training lessened a person's chance of acquiring a pathological condition of the heart provided, of course, that they did not persistently strain themselves (Frymir 1930). Over-training created a problem because it involved the expenditure of more energy by the body than it had attained from rest and food. "Signs of too much training are a lack of initiative and interest, loss of weight, lessening of body resistance to mild infections, and irritability. Plenty of rest rather than exercise is the antidote" (Frymir 1930: 22).

The issue for the amateurs was how to identify if they had overdone it and strained themselves, as well the remedies for rectifying things before irreversible damage occurred. Larrette (nd [1906]: 52) claimed that insomnia and "depression of spirits" were sure signs of being stale. Carry-over fatigue from the previous training session was thought to be a sign of staleness, as was significant thirst and an unhealthy-looking skin, caused by changes in the blood showing up in the face. "Patches of pink appear here and there on the epidermis, the muscles lose their firmness, and the oarsman's eye, instead of being bright and clear, looks dull" (Sportsman 1889: 42). For Beckley (1882: 31), "A man who is 'stale' is nothing less than a sick man. His strength, his energies, his digestion, are impaired, and only careful nursing will restore him to a healthy condition." The renown distance runner, Shrubb (nd [1908]: 28) stated that "the absence of free perspiration after hard work" indicated over-training because, after training or competing, the athlete "should be, perspiring freely then, and the discharge of waste tissue through the pores of [the] skin is at all times a healthy discharge" (76). Galbraith (1895: 77) advised rest when any appreciable fatigue was felt:

> Rapid respiration, palpitation, dizziness, headache, the face becoming pale or pinched, or flushing suddenly, the feeling of great heat or excessive perspiration, are all danger signals, showing that exercise has already been carried too far, and should cease at once. Continued overexertion carried to a point of exhaustion leads to an obstinate irritability of the heart as well as to organic lesions. Contemporary writers agreed that when the failure of

training to increase strength was combined with lassitude and appetite the point of strain had been reached.

Excessive exertion could cause fatigue, inflame vital body parts and even result in premature death. Rather than "assisting in prolonging a healthy life" (Rippon Seymour nd [1898]: 103), continued training when stale was undoubtedly dangerous. Bodily vigor rapidly declined once the finite limits to physical development had been exceeded, opined Harrisson (1869: 5). Conversely, appropriate training—that done moderately, without strain—was thought to improve overall health as well as a person's muscular development.

> Training that does not educate and improve the whole wonderful and complex system of a man, and not merely his external muscles is and must be, on the face of it, *wrong*. A permanent strength cannot be built up from the outside, but when the lungs and heart are practically perfect, then it is the time to look at our *biceps*. (Rippon Seymour nd [1898]: 94, original emphases)

Morgan (1873: 74) asked how regularly and for how long it was possible to go into "hard training" without experiencing staleness? He noted that while highly trained athletes felt themselves to be in a state of "nearly perfect health" they were more liable to succumb to illnesses, "especially those of an inflammatory type." Accordingly, he advised, "A course of hard training therefore should not be taken unnecessarily, nor yet too often" (75).

Optimizing performance by pushing the point of strain to the maximum was therefore a dangerous activity. A fine balance was to be achieved between the good, robust health and well-functioning body attainable from training and pushing the limits of individuals' capabilities that brought with it the threat of over-doing it and ill health. Competition was therefore potentially dangerous. This danger came from both the intensity of the training conducted by athletes in preparation for competition and the strain of the contest itself.

Writing in the early years of organized amateur athletics, when it was still strongly engaged in its separation from professional sport, Michod (1874: 47) critiqued as "redundant athleticism," which would serve only to produce strain, the professional notion that the excitement of competition would enable the athlete to complete the race after running the early stages as hard as possible. But Michod premised his observations on what was promoted by amateurs as the reason for engaging in athletics, which he wrote was "to strengthen the body for the complete enjoyment of perfect health" (1874: 47), which required the avoidance of strain.

Much the same ideas were promoted by Ford (1891–1892) and Bickley (1929) when they advised athletes to under- rather than to over-train. Andrews and Alexander (1925: 51), in working from the same premise, advised athletes to include rest days in their training, not to do any full speed work outside of competition during the final stages of preparation in the racing season and to race not more than once a week, having rested the day before the meet and done only light exercises on the preceding day. Moreover, these authors advised a gradual development of the training program, with the earlier phases concentrating on technique rather than performance, because "the latter will only result in staleness, distaste for training, irritability, and lack of nervous energy, besides bringing disappointment in the results obtained," and "if too much training is indulged in early in the season, staleness or breakdown will be the inevitable result" (Andrews and Alexander 1925: 51, 59).

On the other hand, some writers argued that strain from competition derived from insufficient training. Contrary to the fears that competition could cause strain and injury, Sportsman (1889: 95) drew on the "testimony of eminent medical men" to claim that "a well and carefully trained man" was unlikely to suffer distress from a race. This was because the object of training was "to enable him to accomplish feats which otherwise would be almost, if not practically, impossible without much injury to his system or his health" (Sprinter nd [1906]: 3). Workman (nd [1906]: 17) supported this argument by arguing that it was the practice "so fashionable nowadays" of "racing without the antecedent bother of training" that caused the distress of competitors. This perspective inclined to the view that injuries or illnesses resulted from physical activities when the participants were sickly or under-trained rather than from the preparatory regimes required for participation in sport. Nevertheless, the view that competition did not affect the health of sufficiently trained athletes does not refute the idea of strain. What it meant was that appropriate training pushed the point of strain to a level that was not reached during races—it did rule out strain incurred from over-doing it outside of competition.

Extensive information was provided in the contemporary literature about how to recognize the point of strain, the effects of over-doing it and its resolution. The latter, of course, was thought essential to the health and well-being of the athlete. Having reached the point of strain, the athlete's body was *accumulating* waste matter. Consequently, correcting over-training involved the body regaining its ability to excrete waste materials at a rate that exceeded their build-up. White (nd [ca 1906]: 1024) was aware of the problems associated with strain and advised that they could be minimized, or even avoided altogether, by a training program that slowly brought the athlete to an optimum condition. Many athletes nevertheless experienced staleness, for which the remedy was obvious; the athlete had to adopt measures to temporarily lessen waste production and to accelerate its removal. These measures included the restriction of exercise, a change in diet, the use of purgatives and the consumption of tonics.

Less exercise served to limit further waste production and athletes were advised to ease back on their work (Larrette nd [1906]; Rippon Seymour nd [1898]; Ryle 1912; Sportsman 1889). Constipation was a frequent cause of staleness with the consequence that

This waste material becomes an irritant poison, which clogs the blood vessels and absolutely prevents one from performing the usual work. It is really a case of auto-poisoning, and the only way to get round [it] is to rest for at least a week and take some opening medicine [laxative] (Rippon Seymour nd [1898]: 102–3).

In addition to easing off their training, Larrette (nd [1906]: 52) also advised taking a tonic of Epsom salts, Glauber salts and cream of tartar. Changes in diet were recommended, especially if the staleness was accompanied by a poor appetite (Sportsman 1889: 42–43). Moreover, Abrahams (1912: 39) argued that strain could be avoided altogether if care were taken with diet.

The judicious use of alcohol as a stimulant was thought to be a means of invigorating jaded or sick bodies and overcoming staleness. As "a readily combustible material" alcohol could quickly generate energy (Anonymous 1874: 744). Moreover, it was a taken-for-granted medical opinion that alcohol was "a valuable therapeutical agent" (Berry 1875: 78), with "moderate use absolutely essential to good health and energy" as shown by the "pale, dyspeptic, languid, low spirited" teetotalers (Lowndes 1865: 508). Subject to people not over-imbibing, the medical view that alcohol provided a useful restorative supported its use as a way of overcoming strain. The favored beverage, it seems, was champagne. Ryle's (1912: 52) advice to the stale athlete was to "dose himself with a bottle of champagne," while Graham (nd [1901]: 33) suggested that the problems of fickle sprinters were "best cured by two pints of champagne." Other than the stimulant effect of alcohol helping the recovery of the strained athlete, champagne soothed "the irritated stomach" according to Michod (1874: 18) and its "effervescence stimulates the system to fresher feeling." Of course, that champagne was a regularly promoted stimulant was indicative of the amateurs' class backgrounds!

CONCLUSION

The nineteenth century saw the end of humoral physiology in bio-medical sciences. The positivist epistemology that characterized Enlightenment thinking promoted both empirical research into the functioning of the human body and a marked change in the theorizing about how it worked. These new, emergent physiological theories were employed in the awareness about how exercise impacted the body. Such understandings became especially pertinent when the higher social classes started to actively participate in sporting events—which gave rise to the amateur sporting movement. Existing training practices centered on the preparation of professional athletes. These practices, informed by humoral physiology and conducted under the direction of a working-class trainer, were unsuited to the needs of the gentry. Accordingly, a new system of training was put into place that disparaged and undermined the legitimacy of the professional practices. Contemporary bio-medical theories provided the "knowledge" that the amateur athletes used both to discredit the professionals and justify their new way of training the body.

It is important to bear in mind that the social class backgrounds of the amateur athletes and the bio-medical scientists and practitioners overlapped. Indeed, it is evident from the number of athletics clubs that were established in medical schools that athletes and medical people often were one and the same. Other amateurs were drawn from among aristocrats, men involved in university-educated professional positions and from the civil service. Socially, they were a world apart from the plebeian backgrounds of the sporting professionals. It is no surprise that the amateurs made their sporting world equally separate from that of the lower classes.

Foucault (1980) has noted how power and knowledge establishes dominant discourses and disciplines of the body. This association can be seen clearly here in the way that the amateurs cemented their distinctiveness by using the social power of their classes to construct "truths" about the body and thus about "scientific" training practices. More to the point is that their training regimes were based on a body discipline that developed a somatic form relevant to their class positions. The "capillaries" of power worked to control the behaviors of social elites so that they maintained the signs of their separation from and perceived superiority over the lower classes—which included specific somatic forms. The training practices of the amateurs served to develop the visual imagery of class difference as well provide a demonstration of their pre-eminent knowledge.

In this instance, the knowledge applied by the gentlemen-amateurs concerned the effect of strain on the body. But while the association between performance and body culture was wholly *inferred* from physiological theory, it gained the status of factual knowledge and held sway because of the credibility and legitimacy given to it from the social positioning of the amateur athletes. Exercise had two faces—while it was decidedly beneficial, too much of good thing was fraught with danger. Training was predicated on a physiological theory concerning, in essence, the production of wastes and their excretion from the body. Exercise helped remove wastes, but it also accelerated waste production. When the body could no longer excrete wastes at a rate faster than they were produced, the point of strain was reached and various physical and behavioral symptoms informed the athlete that it was time to lay off training for a while. Thus, through the application of contemporary scientific knowledge and a condemnation of the professional athletes' practices such that following them would have been tantamount to losing caste, the social elite produced a self-regulating physical regime that disciplined them—in the Foucauldian sense—to the body shape of their class position.

NOTES

1. For example, see Borde (1547) and Coghan (1584) for examples of humoral theory applied to humans; and Baret (1618) and Markham (1607) on its application to horses. See Beier (1987) for a recent study on the use of humoral theory in early modern medicine.

2. With the exception of very few "novelty" pedestriennes, professionals and amateurs alike were exclusively male. On pedestriennes see Shaulis (1999).

3. Training for modern sports started in the middle decades of the eighteenth century when established procedures for the preparation of horses were adapted for humans engaged in competitive pedestrianism, pugilism and later, in rowing (Mewett 2002). On the rejection of professional practices by amateurs see, for example, Blaikie (1873); Cortis (1887); Crawley (nd); Hoole (1895); Pollard (1882); Wilkinson (1868).

4. For example, the long distance pedestrian exploits of E. P. Weston in the 1870s were closely montiored by medical people with several reports being written for the *British Medical Journal*. See *British Medical Journal* 28 February 1876: 271–72; 4 March 1876: 297–99; 11 March 1876: 315–56, 334–35; 18 March 1876: 359–62.

5. Proteins and carbohydrates in today's terms.

BIBLIOGRAPHY

Abrahams, A. "Athletics and the Medical Man." *Practitioner* 86 (1911): 429–46.

———. "The Scientific Side of Athletics." *Athletics*, edited by E. H. Ryle. London: Eveleigh Nash, 1912.

Andrews, H., and W. Alexander. *The Secret of Athletic Training*. London: Methuen, 1925.

Anonymous. "Body-Force and Stimulants." *British Medical Journal* (editorial) 12 December (1874): 744–45.

Baret, M. *An Hipponomie or the Vineyard of Horsemanship*. London: George Eld, 1618.

Beckley, G. P. "Second Prize." *Athletic Training: Prize Essays*, edited by R. V. Somers-Smith, G. P. Beckley and A. W. Pollard. London: Simpkin Marshall & Co. and London Athletic Club, 1882:19–34.

Beier, L. C. *Sufferers and Healers: The Experience of Illness in Seventeenth-Century England*. London: Routledge, 1987.

Berry, W. "Alcohol as a Medicine." *British Medical Journal* 16 January (1875): 78.

Bickley, G. *Handbook of Athletics for Coaches and Players*. New York: Barnes, 1929.

Blaikie, W. "Ten Years Among the Rowing Men." *Harper's Monthly* 48 (1873): 407–15.

Borde, A. *The Breuiary of Health*. London: publisher not cited, 1547.

British Medical Journal, 26 February–18 March 1876.

Coghan, T. *The Haven of Health*. London: William Norton, 1584.

Cortis, H. L. *Principles of Training for Amateur Athletes*. 4th ed. London: Iliffe, 1887.

Craven [pseudonym]. *Walker's Manly Exercises, revised or written by 'Craven.'* 9th ed. London: Bohn, 1860.

Crawley, R. *Popular Gymnastics, Athletics, Pedestrianism, etc.* London: Ward, Lock and Co., nd.

Ford, M. W. "Training." *Outing* 19 (1891–1892): 421–24.

Foucault, M. *Power/Knowledge: Selected Interviews and Other Writings, 1972–1977*. New York: Pantheon Books, 1980.

Frymir, A. W. *Track and Field for Women*. New York: Barnes, 1930.

Galbraith, A. M. *Hygiene and Physical Culture for Women*. London: Stevens, 1895.

Graham, H. *Athletics of Today*. London: Ward, nd [1901].

Griffin, H. H. *Athletics*. London: Bell, 1891.

Harrisson, J. *Athletic Training and Health: An Essay on Physical Education*. London: Parker, 1869.

Hoole, H. *The Science and Art of Training: A Handbook for Athletes*. London: Cox, 1895.

Larrette, C. H. "How to Get Fit and Keep So. The Benefits of Walking." *The "Athletic News" Handbook on Training for Athletes and Cyclists*, edited by Sprinter [pseudonym]. London: Athletic News, nd [1906].

Lowndes, H. "Introductory Address: Liverpool Medical Institution." *British Medical Journal* 11 November (1865): 508–9.

Markham, G. *Cavelarice, Or The English Horseman*. London: Edward White, 1607.

Mewett, P. G. "'Nothing is Better for Dinner than a Pint of Good Dry Champagne': The 'Gentleman' Amateur and Sports Training in the Second Half of the Nineteenth Century." Pp. 206–12 in *Proceedings of the Second Australian and New Zealand Leisure Studies Association Conference*, edited by C. Simpson and R. Gidlow. Canterbury, New Zealand: Australian and New Zealand Association for Leisure Studies, 1995.

———. "From Horses to Humans: Species Cross-Overs in the Origin of Modern Sports Training." *Sport History Review* 33, no. 2 (2002): 95–120.

———. "Conspiring to Run: Women, Their Bodies and Athletics Training." *International Review for the Sociology of Sport* 38, no. 3 (2003): 331–49.

Michod, C. J. *Good Condition: A Guide to Athletic Training*. London: Hardwick, 1874.

Morden, W. E. *A New Handbook on Training for Athletic Exercises, etc*. London: Seale, 1887.

Park, R. J. "Athletes and Their Training in Britain and America, 1800–1914." Pp. 57–107 in *Sport and Exercise Science: Essays in the History of Sports Medicine*, edited by J. W. Berryman and R. J. Park. Urbana: University of Illinois Press, 1992.

Pollard, A. W. "Third Prize." Pp. 35–48 in *Athletic Training: Prize Essays*, edited by R. V. Somers-Smith, G. P. Beckley and A. W. Pollard. London: Simpkin Marshall & Co. and London Athletic Club, 1882.

Rippon Seymour, H. *Physical Training: Its Theory and Practice*. Edinburgh: Livingstone, nd [1898].

Ryle, E. H. *Athletics*. London: Eveleigh Nash, 1912.

Sandlands, J. P. *Walking and the Principles of Training*. London: Smith's, 1903.

Shaulis, D. "Pedestriennes: Newsworthy But Controversial Women in Sporting Entertainment." *Journal of Sport History* 26 (1999): 29–50.

Shearman, M. *Athletics*. London: Longmans, 1901.

Shrubb, A. *Running and Cross-Country Running*. London: Health and Strength, nd [1908].

Sportsman [pseudonym]. *The Training Instructor for Aquatics, Pedestrianism, Swimming, Athletics, Bicycling, etc*. London: The Sportsman, 1889.

Sprinter [pseudonym]. *The 'Athletic News' Handbook on Training for Athletes and Cyclists*, 7th ed., edited by "Sprinter." London: Athletic News, nd [1906].

Vertinsky, P. *The Eternally Wounded Woman: Women, Doctors and Exercise in the Late Nineteenth Century*. Manchester: Manchester University Press, 1990.

Westhall, C. *The Modern Method of Training for Running, Walking, Rowing, Boxing, Football, Lawn-Tennis, etc*. New edition revised by E. T. Sachs. London: Ward, Lock and Co., 1890.

White, J. "A Physician's View of Exercise and Athletics." *Lippincott's Magazine* 39, (nd [c1906]): 1008–33.

Wilkinson, H. F. *Modern Athletics*. London: Warne, 1868.

Workman, H. W. "How to Race Successfully. With Hints on Training." *The "Athletic News" Handbook on Training for Athletes and Cyclists*, edited by Sprinter [pseudonym]. London: Athletic News, nd [1906].

12

Throwing like a Brazilian: On Ineptness and a Skill-Shaped Body

Greg Downey

While in Brazil in the 1990s to study capoeira, an Afro-Brazilian martial art and dance, I worked with some of the most physically talented people I have ever known. Oddly enough, however, they could not throw or catch very well at all. Capoeira is an acrobatic genre that combines aspects of dance, sport, martial art, musical genre, and participatory spectacle. Adept capoeiristas are extraordinary athletes, capable of improvising acrobatic kicks, cartwheels, leg sweeps, handstands, and other maneuvers in response to an opponent's similarly fluid movements. Most of my time in the field, a yawning gap separated my own meager abilities as a capoeirista and the extraordinary physical virtuosity of my hosts.

Confronted constantly with my own physical inadequacy, I took a bit of cruel satisfaction from the rare moments when their own distinct ineptness came into clear view, specifically around ballistic skills, that is, the ability to throw and catch small objects with their hands. This inability among my hosts only surfaced when I tossed a set of keys to a colleague in the capoeira academy, unaware that this was not a common way to exchange objects. I've written about this colleague elsewhere, focusing on his exceptional abilities as both a capoeira practitioner and coach (see Downey 2005, 2006). But in the moment when the keys left my hand and arched toward him through the air, he flailed at them awkwardly. The ring of keys hit him square in the chest and fell jangling to the floor to my astonishment. I soon found that my other Bahian colleagues in the capoeira academy also could not catch or throw adeptly with their hands in spite of their uncanny ability to handle incoming objects with their feet, head, and other parts of the body, honed by years of playing soccer with whatever sort of ball they could find.

As a North American of a certain age, especially as a former resident of a university dormitory and fraternity house, I was accustomed to passing a large number of things through the air. Most rubbish bins in my University of Virginia first-year dorm, for instance, had small plastic hoops affixed above them by my basketball-mad colleagues, and trash routinely flew into them. Trained by a childhood with football, baseball, basketball, and even snowball chucking, most American peers were very comfortable with sending or receiving projectiles in a range of contexts: sports, exchanging small objects, even passing food at the dinner table (at least at the fraternity house). Nothing similar happened in Brazil; talented soccer players, samba dancers, and capoeira practitioners, physical virtuosos in many realms, Brazilian colleagues were much less likely to let objects fly as they had no corresponding physical regimen, informal or formal, to acquire manual ballistic skills. Just as cultural regimes of training produced a distinctive set of skills, such as capoeira techniques, these same regimens also left gaps of incompetence around peaks of virtuoso ability. Their culturally distinctive corporeality was defined equally both by competence and incompetence, ability and inability, grace and awkwardness. Far from being uniformly dexterous, these remarkable athletes had pockets of extraordinary skill sitting side-by-side with equally characteristic ineptness.

The anthropological study of physical education and sport is not simply the study of skillful action, expert abilities, and training regimens. Ineptitude, learned inability, and unrealized physical potential are just as characteristic of every culture, and groups or subcultures within each society, as people's positive capacities. This chapter explores the specific comparison between throwing and not throwing, especially the physiological and neurological consequences of learning this ability, in part because throwing is such a crucial, defining ability, not just for Brazilians, but also for women.

The expression "throwing like a girl," common in my own childhood, served an important role in the path-breaking discussion of feminine embodiment advanced by philosopher Iris Marion Young (1990), in the article (and later the book) by the same name. Specifically, Young uses the kinetic character of a distinctively "feminine" way of throwing to highlight the existential state of being a woman, treating ballistic ineptness as both illustration and symptom of female ways of being. Qualitative research backs up her philosophical insights; even proponents of "gender similarity" in psychology acknowledge that overhand throwing is the manual skill in which the gap between men's and women's performance is most marked (see Hyde 2007). This chapter asks what it might mean that Brazilian men (or other groups) also throw "like girls." More important for an anthropological exploration of the relationship of biology to culture in sports, how are we to understand the fact that Brazilian men and (some) North American women throw so poorly? What does ineptness teach us about the development of ability and the biological consequences of physical training?

Robert Sands has elsewhere argued that "the holistic, cross-cultural and ethnographic traditions that define anthropology as an endeavor have never been more pronounced than in the field of sport" (1999: xiv). Not often enough, however, does the anthropological study of sport fulfill this holistic promise, especially when our research confronts the yawning gap in the contemporary discipline between cultural and biological approaches to human difference. Sports offer an ideal place in which to experiment with holistic biocultural approaches because they are a realm of human life where athletic rituals, norms for physical appearance, and ideals for good living become a significant influence on our anatomical and neurological development.

In the specific contrast between skill and ineptness in throwing, we can combine cultural and biological perspectives on human variation, understanding how diverse developmental trajectories, including things like everyday games and physical education, affect or even induce human variation. In a physical practice like learning to throw, cultural values clearly take hold of the individual's development, both psychologically and physiologically, in obvious, tangible practices that we can examine minutely with both empirical and cultural methods, in order to understand their consequences for the individual and society (see, for example, Downey 2005, 2008). As Tim Ingold (1998: 26) encourages, this approach shies away from trying to "complement" cultural or biological approaches with each other, and instead seeks to erase the boundary separating them. Ingold stresses "that throughout life, the body undergoes processes of growth and decay, and that as it does so, particular skills, habits, capacities and strengths, as well as debilities and weaknesses, are enfolded into its very constitution—in its neurology, musculature, even its anatomy."

This chapter brings together current research in sports sciences and physiological plasticity with ethnographic reflection to sketch out some of the biocultural consequences of ineptness and expertise in throwing in order to illustrate this process of bio-enculturation.

THROWING LIKE A GIRL

Many theorists of embodiment, such as Marcel Mauss (1973) and Pierre Bourdieu (1990a, 1990b), have discussed how inhibitions and incapacities form a crucial complement to our habits and proclivities. The late Iris Marion Young, phenomenologist and feminist philosopher, focused specifically on the ability to throw in her exploration of the distinctive inhibitions that marked feminine embodiment. In her landmark article on "throwing like a girl," Young discusses the widespread perception that women have a distinctive, inefficient style of throwing—a signature ineptitude—which is believed to illustrate much more pervasive existential limitations on their bodily mobility and action. When they try to throw, specifically, "Girls do not bring their whole bodies into the motion as much as the boys do. They do not reach back, twist, move backward, step and lean forward. Rather the girls tend to remain relatively immobile except for their arms are not extended as far as they could be" (Young 1990: 145). Journalist James Fallow (1996), in an article about "throwing like a girl," pointed to the body positions of Bill Clinton and Hillary Rodham Clinton in photographs of both throwing out the "first ball" of the season (Bill in Cleveland and Hillary in Chicago). Whereas Bill was captured in a smooth left-arm delivery, Hillary Clinton was snapped in the middle of a motion—facing home plate, elbow up, ball resting on the palm of her hand—that, as Fallow puts it, "can only be described as throwing like a girl" (see also Fredrickson and Harrison 2005).

Young argued that the distinctive unskilled kinesthetic that women used when trying to throw is symptomatic of the feminine style of embodiment, marked by "ambiguous transcendence," "inhibited intentionality," and "discontinuous unity" (Frederickson and Harrison: 147). Specifically, girls were too self-conscious to focus completely on the task, they did not pursue their objectives in an uninhibited bodily fashion but rather restrained themselves physically, and they could not summon the whole of their physical being into any task, whether throwing or anything else, because their body parts and stages of movements did not tend to work together smoothly. In contrast to goal-oriented, uninhibited, whole body movement, the distinctively feminine style that surfaced in "throwing like a girl" was self-conscious, restrained, and awkwardly disunited.

More careful kinematic studies of the development of coordination in children show that girls tend to throw poorly for a number of reasons. Physically, they are often smaller, have less muscle mass in the arms and other relevant muscles, and have shorter limbs, leaving them with less leverage to propel a projectile even when their technique is good. But some of the reasons are not clearly biomechanical. For example, females often use a reduced body motion and do not extend their arms as far as possible, both behavioral or technical rather than anatomical limitations (Robertson and Halverson 1984; see also Thomas and French 1985; Watson and Kimura 1991). Studies of throwing with the non-dominant hand by Williams, Haywood and Painter (1996) found that boys and girls throw with equal force using their non-trained arm, pointing to training effects on the difference in throwing with the favored arm. Other theorists, such as Doreen Kimura (2002), draw on evidence from other spatial tasks and low-effort throwing, such as darts, that suggests women's inability is not merely a deficiency in technique from a lack of practice or anatomical disadvantages, but rather a cognitive difference from men. This distinction in the way that women contend with spatial relations allegedly impedes throwing for accuracy and intercepting a moving target, skills that require coordinating whole body movements with spatial accuracy, more so than it undermines paper-and-pencil tests of spatial reasoning.

Researchers have found that measurable differences in throwing ability, accuracy, velocity, and distance are more marked than other gender disparities in motor ability, with virtually no overlap in the performance range for boys and girls, especially after puberty. In her review of evidence for the overarching similarity of males and females in psychological studies of gender, Janet Shibley Hyde (2007: 260; see also 2005) concedes that certain "exceptions to the pattern of gender similarity exist": foremost among them, throwing velocity and distance are a more pronounced gender difference than even aggression or frequency of masturbation. A meta-analysis of studies of throwing by Thomas and French (1985) found that the gap between average throwing velocity and distance in boys and girls stood at 1.5 standard deviations by three years of age and kept increasing, widening to between three and four standard deviations by puberty (see Thomas and French 1985: 266 and 276). The gap between male and female performance emerges early in children's development and grows so great that Thomas and French argue the difference must be inherent, but reinforced by gender disparities in patterns of education, play and other activities. Relatively small, but significant differences in arm length, bicep size, and arm composition might be compounded by environmental feedback, informal training, and encouragement. In a study of discipline in an American preschool, for example, Karin Martin (1998) found that boys were allowed to take up more space and engage in more vigorous, louder play. Girls were disciplined to stay quiet, avoid conflict, and control their bodily movement so that they did not tend to do the same sorts of vigorous whole-body motions in which boys regularly engaged, the type of collateral activities that might train the body in the sort of integrative biomechanical effort that produces the highest velocities of throwing.

Within each sex, however, throwing performance varies widely. A study of German children (Ehl, Roberton, and Langendorfer 2005) found that, while a gender gap existed there, most of the gap could be attributed to technique differences, and that German boys, with less experience than their American counterparts, threw much like American girls (but still better than German girls). In a study of adolescent girls, Fredrickson and Harrison (2005) found that girls were not all equally "self-objectifying" and that the degree of each girl's self-objectification, measured as her concern for personal appearance, predicted her inability to throw a softball at high velocity. Frederickson and Harrison highlight that self-objectification is both an enduring trait and an even more pronounced temporary condition in certain contexts, and that multiple channels socialize girls to become self-conscious in ways that inhibit their bodily actions (Frederickson and Harrison: 81–82). Similarly, Evaldsson (2003) found that "ineptness" at throwing was partially shaped by interactional dynamics; that is, girls' throwing ability in a multiethnic school in Sweden seemed to vary depending upon the context in which they were playing the children's game, foursquare. The girls who were most accomplished reorganized their own ability when playing with less competent girls but were capable of vigorous, well-coordinated throwing movements when playing against equally accomplished girls or boys.

Sexual variation in gender behavior, in some studies, produces significant modifications to the gender pattern of proficiency. Hall and Kimura

(1995) examined homosexual subjects' ability to throw overhand and found that gay men did not perform as well as heterosexual men and that lesbian women outperformed heterosexual women. Although the researchers take this as possible evidence of the neurological consequences (or causes) of homosexuality, one could just as easily argue that the results are consistent with homosexual individuals conforming less to gender expectations of bodily movement styles or participating less in the activity patterns of heterosexual members of the same sex. Whichever interpretation one takes, the study suggests that the male-female difference in throwing ability is not immune to influence from non-biological factors.

When Young (1998) returned to reconsider the subject of "throwing like a girl" twenty years after her ground-breaking article, passage of the Patsy T. Mink Equal Opportunity in Education Act (Title IX) had opened new athletic opportunities for young women. Many girls had responded to Title IX enthusiastically, developing an increasing range of sporting abilities. Women's sport had grown more visible, including more widespread participation in women's collegiate sports and collegiate sports scholarships in the United States, and the inclusion of fast-pitch softball in the Olympics for the first time in 1996. Young had watched her daughter, growing up in a post–Title IX world, learn how to throw in sports, in a broader context where young women seemed to behave in new ways, changing their styles of comportment, and learning novel physical skills as they seemed to shed distinctive inhibitions. Young began her retrospective reconsideration of her older article by pointing out that these changes affected the very foundational practices that she found so important to feminine embodiment in the earlier essay. And yet—ironically—she was satisfied to say that her original position still resonated with young women, even though many of them played softball and other sports that required them to throw as adeptly as their male peers. Young argues that the bodily style of being that is illustrated in "throwing like a girl" still captured the existential condition of being feminine.

One of the ironies of Young's account, and her seemingly odd insistence twenty years later that "throwing like a girl" still provided an essential window on the feminine condition, even though her daughter's peers increasingly did not "throw like girls," is that her conclusion virtually demands a naturalizing, biological explanation for differences in men's and women's throwing styles, an explanation she would have likely found unpalatable (see Dowling 2000; Thomas and French 1995).[1] That is, explaining the distinctive style of movement that constitutes "throwing like a girl" as a result of an underlying existential condition—being a girl—rather than as illustrative of a changing pattern of gender-differentiated behaviors, with many exceptions, commits Young to a model that finds bodily change and variation hard to explain. How do we explain the women who do not "throw like girls," if the kinesthetic is a product of essential femininity? Or, for that matter, what do we say about the Brazilian men who throw just as ineptly?

In fact, some women, without losing their femininity in any existential sense, learn to throw overhand adeptly. For example, many young women likely took up sports after the passage of Title IX and developed extraordinary athletic ability without breaking from the broader pattern of embodiment Young indentifies of ambiguous transcendence, inhibited intentionality, and discontinuous unity; this is probably why Young (1998; see also 1990: 15) still finds her earlier account compelling twenty years after it first appeared, even though its central metaphor was in athletic jeopardy in a new generation of women athletes. Understanding the biocultural processes that produce ineptitude, and the debilitating physiological consequences of lacunae in training regimes, in my opinion, places us in a much better position to understand patterns of bodily proficiency in different societies.

FROM INEPTNESS TO SKILL

Expert overhand throwing is one of the fastest and most powerful athletic movements that the human body can generate, recruiting a large portion of the body's muscular resources into a kinesthic chain that can launch a projectile from the hand of an expert cricket bowler or baseball pitcher at speeds in excess of 90 mph (around 145 km/hr). Even at lower levels of proficiency, skillful techniques can produce significant force and accuracy; high school baseball pitchers can produce velocities over 70 mph (110 km/hr). From an evolutionary perspective, many theorists, starting with Darwin in the 1870s (see 1901) have argued that overhand throwing was a crucial development in the distinctly human behavioral arsenal, allowing our ancestors to deliver force at a distance, defend themselves against or intimidate predators, and in the process, transforming our hands, arms, and even our cognitive capacities (see Calvin 1983, 1991; Darlington 1975; Dunsworth, Challis and Walker 2003; Isaac 1987; Noble and Davidson 1996; Rhodes and Churchill 2008; Young 2003).[2]

The biomechanics of overhand throwing have been carefully studied by researchers interested in both elite-level performance and developmental dynamics (see Stodden et al. 2006a, 2006b, for a recent discussion). Expert throwing techniques such as those used in softball, Olympic handball (called "team handball" in the United States), javelin throwing, or water polo recruit a number of successive movements, tightly orchestrated, so that force generated in one part of the body can be transferred to and increased by the next body part in the sequence, buffered and stabilized, and, finally, dissipated after release. Developing skill at throwing requires improving the body's brute physiological capacity and resilience to the motion, but it also involves learning to better coordinate this complicated technique so that each body part can contribute to the overall movement.

Many discussions of baseball pitching, for example, segment the motion into six stages: windup, forward stride, cocking of the arm, acceleration, deceleration, and follow through (see, for example, Bartlett 2000; Whiting and Rugg 2006: 171–72). During the preparatory phase of the windup, the pitcher's body turns backward on the throwing side, especially the pelvis and trunk, the opposite leg is raised, the shoulder is extended sideways and rotated, the elbow is flexed, and the wrist hyper-extended. Beginning with the forward stride of the opposite (contralateral) leg, a baseball pitcher unleashes the stored potential energy in this posture, dragging the ball with a kind of cooperative whiplash motion. The resulting technique generates enormous force, in part by leaving the projectile back as long as possible and accumulating forward momentum by linking a cascade of rotational generators in the body (like the trunk, shoulders, and pelvis) together with a lunging, twisting forward step. Orchestrating the finely tuned chain of movements of the legs, pelvis, torso, shoulder, elbow, forearm, wrist and hand is a complicated task, made more difficult by the fact that it is all done in around two seconds: approximately 1.5 seconds for the preparatory phases (the windup, stride and cocking the arm), 350 milliseconds for the deceleration and follow-through at the end, and less than one-tenth of a second accelerating in the middle of the technique (Pappas, Zawacki, and Sullivan 1985; see also Hore et al. 1995; Wilk 2000). Other throwing motions, such as in javelin, cricket, or even skipping rocks, require a similar kinetic chain, although the particular stages are affected by the object being thrown, the objective, and the restrictions placed on a thrower's movement, such as whether a thrower can use a run up to the launch.

Faced with such complex kinesthetic demands, when children first learn to throw, especially if they seek to throw accurately, they typically "throw like girls." They hold one arm up facing the target and immobilize the rest of their bodies. Then, reaching back slightly, they throw by extending the elbow alone, sometimes with a bit of additional movement in the upper body (Robertson and Halverson 1984). Kinesiologist Monica Wild (1938) was one of the first researchers to analyze the development of throwing ability in children. Using photographs in a longitudinal study of subjects from aged two- to twelve-years-old, she identified specific techniques that, while ineffective, built toward growing expertise. Wild divided the learning process into four stages, arguing that the first was simple movement in the direction of the throw in the upper body, and that subsequent stages added the rotation of the torso, a weight shift and step with the same foot, and, finally, a more complex motion including a step with the contralateral foot, cocking of the arm, and torso rotation. Early processes were simpler, demanding fewer body parts or sources of momentum, although they sometimes involved movement that, at later stages, had to be rectified (such as stepping with the wrong foot at first).

Mary Ann Roberton (1977, 1978), in a series of studies, broke with models of developmental stages in skill acquisition when she discovered that children did not progress uniformly or in fixed series of clear steps, but rather developed unevenly. She eventually decided that the throw was composed of five separate anatomical regions or movements: humerus action, trunk rotation, forearm movement, stepping action, and stride length (see Roberton and Konczak 2001: 92; see also Burton and Rodgerson 2003: 233–34). Roberton argued that development might occur unevenly, achieving more advanced dynamics in one area before growing more sophisticated in a linked motion, or refinement of one part of the movement dependent upon an improvement somewhere else first. Roberton's fine-grained "component approach" to studying skill improvement allowed her and Langendorfer to chart diverse developmental trajectories in throwing techniques across a number of children (Langendorfer and Roberton 2002).[3] They found that some trajectories or developmental series were more common or stable than others, but that some children assembled idiosyncratic combinations in their techniques, or advanced in distinctive ways. A stage-based approach to understanding skill development tended to erase this variation. Langendorfer and Roberton (2002) also found that the same child sometimes varied his or her technique on multiple throws at the same trial, suggesting that bodily coordination could be unstable, especially as new motions developed in one part of the technique.

MANAGING THE BODY'S MOTION

"Throwing like a girl," then, is common in novice throwers as a kinesthetic adaptation to solve, however temporarily and unsatisfactorily, two closely related corporeal challenges: the difficulty of controlling all of the degrees of freedom in the body at once, and limits on a novice's ability to recruit all the various components successfully into a unified throwing motion. First, to throw "like a girl" involves limiting the joints and muscles that move, freezing most of the body simply to stabilize the action. This approach to throwing is a normal and reasonably successful way of contending with what Russian kinesiologist Nicholai Bernstein (1996) identified as the "degrees of freedom" problem in the face of attempting a new task. Even experts, asked to throw for accuracy, often revert to a similar strategy, immobilizing the body and throwing primarily with the wrist and elbow, as when throwing darts or aiming for small targets.

Bernstein identified the body's own range of motion as a challenge to novice attempts at any new activity. He argued that mastering the many "degrees of freedom," learning to control the potential movement of the many joints and muscles, was an essential part of developing skilled action. As Bernstein writes:

> Apparently, the immense richness of the moving organs, whose boundlessness we are just beginning to realize, can be mastered and used for our needs rather than leading to total anarchy only if each and every degree of freedom is tamed and bridled by a specialized sensory system that closely monitors it. (1996: 36)

Newell (1996: 413), drawing on Bernstein, argues that the first stage of motor learning is characterized by "freezing" of much of the body in order to manage this excessive freedom:

> Because the basic problem of coordination is the harnessing of the extreme abundance of degrees of freedom of the system, the first stage in learning is characterized by coordination solutions that reduce the number of degrees

of freedom at the periphery to a minimum. The freezing strategy effectively reduces the number of biomechanical degrees that need to be coordinated and controlled.

When most of us first learn to throw, or do any other complex physical task, the sensation of so many body parts moving is impossible to control. Most children (and what Young classifies as the "feminine" avenue) make the sensory management technique less difficult by immobilizing the majority of the body, isolating the arm to make it the sole locus of control.

Some young children, with idiosyncratic developmental trajectories, may adopt a different management strategy, for example, flailing the whole body and throwing wildly and out of control. But this difference is simply another, more-or-less successful management strategy, Roberton's model would suggest. Both inhibited and uninhibited strategies might appear in male or female children, and both can, through gradual refinement, converge on expert technique through trial and error, coaching, and emulation.[4]

The most basic forms of inept overhand throwing tightly restrict motion both because this limits extraneous movement and because the novice thrower cannot successfully draw on all the body's resources, some of which will not become apparent until sufficient force or technical skill is developed in a linked movement component. For example, Langendorfer and Roberton (2002: 254) hypothesized that some of their subjects did not develop the most sophisticated throwing motion in the upper arm because these subjects "never received the throwing experiences necessary to allow trunk acceleration to reach the critical values necessary to elicit a lagging humerus," one of the hallmarks of expert technique. That is, until they developed sufficient trunk speed and rotational force in the throw, the expert arm motion likely was difficult to discover or execute. Developing one segment of the bodily skill generated the possibility of exploring more advanced kinesthetic techniques with other body parts (see also Ehl, Roberton, and Langendorfer 2005).

In other words, two of the three qualities Young (1990) describes as inherently "feminine" in the "throwing like a girl" style of movement—inhibited intentionality and discontinuous unity—are traits of virtually all inexperienced attempts, not because of the thrower's "femininity," but rather as positive strategies for contending with the difficulties of the task.[5] Bernstein's theory, Newell's refinement, and Roberton's observations all suggest that a "feminine" style of throwing, with excessive control and incomplete mobilization, is most likely—but not universally—to be the first stage in any development of throwing ability, whether the individual stalls at this stage or develops more skillful technique. If a person gains appropriate experience, models, and training, he or she may eventually release additional degrees of freedom and learn to exploit the interaction of different body parts within the movement (Newell 1996: 413–14), such as the way that the torso and humerus can interact to produce greater momentum through lagged linkage. In other words, discontinuity and inhibition, two traits that Young identifies as "feminine," and can be found in my Brazilian friends' styles of throwing, are actually productive strategies for building a skilled movement from an unskilled throwing technique, found across much of motor learning.

Fallow (1996) asks, "Why, exactly, do so many women 'throw like girls'?" Young's (1990) answer is that this is the essence of feminine nature, to be self-conscious, inhibited, and unable to coordinate one's body. When we shift the question, asking why exactly some Afro-Brazilian men throw like girls, we find no pattern of disunity and inhibition to explain their inept attempts to throw. In fact, my Brazilian subjects were otherwise exceptional athletes, experts in capoeira and often accomplished soccer players. I routinely saw them juggling soccer balls with most parts of their bodies—except their hands, of course. Their capoeira training specifically involved drills intended to "tear the shame" from their bodies, to remove what inhibitions they had. Paradoxically, Afro-Brazilian men from poor and working-class backgrounds—the worst at throwing overhand in my experience—were believed by my capoeira instructors to be the least inhibited students to teach movement techniques, as most were also accomplished samba dancers (Downey 2005: 186–202). They flung their bodies into unpredictable acrobatic moves with abandon. Far from "ambiguous," their capoeira performances were emphatically "transcendent" in a phenomenological sense, including pronounced aggression, physical assertiveness, and complete immersion in the task at hand. Capoeira techniques demanded extraordinary body coordination, a trait that was hammered home to me when I finally realized that my veteran colleagues were able to push themselves up from a headstand to a handstand because they adroitly used their legs, held all the time in the air, to generate upward momentum. My Brazilian colleagues' inability to throw was not part of a larger "feminine" pattern of inhibition or bodily disunity in everyday life; from my perspective, the reason I noticed the odd trait in the first place, the hapless throwing style seemed so strangely out of character, a startling glitch in what were otherwise well-honed athletic skill sets.[6]

If (most) Brazilian men and (many) women (and some men) in the United States (and Germany, but not the same ratios) stall at early developmental stages of throwing skill, femininity may not be the most likely or parsimonious explanation for patterns of ineptness. Because throwing expertly from a standing start requires several counter-intuitive movements, it may require coaching, imitation, or significant experimentation to discover. For example, athletic overhand throwing demands the thrower turn sideways to the target and that the object to be thrown is first moved, almost as far as the body will allow, away from the target. As Langendorfer and Roberton (2002) observed, children do not always make these transitions without practice or even explicit coaching.

When I was growing up in St. Louis, very much a "baseball town," I remember being taken to a classroom by my first baseball coach, Dr. Wickersham, to be instructed on how to throw properly. Although the memory is hazy, I do recall clearly being taught, explicitly, with chalkboard diagrams and many patient demonstrations, about the need to turn sideways and cock the ball back behind us, away from the direction of the throw. Even with this explicit coaching, and with enormous stigma attached to "throwing like a girl" beyond a certain age, I still recall many throwing-related mishaps during that first baseball season, when it was clear that our developing skills were technically unstable and easily unraveled by stress, varying conditions, or lack of concentration. Anthropologists tend to underestimate the importance of coaching in the development of corporeally techniques, as I have argued elsewhere (Downey 2006, 2008), in part because bodily learning through unconscious imitation is crucial in some of our theoretical paradigms.

THE PHYSIOLOGY OF OVERHAND THROWING

In her discussion of "throwing like a girl," Young shies away from the question of whether the difference in throwing motion is innate or a consequence of biology. Instead, she shifts the focus to psychologist Erwin Strauss (1966), whose initial comments on girls' throwing motions inspired her essay. She suggests that, for Strauss, the origin of the difference is "biologically based" but that Strauss "denies that it is specifically anatomical" (Young 1990:142). Young does not return to the question, nor does she comment on Strauss's difficult distinction between difference that is "anatomical" and that is "biologically based."

The semantic tangle is symptomatic of a broader problem: the tendency to divide influences on performance into the "biological" and the "experience-based," and then to assume that the "biological" is inherent, immutable, or genetic.[7] In fact, throwing has biological consequences, as well as preconditions. That is, we are capable of overhand throwing because most humans, barring skeletal abnormality or disability, can reach over their heads, the evolutionary consequence of our descent from primates who traveled by brachiating, or hanging by their arms in trees (Dunsworth, Challis and Walker 2003). The behavior of these primates became part of our anatomy because the active behavior-niche relationship made this trait relevant in selective processes. However, without the contribution of a number of developmental factors in the life of a growing child, not all of which we fully understand (see Duffy, Ericsson and Baluch 2007), the child will not be capable of expert overhand throwing. My Brazilian colleagues and (some) women cannot throw well for biological reasons, I will suggest, but those anatomical and neurological traits are both the consequences of not throwing, as well as the causes of being unable to throw.

As soon as we begin to throw, our bodies begin to adapt to this pattern of activity. Human tissue, like other animal tissue, remodels itself in order to become better able to do tasks for which it is frequently employed. Some biologists refer to this characteristic as "activity dependent phenotypic plasticity," but it is also designated "phenotypic adaptation," "developmental plasticity," "cardiac remodeling," and "metabolic plasticity" in the various research disciplines that observe it (see Garland and Kelly 2006: 2347; Pigliucci 2001; West-Eberhard 2003). In the case of skilled action, any activity in which there is the possibility of expertise arising, such as throwing, requires physiological change, whether in subtle neural modification or more easily observed gross anatomical adaptation (see Ericsson and Lehman 1996). For example, abundant evidence suggests that skeletal structure, including bone density and morphology, are affected significantly by mechanical loading, making bones better suited to bear habitual mechanical stresses (see Flück 2006; Ruff, Holt and Trinkaus 2006). Muscles become stronger if they are taxed (up to a certain point), and the nervous system, including the brain, adapts to the demands placed upon it (see, for example, Booth and Baldwin 1996; Doidge 2007; Hood et al. 2006; Staron and Hikida 2000).

Because many of these physiological demands in humans actually arise from socially and culturally determined contexts, phenotypic adaptation in humans is a bio-enculturation of the body, a deep, slow modification of tissue and bone. Although we may consider sport to be a form of "play," even less significant for determining our nature than "work" or "family," the extraordinary physical demands that elite athletes place on their bodies can make sport one of the most powerful contemporary determinants affecting how our physiology unfolds through time. Through their dedicated pursuit of increased ability, athletes help map out some of the boundaries of human anatomical plasticity by driving their bodies as hard as they can into modified configurations for elite performance.

The ability to throw overhand may be crucial in human evolution, a kinetic possibility in almost any human body, but the evidence that (some) women and (some) Brazilian men throw "throw like a girl" suggests that it is not inevitable that we learn to throw, even if the possibility is inherent anatomically in the human body. The development of throwing skill and the necessary physiological traits require the appropriate context for realization, such as childhood baseball or using rocks to scare off predators (see Newell 1996). In fact, the forces involved in overhand expert throwing can be so arduous, persistent, and violent that practice in the technique significantly changes the thrower's soft tissue and skeleton. At elite levels, a baseball or softball pitcher's arm reaches velocities that would spin it around the shoulder twenty-one times a second, if it could be maintained longer than a few milliseconds (see also Chant 2003; Fleisig et al. 1995). Hans-Gerd Pieper (1998: 247) reports that European handball players perform at least 48,000 throwing motions in a single year of training and competition with a ball that weighs between 425 and 475 grams (around one pound) at speeds reaching 130 km/hr (80 mph). Just as muscles and tendons must be cultivated over time to generate this enormous force, ligaments of the elbow must become capable of absorbing this energy at the end of the throw, in the deceleration phase.

THE SKELETAL CONSEQUENCES OF THROWING

Henry Jones and colleagues (1977) found that asymmetrical patterns of upper-body exercise and strain could lead to greater bone mass in the dominant arm (see also King, Brelsford, and Tullos 1969; Nevill, Holder and Stewart 2004). They examined eighty-four active professional tennis players and found that the cortex in the humerus of their dominant arm was approximately 35 percent thicker in men and 28 percent thicker in women than in their non-dominant arm (when tennis players favored one-handed hitting techniques) (see also Huddleston et al. 1980; Nilsson and Westlin 1971; Trinkaus, Churchill and Ruff 1994). Studies of tennis players and other athletes using one dominant arm are frequently cited as clear indication that mechanical stresses can affect bone density and composition, in part because of the built-in control offered by the non-dominant arm. If the arm used most heavily is significantly different from its opposite counterpart, clearly such factors as diet and genes cannot explain the asymmetry as these variables likely influence both arms equally.

German anatomist Julius Wolff (1896) first recognized that the skeleton was not an inert structure, but rather responded dynamically to mechanical strain, adapting structurally to patterns of use. Specific mathematical formulations of "Wolff's law" have been subject to critique, including the recognition that age affects the degree to which bones can be altered and that not all skeletal parameters are equally malleable; cortical thickness of bones and their density, for example, but not their length, can be powerfully influenced by ballistic overhand motions.[8] Nevertheless, the basic principle of "bone functional adaptation," to use the formulation preferred by Ruff, Holt, and Trinkaus (2006), holds true in the case of adolescent training for overhand hard throwing.

The point is not simply that use modifies the "natural" state of our skeleton, but rather that the emergence and development of the skeleton is inherently dependent, in part, upon patterns of loading and strain, among other factors (such as diet, hormones, disease, and genetic influences). Without ongoing mechanical stresses, the balance between the constant bone dissolution and regeneration that supports our skeleton shifts. Astronauts and cosmonauts discovered, for example, that being removed from the constant pull of gravity (in addition to other factors, such as lack of sunlight and changed diet) led them to shed calcium, especially from their hips and lower body, much as bed-ridden patients do (Buckley 2006: 3–32).

Activity patterns affect overall mass and density of bones, but also their morphology, within limits. On the detrimental side, if training starts too early and is pursued with too much vigor, exercise can overtax the developing arm, leading to tears in the growth plate on the humerus or pain from rapid osseous transformation, commonly referred to as "Little League Shoulder Syndrome" (see Osbahr, Cannon and Speer 2002: 352). If skill acquisition is not rushed, however, the shoulder can adapt to the persistent demands placed upon it by the cocking and acceleration phases of the throw by gradually turning to the rear, or undergoing retroversion. Because the highest throwing velocities can be obtained by twisting the shoulders vigorously while leaving the upper arm or humerus to lag behind cocked, enormous strain can arise as expert movement stretches the arm to the rear and side of the shoulder. Heber Crockett and his colleagues (2002) found that, when pitchers started their training early, before ten years of age, the shoulder joint underwent humeral retroversion (i.e., turned or tilted) up to 17 degrees measured against their non-throwing shoulder (see also Chant 2003; Osbahr, Cannon and Speer 2002; Reagan et al. 2002). These results confirmed earlier research by Hans-Gerd Pieper (1998: 251) on humeral retroversion in the shoulders of professional European handball players, whose dominant shoulder had, on average, a shoulder retroversion of 9.4 degrees, with some extreme examples reaching 29 degrees. Pieper demonstrated that increased range of motion was not due to relaxation in the joint capsule or ligaments of the shoulder, but due to actual bone remodeling.

The elite pitcher's or handball player's shoulder is not necessarily more flexible than a normal shoulder, in the sense that the total range of motion is much the same, but the range is shifted backward, much as ballet dancers shift their range of leg rotation outward by spending so much time in "turned out" positions (see Ericsson and Lehman 1996: 279–80). Pieper's (1998) findings were especially interesting because he observed that the average angle of retroversion was smaller (5.2 degrees compared to 14.4 degrees) in those athletes complaining of chronic pain compared to those who experienced no symptoms. This finding suggests that retroversion is adaptive, decreasing the chance of damage to the shoulder, as well as allowing greater rotation for increased throwing velocity (see Stodden et al. 2006b).

Although professional athletes might appear an unfair comparison to normal skeletal development, and they are admittedly extreme examples of bio-enculturation, osteoarchaeologist Jill Rhodes (2006) found that some medieval British skeletons evidenced even greater asymmetry than that found in professional tennis players and baseball pitchers. Their asymmetrical skeletal development was evidence, not just of single-arm dominance in activity patterns, but of strenuous, repeated, long-term asymmetrical activity, including professional specialization.

One reason that (some) Brazilian men and (some) women "throw like a girl" is likely that they have not developed sufficient shoulder rotation, either in soft tissue or in the joint; they are "anatomically," to use Srauss's term, different from those who can throw, but not because of an innate ineptness. Levine and colleagues (2006) found, in a study of young baseball players, that asymmetrical shoulder flexibility was apparent even in the youngest age bracket (aged eight to twelve years old), and the range of the throwing arm in relation to the non-throwing one increased over time. Their findings support earlier hypotheses by anatomists like Pieper and Crocket that the extreme retroversion found in adult professional athletes was founded upon extensive practice initiated prior to adolescence. The pattern of throwing, especially during stages of development in which the skeleton was growing quickly, established the physiological foundations for sport-related adaptation later in life.

REFINING THE THROW, REMODELING THE NERVOUS SYSTEM

Throwing for accuracy is neurologically demanding, both in terms of bodily coordination and the need to release the projectile at the correct point in the arm's trajectory. When we throw harder, our arm moves more quickly, making the timing of release progressively more difficult. As William Calvin (1983) first highlighted, the "launch window" for releasing a projectile shrinks to a few milliseconds as the arm moves fast enough to throw beyond a couple of meters (see also Chowdhary and Challis 1999; Hore et al. 1995). In his discussion of throwing in a prehistoric context, Calvin calculates that hitting a target ten by twenty centimeters—a size he calls, "one standard rabbit"—from a four-meter distance requires a release timed within an eleven millisecond time frame, in addition to being on the correct bearing laterally (1983: 125). When an athlete is throwing at high speeds, the arm can rotate 70 degrees in less than a tenth of a second; even a slight timing error will send the projectile over the target, or into the ground before it reaches its intended destination. In a study of throws with the non-dominant arm, Hore and colleagues (1996) found that the timing of the finger release varied significantly and was the most important cause of inaccuracy with the non-dominant arm. Increasing accuracy requires better control over the many degrees of freedom in the limb, and less variability at every joint, but the timing of the release is especially crucial because any error is exacerbated by the fact that the hand is at the end of the limb, where a few degrees of inconsistency will be magnified.

Single neurons cannot achieve such dependable timing accuracy due to neural noise, so Calvin (1983: 117–18) suggests that the neural precision required likely arises from bundling together redundant timing neurons. The sum of their activity is more accurate than any single one, as redundancy offsets the variability in any one neuron by massing multiple timing "circuits." Calvin argues that throwing may have offered a selective advantage to hominids that shaped the human brain's ability to sequence chains of rapid motor movement, an ability that would prove crucial in a range of other behaviors, such as speech and tool manufacture and use. Although some accounts of human brain evolution focus on cognitive abilities, humans have significant advantages over other animals in this ability to assemble complicated sequences of movements to build skillful actions.

Skillful throwing also requires orchestrating various muscles and joints to exploit interactions among them; the expert motion is a series of component movements that cascade through the body and accumulate momentum until the projectile leaves the hand at maximum velocity. Unskilled throwers, like the nondominant arms of skilled throwers, are not able to coordinate these relations at high speed (see Gray et al. 2006). For the body to reliably produce high performance, the body likely has to reallocate neural resources, such as has been found in other manual tasks like playing the violin (Edelman 2006: 56–57; Kelly and Garavan 2005; Münte, Altenmüller and Jäncke 2002). These forms of neural enskillment are material changes in the brain and nervous system; computer metaphors sometimes mislead us into thinking that a brain learns by storing information on an unchanged organ. In fact, learning is material change. Like muscular hypertrophy, neural refinement can lead to significant strength gains, even in simple motor movements, without any change in the muscle tissue itself. For example, Yue and Cole (1992) found that imagining hand exercises led to significant gains in strength, likely due to improved neural organization of the movement. In a sense, the nervous systems, with repeated practice, becomes better at squeezing performance out of the body at the same time that the body becomes better suited for performing the task.

This holistic approach to skill development casts a new light on the fact that throwing technique, using the component analysis advocated by Mary Ann Roberton, strongly predicts throwing velocity, even making a person's sex a redundant variable (see Roberton and Konczak 2001: 101). That is, from an analysis of how a person throws kinematically, Roberton and Konczak could predict how fast a person could throw even if they were blind to whether the subject was a boy or girl. "Throwing like a girl" was more important than actually being a girl to predict how hard a person could throw overhand. This result not only demonstrates the greater importance of technique than sex, but also likely arose because at each stage of development, throwing techniques affect physiological development. Greater joint mobility and more cooperative whole body motions produce neural adaptations and lay the musculoskeletal foundation (or obstacles) for subsequent stages of technical development in a self-reinforcing cycle; throw harder and the body and brain get better at throwing so that one can throw harder still. For example, early stage throwing may increase shoulder flexibility and strength, producing the musculature necessary for subsequent skill refinement, or more sophisticated throwing techniques must await sufficient muscular maturation. "Throwing like a girl" does not place enough stress on the body or nervous system to change them and adapt them for expert throwing.

CONCLUSION

One of the great challenges of sports research, as Sands' (1999) discussion of holism suggests, is that physical training blurs the distinction between biology and culture. In sports, ideologies about gender, expectations of moral character, models of racial identity, and national traits influence the creation of physical regimens that end up shaping individual behavior, psychology, and physiology. Many studies of human biological malleability have focused almost entirely on neuroplasticity; sports encourage us to see plasticity throughout the human organism, evidenced broadly in traits from bone density and composition to endocrine function, organ performance, and baseline metabolic dynamics. Analyzing physical training as deep enculturation affecting organic physiology, as bio-enculturation, demonstrates much more clearly "top-down" influences—social, cultural, behavioral, ideological, technological, and aesthetic—on biological

dynamics, even to the cellular level. Strauss's slippery distinction between the "anatomical" and the "biologically based" is a reflection, not of
conceptual confusion, but of the empirical difficulties of separating biology from culture when studying the development of the human organism
over time, especially in a sphere of activity like sports.

The point is not that athletes are unique, but that activity patterns and
programs of skill acquisition—influenced by cultural norms, shaped by
social structures—are constantly cultivating all human tissue, conditioning our neurological systems and sculpting our skeletons, even if this is
through neglect or sedentariness. Our ways of life shape our bodies. Athletes make that process more obvious, exaggerated, and better scrutinized,
but we are all subject constantly to similar processes through which our
culture helps to determine the conditions in which our physiology and
psychology develop.

Hard overhand throwing is an excellent test case for a number of reasons: the activity places enormous demands on the body and is likely to
have been significant in the evolution of our species, and yet, for those
groups that "throw like girls," the unexplored bodily potential becomes
a territory of ineptness, a learned disability (see Marks 2003: 180–81).
In fact, the vast majority of North Americans, men and women, are
inept throwers, in comparison both to elite professional athletes and to
ethnographic accounts of the accuracy of some foraging peoples. Professional tennis players' and baseball players' shoulders may look aberrant
in comparison to their contemporaries, but they often appear normal
relative to examples from non-industrial societies or pre-industrial archaeological remains.

The enormous gap in proficiency between virtuoso athletes and people
with average ability highlights the role that training plays in the production of biological differences among humans and the way that research
on physical abilities finds the boundary between culture and biology
erased in the developmental emergence of skill. The close study of the
biocultural consequences of skill acquisition collapses clear distinctions
between "learning," "development," and "phenotypic adaptation" (see
Roberton and Konczak 2001: 92). Each term focuses on a different part
of an unbroken continuum of ways that a person can change—bodily,
behaviorally, neurologically, consciously, or in some combination—depending upon the situation and activities with which he or she engages.
Although athletes may be virtuosos of bodily self-cultivation, they also

stand as reminders that we are all, whether conscious of it or not, engaged in patterns of behavior that profoundly shape our bones, muscles, brains, and nervous systems. Brazilians (and some women) throw like they do, not because of who they are, but because of the bodies that they have made for themselves. Their ineptness is certainly biological, but it is not predestined or foreordained. Rather, it is a product of the same physical enculturation that produces the skill-shaped body.

NOTES

The Wenner-Gren Foundation for Anthropological Research Inc. generously provided support for this article through the Richard Carley Hunt Fellowship (GR 7414). The author would like to thank especially Robert Sands, Neil Maclean, John Sutton, Paul Mason, and Daniel Lende, as well as colloquium audiences at both Macquarie University and the University of Sydney, for conversations that helped to shape the final version of this piece. Thanks also to Tonia Gray for support during the preparation of this chapter.

1. Even though differences in physical ability emerge early in childhood, they may or may not be strictly inevitable. In studies of bias about infant crawling ability, for example, Mondschein, Adolph, and Tamis-LeMonda (2000) found that mothers' consistently underestimated their daughters' ability and overestimated sons' ability despite no observable differences in their performance on basic tests. Barbara Rogoff (2003: 159) discusses how community expectations across cultures affects the time at which various physical skills emerge, even with such basic abilities as walking and sitting.

2. Although the velocities attained in throws by professional and highly trained amateur athletes may seem extreme, archaeological evidence suggests that our ancestors engaged in comparably vigorous, asymmetrical activities like one-arm throwing or hammering. For example, asymmetries between the bones in the dominant and non-dominant arms, evidence of a pattern of vigorous one-armed activities, are more pronounced in pre-industrial populations than modern groups, in some groups approaching the high levels of asymmetry found in professional athletes who use a dominant arm, like pitchers or handball players (see Auerbach and Ruff 2006; Rhodes 2006).

3. Langendorfer and Roberton's (2002) approach also draws heavily on Newell's (1986) constraint theory of the development of coordination and on dynamic systems approaches to the emergence of bodily control (see, for example, Muchisky, Gershkoff-Stowe, Cole and Thelen 1996; Thelen 1995; Thelen and Smith 1996).

4. Slight variations, even at elite levels, have been found in throwing techniques as well, although overhand throwing is likely a biomechanical skill for which maximal solutions are convergent. Rafael Escamilla and colleagues (2001) examined baseball pitchers in the 1996 Olympics and found small but significant national differences in the biomechanics of throwing fast pitches, especially in the angle of shoulder abduction when the striding foot contacted the ground. Although they could not conclude on the

reason for the differences, especially in the Cuban and U.S. pitchers' motions, they suggest that training techniques or coaching, including patterns of concern about what degree of abduction might be dangerous, may influence throwing movement even at these high levels of elite performance.

5. The only quality absent from Young's description is the inhibition provoked by excessive self-awareness or concern for how one appears when acting. Frederickson and Roberts (1997) emphasized this quality of feminine embodiment and the degree to which it affected women's ability to throw, demonstrating empirically that higher levels of self-consciousness correlated with less effective styles of throwing. Although children may not experience this type of detrimental self-awareness, I suspect that many Brazilian men, asked to throw and aware of their awkwardness, would likely also score similarly high on the types of test that Frederickson and Roberts used to determine self-consciousness (for example, self-reports after attempting the throw in front of a video camera).

6. Ironically, Young (1998) herself discusses similar inconsistency in a retrospective reflection on her original article; she points out that her daughter, following the expansion of athletic opportunities, learned how to throw, in spite of the fact that Young thinks she still has an inhibited, disunified, non-transcendent style of bodily being. Given one's area of focus, it can be hard to argue that even typical Western middle-class women are more inhibited or corporeally disunited than men; for example, my experience as a salsa and tango instructor, and attending many types of dance classes, undermines the argument for men's corporeal comfort and innate kinesthetic superiority over women.

7. The term "experience" is used here rather than "environment" to highlight the focus on activity patterns generated by social institutions and cultural values (see also Fausto-Sterling 2005:1495).

8. For significant critiques of treating bone remodeling as subject to a single "Wolff's Law," see, for example, Bertram and Swartz (1991) and Pearson and Lieberman (2004). A twin study by Pocock et al. (1987) suggested that some bones (in the case of their study, the lumbar spine) were less subject to environmental influences than others (such as the hip and forearm).

BIBLIOGRAPHY

Auerbach, Benjamin M., and Christopher B. Ruff. 2006. "Limb Bone Bilateral Asymmetry: Variability and Commonality Among Modern Humans." *Journal of Human Evolution* 50: 203–18.

Bartlett, R. 2000. "Principles of Throwing." In Vladimir Zatsiorsky, ed. *Biomechanics in Sport: Performance Enhancement and Injury Prevention*. Pp. 365–80. Malden, Mass.: Wiley-Blackwell.

Bernstein, Nicholai A. 1996. "On Dexterity and Development." Translated by Mark L. Latash. *In Dexterity and Its Development*. Edited by Mark L. Latash and Michael T. Turvey. Pp. 1–244. Mahwah, N.J.: Lawrence Erlbaum Associates.

Bertram, John E. A., and Sharon M. Swartz. 1991. "The 'Law of Bone Transformation': A Case of Crying Wolff?" *Biological Reviews of the Cambridge Philosophical Society* 22(3): 245–73.

Booth, Frank W. and Baldwin, Kennety M. 1996. "Muscle Plasticity: Energy Demand and Supply Processes." In *Handbook of Physiology*. Section 12. Exercise: Regulation and Integration of Multiple Systems. Loring B. Rowell and John T. Shepherd, eds. Pp. 1074–123. New York: Oxford University Press.

Bourdieu, Pierre. 1990a. *In Other Words: Essays Towards a Reflexive Sociology*. Translated by M. Adamson. Stanford: Stanford University Press.

———. 1990b (1980). *The Logic of Practice*. Translated by Richard Nice. Sanford: Stanford University Press.

Buckley, Jay C., Jr. 2006. *Space Physiology*. New York: Oxford University Press.

Burton, Allen W., and Richard W. Rodgerson. 2003. "The Development of Throwing Behaviour." In Geert J. P. Savelsbergh, Keith Davids, John Van Der Kamp, eds. *Development of Movement Co-ordination in Children: Applications in the Field of Ergonomics, Health Sciences, and Sport*. Pp. 225–40. New York: Routledge.

Calvin, William H. 1983. "A Stone's Throw and Its Launch Window: Timing and Precision and Its Implications for Language and Hominid Brains." *Journal of Theoretical Biology* 104: 121–35.

———. 1991. "Did Throwing Stones Lead to Bigger Brains?" In *The Throwing Madonna: Essays on the Brain*. New York: Bantam.

Chant, Chris B. 2003. "Rotational Adaptation: Humeral Head Retroversion in Throwing Athletes." *Biomechanics* (April 2003): 22–34.

Chowdary, Aasim, and John H. Challis. 1999. "Timing Accuracy in Human Throwing." *Journal of Theoretical Biology* 201(4): 219–29.

Crockett, Heber C., Lyndon B. Gross, Kevin E. Wilk, Martin L. Schwartz, Jamie Reed, Jay O'Mara, Michael T. Reilly, Jeffrey R. Dugas, Keith Meister, Stephen Lyman, and James R. Andrews. 2002. "Osseous Adaptation and Range of Motion at the Glenohumeral Joint in Professional Baseball Pitchers." *American Journal of Sports Medicine* 30 (1): 20–26.

Darlington, P. J., Jr. 1975. "Group Selection, Altruism, Reinforcement, and Throwing in Human Evolution." *Proceedings of the National Academy of Sciences* (USA) 72(9): 3748–52.

Darwin, Charles. 1901 (1871). *The Descent of Man, and Selection in Relation to Sex*. London: Murray.

Doidge, Norman. 2007. The *Brain That Changes Itself: Stories of Personal Triumph from the Frontiers of Brain Science*. New York: Penguin.

Dowling, Colette. 2000. *The Frailty Myth: Women Approaching Physical Equality*. New York: Random House.

Downey, Greg. 2005. *Learning Capoeira: Lessons in Cunning from an Afro-Brazilian Art*. New York: Oxford.

———. 2006. "Coaches As Phenomenologists: Para-ethnographic Work in Sports." Proceedings of the 2006 Annual Conference of the Australasian Association for Drama,

Theatre and Performance Studies. Ian Maxwell, ed. Available online at: hdl.handle .net/2123/2490 (accessed July 12, 2010).

———. 2008. "Scaffolding Imitation in Capoeira: Physical Education and Enculturation in an Afro-Brazilian Art." *American Anthropologist* 110(2): 204–13.

Duffy, Linda J., K. Anders Ericsson, and Bahman Baluch. 2007. "In Search of the Loci for Sex Differences in Throwing: The Effects of Physical Size and Differential Recruitment Rates on High Level Dart Performance." *Research Quarterly for Exercise and Sport* 78(1): 71–78.

Dunsworth, Holly, John H. Challis, and Alan Walker. 2003. "Throwing and Bipedalism: A New Look at an Old Idea." *Courier Forschungsinstitut Senckenberg* 243: 105–10.

Eagly, Alice H. 1995. "The Science and Politics of Comparing Women and Men." *American Psychologist* 50: 145–68.

Edelman, Gerald M. 2006. *Second Nature: Brain Science and Human Knowledge*. New Haven and London: Yale University Press.

Ehl, Tanja, Mary Ann Roberton and Stephen J. Langendorfer. 2005. "Does the Throwing 'Gender Gap' Occur in Germany?" *Research Quarterly for Exercise and Sport* 76(4): 488–93.

Escamilla, Rafael F., Glen S. Fleisig, Nigel Zheng, Steven W. Barrentine, and James R. Andrews. 2001. "Kinematic Comparisons of 1996 Olympic Baseball Pitchers." *Journal of Sports Sciences* 19: 665–76.

Ericsson, K. A., and A. C. Lehmann. 1996. "Expert and Exceptional Performance: Evidence of Maximal Adaptation to Task Constraints." *Annual Review of Psychology* 47: 273–305.

Evaldsson, Ann-Carita. 2003. "Throwing Like a Girl?: Situating Gender Differences in Physicality Across Game Contexts." *Childhood* 10: 475–97.

Fallow, James. 1996. "Throwing Like a Girl." *The Atlantic* 278(2): 84–87.

Fausto-Sterling, Anne. 2005. "The Bare Bones of Sex: Part 1—Sex and Gender." *Signs: Journal of Women in Culture and Society* 30(2): 1491–527.

Fleisig, Glenn S., James R. Andrews, Charles J. Dillman, and Rafael F. Escamilla. 1995. "Kinetics of Baseball Pitching with Implications About Injury Mechanisms." *American Journal of Sports Medicine* 23(2): 233–39.

Flück, Martin. 2006. "Functional, Structural and Molecular Plasticity of Mammalian Skeletal Muscle in Response to Exercise Stimuli." *Journal of Experimental Biology* 209(12): 2239–48.

Frederickson, Barbara L., and Kristen Harrison. 2005. "Throwing Like a Girl: Self Objectification Predicts Adolescent Girls' Motor Performance." *Journal of Sport and Social Issues* 29(1): 79–101.

Fredrickson, Barbara L., and Tomi-Ann Roberts. 1997. "Objectification Theory: Towards an Explanation of Women's Lived Experiences and Mental Health Risks." *Psychology of Women Quarterly* 21(2): 173–206.

Garland, Theodore, Jr., and Scott A. Kelly. 2006. "Review: Phenotypic Plasticity and Experimental Evolution." *Journal of Experimental Biology* 209(12): 2344–61.

Gray, S., S. Watts, D. Debicki, and J. Hore. 2006. "Comparison of Kinematics in Skilled and Unskilled Arms of the Same Recreational Baseball Players." *Journal of Sports Sciences* 24(11): 1183–94.

Hall, J. A. Y., and Doreen Kimura. 1995. "Sexual Orientation and Performance on Sexually Dimorphic Motor Tasks." *Archives of Sexual Behavior* 24(4): 395–407.

Hood, David A., Isabella Irrcher, Vladimir Ljubicic, and Anna-Maria Joseph. 2006. "Coordination of Metabolic Plasticity in Skeletal Muscle." *Journal of Experimental Biology* 209(12): 2265–75.

Hore, J., S. Watts, J. Martin, and B. Miller. 1995. "Timing of Finger Opening and Ball Release in Fast and Accurate Overarm Throws." *Experimental Brain Research* 103(2): 277–86.

Hore, J., S. Watts, D. Tweed, and B. Miller. 1996. "Overarm Throws With the Nondominant Arm: Kinematics of Accuracy." *Journal of Neurophysiology* 76(6): 3696–704.

Huddleston, A. L., D. Rockwell, D. N. Kulund, and R. B. Harrison. 1980. "Bone Mass in Lifetime Tennis Athletes." *JAMA: Journal of the American Medical Association* 244(10): 1107–109.

Hyde, Janet Shibley. 2005. "The Gender Similarity Hypothesis." *American Psychologist* 60(6): 581–92.

———. 2007. "New Directions in the Study of Gender Similarities and Differences." *Current Directions in Psychological Science* 16(5): 259–63.

Ingold, Tim. 1998. "From Complementarity to Obviation: On Dissolving the Boundaries Between Social and Biological Anthropology, Archaeology and Psychology." *Zeitschrift für Ethnologie* 123(1): 21–52.

Isaac, Barbara. 1987. "Throwing and Human Evolution." *African Archaeological Review* 5(1): 3–17.

Jones, Henry H., James D. Priest, Wilson C. Hayes, Carol Chinn Tichenor, and Donald A. Nagel. 1977. "Humeral Hypertrophy in Response to Exercise." *Journal of Bone and Joint Surgery* 59(2): 204–8.

Kelly, A. M. Clare, and Hugh Garavan. 2005. "Human Functional Neuroimaging of Brain Changes Associated with Practice." *Cerebral Cortex* 15(8): 1089–102.

Kimura, Doreen. 2002. "Sex Hormones Influence Human Cognitive Pattern." *Neuroendocrinology Letters* (Suppl.4): 67–77.

King, Joe W., Harold J. Brelsford, and Hugh S. Tullos. 1969. "Analysis of the Pitching Arm of the Professional Baseball Pitcher." *Clinical Orthopaedics and Related Research* 67: 116–23.

Langendorfer, Stephen J., and Mary Ann Roberton. 2002. "Individual Pathways in the Development of Forceful Throwing." *Research Quarterly for Exercise and Sport* 73(3): 245–56.

Levine, William N., Mark L. Brandon, Beth Shubin Stein, Thomas R. Gardner, Louis U. Bigliani, and Christopher S. Ahmad. 2006. "Shoulder Adaptive Changes in Youth Baseball Players." *Journal of Shoulder and Elbow Surgery* 15(5): 562–66.

Marks, Jonathan. 2003. *What It Means to Be 98% Chimpanzee: Apes, People, and Their Genes.* Berkeley: University of California Press.

Martin, Karin A. 1998. "Becoming a Gendered Body: Practices of Preschools." *American Sociological Review* 63(4): 494–511.

Mauss, Marcel. 1973 (1935). "Techniques of the Body." Translated by B. Brewster. *Economy and Society* 2(1): 70–87.

Mondschein, Emily R., Karen E. Adolph, and Catherine S. Tamis-LeMonda. 2000. "Gender Bias in Mothers' Expectations about Infant Crawling." *Journal of Experimental Child Psychology* 77: 304–16.

Muchisky, Michael, Lisa Gershkoff-Stowe, Emily Cole, and Esther Thelen. "The Epigenetic Landscape Revisited: A Dynamic Interpretation." In *Advances in Infancy Research*. Vol. 10. Harlene Hayne, Lewis P. Lipsitt, and Carolyn Rovee-Collier, eds. Pp. 122–59. Westport, Conn.: Greenwood.

Münte, Thomas F., Eckhart Altenmüller, and Lutz Jäncke. 2002. "The Musician's Brain as a Model of Neuroplasticity." *Nature Reviews Neuroscience* 3(6): 473–78.

Nevill, Alan M., Roger L. Holder, and Arthur D. Stewart. 2004. "Do Sporting Activities Convey Benefits to Bone Mass Throughout the Skeleton?" *Journal of Sports Sciences* 22: 645–50.

Newell, Kari M. 1986. "Constraints on the Development of Coordination." *In Motor Development in Children: Aspects of Coordination and Control*. M. G. Wade and H. T. A. Whiting, eds. Pp. 341–60. Dordrecht, Netherlands: Martinus Nijoff.

———. 1996. "Change in Movement and Skill: Learning, Retention and Transfer." *In Dexterity and Its Development*. Edited by Mark L. Latash and Michael T. Turvey. Pp. 393–430. Mahwah, N.J.: Lawrence Erlbaum Associates.

Nilsson, B. E. and N. E. Westlin. 1971. "Bone Density in Athletes." *Clinical Orthopaedics and Related Research* 77: 179–82.

Noble, William, and Iain Davidson. 1996. *Human Evolution, Language and Mind: A Psychological and Archaeological Inquiry*. Cambridge: Cambridge University Press.

Osbahr, Daryl C., David L. Cannon, and Kevin P. Speer. 2002. "Retroversion of the Humerus in the Throwing Shoulder of College Baseball Pitchers." *American Journal of Sports Medicine* 30: 347–53.

Pappas, Arthur M., Richard M. Zawacki, and Thomas J. Sullivan. 1985. "Biomechanics of Baseball Pitching." *American Journal of Sports Medicine* 13: 216–22.

Pearson, Osbjorn M., and Daniel E. Lieberman. 2004. "The Aging of 'Wolff's Law': Ontogeny and Responses to Mechanical Loading in Cortical Bone." *Yearbook of Physical Anthropology* 47: 63–99.

Pieper, Hans-Gerd. 1998. "Humeral Torsion in the Throwing Arm of Handball Players." *American Journal of Sports Medicine* 26: 247–53.

Pigliucci, Massimo. 2001. *Phenotypic Plasticity: Beyond Nature and Nurture*. Baltimore: Johns Hopkins University Press.

Pocock, Nicholas A., John A. Eisman, John L. Hopper, Michael G. Yeates, Philip N. Sambrook, and Stefan Eber. 1987. "Genetic Determinants of Bone Mass in Adults: A Twin Study." *Journal of Clinical Investigation* 80(3): 706–10.

Reagan, K. M., Keith Meister, Mary Beth Horodyski, Dave W. Werner, Cathy Carruthers and Kevin Wilk. 2002. "Humeral Retroversion and Its Relationship to Glenohumeral Rotation in the Shoulder of College Baseball Players." *American Journal of Sports Medicine* 30(3): 354–60.

Rhodes, Jill A. 2006. "Adaptations to Humeral Torsion in Medieval Britain." *Journal of Physical Anthropology* 130: 160–66.

Rhodes, Jill A., and Steven E. Churchill. 2008. "Throwing in the Middle and Upper Paleolithic: Inferences from an analysis of humeral retroversion." *Journal of Human Evolution* 56(1): 1–10.

Roberton, Mary Ann. 1977. "Stability of Stage Categorizations Across Trials: Implications for the 'Stage Theory' of Overarm Throw Development." *Journal of Human Movement Studies* 3: 49–59.

———. 1978. "Longitudinal Evidence for Developmental Stages in the Forceful Overarm Throw." *Journal of Human Movement Studies* 4: 167–75.

Roberton, Mary Ann, and Lolas E. Halverson. 1984. *Developing Children: Their Changing Movement*. Philadelphia: Lea & Febiger.

Roberton, Mary Ann, and Jürgen Konczak. 2001. "Predicting Children's Overarm Throw Ball Velocities from Their Developmental Levels in Throwing." *Research Quarterly for Exercise and Sport* 72(2): 91–103.

Rogoff, Barbara. 2003. *The Cultural Nature of Human Development*. Oxford and New York: Oxford University Press.

Ruff, Christopher, Brigitte Holt, and Erik Trinkaus. 2006. "Who's Afraid of the Big Bad Wolff?: 'Wolff's Law' and Bone Functional Adaptation." *American Journal of Physical Anthropology* 129: 484–98.

Ruff, Christopher, Alan Walker, and Erik Trinkaus. 1994. "Postcranial Robusticity in Homo, III: Ontogeny." *American Journal of Physical Anthropology* 93(1): 35–54.

Sands, Robert, ed. 1999. *Anthropology, Sport and Culture*. Westport, Conn.: Bergin and Garvey.

Staron, Robert S., and Robert S. Hikida. 2000. "Muscular Responses to Exercise and Training." *In Exercise and Sport Science: Basic and Applied Science*. William E. Garrett, Donald T. Kirkendall, eds. Pp. 163–76. Philadelphia: Lippincott, Williams & Wilkins.

Stodden, David F., Stephen J. Lagendorfer, Glenn S. Fleisig, and James R. Andrews. 2006a. "Kinematic Constraints Associated with the Acquisition of Overarm Throwing Part I: Step and Trunk Actions." *Research Quarterly for Exercise and Sport* 77(4): 417–27.

———. 2006b. "Kinematic Constraints Associated with the Acquisition of Overarm Throwing Part II: Upper Extremity Actions." *Research Quarterly for Exercise and Sport* 77(4): 428–36.

Thelen, Esther. 1995. "Motor Development: A New Synthesis." *American Psychologist* 50(2): 79–95.

Thelen, Esther, and Linda B. Smith. 1996. *A Dynamic Systems Approach to the Development of Cognition and Action*. Cambridge, Mass.: MIT Press/Bradford Books.

Thomas, Jerry R., and Karen E. French. 1985. "Gender Differences Across Age in Motor Performance: A Meta-Analysis." *Psychological Bulletin* 98: 260–82.

Trinkaus, Erik, Steven E. Churchill, and Christopher Ruff. 1994. "Postcranial Robusticity in Homo, II: Humeral Bilateral Asymmetry and Bone Plasticity." *American Journal of Physical Anthropology* 93(1): 1–34.

Watson, Neil V., and Doreen Kimura. 1991. "Nontrivial Sex Differences in Throwing and Intercepting: Relation to Psychometrically Defined Spatial Functions." *Personality and Individual Difference* 12(5): 375–85.

West-Eberhard, Mary Jane. 2003. *Developmental Plasticity and Evolution*. Oxford and New York: Oxford University Press.

Whiting, William C., and Stuart Rugg. 2006. *Dynatomy: Dynamic Human Anatomy*. Champaign, Ill.: Human Kinetics.

Wild, Monica. 1938. "The Behavior Pattern of Throwing and Some Observations Concerning Its Course of Development in Children." *Research Quarterly* 9: 20–24.

Wilk, Kevin E. 2000. "Physiology of Baseball." *In Exercise and Sport Science: Basic and Applied Science*. William E. Garrett, Donald T. Kirkendall, eds. Pp. 709–731. Philadelphia: Lippincott, Williams & Wilkins.

Williams, Kathleen, Kathleen M. Haywood, and Mary Painter. 1996. "Environmental vs. Biological Influences on Gender Differences in the Overarm Throw for Force: Dominant and Nondominant Arm Throws." *Women in Sport and Physical Activity Journal* 5(2): 29–48.

Wolff, Julius. 1896 (1892). *The Law of Bone Remodeling*. Trans. By P. Maquet and R. Furlong. Berlin: Springer Verlag.

Young, Iris Marion. 1990. *Throwing Like a Girl and Other Essays in Feminist Philosophy and Social Theory*. Bloomington and Indianapolis: Indiana University Press.

———. 1998. "'Throwing Like a Girl': Twenty Years Later." *In Body and Flesh: A Philosophical Reader*. Donn Welton, ed. Pp. 286–90. Oxford: Blackwell Publishers.

Young, Richard W. 2003. "Evolution of the Human Hand: The Role of Throwing and Clubbing." *Journal of Anatomy* 202(1): 165–74.

Yue, Guang, and Kelly J. Cole. 1992. "Strength Increases from the Motor Program: Comparison of Training with Maximal Voluntary and Imagined Muscle Contractions." *Journal of Neuropsychology* 67(5): 1114–23.

13

The DREAM Gene for the Posthuman Athlete: Reducing Exercise-Induced Pain Sensations Using Gene Transfer

Andy Miah

Downstream Regulatory Element Antagonistic Modulator, or DREAM for short, is a protein critical to pain sensations experienced by organisms. Recent research has suggested that it might be possible to exploit this genetic modulator of pain for the purpose of pain management (Cheng et al., 2002; Cheng and Penninger, 2003). This chapter discusses the ethical implications of modulating DREAM expression for sport; to advance the debate on what constitutes a legitimate method of performance modification. Initially, it is argued that DREAM presents a more complex problem for anti-doping authorities than other methods of gene doping, since it cannot easily be characterized as enhancing or therapeutic. Indeed, the basis of this distinction is criticized by exploring a biocultural definition of health. On this model, which seems unlikely to be endorsed by anti-doping authorities, but, nevertheless, which is perpetuated by sport physicians, the use of DREAM manipulation would seem more difficult to prohibit on medical grounds. Its use is consistent with a medical desire to alleviate suffering, even where it is self-induced. A similar dichotomy exists when discussing the relevance of pain from a sporting perspective. While one might presume that the ethics of sport is such that any legal mechanism to improve performance is desirable for an athlete, pain tolerance appears to have a symbolic value that would undermine the usefulness of DREAM manipulation. This tension demonstrates greater complexity to the debate about the role of technology in sport and its ideological connotations about what it means to be an athlete.

Since the discovery of the double helix by Francis Crick and James Watson in 1953, the gene has become an important and powerful symbol in society. Genetic science is seldom out of the news and has been the inspiration for many controversial descriptions about our imminent "posthuman future" (Fukuyama, 2002). Indeed, various examples can be cited that describe a *contested* history of genetic technology. Even the discovery of the structure of DNA was steeped in controversy over who could claim credit for having identified its *twisted helix* structure (Hubbard, 2003).[1] Sport is no exception to this controversy. The nature-nurture discussion about athlete performance is ongoing and its veracity is fueled by the continued acceptance of performance as a guiding value in elite sport, which prioritizes quantifiable achievements of athletes over qualitative ones. To this end, sport scientists are constantly trying to find ways to develop a better understanding human biology in an effort to legally enhance performance.

In recent years, a number of ethicists have begun to discuss the role of gene transfer technology in sports (Miah, 2004; Munthe, 2000, 2002; Tamburrini, 2002). Such discussions have questioned the ability to maintain anti-doping policies in an era of genetic modification and have revealed some of the complex circumstances that arise as a consequence of genetic modification. For example, one challenging situation for anti-doping agencies would be the prospect of the genetically modified athletes who could not be called cheats, just because they were modified before they were born. While such troublesome cases might not occur until some time in the distant future, they bring into question what should be the basis of inclusion within elite sports. Such circumstances require sport policy makers to recognize the broader implications of genetic technology and radically rethink sporting values.

The literature says little about the social and cultural significance of genetic modification in sport, despite some obvious overlaps. The sorts of questions that have dominated the discourse in sport have been the ethical legitimacy of genetic modification, where it is usually conceptualized as a form of performance enhancement. Alternatively, discussions have been concerned with the ideological implications of characterizing sport performance as genetically determined, for the potentially divisive consequences such conclusions might have. As well, authors have attempted to place this in an ideological context, discussing whether the tendency toward excessive achievement in sport leads necessarily to a technologized future for athletes. Such arguments introduce notions of cyborgism (Butryn, 2003a), transhumanism (Miah, 2003), and posthumanism (Butryn, 2003b) as a way of characterizing the postmodern athlete. However, athletes do not fit neatly into this technological characterization, since naturalness and being human are also championed as athletic virtues, where the use of doping undermines these values. Moreover, this paper aims to suggest that one cannot easily relate technologization with a desire to transcend human limits. Indeed, one could argue that there is resistance to the technologization of sport, on this basis. Consequently, how elite sports reconcile the use of high-technology and its resistance has led to interesting debates (Miah and Eassom, 2002).

Nearly all of these discussions problematize the legitimacy of enhancement in sport, specifically concerned with the distinctions between acceptable and unacceptable methods of performance modification. This paper is less concerned with that distinction, and rather, inquires into the legitimacy of what would typically be described as therapeutic modification, specifically, pain management. This example is particularly intriguing since it has an ambiguous status as both an example of high-technology (genetic modification) and, as an application, something that is morally conservative (reducing pain). Where sports authorities have dismissed genetic enhancement or "gene doping" as unequivocally unethical, the use of gene therapy is considered to be legitimate. Potentially, the genetic modification of pain sensations could be conceptualized as therapeutic, yet it would have clear implications for the capacity of an athlete to perform in sport, which would most likely make it controversial.

In this context, the paper proceeds by explaining the scientific research underpinning the potential genetic manipulation of pain sensations. This research is then placed into a medical context, from which I will discuss how the possibility for reducing pain sensations might be medically desirable and ethically consistent with what is athletically relevant in sport contests.

DREAM, FOR SHORT

Downstream Regulatory Element Antagonistic Modulator (DREAM) is a "critical repressor for pain modulation" (Cheung, January 11, 2002), which means that it has some role in how we interpret the sensations of pain. Recent research suggests that it could provide useful information about the function of pain and how it might be managed, which could revolutionize how pain is addressed by medicine (Cheng et al., 2002; Cheng and Penninger, 2003). The DREAM protein functions by blocking the production of prodynorphin (the precursor to dynorphin, an endogenous analgesic), which is a chemical produced in response to pain or stress. Research with mice suggests that the absence of DREAM (the gene) leads to increased levels of dynorphin and a decreased sensitivity to inflammatory, acute, and neuropathic pain.

The possible applications of this research are diverse, though it is important to note that further work must take place to clarify what is possible to achieve in relation to this gene. It is not yet clear how it will be possible to alter sensations of pain and research remains pre-clinical, which means it has yet to be applied to human subjects. As yet, no connection has been made between this discovery and the possible applications to sport. Indeed, no scientist researching this gene is likely to envisage it being used in any sporting context. Yet, some applications of related research have taken place, which provide a useful way of understanding how DREAM might be addressed in sport. For example, for many years athletes have used medical technology, such as ultrasound, to promote the repair of muscle tissue. More recently, this has been considered possible on a genetic level by using various growth factors to promote the repair of damaged tissue (Lamsam et al., 1997).

Repair versus Enhancement: An Ethical Distinction

When discussing the ethics of modifying performance in sport, authorities are very clear on the distinction between therapy and enhancement. However, it is critical to note that the use of the concept "enhancement" is somewhat misleading. The intention of sporting authorities is not specifically to prohibit technologies that would lead to the existence of super-humans. Rather, "enhancement" is defined largely as the "non-therapeutic" use of medicine, which is often the use of a therapeutic medicine by somebody who has not been diagnosed by a qualified physician as requiring the treatment. Thus, it is not necessarily the case that the pro-enhancement position relies on the use of any unusual or untested technology.

Rather, the pro-enhancement position might, less controversially, be challenging the basis of medical prescription. For example, in consideration of whether a patient requires something like growth hormone—a physician would base the distinction largely on a biomedical concept of health and specifically on the symptoms associated with growth. However, the pro-enhancement position would argue that this biomedical model is not sufficient to determine what is best for the patient and that, for example, other factors, such as the social circumstances of an athlete must also be taken into account. Thus, even if it is not biomedically necessary for an athlete to receive supplements of growth hormone, she might argue that her career would benefit significantly by the use of such medication, say, by ensuring that she will be taller than she otherwise would be to aid her as a basketball player. By making such a case the athlete would be arguing that the biomedical articulation of health is not sufficient, and that physician's concern for health should also encompass the specific circumstances of somebody's life. Indeed, this argument is often made in sport, and sports physicians regularly make a decision of this kind when treating an athlete. Something as simple as muscular spray that permits an athlete to continue training through a muscle cramp is a form of applying a medical treatment for the purpose of permitting the athlete to continue performing through injury.

The broader context of this debate concerns the proper role of medicine in sport. Discussions of this kind arise frequently in relation to cosmetic surgery. In this case, there is a generally accepted norm in some countries that, if surgery is used to correct some deformity that the individual finds difficult to live with, then surgery should be made freely available to the patient. Conversely, if the surgery is used to correct what some would describe as "trivial" deformities, then society does not have a responsibility to correct that deformity. In the latter case, any surgery to correct the deformity would have to be paid for by the individual. This is not an easy distinction to make, though Welie (1999) argues that the guiding premise must be individual "integrity" (p. 173) rather than the normative distinctions between therapy, enhancement, and the aesthetics. When making a broader claim about the limits of medicine, Welie (1999) even refers to athletic enhancements to make the point.

In sum, when discussing the ethical distinction between therapy and enhancement (or, more accurately, non-therapy), it is important to note that the pro-enhancement position is not necessarily about radically augmenting humans to create grotesque beings that are unrecognizable as humans. Moreover, the anti-doping rejection of enhancement is more accurately an assertion of a particular view of health, which follows a biomedical rather than biocultural model. Thus, it gives less importance to the cultural basis on which a patient might claim their desire for medical intervention.

Because of this biomedical model, it is probable that all anti-doping sporting organizations, such as the World Anti-Doping Agency and the International Olympic Committee, would condemn the manipulation of DREAM for sport, since it would be seen as dangerous and unnecessary. Some evidence of this can be found in the recent statements by both of these institutions about the use of genetic technology in sport (WADA, 2002; IOC, 2001). Such a position would reflect the dominant ethical stance in relation to medical technologies and, coupled with the need to apply policy into a context where norms and rules applicable to all are seen as necessary, sport policy on performance demands taking the view that an individualized approach to the ethics of modifying performance is not possible.[2]

Yet, DREAM (and genetic modification more broadly) challenges the credibility of this distinction. It is not clear whether the modification of DREAM would be seen as therapeutic or non-therapeutic. More precisely, it is not clear when a physician would feel justified in utilizing this tech-nology for the benefit of a patient. If we consider its use outside of sport for a moment, it is also unclear, though there would almost certainly be a motivation to utilize the technology in pain management, which is widely recognized as a significant problem for patients. The current understanding of pain is such that the methods of pain management come with a number of burdens and obstacles. Consequently, the prospect of a more effective method would be highly desirable. Yet, it begs the question as to what kinds of pain would justify the use of a given form of treatment. Indeed, it also requires understanding precisely what kind of pain should be treated by medicine or described as a health-deficit. One imagines the classic case of the patient who visits his physician seeking a remedy for his broken heart. Coming to a conclusion about this requires understanding more about the nature of pain in sport. The next section of this paper aims to inform that debate, to understand whether there can be a medical justification for want-ing to lessen sensations of pain when competing at elite levels in sport.

WHICH PAINS MATTER?

The question concerning DREAM requires us to ask whether there are some applications where treatment might not be appropriate. In our case, the question is whether sporting pains deserve medical treatment and, sub-sequently, whether this is a good reason to legalize DREAM manipulation as a method of altering performance. The idea that some pains are more worthy of treatment than others is highly contested. Perhaps one of the most controversial recent discussions has been in relation to how health care is utilized by smokers who, some argue, voluntarily induce their ill-ness and, on this basis, should be not given treatment. Less radically, this argument often forms part of the decision-making process when having to make difficult moral decisions about the provision of care when resources are scarce or where a reasonable decision is made based upon the likely effectiveness of the treatment. Thus, if a physician has reason to believe that a patient will not benefit from a treatment, because they will most likely resort to behavior that will make the treatment ineffective, such as through continuing to smoke, then this is regarded as less worthy a case than a patient who is likely to benefit from a treatment in their subsequent behavior. A comparable example can be found in sports, particularly in relation to extreme sports, where individuals take risks and often rely on a state-funded rescue service to assist them when in trouble. However, the debate about enhancement is not merely a matter of allocating re-sources and, in sport, this concern is unlikely to be a priority, given that performance technology would not derive from public health care–funds (although the care for long-term consequences of, say, drug use in sport, might be a basis for re-visiting this argument).

Understanding what kind of pain deserves treatment requires first un-derstanding what counts as a legitimate instance of pain and why it calls for attention from medicine. Defining pain has been central to a number of ethical and sociological discussions about the role of medicine, though an answer to the rather straightforward question "what is pain?" remains contested. One of the key points of contention has to do with what counts as an experience of pain. The importance of answering this question has frequently provoked a reference to the fetus and its capacity (or lack of) to experience pain. It is suggested that the experience of pain reveals something about our moral and legal obligations to that life or, more spe-cifically, to seek the alleviation of pain experienced by that life. Thus, if a life is capable of feeling pain, then we have an obligation to minimize that pain and/or ensure that we do not contribute to the experience of any unnecessary pain. An obvious implication of how we describe the fetus example is in relation to abortion. On one view, one might argue that the pro-life campaign would gain credibility, if it can show that fetuses experience pain at a very early stage in their lives in a similar way to how a fully developed person feels pain.[3] Thus, the experience of pain is a measure to which a sense of moral responsibility must adhere.

A genetic worldview has become central to how these problems are addressed, which is particularly pertinent to the analysis of DREAM. The ability to perceive genes through medical technology provides a way of making genes meaningful to people. Increasingly, a scientific view of pain dominates and assumes that, for example, if a fetus displays specific chemical reactions, then it is agitated or, potentially, in pain. Yet, the meaning of this demonstration of pain and how it has come to be viewed as "pain" rather than *nociception* is not obvious. As Benatar and Benatar (2001) explain, nociception is:

> the neural activity in those peripheral receptors and centripetal (that is, afferent) pathways via which noxious stimuli are transmitted to the brain. Put more simply, it is the process whereby noxious stimuli are sensed and transmitted to the brain. Thus, while nociception is neural activity, pain is an unpleasant feeling (p. 59).

In recent years, it has become clear that such a biomedical model of understanding pain is inadequate. Certainly, most people are capable of *feeling* pain in some sense that can be explained biologically, but the ways in which this is expressed and the kinds of circumstances associated with pain differ. For example, Hoffmann (2001) describes how it is possible to identify differences between the ways that men and women experience pain. Also, race and ethnicity is suggested to be an important factor in how the articulation of pain is approached by medical practitioners. As Bonham (2001) describes, "People interpret and react to health symptoms, including pain based on their life experiences and their cultural norms" (p. 52). This does not mean that, if a man and a woman were each to burn themselves, they would feel different kinds of pain (though in some circumstances, it does mean this). Rather, people engage with their pain in various ways, which makes us aware that the experience of pain is not just a biological fact, but is also a cultural construct. This point is critical, since the medical profession relies heavily on an individual's capacity to *articulate* their pain, which is itself one instance of how pain is culturally mediated through language. Indeed, the point relates partly to the earlier discussion about the pain experienced by the fetus and the problems associated with that argument. These discussions inform us of how it would be inadequate to dismiss the importance of pain in sport on the basis of it being self-induced. *Prima facie*, the removal of pain in sport would reduce suffering and would, thus, appear to be medically justified in the same way that other pain-management treatments are justified.

THE (IR)RELEVANCE OF PAIN IN SPORT

In the context of sport, Elaine Scarry's *The Body in Pain* (1985) is a useful, if unlikely, place to begin discussing the ethics of DREAM manipulation from a sports ethical perspective. In short, the question that remains to be answered is whether there is any basis on which we can justify the circumvention of pain experiences in sport, or whether the experience of pain plays some important role in what makes sport valuable. Scarry offers an explanation for why injuring others has a special status as a means of distinguishing between opponents in contests. Scarry contrasts the use of injury in "war" with other possible ways of settling contests, particularly sporting contests. She sets up the question by asking "What Differentiates Injuring from Other Acts or Attributes Upon Which a Contest Can be Based" (p. 91). Scarry then argues that injurious acts are different, just because other kinds of acts are *externally irrelevant* to the nature of a particular contest. To explain this argument, the example Scarry gives is, again, war. She argues that war could not be settled on the basis of a sports contest, such as a tennis or chess match, even if rival countries agreed upon the rules. This is because "sports" are not relevant to the nature of the dispute. In other words, the test of a sport is not relevant to political disputes. In contrast, if the test were to decide who had the sharpest mind, then a chess match might be appropriate (and a war would not). However, it is unlikely that, for example, a test to see who could drink the most alcohol would, in this case, be relevant.

Scarry's argument informs us that the act of injury is *not* a relevant aspect of a contest in the majority of circumstances. Thus, the basis upon which political disagreements should be settled has nothing to do with violence or war. Therefore, to enter into injurious acts as a basis for resolving such disputes actually fails to grasp the notion that what lies at the heart of the dispute is not a violent issue, but a matter of contested discourses. In this sense, war is a desperate attempt at trying to make oneself heard, when one's arguments are not met with sympathy. Scarry claims that sports contests would not be useful to settle political disputes, since parties could always break the rules of the sport to gain an advantage or claim that they were cheated by opponents, thus giving them reason to reject the contest's outcome. If the dispute is settled by war—where there are, theoretically, no rules—then competitors could not resort to other tactics to gain an advantage, since there is an assumption that opponents already employ any such means.[4]

In this context, what gives sport value does not derive from the infliction of pain on the opponent or, more specifically, the achievement of athletes is not measured in their capacity to withstand pain during their performance. Even in blood sports, the importance of pain is secondary to the demonstration of skill. Contests are not won by demonstrating the greatest capacity to withstand pain. In this sense, pain is irrelevant to sporting performances and is not an indication of sporting prowess. On this basis, it would be desirable to find ways of equalizing pain sensations in sport.

THE SYMBOLIC VALUE OF SPORTING PAINS

This view might appear to conflict with Safai's (2003) claims about the role of pain in sport: "Pain tolerance become physical and symbolic markers of character for many athletes" (p. 129). On Safai's view, being in pain is "normal" in sport and sports are unavoidably violent. Pain is a vehicle for knowing that one is working hard and trying, and by embodying those values we (and athletes) believe are important for athletes to exhibit. The phrase "No pain, no gain" derives out of circumstances where this means something to athletes. Yet, these findings do not constitute a medical endorsement of these circumstances, which is the central position that must be addressed. Moreover, neither is it clear whether this kind of pain is the kind that is under critique. Thus, we would wish to distinguish between the pain felt by performing through, say, a sprained wrist or dislocated shoulder and that which is felt in the legs during the final mile of a marathon. One would suspect that it is the latter of these that is described in Safai's findings. Yet, for either case, my position remains that, despite this endorsement of pain experiences within sporting ethos, the value of sport does not derive from this ethos. Indeed, Safai offers some criticisms about this pain discourse in sport:

Pain and injury tolerance in sport warrants in-depth investigation not only because of the social processes that normalise pain and injury in sport, but also because of the damaging, potentially devastating, consequences to the health and well-being of many people. Pain and injury occur in an environment that is often cloaked in uncritical and unquestioned acceptance and idealisation (p. 127).

The concerns about the way athletes value pain reinforces the uncertainty about how DREAM manipulation might be evaluated or used. Arguably, the fact that athletes would appear to value pain tolerance as a symbolic characteristic of athletic superiority seems desirable to undermine. After all, it would be difficult for the medical profession to endorse a discourse that legitimizes such sentiments. Yet, because of this possible resistance from athletes, it is very difficult to conclude the ethical status of such technology. Thus, where one might find it easier to argue that the enhancement-seeking athlete recognizes their chosen pursuit as constitutively technological (and even trans-human), the possible resistance to DREAM manipulation would suggest otherwise. In short, it would appear that the high-tech athlete would not seek to utilize this technology for performance, because it would undermine something presumed to be of value to sport. Safai's research suggests that its use would be resisted and this disrupts the idea that athletes (cheating or not) are engaged in a pursuit of trying to undermine biology by using technology.

Specifically, it is not possible to assume that athletes would desire the use of genetic technology to circumvent pain or, at least, that there are competing views on the value of performance that would emerge with the prospect of DREAM manipulation. The first would entail the desire to minimize pain sensations so as to optimize sporting capacity. The second would seek to ensure a performance is not seen as any less valuable because it did not require as much suffering as it would without the pain management technology.

A WORTHWHILE DREAM?

The purpose of this inquiry has been to recognize the conceptual overlap between therapy and enhancement when considering the utilization of emerging, preventive medicine, such as genetically driven pain management. Understanding the complexity of the distinction between therapy and enhancement requires taking to task the ethical assumptions about each. This is why the discussion has focused mainly on the ethical status of therapeutic technology in sport. While it can be argued that the capacity to endure pain in sport is medically unconscionable, its tolerance has a symbolic and functional status that challenges the idea that athletes would willingly use this technology to enhance their performance. Such use would be conceptually different from, say, using hormone therapy to build muscle mass. On this basis, whereas it has been commonplace for anti-doping rhetoric to condemn enhancement and embrace therapeutic medicine, this distinction underestimates the complexity of both terms and the inadequacy of basing an ethical distinction on their assumed characteristics.

DREAM manipulation problematizes what constitutes an ethical performance in sport. It brings into question what values underpin sport and the medical principles on which anti-doping codes have been based, which lead to making such distinctions as that made between therapy and enhancement. Moreover, it raises the question about what sporting authorities are trying to protect when they base arguments against doping on the well-being of athletes. It is important to note the value of this distinction is asserted largely from the medical side of sport. Sport has a legitimate interest in performance enhancement and it is widely understood that the only obstacle to athletes using any biochemical method of performance enhancements is the ethical permissibility of the technology. It has been argued here that pain tolerance does not contribute to establishing who is the better athlete and, for this reason, technology that can equalize this human characteristic would be a desirable innovation for competition.

NOTES

Thanks to my dear friend and colleague Parissa Safai, University of Toronto, for her critical insights on this topic and for bringing DREAM to my attention.

1. Specifically, at least two other researchers seemed important in the process of this historic finding, Rosalind Franklin and Maurice Wilkins.

2. However, if one looks to other kinds of enhancements, there is some evidence to support an individualized perspective on what is ethical. For example, in many sports there

is considerable flexibility on what kind of equipment an athlete is allowed to use, even if the equipment must fall within some minimal parameters.

3. Though it is interesting that the burden of proof appears to rest with demonstrating that fetuses do experience pain, rather than being able to demonstrate that they do not, despite the relative strength of each position.

4. This omits a significant discourse on the art of war, as well as saying very little about some means that are not used by opponents for various reasons. Biological weapons and weapons of mass destruction are examples of such means that are part of these unwritten rules of war and their instable status is the basis of many ethical discussions about agreements on nuclear weapons and so on, Scarry implies that war is supposed to entail a "win at all costs" approach, where any means are legitimate. This is qualitatively different from the "win at all costs" approach in sport, athletes accept only the use of specific means and where far greater rules exist on what is acceptable.

BIBLIOGRAPHY

Barendse, M. A. "Individualism, Technology and Sport: The Speedway Nexus." *Journal of Sport & Social Issues*, 7, no. 1 (1983): 15–23.

Benatar, D., and M. Benatar. "A Pain in the Fetus: Toward Ending Confusion About Fetal Pain." *Bioethics*, 15, no. 1 (2001): 1–31.

Bonham, V. L. "Race, Ethnicity, and Pain Treatment: Striving to Understand the Causes and Solutions to the Disparities in Pain Treatment." *Journal of Law, Medicine & Ethics*, 29 (2001): 52–68.

Bostrom, N. "What is Transhumanism?" www.nickbostrom.com/old/transhumanism.html (accessed May 4, 2010).

Breivik, G. "Limits to Growth in Elite Sport: Some Ethical Considerations." Twentieth World Congress of Philosophy, Boston. 1998. Available online: www.bu.edu/wcp/Papers/Spor/SporBrei.htm (accessed July 12, 2010).

Butryn, T. "Cyborg Horizons: Sport and the Ethics of Self-Technologization." Pp. 111–33 in *Sport Technology: History, Philosophy and Policy*. Edited by A. Miah and S. B. Eassom. Oxford: Elsevier Science, 2002.

Butryn, T. M., and M. A. Masucci. "It's Not about the Book: A Cyborg Counternarrative of Lance Armstrong." *Journal of Sport and Social Issues*, 27, no. 2 (2003): 124–44.

Butryn, T. M. (2003b) "Posthuman Podiums: Cyborg Narratives of Elite Track and Field Athletes," *Sociology of Sport Journal*, 20, no. 1 (2003)

Cheng et al. "DREAM Is a Critical Transcriptional Repressor for Pain Modulation." *Cell*, 108, no. 1 (2002): 31–43.

Cheng, H.-Y. M., and J. M. Penninger. "When the DREAM Is Gone: From Basic Science to Future Prospectives in Pain Management and Beyond." *Expert Opinion on Therapeutic Targets*, 7, no. 2 (2003): 249–63.

Cole, C. "Hybrid Athletes, Monstrous Addicts and Cyborg Natures." *Journal of Sport History*, 21, no. 2 (1994): 228–39.

Davidson, J. "Sport and Modern Technology: The Rise of Skateboarding." *Journal of Popular Culture*, 18, no. 4 (1985): 145–47.

d'Agincourt-Canning, L. "Experiences of Genetic Risk: Disclosure and the Gendering of Responsibility." *Bioethics*, 15, no. 3 (2001): 231–47.

Derbyshire, S. W. G. "Locating the Beginnings of Pain." *Bioethics*, 13, no. 1 (1999): 1–26.

———. "Fetal Pain: An Infantile Debate." *Bioethics*, 15, no. 1 (2001): 77–84.

Delgado, R. "Forget Exercise, Pop a Fitness Pill." *Chronicle* (2002).

Fukuyama, F. *Our Posthuman Future: Consequences of the Biotechnology Revolution.* London: Profile Books, 2002.

Gelberg, J. N. "The Lethal Weapon: How the Plastic Football Helmet Transformed the Game of Football 1939–1994." *Bulletin of Science, Technology, and Society*, 15, no. 5–6 (1995): 302–9.

———. "The Rise and Fall of the Polara Asymmetric Golf Ball: No Hook, No Slice, No Dice." *Technology in Society*, 18, no. 1 (1996): 93–110.

———. "Tradition, Talent and Technology: The Ambiguous Relationship between Sports and Innovation." Pp. 88–110 in *Design for Sport*. Edited by A. Bush. London: Thames & Hudson, 1998.

Gibson, J. H. *Performance vs. Results: A Critique of Values in Contemporary Sport.* Albany: State University of New York Press, 1993.

Gray, C. H. *Cyborg Citizen: Politics in the Posthuman Age.* London: Routledge, 2002.

Gray, C. H., and S. Mentor, eds. *The Cyborg Handbook.* London: Routledge, 1995.

Have, H. A. M. J. t. "Genetics and Culture: The Geneticization Thesis." *Medicine, Health Care and Philosophy*, 4, no. 3 (2001): 295–304.

Hayles, N. K. *How We became Posthuman: Virtual Bodies in Cybernetics, Literature, and Informatics.* London: University of Chicago Press, 1999.

Hoberman, J. M. *Mortal Engines: The Science of Performance and the Dehumanization of Sport.* New York: Free Press, 1992.

Hoffmann, D. E., and A. J. Tarzian. "The Girl Who Cried Pain: A Bias Against Women in the Treatment of Pain." *Journal of Law, Medicine & Ethics*, 29, no. 4 (2001): 13–27.

Hubbard, R. "Science, Power, Gender: How DNA Became the Book of Life Signs." *Journal of Women in Culture and Society*, 28, no. 3 (2003): 791–99.

Hummel, R. L., and G. S. Foster. "A Sporting Chance: Relationships Between Technological Change and Concepts of Fair Play in Fishing." *Journal of Leisure Research*, 18, no. 1 (1986): 40–52.

Illich, I. *Limits to Medicine: Medical Nemesis: The Expropriation of Health.* London: Penguin Books, 1990.

International Olympic Committee. "Press Release: IOC Gene Therapy Working Group—Conclusion. Lausanne, International Olympic Committee," 2001. www.olympic.org/uk/news/publications/press_uk.asp?release=179.

Lamsam, C., F. H. Fu, et al. "Gene Therapy in Sports Medicine." *Sports Medicine*, 25, no. 2 (1997): 73–77.

Lewis, B. E. "Prozac and the Post-human Politics of Cyborgs." *Journal of Medical Humanities*, 24, nos. 1 and 2 (2003): 49–63.

Lippman, A. "Led (Astray) by Genetic Maps: The Cartography of the Human Genome and Health Care." *Social Science and Medicine*, 35, no. 12 (1992): 1469–76.

Loland, S. "The Record Dilemma, 20th World Congress of Philosophy." 1998. www .bu.edu/wcp/Papers/Spor/SporLola.htm (accessed July 12, 2010).

McCrory, P. "Ethics, Molecular Biology, and Sports Medicine." *British Journal of Sports Medicine*, 35, no. 3 (2001): 142–43.

Melzer, D., and R. Zimmern. "Genetics and Medicalisation: Genetics Could Drive a New Wave of Medicalisation if Genetic Tests are Accepted without Appropriate Clinical Evaluation." *British Medical Journal*, 324, no. 7342 (2002): 863–64.

Miah, A. *Genetically Modified Athletes: Biomedical Ethics, Gene Doping and Sport.* London: Routledge, 2004.

Miller, P. S. "Genetic Discrimination in the Workplace." *Journal of Law, Medicine & Ethics*, 26, no. 3 (1998): 189.

Moynihan, R., and R. Smith. "Too Much Medicine?: Almost Certainly." *British Medical Journal*, 324, no. 7342 (2002): 859–60.

Munthe, C. "Selected Champions: Making Winners in an Age of Genetic Technology." Pp. 217–31 in *Values in Sport: Elitism, Nationalism, Gender Equality, and the Scientific Manufacture of Winners*. Edited by T. Tännsjö and C. Tamburrini. London: E & FN Spon, 2002.

Rintala, J. "Sport and Technology: Human Questions in a World of Machines." *Journal of Sport and Social Issues*, 19, no. 1 (1995): 63–75.

Rosner, M., and T. R. Johnson. "Telling Stories: Metaphors of the Human Genome Project." *Hypatia*, 10, no. 4 (1995): 104–29.

Safai, P. "Healing the Body in the 'Culture of Risk': Examining the Negotiation of Treatment Between Sport Medicine Clinicians and Injured Athletes in Canadian Intercollegiate Sport." *Sociology of Sport Journal*, 20, no. 2 (2003): 127–46.

Scarry, E. *The Body in Pain: The Making and Unmaking of the World.* Oxford: Oxford University Press, 1985.

Shogan, D. *The Making of High Performance Athletes: Discipline, Diversity and Ethics.* Toronto: University of Toronto Press, 1999.

———. "Disciplinary Technologies of Sport Performance." Pp. 93–109 in *Sport Technology: History, Philosophy and Policy*. Edited by A. Miah and S. B. Eassom. Oxford: Elsevier, 2002.

St. Louis, B. "Sport, Genetics and the 'Natural Athlete': The Resurgence of Racial Science." *Body and Society*, 9, no. 2 (2003): 75–95.

Tamburrini, C. M. "After Doping What? The Morality of the Genetic Engineering of Athletes." Pp. 253–68 in *Sport Technology: History, Philosophy and Policy*. Edited by A. Miah and S. B. Eassom. Oxford: Elsevier Science, 2002.

Thacker, E. Bio-X: Removing Bodily Contingency in Regenerative Medicine. Journal Medical Humanities of proxy-4.pdf in desktop articles folder. 2002

World Anti-Doping Agency. "Press Release: WADA Conference Sheds Light on the Potential of Gene Doping. New York, World Anti-Doping Agency." 2002. www.wadaama.org.

Welie, J. V. M. "Do You Have a Healthy Smile?" *Medicine, Health Care and Philosophy*, 2, no. 2 (1999): 169–80.

Index

performance gap, 302; and the nervous system, 315–19; physiology of, 310; and "self objectification," 302; skeletal consequence of, 312–15; "throwing like a girl," 298, 299–319

training, 282; and diet, 283; and physiology of, 283–86

unitary systems of analysis, 50

West African and descent, 245–53; and Jamaican sprinting, 243; and non-genetic explanation, 256; and sickle cell hemoglobin, 245; and slave trade, 246

World Anti-Doping Agency, 332

world records for running, 206, *244*

Young, Iris Marion, 300–303, 308–10, 320nn5–6

Contributors

Vilma Charlton is a lecturer in physical education. She is the third vice president of the Jamaica Amateur Athletic Association, an IAAF track and field course instructor and an executive member of the Jamaica Physical Education Association. In athletics she is an Olympian, having represented Jamaica in sprinting at three Olympics—1964, 1968, and 1972—and has been awarded the Order of Distinction, an honor given by the Jamaican government for outstanding service in the field of sport and physical education.

Dirk L. Christensen is currently a post-doctorate research fellow at the Department of International Health, University of Copenhagen, Denmark. Following a bachelor's degree at University of Southern Denmark in Odense and Auburn University, United States, he finished his master's degree in exercise physiology and later in African studies, both at the University of Copenhagen. His PhD degree was obtained at the University of Copenhagen and Steno Diabetes Center, Denmark, in the field of diabetes epidemiology. Christensen has worked extensively with running and physical activity in the context of sports as well as health since the early 1990s, especially in an African context. Among others, studies have included dietary intake of Kalenjin runners and physical activity in the general population in relationship to diabetes and other chronic diseases, both carried out in Kenya. He has also been involved in sports and health studies in México and Tanzania.

Loren Cordain is a professor in the Department of Health and Exercise Science at Colorado State University in Fort Collins, Colorado. His research emphasis over the past fifteen years has focused upon the evolutionary and anthropological basis for diet, health and well-being in modern humans. Cordain's scientific publications have examined the nutritional characteristics of worldwide hunter-gatherer diets as well as the nutrient composition of wild plant and animal foods consumed by foraging humans. More recently his work has focused upon the adverse health effects of the high dietary glycemic load that is ubiquitous in the typical western diet. A number of his recent papers have proposed a common endocrine link between dietary-induced hyperinsulinemia and acne, early menarche, certain epithelial cell carcinomas, increased stature, myopia, ancanthosis nigricans, cutaneous papillomas, polycystic ovary syndrome, and male vertex balding. Cordain is the author of more than one hundred peer-reviewed publications, many of which were funded by both private and governmental agencies. He is the recent recipient of the Scholarly Excellence award at Colorado State University for his contributions into understanding optimal human nutrition. He has lectured extensively on the "Paleolithic Nutrition" concept worldwide, and has written three popular books (*The Paleo Diet* [2002]; *The Paleo Diet for Athletes* [2005]; *The Dietary Cure for Acne* [2006]) summarizing his research findings.

Søren Damkjær (d. 2007) was a sociologist who took his university degree from the University of Copenhagen. He also studied at Dartmouth College, United States, Moscow State University, and Sorbonne University and Grande Ecóle–Institute of Political Science, the latter two of which are in Paris. Damkjær's university career at the University of Copenhagen was divided between sociology and sport and it eventually joined into the sociology of sport. He taught, researched, and published extensively in the topics of the sociology of the body and the sociology of sports science during the period of 1992–2006, after which he retired from a position at the Institute of Sports Science, University of Copenhagen.

Greg Downey (BA, University of Virginia; MA, University of Chicago; PhD, University of Chicago) is senior lecturer in anthropology at Macquarie University, in Sydney, Australia. He is author of *Learning Capoeira: Lessons in Cunning from an Afro-Brazilian Art* (2005) and co-editor with

Melissa Fisher of the collection *Frontiers of Capital: Ethnographic Reflections on the New Economy* (2006). He is currently completing work on a book, *The Athletic Animal: Sport and Human Potential*, exploring the malleability of the human body and nervous system. His research interests involve a range of sports and physical education, including the Afro-Brazilian martial art, capoeira, "no-holds-barred" fighting, Latin dancing, and rugby in Australia, New Zealand, and Fiji.

Jon Entine is an internationally respected corporate and leadership consultant, author, and public-policy expert. He is a visiting fellow at the American Enterprise Institute for Public Policy Research in Washington, D.C., a columnist for the British-based international magazine *Ethical Corporation*, and co-founder of ESGMetrics, which advises businesses and NGOs on environmental, social, and governance issues, including sustainability and executive leadership, and includes among his clients the Bill and Melinda Gates Foundation. Entine has authored five books, among them *Taboo: Why Black Athletes Dominate Sports and Why We're Afraid to Talk About It* (2000). This work was based on the documentary *Black Athletes: Fact and Fiction*, written and produced with Tom Brokaw at NBC News, and named best sports film of the year at the International Sports Film Festival in 1989. He has also written hundreds of academic and popular articles on science and public policy and sustainability. Entine has been a lecturer and professor at various universities, including Columbia University, the University of Michigan (where he studied on a National Endowment for the Humanities fellowship), Arizona State University, New York University, and most recently Miami University (Ohio), where he was scholar-in-residence.

Joe Friel is founder and president of TrainingBible Coaching, LLC, a group of elite endurance coaches in the United States, United Kingdom, and South Africa. He also founded and is president of TrainingPeaks.com, a company providing software for endurance athletes and sport-device manufacturers. His ten books include *The Cyclist's Training Bible* and *The Triathlete's Training Bible*, both the best-selling-ever books within their sport genre. Friel has coached athletes in a wide range of endurance sports from novice to Olympian. He was one of the first freelance coaches of endurance athletes in the United States, having started in 1980. He lives and trains both in Scottsdale, Arizona, and in Boulder, Colorado.

Clifford Geertz (1926–2006), PhD Harvard, 1956. His first position was at the Center for International Studies at the Massachusetts Institute of Technology in 1957. From Massachusetts, Geertz moved to Stanford (1958–1959), the University of California, Berkeley (1958–1960), the University of Chicago (1960–1970), and then to the Institute for Advanced Study, with joint appointments at Oxford University (1978–1979) and Princeton University (1975–2006). Geertz was the recipient of numerous honorary degrees and scholarly awards, the author of twelve books, and the co-author and editor of a number of others. He received the National Book Critics Circle Prize for criticism in 1989 for *Works and Lives: The Anthropologist as Author*. He was a member of the advisory board of the *Antioch Review* and a frequent contributor to *The New York Review of Books*.

Bernd Heinrich, following in the tradition of E. O. Wilson, is a consummate naturalist and noted researcher and author. Heinrich works in the interface between the field and the laboratory to examine physiological and behavioral adaptation to the physical environment. Author of such recognized books as *Ravens in Winter* (1989), *Mind of the Raven* (1999), and *The Winter World* (2003), Heinrich's 2001 *Why We Run: A Natural History* was a highly acclaimed treatise that explored the implications of endurance running in human evolution. Heinrich is professor emeritus of biology at the University of Vermont.

Rachael Irving is a lecturer in the Department of Basic Medical Sciences at the University of West Indies, Jamaica. Dr. Irving is project manager of the first genetic study of elite Jamaican sprinters aimed at unraveling their superior performance. Her research interests are interactions between genes, nutrients, and the environment in both health and disease with application to treatment interventions in a variety of disorders.

Kerrie Lewis first became interested in play behavior during her undergraduate degree in anthropology at University College London, where her BS dissertation focused on play and social cognition in primates. Her doctoral research at Durham University (U.K.) investigated the evolution of play in primates and carnivores. Moving to the United States, she enjoyed two postdoctoral positions, first at Duke University in Durham, North Carolina, and then at Washington University in St. Louis, conducting research into numerical cognition and human brain scaling, respectively. Lewis is currently an assistant professor in anthropology at Texas State University–San Marcos, where she continues her research. She is the co-author of two recent articles on play and neural structure and organization in non-human primates in the *Journal of Comparative Psychology* and the journal *Human Nature*.

Peter Mewett teaches sociology at Deakin University in Australia. He received his first degree from the University of Hull, followed by postgraduate degrees from the universities of Manchester and Aberdeen, in most part spanning the disciplines of anthropology and sociology. Originally he researched and published on British rural ethnography, having conducted his doctoral fieldwork on migration from the Isle of Lewis (Scotland). After moving to Australia, his interests shifted to the study of sport and he has engaged in research on professional running; a socio-historical study of the origins and development of sports training in modernity; and is currently researching women football fans.

Andy Miah, BA, MPhil, PhD, FRSA, is professor in ethics and emerging technologies in the Faculty of Business and Creative Industries at the University of the West of Scotland, Fellow of the Institute for Ethics and Emerging Technologies, U.S.A. and Fellow at FACT, the Foundation for Art and Creative Technology, United Kingdom. He is author of *Genetically Modified Athletes* (2004) and co-author with Dr. Emma Rich of *The Medicalization of Cyberspace* (2008) and editor of *Human Futures: Art in an Age of Uncertainty* (2008). Miah's research discusses the intersections of art, ethics, technology and culture and he has published broadly in areas of emerging technologies, particularly related to human enhancement. He has published more than one hundred academic articles in refereed journals, books, magazines, and national media press on the subjects of cyberculture, medicine, technology, and sport. He has also given more than one hundred major conference presentations and he is often invited to speak about philosophical and ethical issues concerning technology in society. Miah regularly interviews for a range of major media companies, which have included BBC's *Newsnight* and *Start the Week* with Andrew Marr, ABC's *The 7:30 Review*, and CBC's *The Hour*. He currently writes a monthly column for the *Guardian* on contemporary ethical issues in science and technology.

Tim Noakes is professor in the Discovery Health Chair of Exercise and Sports Science at the University of Cape Town. He is also director of the UCT/MRC Research Unit for Exercise Science and Sports Medicine and co-founder of the Sports Science Institute of South Africa. He is a Fellow of the American College of Sports Medicine and was elected a Fellow of the University of Cape Town for sustained excellence in original scientific work. He was the team doctor for the Proteas Cricket Team in the 1996 Cricket World Cup and assisted long-distance swimmer Lewis Pugh in cold-water swims in the Arctic and Antarctic and at the North Pole. He has also served on the Ministerial Commission into High Performance Sport in South Africa. In 2004 he received the National Research Foundation rating as an A1-rated scientist. He has won many awards over the years, among them the National Foundation for Research and Technology Award for Individual over a Lifetime and the Men's Health Annual Award for Recipient of Best Man Award in the category for Science and Technology. In 2008 he received the Order of Mapungubwe, Silver from the State President for "excellent contribution in the field of sports and the science of physical exercise." He has authored many books and papers over the years including his book *Lore of Running* which is in its fourth edition and which has been published in countries worldwide. His latest book is *The Art and Science of Cricket* (2008), which he co-authored with Bob Woolmer.

Yannis Pitsiladis is a reader in exercise physiology at the Institute of Biomedical and Life Sciences at the University of Glasgow and founding member of the International Centre for East African Running Science, or ICEARS, set up to investigate the physiological, genetic, psycho-social and economic determinants of the phenomenal success of East African distance runners in international athletics. Recent projects include the study of West African sprinters (including elite sprinters from Jamaica and the United States) and the study of working-class swimmers (for example, why are there very few black swimmers?). He is a visiting professor in exercise physiology at Moi University (Kenya) and Addis Ababa University (Ethiopia).

Linda R. Sands is a wildlife biologist and project scientist with CH2M HILL.

Robert R. Sands is a consultant for the Department of Defense for Language, Regional Expertise and Culture programs. His graduate degrees in anthropology were from Iowa State University (MA) and University of Illinois (PhD). He has published six books and several book chapters on the topic of sport and culture, including *Sport Ethnography* and *GutCheck! An Anthropologist's Wild Ride into the Heart of College Football*, and edited and contributed to the pioneering reader in anthropology of sport, *Anthropology, Sport and Culture*. Sands formerly was chair of the Department of Cross-Cultural Competence, Air Force Culture and Language Center, Air University. Sands has researched and written on biological/physical anthropology and human evolution. He also has extensive experience in the applied anthropology fields of cultural resource management and environmental security and has published on natural origins of religion.

Robert Scott is a post-doctoral research associate at the University of Glasgow investigating the genetic determinants of health and fitness-related phenotypes. During his PhD, Scott undertook some of the first genetic studies of elite East African distance runners in an attempt to understand their superior performance, and, more recently, has worked on projects attempting to understand the genetic basis to elite athletic performance by studying U.S. and Jamaican sprint athletes.

CPSIA information can be obtained at www.ICGtesting.com
Printed in the USA
BVOW020852200412

288139BV00001B/5/P